College and Career Success for Those with Physical Disabilities

How to Transition from Motivated Student to Happily Employed Graduate

Julia Nelson

Published by Justicia Press

ISBN 978-0-9863260-4-2

https://www.facebook.com/AuthorJuliaNelson/

 https://twitter.com/CollegeDisabled

Author's Blog: https://greenbandblog.com/

Cover and Book Design done by Beehive Book Design

To my loving parents, Mom, Dick, and Dad;

My dearly departed Grandparents, Frank and Betty Vernamonti;

And my Aunt Sara.

Thank all of you for teaching me to live out my dreams.

Without you I couldn't have done any of it.

Table of Contents

Acknowledgments

I wish to express my deepest gratitude to all these kind folks who played a role in my getting this book written.

First, I thank all of those behind the hundreds of websites mentioned in this book, which are an integral part of the benefits to my readers offered by the book. Special acknowledgment goes to Washington.edu for leading me to many invaluable resources.

Heartfelt thanks also to all those who offered their personal success stories to be part of this book.

> Barbara Wexler: Without you I wouldn't have gotten through the first two years of college and this book wouldn't have been written.

> Jeffery Vernamonti: High school guidance counselor extraordinaire, who was always available to provide information.

> Larry Vernamonti: Who told me it that took Thomas Edison a lot of tries to figure out how to invent the perfect light bulb at a moment when I so needed to h/ear that.

> Renee Donahoe: Expert in the field of Pediatric Physical Therapy, who taught me so much about mobility and ADLs. And, how important it is to assess the needs of every individual to come up with their best plan. She has been encouraging me to grab 'my plan' since age eleven. I feel such gratitude to always have had her in my corner.

> Thomas Sicoli: Who started my interest in both college planning and assistive technology.

And last but not least, my editor Gregg Roberts, whose tireless efforts and brilliance made this book a reality.

Preface

"Be the change you want to see in the world."

– Mahatma Gandhi

As an adult with cerebral palsy who has experienced both success in the educational system and challenges securing employment, I was inspired to write this book. Like many people with disabilities getting an appropriate education in the least restrictive environment was a battle for my parents and then myself, despite being born after the passage of IDEA. Some with disabilities and their families are still fighting this battle, even in 2019 This made both my high school and college graduations even more triumphant! Yet it also made it even scary wondering if I'd have the opportunity to use my education that I had to fight so hard for?

As an 18-year-old college freshman attending Ramapo College of New Jersey, I worried (when being totally honest with myself) that no one would hire me. I thought that I had to just try to suppress my fear, as if with brute force. Just pretend it was not there … put on the best act I could to convince everyone, mostly myself, that I had everything handled. Looking back, I realize it would have been better to fully acknowledge my fear and discuss it with the people in my life who were the most supportive.

Things finally got better when I was accepted into a highly competitive major in my junior year of college. Despite the discrimination I had faced both in middle school and high school and despite struggling with self-doubt, during my first two years at Ramapo I felt more confident after transferring to The University of Arizona and decided to apply for the Management Information Systems program. This was a highly competitive program, and everyone said, "it's impossible to get into." When I was admitted to the program, I felt as if I had won an almost decade-long battle. I had "won the golden ticket" to a lucrative job when I graduated. A golden ticket that could provide the opportunity to earn the life that I had always envisioned for myself.

This 'victory' translated into the worst mistake I made during college. Not only was I succeeding in a sought-after major, I had a double major, a minor, and an internship and was president of my residence hall. All of this lulled me into a false sense of security. I thought, I am majoring in something marketable and practical, and I had to work hard to get in. I'm involved in a couple of clubs, I interned the summer before senior year, and started my job hunt in my last semester. How can I go wrong?

In hindsight I see that there was so much more I could have done in college to get not only the job I deserved, but more importantly, the future that I so desired. Aside from a list of things that I personally could have done, there were also several programs that could have helped me-- if *only* I or my family had known about them. For example, there are currently over 200 colleges that offer the Workforce Recruitment Program, a tremendously effective program that I wish I had known about. I have included the contact information to this program in my book.

I wrote this book to give students with physical disabilities a road map and information about resources that I did not have.

My wish for you is to graduate from the college of your choice and/or to get the career you want! My main goal is for my reader to get the point that the earlier they start planning for their job hunt the better! My main message is simple. The antidote to fear is planning … the antidote to discrimination is planning … the antidote to any obstacle is, you guessed it, planning.

I congratulate you and am in humble admiration of your commitment to your success. I hope this book helps you achieve the future that you deserve!

Part I: Getting to College

Chapter 1: Setting Yourself Up for College and Career Success

This first chapter is geared toward putting into place a framework that will best enable you to graduate from the college of your choice and be well on your way to a satisfying career in your chosen field.

Throughout my school years I often thought no one would ever hire me because my disability is too severe. A wonderful plan to counteract this kind of thinking is internships. Did you know the statistics above about internships and college? Did you know that there are internships that actively seek applicants with disabilities? Did you know that those internships could be pathways to jobs after graduation? I wish someone had told that scared 13-year-old that used to be me, "Hey, you can get hired. All you need to do is get into a college. You're smart, and I know you can do that. After you get into college, join a couple clubs and get good grades. All that will lead you to an internship, which statistics prove will lead to a job." If someone had put it like that to me, I would have felt better. Those closest to me always acted as if I was completely capable of graduating from college. To me this speaks volumes about how I was raised to believe I could do whatever I wanted. However, the devil was in the details of HOW. That's what I figured out later, and what I've been sharing with you in these hundreds of pages.

As I approached adolescence, I knew I wanted to do many things that people associate with the passage of becoming a full adult, I just didn't know how it will happen with the magnitude of my disability. This book has been designed to give you the tools so that you can answer that all-important question of how. This chapter starts out with driving because that was the number one 'adult thing,' that I wanted, immediately after driving on this list was a good job, immediately after a good job was my own place near my loving family. As I dreamt of my life as an adult, I only really wanted those three things. Reflecting on my life, I wish there was a roadmap to things. That is what this book is about.

Driving

Driving is an important part of becoming an adult and achieving independence. It also will greatly help you in pursuing both your educational and professional goals. It's another big area where your disabilities don't have to prevent you from enjoying a high level of functioning, including pursuing higher education and higher paying, more interesting employment.

I feel all teens who have physical disabilities should try – with appropriate instruction and safe practice – to learn to drive. It astounds me how many folks with disabilities I've met who have never tried. If your physical disabilities are less severe, you might be able to learn like any "typical" driver. This would be either by your parents teaching you, or by going to a "normal" driving school.

If your physical disabilities are more severe, or you are having trouble learning from either your parents or another person, then you need an evaluation from an *adaptive driving instructor*.

Learn the Lingo
As with any specialized area, there are terms to understand that are either unique to the area or are used in a special way. This webpage aligns you with a useful set of terms and definitions that relate to drivers with disabilities:

> http://www.mobilityawarenessmonth.com/local-heroes/mobility-solutions/

Finding an Adaptive Driving Instructor
The website http://www.driver-ed.org has a list for each state. Before your evaluation date, you will need to get both a prescription from your doctor and a learner's permit.

Please note that just because your doctor writes you a prescription or a referral for an evaluation it does not mean you can legally drive, yet.

Once you have your permit, the date of the evaluation will come. On that day, there are typically two parts. The first will be in an office, where the evaluator will give you a series of short tests to assess abilities such as cognitive reasoning and spatial perception. For those of you who were classified in school by an educational physiologist, this part will feel very similar to that previous testing, but lots shorter.

The second part will be a behind-the-wheel evaluation, where you actually drive for maybe the first time in your life! Everyone is nervous the first time. During this evaluation you might try different equipment to try to compensate for your disability. For example, if you are paralyzed, you will use hand controls for the gas and brake instead of pedals.

After the initial evaluation the instructor will tell you whether they feel you are able to learn to drive safely. For me this moment was akin to finding out whether I had cancer. In fact, the year before this, I had had an MRI, and waiting for those results didn't worry me as much!

If you are declared able to learn to drive, then they will make up a treatment plan, which will include how many sessions you will need before they will take you back to the DMV for your road test, the last step before you become a licensed driver. The instructor will also tell you if you need any vehicle modifications or special equipment, and where you can obtain them.

Do not let safety concerns stop you from pursuing the possibility of driving! It is being done in a medical setting, where safety is the #1 concern.

If You Fail

Regardless of the outcome of your evaluation, ask the instructor to mail a copy of the final report to your house. You will need this, particularly if you failed the evaluation. The report will help you work on the issues that got in the way of your being able to safely learn to drive. I have a folder with all my medical reports that are related to driving because I am still looking for a specialist who can help me. If I seek further medical advice in this regard, it will be helpful to have all the records.

If you find out you cannot learn to drive right now, all you can do is go on with life. I felt okay, got some bad news, now I still need to focus on getting into college, being a friend, daughter, sister, niece. I still need to look toward high school graduation and moving on. I had to feel that I would deal with logistical challenges such as getting to work, as they come up.

Paying for an Adaptive Driving Evaluation

As all things in life, adaptive driving evaluations are not free. Typically it is not covered by health insurance. You can either pay for the evaluation and training out of pocket, go through your state's department of vocational rehabilitation, or your school district might be obligated to pay for it. If your district provides six hours of behind the wheel training for their students, as my school district did, then they have to pay for an adaptive instructor for you. This is because the school's PE teachers, who teach the driving classes, were not trained in adaptive driving.

Your school district is not responsible for paying for any adaptive equipment because they don't purchase a car for any student. At your next IEP meeting, you can ask if your district provides behind-the-wheel training. Lots of districts have cut this expense as schools budgets keep getting slashed. If your district still does provide this, ask for an adaptive instructor. If they don't provide this, then your options are either to have your parents pay out of pocket or go through a VR department.

Other Things You Can Do to Help Prepare to Drive

One thing you can do at any age to prepare for driving is called *spamming*. No, not the email kind. Often, those of us with cerebral palsy have what is called a hyperactive startle reflex. That means we jump or flinch easier than others. As with all other symptoms that are associated with physical disabilities this varies widely from person to person. If you feel you have this, it will be one of the many factors considered during your driving evaluation.

You may be able to improve upon this with practice. What you do is really simple; get a beach ball and have anybody throw it at you for a couple of minutes a day. It could turn into a game of catch but does not have to – all they must do is throw the ball at you. If after a few weeks you are feeling less "flinchy," you are improving! Also, at first all you do is flinch and then after a while you are able to either catch or swat it back to them. That's a thrilling feeling of progress!

If my physical therapist at school had told me about this exercise, my little brother and I could have had fun doing it. And I would have felt better knowing that there was something, *anything*, I could do to get the future I want. It was so good to know that I wasn't helpless!

I sometimes had the impression that professionals who work with young people with disabilities are afraid that if they tell kids they work with how to work towards a goal, their students or patients will mistake that as almost a promise that they will accomplish the goal one day.

While I understand the concern, I have a different view. There are so many teens, even young teens, who actively pursue activities or lifestyles so that they can have a shot at playing professional sports. These thousands or even millions of hopefuls certainly know there are no guarantees. Nonetheless, it does not stop them from trying, nor does it stop coaches or others from advising kids on how to improve in their chosen sport. The way I see it, our situation as kids with disabilities isn't all that different. Everybody has to learn to handle failure. It doesn't matter that much whether the failure arises because of a formally recognized disability, bad planning, poor execution, bad luck, or whatever else. We all still have to choose whether to try again when we have already tried a whole bunch of times – or accept in good spirits something that seems to be a real limitation.

Eye Tracking

If you see an ophthalmologist, ask them if your eye tracking is affected by your disabilities. If they say yes, ask them for any exercises that may help you improve in this area. You are never too young to start doing this to boost your chances of driving when you are old enough.

When you are being driven anywhere try practice keeping your eyes focused on the road, as if you were driving. This will also start to train eye your muscles how to work for driving.

Another way to prepare is to ask your parents to start narrating as they drive. This is them saying "I am getting ready to turn, change lanes or stop, so to prepare for that I am doing *this* and *this*...". Or "That was a tricky situation, with that driver not signaling..." After a while you can practice talking through situations on the road, to test your awareness of what's going on around you on the streets and how to safely respond. The early teen years are not too early to start this!

A Note to Parents

As with all ADL training or with raising any child, I understand it's not realistic that every time you do a task, you use it as a teaching activity. Sometimes you just need to get the laundry done, a meal made or quickly run to the store. You do not always have time to include your five-year-old and teach them whatever you are doing. However, if you can get your small kid involved in even making one meal or doing one load of laundry a week or one shopping trip a month, this is good parenting.

The same is true when you have a child with disabilities. It is generally not practical to work with them every time a skill needs to be done but do so some of the time. Same applies to the driver narration technique. If you can do this with your teen once a week, it will help a lot.

Adaptive Equipment Rebate Programs

These programs were established to help disabled people pay for the vehicle modifications they need to be able to drive, such as hand controls.

https://wwwc.discountramps.com/info/mobility/auto-modification-reimbursement-programs/a/B57/

Importance of Early Employment Experience

Because of my experience of trying to find employment after college, I am a huge advocate of students getting work experience while they are still in school. I talk about this in Chapter Seven and urge college students to get a job. This is because building a work history when you are still in school will give you an invaluable edge when you seek a job after graduation.

If you already know that you don't want to go to college straight out of high school, then you should do this in high school.

This may be more challenging because your disability may make it very difficult or even prohibit you from doing the jobs that teens normally do. In my case, I knew that my neighbors weren't going to hire me to babysit their kids. Neither was my dad's friend going hire me to work in his pizza parlor. These were both jobs that my incredibly industrious sister did as a teen. This was not because my neighbors or my dad's friends were ignorant! My disability realistically did prevent me from carrying out the functions of those two jobs. I had to just accept that and find a job that a high school student with my disability could do.

This is an example of counteracting my limitations by coming up with an action plan *that took my real abilities into account.* My high school hired juniors and seniors to work in the library after school, so that's what I decided to go for. This plan solved my three obstacles to getting a job as a teen: it was something I could do, they were looking for applicants my age, and I would have transportation despite not having a bike or a car. During my high school years, that was the best way for me to earn my own money. The extra money, not the experience, was my main motivation for wanting the position. I really wanted my own money!

Your high school could be a great resource for you to get work experience! Talk to your school counselors about this issue – perhaps at your next individualized education plan (IEP) meeting. If you are not comfortable with IEP team, talk to your favorite teacher, guidance counselor or administrator. Talk to someone at your school and say "I just do not have the same opportunities to do the same kinds of jobs that many other teens get due to my disability. So, what can I do?"

You might also want to tell them that adults with disabilities face far higher unemployment rates than those without. Tell them that you are trying to take proactive steps not to get caught in this statistic. Ask them if there is anything at your school that you could do. Maybe you could work a couple of hours a week in the library or the office.

You might be able to have this activity written into your IEP, or it could be something separate that you are doing. Identify who best to talk to. Back to my example, I did not feel that my IEP team would be the most sensible way to get the position I wanted. I did feel that one of the assistant librarians liked me. I tried to cultivate a friendly rapport with her during sophomore year and figured I would approach her first to request an interview. *If you do not ask, you will never receive!*

Many high schools have programs that allow students to work for credit. If you intend to go right into the workforce after high school, you would be well served by such a program to establish a work history! If you are set on gaining admission to a top university, you would be better served just taking classes in high school, and then during *college* start working. An after-school job looks good on a college application; however, so do volunteering or extracurricular activities.

Resources for Employment Straight out of High School

As with all 'resource sections' in this book, please keep in mind that websites get taken down and web addresses get changed. Information was current within a few months before publication of this book. The program names you find here can be used to do internet searches of your own for up-to-date links.

AmeriCorps

https://www.nationalservice.gov/node/36515

AmeriCorps engages more than 75,000 Americans in intensive service each year at nonprofits, schools, public agencies, and community and faith-based groups across the country.

Since the program's founding in 1994, more than 900,000 AmeriCorps members have contributed more than 1.2 billion hours in service across America while tackling pressing problems and mobilizing millions of volunteers for the organizations they serve.

Disability & Inclusion Advisor:
Email: disability@cns.gov

Career OneStop

http://careeronestop.org/

CareerOneStop is a Department of Labor-sponsored web site that offers career resources and assessment tools for job seekers.

Goodwill Industries International Inc.

http://www.goodwill.org

Goodwill is one of the world's largest nonprofit providers of education, training, and career services for people with physical, mental and emotional disabilities, as well as those with disadvantages such as welfare dependency, homelessness, and lack of education or work experience.

Goodwill Industries
15810 Indianola Drive
Rockville, Maryland 20855

Phone: (800) 664-6577 or (301) 530-6500
Fax: (301) 530-1516

Javits-Wagner-O'Day / AbilityOne Program

http://www.abilityone.org

The Javits-Wagner-O'Day (JWOD) program is now called the AbilityOne Program. AbilityOne is a Federal initiative to help people who are blind or severely disabled find employment by working for nonprofit agencies that sell products and/or services to the U.S. Government. In 2006, nearly 47,000 people were employed through the program, making AbilityOne the largest source of work opportunities for people who are blind or have other severe disabilities in the U.S.

Job Corps

http://recruiting.jobcorps.gov

Job Corps is the nation's largest and most comprehensive residential education and job training program for at-risk youth, ages 16 through 24. Job Corps combines classroom, practical, and work-based learning experiences to prepare youth for stable, long-term, high-paying jobs.

Job Corps is administered by the Department of Labor's Office of the Secretary. For information on Job Corps, including eligibility requirements and location of the center nearest you, call (800) 733-JOBS.

Marriott Foundation for People with Disabilities: Bridges from School to Work

http://www.bridgestowork.org/

National studies show that well over 50% of the 250,000 youth who exit special education each year remain unemployed one year later, with many more significantly underemployed. Meanwhile, employers continue to state that attracting and retaining a strong workforce is one of their greatest challenges, while more than 60% of them say that they have never knowingly employed an individual with disabilities. To help close this gap, the Foundation developed Bridges from School to Work." This acclaimed program matches the interests and abilities of young people with the workforce needs of employers, creating and supporting strong employment relationships that work to the benefit of all.

Marriott Foundation for People with Disabilities
10400 Fernwood Road
Bethesda, MD 20817

Phone: (301) 380-7771
Fax: (301) 380-8973
TTY: (301) 380-6600
Email: Linda.bender@marriott.com

National Statler Center for Careers in Hospitality
http://www.statlercenter.org

The Statler Center is a free 13-week training program located in Buffalo, NY. The Center trains blind and physically disabled people for great careers in the hospitality industry. The Center aims to prepare people with disabilities for hospitality careers by providing them with an overview of the industry as well as job-specific knowledge. Graduates of its program will be "computer-literate, equipped with a thorough knowledge of industry standards, and ready for successful, long-term careers." Potential employers may be hotels, convention centers, travel agents, restaurants, etc. There is no cost to attend this training program, and the Center states [that] its job placement rate is approximately 85%.

1160 Main Street
Buffalo, New York 14209
Phone: 716/882-5690
Fax: 716/882-5577
Email: info@statlercenter.org

Project Search
http://www.projectsearch.us/OurPROGRAM.aspx

Project SEARCH is a one-year, school-to-work program that takes place entirely at the workplace. This innovative, business-led model features total workplace immersion, which facilitates a seamless combination of classroom instruction, career exploration and work site-based training and support.

State Directory of Office for Apprenticeship
https://www.doleta.gov/OA/stateoffices.cfm#NC

All 50 states offer a wide range of apprenticeship programs leading to meaningful careers and credentials. Because of the new workforce law, these programs now are legally open and accessible for job seekers with disabilities.

State Vocational Rehabilitation Agency
http://wdcrobcolp01.ed.gov/Programs/EROD/org_list.cfm?category_ID=SVR

Find a VR office in your state from the list at this webpage

The ABCs of SCHEDULE A
https://www.eeoc.gov/eeoc/publications/abc_applicants_with_disabilities.cfm

Tips for Applicants with Disabilities on Getting Federal Jobs

Year Up
http://www.yearup.org/about/main.php?page=program

Year Up is a one-year, intensive training program that provides low-income young adults, ages 18-24, with a combination of hands-on skill development, college credits, and corporate internships. If you have an Individual Education Program (IEP), Year

Up will work with you to implement it at Year Up to the extent it is reasonable to do so.

Taking Part in Your IEP Process

A 2004 amendment to the Individuals with Disabilities Education Act (IDEA) requires that any student who is 14 years old be invited to his or her IEP meeting. I feel that it can be appropriate for even younger students to attend. I started attending IEP meeting when I was 12 years old.

As a student, it can be a little intimidating to attend a meeting with a lot of adults who are all talking about you. Your parent(s) were probably slightly intimidated when they went to your first IEP meeting because it was all new to them as well. It is okay if you do not say much, and just watch and listen. At my first meeting I didn't say much, I just wanted to know what "they" were saying about me.

I suggest that you listen respectfully to whoever is talking; even if you disagree, don't interrupt. When that person is finished speaking, make good eye contact and say "I understand what you said and where you're coming from. However, this is how I see it because…"

Before you attend, think about any issues that you want to discuss so that you will be in a better position to "sell" your proposal to the IEP team. Examples might include starting to use a paraprofessional/para-pro, formally called an aide, or ceasing to use one. Or maybe you feel you need a modification to the curriculum in one of your classes so that you receive alternative assignments. Another example is you need an accommodation to get from class to class easier.

When you have identified the area(s) where you want to make some changes, ask yourself *how* you want them changed, what is/are the alternative(s)? Then ask yourself why your plan would work better for your needs. It's also a good idea to consider how your change might benefit the school – for example by saving them some money.

I also recommend that you talk with your parent(s) ahead of time about what you want from the meeting, for two reasons. First, your parents will be your best allies for getting what you want. If you talk to them before the meeting, they can help you prepare alternate solutions and how to explain how those solutions would benefit the interests of the school (or at least not hurt those interests).

Second, if you are uncomfortable talking to the other adults in the IEP meeting, your parents could do most of the talking for you. This way, you do not have to talk a lot, but you can still get your point of view expressed. And of course, you are still there, hearing what's being said about your case.

At your IEP meeting you should make your educational and career goals known. As I've said, you don't have to be extremely specific or certain about what you want it. But just being clear that you want to attend college or that you want to work with children, or with animals, or to be an artist, is great!

If you really do not want to go to your IEP meeting, that's your choice. You can still be involved in the process by talking to your parent(s) beforehand about what you want and then asking them what happened.

High School IEP Tips

With every grade level that you advance, the importance of your participation goes up. Some of the challenges you face will remind you of your disabilities, which may be less than pleasant.

But remember that one of the benefits of high school is that you get to practice life as an adult while you still have the support of your parents for most of your day-to-day activities. However, you feel now about your disabilities, they are probably going to be something you'll need to manage one way or another throughout your life. The transition to having less support is best if it is gradual. You and your parents can work together throughout your teenage years at managing this area of your life.

In the paragraphs below, I use an asterisk (*) to denote issues that could also be discussed during a less formal meeting with your case manager or at your IEP. Where you discuss these issues depends on what you feel is best and how accessible these folks are to you during other times. However, you might want to raise these issues at your actual IEP meetings, because those meetings are the forum where the most people are together to focus on your goals.

- **Plan for the meeting.** What's working and what's not? What do you want to change? Know what courses you signed up for and what and (if any) accommodations or modifications you feel you need for each.

- **Decide beforehand whether you will want a longer meeting timeslot.** Typically, only 20 to 30 minutes is scheduled for each student's meeting, because they have a lot of students to meet with. If you feel you need to discuss multiple changes to your current program, you may want to request that a longer meeting time slot be scheduled for you. In both tenth and eleventh grades, after one of my meetings had been going on for 45 minutes, we needed to schedule a second meeting due to time running out. This was because, I needed to make some major changes in how I was being accommodated, and most of my IEP team were opposed my needs.

- **Know the difference between *accommodations* and *modifications*.** *Accommodations* are adaptations to the existing curriculum or school routine. *Modifications* are changes to the curriculum. When you are in high school the law entitles you to both. This differs from college and employment, when you are only entitled to accommodations.

I most certainly should have had some modifications in addition to accommodations. For example, instead of being required to make posters – dioramas – that I couldn't make because I had no fine motor skills, I should have gotten permission to do a writing assignment instead. In addition, I could have arranged for a reduced number of math homework problems and extended deadlines for those assignments.

- **Discuss accommodations**. You might need adaptations for laboratory activities, for example, to make sure the equipment is accessible to you. Or, you might need para-pro to help you conduct the activities. Or, you might just need alternative assignments. This will vary depending on your physical limitations and the course.

- **Consider Standardized Tests or AP Exams:** Consider what accommodations you will need to take either of these. Ask about the procedures for requesting accommodations from outside agencies who might oversee such tests.

- *** Share your thoughts about college and career.** Tell the team as much as you know about what you want after high school. If you know what college you want to go to, say so. You never know what help or tips they will volunteer.

- *** Invite suggestions.** This could be about what you should do over the summer to raise your prospects for a first job after high school or college admission. You do not have to accept all suggestions! My IEP team would have suggested a day camp for people five through twenty-one! *No, thank you!* But you have nothing to lose by asking for suggestions. Someone on your IEP team could be particularly discerning or well-connected and could set you up with something you really want to do, either to get into college or for yourself.

- *** Ask about scholarships for disabled students.** If anyone there has knowledge, ask what the process is, how to get application materials and when the application deadline(s) are.

- **Ask yourself who you would like to be there and arrange to invite them.** Who works at your school and would add valuable input towards your goal(s) for the meeting? You would probably not want the room crowded with all your teachers. But I was comforted in one meeting when I entered the room and saw not only my parents – whom I knew were going to be there – but also another staff member who I felt "got it." It was a big help to have *three* people there who I felt confident were on my side. I had not thought to invite this other staff member to the meeting, but since she had become involved in my situation at school, she came.

If you feel one teacher is doing an especially good job of accommodating you in his or her class, and you would like similar accommodations in your other classes that would be a good person to invite! Or, if problems have arisen in the previous school year and a faculty member, staff member or administrator have been helpful in solving them, they also would be good for you to invite.

You can either ask them to come, or drop them a note or an email, saying the date and time, and "I would appreciate it if you could come to this meeting because..."

- **Case for Independence:** If you want to be more independent or receive fewer services, a good way to support this is to say you need to know whether you can do college without the help of (fill in the blank). Colleges are not legally required to accommodate you to the same extent that high schools are.

- **Lean on your support team!** For me, this was mostly my mom. Communication both before and after was crucial. Before, I needed to tell her what I wanted and after, I needed to vent. Sometimes we both needed to vent to each other!

TMI!
Finally, I will not tell you to read your IEP. But after I read part of mine once, I never did so again. I was put off by the language that was used regarding social, communication, or self-advocacy objectives. I understood why those sections were there: schools are mandated to write all sections for all students who require an IEP. But I would just get mad when I read the material. I decided there was no point in putting myself through that reaction again; it would have been counterproductive for me. I could successfully advocate for myself during the planning process to get what I needed without reading more of it.

Nonetheless, I do advise you to keep copies of your high school IEPs. Should you ever need accommodations to take the LSAT, GMAT, or other tests in college, it will be easier to prove that you need such accommodations can point to the history of your disability and accommodations that you received in the past. The agencies that manage these test administrations will scrutinize your requests and look for reasons to deny them. The further back that you can produce documentation that you have received accommodations, the better chance you have to get them again, or new ones, as needed.

It is better to have something and not need it than to need it and not have it! I had no clue about this issue in high school! Why would I? My school never told me about this. It seemed to me that was they never thought about the students' futures beyond high school. If I now tried to contact my old high school requesting my IEPs from '93 to '96 because I now need to sit for the bar, I doubt I would even get a response – and if I did, it would be "Sorry, we don't have your records anymore"!

If you receive any accommodations to take the SAT, ACT or any Advanced Placement exams, keep the documentation of it such in the same file.

School and Walking

As an adult with cerebral palsy (CP), looking back on the way my disability was treated when I was a child, I believe there was too much emphasis on trying to get me to walk at school. To me, school serves two main purposes:

- Academic preparation for college and later life, and
- A fulfilling social life while in school that will provide you with connections after graduation.

If trying to walk at school is making you miss the beginning or end of each class because you need to leave early to avoid the crowded hallways ... or if walking takes up a lot of your energy that you need to use for more important things ... is it worth it?

In middle school, I did not want to be in a wheelchair. If I had to relive middle school, I would have used my wheelchair exclusively at school. I don't think I retained any gains in my physical abilities by trying to walk so much. It was more hassle than it was worth.

Finally, in high school, the building was way too big for me to walk from class to class, hence I settled in to using my manual wheelchair all the time during school hours. It made my life so much simpler, and actually made me feel more "normal." Don't underestimate the value of normalcy! If you are always thinking you look different or are being kept out of a social group because you look awkward, you'll be stressed out and distracted. That will keep you from doing as well as you otherwise would. If you basically need a wheelchair, don't be afraid to use one.

No matter where they are on the academic scale, most people have the fondest memories – or their most painful ones – regarding their social connections. If you must leave class five minutes early to avoid crowded halls because you have trouble keeping your balance, you are missing out on the opportunities that the other kids have to catch up with each other. So, give yourself the support you need to take advantage of this special time in your life. It is both fun and good for you!

When and How to Consider Mobility Assistance

Typically, middle school is when students start to need to change classrooms several times a day. Because of this, students with physical disabilities should do a mobility evaluation at least three times: when they enter middle school, when they enter high school, and just before they go to college.

For those of you who walk without struggle, great! Otherwise consider every alternative. Make the decision that lets you focus on your academics and social life. If you have a physical therapist (PT), include him or her in this decision. My parents, my PT, and I understood that I could not keep walking during school. They thought I should have had a power chair starting in high school. I kept choosing to use a manual chair because that was the option that made me feel the most normal, or the least "disabled." The result of that decision was that mobility did not hinder or impact my life while I was at high school, during those crucial years. I kept walking around my home and short distances in the community when it was practical to take the extra time that that required.

That whole conversation and decision was a great example of my caregivers helping me think through my needs and options, and then letting me make the choice that I knew was right for me. If your caregivers are not like that, look for some it's important that you find some who *are*.

Using a wheelchair is not giving up. It is just giving yourself a fair chance at having the most normal and fulfilling life that you can, by setting yourself up for success – in school and after!

Surgeries and Timing

Physical disabilities vary a great deal, as do the treatments for them. With some disabilities, such as CP and Spina Bifida, orthopedic surgeries may be common. Again, this varies widely; I know adults with CP who have had no surgeries. Others have had surgeries numbering well into the double digits.

Would It Be Worth the Risks?

From my perspective as an adult with CP, when faced with a decision as to whether a child with a disability should have surgery, one of the questions to be asked and answered is, "If things go well, will it really raise the probability that my child will achieve his or her full potential in the long run?" It is easy to define a surgical goal as to walk better. But then you need to ask yourself, *will walking better increase independence or the likelihood that my child will fulfill his or her educational, professional, or personal goals?* If the answer is yes, go for it. If the answer is no, you may need to discuss it further with your medical team.

When Should We Schedule the Surgery?

Based on my personal experience, I strongly advocate having these types of surgeries done in the summer. The simple reason is that your body and perhaps your mind also will need time to recover from the surgery. Having to go back to school as soon as possible or start doing five subjects worth of work at home, is a challenge that you can avoid without any real penalties if you have your surgery in the summer.

Here's how it went for me. It was first proposed that I have surgery in the middle of my high school junior year, then be on home study for however long I needed to recover. My mom and I said, "Absolutely not!" We both knew that that would have put me at a huge disadvantage academically. I knew that keeping up with my studies from home would have been beyond what I could handle. We held firm and got a surgery date during summer. In doing so, I was what I needed to do to balance my medical and academic responsibilities.

Get Surgeries Done Before 11th Grade

To fine-tune all this, don't schedule any surgeries during the summers after tenth or eleventh grades. Why?

First, it will cost you a summer of participation in activities that will help you get into college.

Second, and more important, if something goes wrong, it could affect most of your next school year. Your junior year and the first semester of your senior year are the most important times of your high school career in terms of how good you look to college admission boards. I don't think it's usually worth the risk.

Of course, there will be exceptions. If the purpose of the surgery is to alleviate pain, and the surgery goes well, it could very well make up for the risks. You can't do your best in school when you are frequently in pain. Anybody can get an illness such as appendicitis or experience an injury that requires emergency surgery. All high schools have procedures to deal with those issues. However, if you need to schedule surgeries such as an osteotomy, bone lengthening, or muscle/tendon lengthening/transfers, I would advise you to try to come up with another option.

If you don't find out that you need a procedure in time to follow this advice, another option is to wait until the "lame-duck" session of high school – right after the mid-terms of your senior year. By then your college applications will already have been sent out. All you will need to do on home study is enough to pass your subjects. If you do a surgery in January or February, you will be well enough to go to any senior activities that are important to you, even if you are not back at school full-time.

Should you opt for this, try to work with a college admissions coach. This is so they can work with you to set up a schedule to get all your college applications and financial aid forms out before your surgery date. Also, inform your guidance counselor about a month before, so arrangements can be made to have assignments sent home and/or your teacher(s) come to your house – or both – after a certain target date.

You might think that having surgery this close to going to college will make everything too hectic, especially if you have complications. In that event, you could delay starting college for a semester, or even a whole year. Once you have been accepted, all you need to do is contact the institution you plan on attending and find out their procedures for applying for a medical deferment.

During your "gap semester/year" there are a lot of things you can do to be better prepared for college and career. Concentrate on your recovery and then on preparing to go to college. If you are bored, take a class or two online, or take a volunteer position that relates to your tentatively chosen career goals. People who are in positions to accept you into programs or introduce you to those who can, will be impressed if you stay busy and can show them a record of consistent focus toward your goals.

While you may feel fully recovered and ready to go to college by the following January, there are benefits to starting in the fall with the next freshman class. It allows you to go through a full orientation with all other freshmen. Otherwise you might very well feel like the odd man out because you missed the orientation the others all went through – as well as a semester of making friends that most of the other students experienced.

The school you attend should also factor into this decision. Some colleges do a lot to try to inspire freshman cohesion and unity. Others do the same boring orientation where they just give students basic information. At those schools the orientation isn't much of a social experience, so it would not matter much if you started in the spring at such a school. To me the purpose of going to orientation is simple: to meet new people on your new campus!

To Sum Up
Again, every situation is different. Obviously, I cannot give any medical advice. I'm just encouraging you to consider whether any proposed surgery will help you reach your goals. Then think hard about the timing and how it will factor into your college admissions!

Lastly, share your thoughts, concerns and priories with your medical team. They might not be thinking about it from the angle of how it will affect your life at school.

Early Assessment of Your ADLs

Activities of Daily Living (ADLs) is a medical term used to refer to daily self-care activities.

I am talking about this because, if things such as taking a bath and getting dressed are challenging for you, you need to have a plan in place for managing these things when you either go to college or move out. The earlier you start to think about and practice these issues, the better off they will be when you have places to be and people to see every day of the week!

There may be some areas where you will always need more help because of your disabilities, and that's OK. Part of making your individual plan is to consider how you will handle the areas in which you cannot be independent. You may need a Personal Care Assistant (PCA). This will not stop you from moving out, going to college, or working! Plenty of adults who need daily PCA care live on their own, leading full professional lives.

Refer to Chapter 5 for more about PCA care. You might be like me when I went away to college. I was not functional at the level that I would have liked to be at, however, I was able to "make do." The situation was not ideal. If you think about it, everyone on the planet is making do with whatever they have. The important thing is, it did not stop me from achieving my goal of a college degree. It also did not stop me from living on my own, as I feared it would during my adolescence.

Aim High, Aim Early
I was grateful that the first week of college was not the first time I started to confront these issues. I started at age eleven and was able to make some progress by 18 that did help me be able to live in a dorm as a college freshman. However, on a personal level, I am not at the level I was aiming for when I first did an evaluation of my ADLs

Occupational Therapists (OTs) normally work with ADLs, while physical therapists (PTs) work mainly with mobility issues. If you feel you are a little behind what a person your age is doing for themselves, your OT would be a great person to talk to. Tell your OT what area(s) you want to improve on. And then ask what a realistic starter goal is in that area for you and enlist the OT's help to devise and work a plan for reaching it.

If you do not have an OT, then talk with your parent(s) about where they are with still helping you. Often, parents of children with disabilities automatically get into habits of helping their children where they are struggling. This is no one's fault. As a child grows up, it is important to question these habits. Will help really be needed throughout the child's life? Or can it be gradually withdrawn as the child becomes more able to manage his or her own needs?

What to Work on
Start looking at working on areas that you need help with. This process can start slowly. For example, if the issue is dressing, the goal could be you try to dress yourself once a week, not on a school morning where you are pressed for time. If you are able to make steady progress towards this goal until you reach it, then you can increase the frequency of which you do this task by yourself.

Summers are a great time to work on these issues since you usually have more free time then. A good habit would be to revisit this list at least once a year, the start of your summer break. Make a realistic goal list have your parent(s) and/or your OT help. Then devote a small percentage of your summer break to working toward your goals.

When one has significant physical disabilities, being self-reliant for your ADLs can take years of both trial and error and repeated evaluation. This is okay! Remember, small gains will usually get you at least closer to where you want to be. Just keep working at it.

If you and your parents feel that you are not making any progress towards your ADL goals despite consistent effort, then your parents can navigate either the educational or medical system to get you an evaluation and maybe sessions with an OT. Or, you might just have to accept that you will need help with certain ADLs your whole life, especially if your disability is of a type that tends to get worse over time.

Assistive Technology (AT)

Assistive technology (AT) is a broad term for any device that helps an individual with a disability compensate for such to perform any task. A wide range of products are covered under this term. Examples include:

- Wheelchairs or other mobility aids
- Hearing aids
- Computer hardware and software
- ADL aids
- Voice-activated environmental controls

There are always going to be two main areas in your life where you might need AT: home, and school or work. Assistive technology can help you become more self-sufficient in both. It is common for schools to send students with disabilities for an AT evaluation. I was evaluated a couple of times when I was a student. If the evaluation is centered on the student's academic need, the focus will usually be on which types of computer equipment will help. If the evaluation is due to either needs with basic ADLs or mobility, durable medical equipment (DMEs) will be considered. A DME is a product such as a wheelchair, walker, shower bench button hook, or adaptive utensils.

I have had the use of assistive technology dramatically improve my life at school. A very talented AT expert, Dr. Tom Sicoli, whom I had originally been evaluated by several years earlier, ran into me when I was at the DuPont Institute for a medical visit. He said, "I have something new I want to show you; stop up before you leave." What he wanted to show me was a handheld computer designed for people with disabilities, called Alpha Smart Pro. When I saw this product I instantly knew that it would eliminate the obstacles that I had been encountering with using a traditional laptop to become independent at school. It was also a lot cheaper than a traditional laptop, which meant my parents could afford to buy one. That in turn meant we owned it, so the school could not restrict how I transported it. It also meant that I could take it to college, which I ended up doing.

The lesson with that is the most expensive piece of equipment may not be the option that works best for you. This affordable product worked wonderfully for me and made my life at school easier. I used it both to take my own notes and complete most of my assignments during my senior year of high school and throughout college. With my Alpha Smart Pro, who needed a para-pro? Not me; the product replaced a whole person. I wished I had found it at the beginning of my school years rather than just before I started twelfth grade. For me, it was a miracle product!

I have included this story not to endorse this particular product, because technology changes rapidly. I included it to make the larger point that *the right assistive technology can make a huge difference in your quality of life*. If you have a physical problem doing anything, whether it be at home or school, do some research to find out whether there might be a product out there that can make things easier for you. The links below will get you started.

Assistive Technology Disclaimer

Millions of AT products exist. As my story illustrates, AT can change your life. Yet it is not as simple as going after the first product that promises to solve your problem. Everyone's different and verbal descriptions might just fail to capture your precise mix of needs. There is no substitute here for trial and error – but start by reading carefully and asking lots of questions.

I have tried lots of products that did not help me at all. Two examples are key guards and writing aids: I don't type any better with a key guard than without one. The less equipment I need, the better. If it doesn't help significantly, I don't want it.

My second example is handwriting aids. It is just not possible for me to write so I use a computer to type everything. Most new devices take practice to learn their optimal use, but after you've given a device a fair shake, move on rather than frustrate yourself.

State Libraries for Assistive Technology

Every state has an assistive technology lending library. These are like any other libraries in that they are completely free and available to everyone. The one difference is that instead of each school or community having a branch of a library, generally there is one assistive technology library per state. You can still elect to pick or drop things off. However, because there is only one in each state assistive technology libraries are in the habit of shipping items to you free of charge. When they ship something to you, a pre-payed return label comes with it for you to return it without incurring any charge.

This grants you an excellent opportunity to try a wide array of items prior to buying. This is huge, because you can see if something works for you, easily. Loaner periods are usually a few weeks. Some libraries may arrange a longer loaner period for certain items upon request.

I love this because anyone and everyone can use these libraries, you do not have to be a teacher or a medical professional. Type in your state plus assistive technology lending library into your search engine to find you're states library's website or see the web address below. You can then browse their inventory and find out how to start the simple process of being able to get items sent to you. In my state, all I needed to do was sign a form, and there was five different ways to get it to them. You can sign it, take a picture and text it back, it's designed to be easy for you to access and I found those who work there were very helpful!

If you find an item that works for you but is expensive, these libraries are also great to ask about what funding sources are available so that you can purchase one.

I really love that these exist because I feel there are super useful and helpful to us.

State Assistive Technology Library Directory

http://soar.askjan.org/IssueConcern/217

Assistive Technology (AT) Resources

ABLEDATA

http://www.abledata.com

Provides objective information about assistive technology products and rehabilitation equipment available from domestic and international sources. Although ABLEDATA does not sell any products, they can help you locate the companies that do.

Assistive Technology Forum

http://www.rehabtool.com/forum/discussions/98.html

Discuss your needs, questions, and options with others online. Someone out there may have a solution to your challenge.

Lilly Walters' About One Hand Typing

http://www.aboutonehandtyping.com

Lilly Walters, who is a one-hand typist and an author of two books on the topic, offers this site providing information on the options available for one-hand typists, as well as some motivational success stories, and available products.
Email: lilly@aboutonehandtyping.com

Funding Assistive Technology Through State Medicaid Programs

http://nls.org/Disability/NationalAssistiveTechnologyProject

Funded through a grant from the National Institute on Disability and Rehabilitation Research (NIDRR), this project provides nationwide support services to Protection and Advocacy (P&A) and Client Assistance Program attorneys and advocates, as well as Legal Services and private attorneys who are working on AT advocacy issues. The project's web site features downloadable booklets on funding AT through Social Security, SSI (Supplemental Security Income), Medicaid, vocational rehabilitation, and the public schools' special education system. The project's online newsletter is the AT Advocate.

Phone: 716-847-0650
TTY: 716-847-1322

National Library Service for the Blind and Physically Handicapped

http://www.loc.gov/nls/

The NLS is provided by the Library of Congress. The site includes information on library services for the blind, an on-line catalog listing braille and recorded books available from the NLS and other library services around the world, and reference circulars on a variety of blindness-related topics.

Phone: 800-424-8567 or 202-707-5100
TTY: 202-707-0744
Email: nls@loc.gov

Patterson Medical

http://www.pattersonmedical.com

This is a catalog geared toward medical professionals. If you need it for your home, it would be expensive to cover out of pocket. However, they also have less expensive products that can help with ADLs and mobility. If you see a product here that you think might help, but you can't afford it, talk to your medical team or OT about it. Maybe there's a way to try one before you buy it or even get it covered by insurance.

If you need a product to help you at school, it's the school's responsibility to pay for it if you want them to. You can start by talking to your school therapist or your IEP Team. However, you'll often be better off buying the product for yourself. For example, if you need a book bag for your wheelchair, yes, you will use it mainly at school; however, it may make the most sense and be easiest for you or your parents to buy it. If the school buys it, they own it, not you. They can prohibit you from taking it home at night, and you probably will not get to keep it after that year. But if a product seems very promising in terms of how much it will help you be more independent, less stressed out, and so on, and it's beyond your means, it would be better for the school to buy you one and keep control over it than for you not to have the AT product at all.

RESNA

http://www.resna.org/

The Rehabilitation Engineering and Assistive Technology Society of North America is the premier professional organization dedicated to promoting the health and well-being of people with disabilities through increasing access to technology solutions. RESNA advances the field by offering certification, continuing education, and professional development; developing assistive technology standards; promoting research and public policy; and sponsoring forums for the exchange of information and ideas to meet the needs of our multidisciplinary constituency.

TechMatrix

http://www.techmatrix.org/

The TechMatrix is a dynamic, searchable data base provides information on resources for students with special needs. Funded by the U.S. Department of Education's Office of Special Education Programs and developed by the National Center for Technology Innovation (NCTI) and the Center for Implementing Technology in Education

(CITEd), the database enables educators and parents to make technology choices based on reviews and research.

Phone: 202-403-5323
Email: techmatrix@air.org

It is NEVER Too Early to Start Thinking about Career Paths

Most students have no clue what they want to do as adults once they figure out that "Fairy Princess" or "Superhero" are probably out. There is nothing wrong with this. Many do not know what they really want to do, even after several years in the post-high school or college job market.

The average American changes careers three to five times in their lifetime, according to the US Department of Labor. Most people change jobs within the same career area even more frequently than that.

In most cases, it's not a question of knowing what you want to do with the rest of your life, but just knowing what you want to do *next* – or for the next few years. You will be revisiting this question most of your life.

If you don't want to be disadvantaged relative to other people, you will get up and go to school – 180 days out of the year. Yet, it is rarely discussed in school why you are there. They just expect you to show up and do your work because they tell you so. I believe part of the reason that the high school drop-out rate is so high in the US is that not enough is done to emphasize to students why they are there. I will tell you the reason as I see it in one word: *freedom!* You will have more and better options *the rest of your life* if you do well in high school.

If you already know that your chosen profession requires an advanced degree, then the classes you take and the grades you earn are important NOW. One thing builds on the next: good class choices and grades will help you attend the college of your choice. Getting into the college of your choice and making good grades there – along with other crucial tricks I'll be telling you about later in the book – will help you be more confident and successful when you apply for jobs.

If you don't already know for sure the career area where you want to work, you at least know that you want to have as many choices as you can. It's okay to be indecisive about career at your age, but you don't want that indecisiveness to translate into closed and locked doors. Keeping your options open means working hard and working smart now, with what is right there in front of you.

Hopefully this gives you a stronger and healthier motivation to do your homework in your least favorite class than because someone in authority told you to.

Picture It
Aside from keeping you fired-up to do well in school, adopting some career goals early on will also help you envision your future, making decisions easier. If you know what you want to major in, it is easier to figure out what college to go to. The sooner you know the industry where you want to work, the sooner you can start making contacts that will help you on your way. This is important for everyone – but it's *vital* if you have a disability. The sooner you

start trying to get ahead of your competition, the more likely it is that you will succeed in getting that all-important first job after you have completed school.

Career Clusters

A great way to know what your options are and then start to narrow them down is to use the career cluster system. This was developed by the US Department of Education. It breaks the available occupations down into sixteen groups.

The good news is the possible choices for a future vocation are ample. The bad news is that there are so many choices it may be overwhelming. But looking over these 16 categories is a lot less intimidating than looking at a list of more than 100 jobs!

Source: http://www.glencoe.com/sec/careers/cclusters/student/introclusters.shtml

Once you have glanced over these "clusters," my advice is to first find the area that interests you without considering your disabilities. Then, find the jobs within that area that reasonably match your physical abilities.

The last step is to determine what level of education is required for each possible job that you have selected. Ask yourself, "How long can I see staying in school?" and "How well does that match up with the education that's typically required for the jobs I selected?"

Then, start researching these jobs by both using the internet or by talking to the adults in your life about the jobs you are considering. If you have an opportunity to take an elective in school, go to a summer program or take part in an extra-curricular activity to try out what you are thinking – go for it!

Pencil It In

Nothing is ever set in stone. You might change your mind ten times in a few short years. That's okay! In fact, it is great! You don't have to be sure of your preference in order to start acting on it. Just by taking your desires seriously and taking sensible steps to explore them, you will put yourself near the front of the pack. This will help you at every point when you need to make choices about your education – and it will help you stay motivated.

Find a Mentor – or More Than One!
It is never too early to have a mentor. The sooner you can start networking and building what will be your future résumé, the better! By taking actions to prepare for a career, even if you still in middle school, you are counteracting the fear that your disability will hold you back. I had this fear in middle school and I wished that I had dealt with it by finding a mentor and seeking out opportunities to both define my career goals and begin to work towards them.

Job Shadowing

For each career cluster that you have identified, ask your fellow students or the adults in your life if they know anyone in that profession that you might be able to spend a half-day or a day at work with. The goal of this is to make it real. Is what they did and what happened to them throughout the day, the same as the way you pictured that job? Could you see yourself doing that job for at least a year or two?

Ask about the education and experience that it took to get that job. Is it an entry-level job, or is it the kind of job that they worked their way up to for 10 years? How straightforward was this person's path into that job?

Also ask if they know of anything you can take part in during high school or college, such as mentorship programs, volunteering or an internship, to help get established in the field.

ALWAYS write a thank-you note for this person's time. I say this needs to be done within a week. I also say a formal email is an acceptable.

If you are still interested in doing what they do after you observe them, try as best you can to keep in contact with them. Hint, holiday cards or a note when you graduate high school or college are a perfect way to do this. Don't let them only hear from you when you need something.

It is *never* too early to start making contacts. You never know who will help you get you your first internship or job! Of course, if you job-shadow your aunt, keeping contact will take a different form than if you job-shadow a friend of your dad's co-worker.

Ideally, you should job-shadow in a couple of different fields. If this tells you that a career is not what you thought, and you do not feel you see yourself in that job, that's excellent! Knowing what will not work for you is as important as knowing what will. This will help you make informed decisions and solid plans.

Informational Interviews
An alternative to job shadowing is an informational interview. This can take as little as ten to fifteen minutes, and it asks less of you and of the other person than job-shadowing.

This kind of interview can be done in person, by phone, email or even instant messaging, but any method should usually be done by appointment. Visit Jobshadow.com for a collection of suggested questions.

Again, follow up with a thank-you note.

Web-Based Resources for Career Exploration or Mentorship

DO-IT Pals

https://www.washington.edu/doit/do-it-pals-application

Frequent electronic mail and personal contacts with Mentors support DO-IT Pals' academic, career, and personal goals. Mentors are college students, faculty, and practicing engineers, scientists, and other professionals. Many DO-IT Mentors have disabilities themselves. Experienced DO-IT Pals also develop and practice communication and leadership skills by acting as peer mentors for incoming DO-IT Pals. They make friends and motivate each other to achieve their goals.

Connecting to Success

http://ici.umn.edu/ementoring/

Connecting to Success is an electronic mentoring program, begun in 1999, designed to promote successful transition of youth with disabilities to adult life. Electronic mentoring, also called e-mentoring, uses a combination of e-mail and face-to-face meetings to facilitate mentoring relationships between young people and caring adults. For further information, please contact Joe Timmons at 612-624-5659 or timm0119@umn.edu.

Job Shadow

http://www.jobshadow.com/

Read real interviews from people as they talk about the jobs they do and the careers they have.

Mentoring

http://www.mentoring.org

Great website to see what mentoring is about. Includes resources for finding a mentoring program or a mentor in your local

MyPlan.com

http://www.myplan.com/

Helps students and professionals plan more fulfilling lives by making well-informed decisions about their education and careers. Whether you're deciding on what college to go to, choosing a major, planning for your first career, or thinking about making a career change, MyPlan.com can help you explore options and bring clarity and insight into figuring out what's right for you. 100% independent and unbiased, MyPlan.com gives you the truth about colleges, careers and majors. Our research and data are the most comprehensive you'll find anywhere on the subject. And, with dozens of easy-to-use tools, we've made getting to that information convenient, simple and fun.

National Career Development Association (NCDA)

http://www.ncda.org/aws/NCDA/pt/sp/home_page

The National Career Development Association (NCDA), a division of the American Counseling Association (ACA), promotes the career development of all people over the life span. Resources on this site include an extensive set of links on the topics of

Self-Assessment; Career Development Process; Occupational Information; Employment Trends; Salary Information; Trade and Professional Associations; Military Information; Educational Information; Distance Education; Seminars, Short Courses, and Certification Opportunities; Financial Aid Information; Apprenticeships and Other Alternative Training Opportunities; Job Search Instruction and Advice; Job Banks; Industry and Occupation Specific Information; Researching Employers; Directory of Online Employment Information; Online Counseling.

Occupational Outlook Handbook

http://www.bls.gov/oco/

The Occupational Outlook Handbook is a publication released biennially by the United States Department of Labor's Bureau of Labor Statistics that includes information about the nature of work, working conditions, training and education, earnings, and job outlook for hundreds of different occupations.

The American Association of People with Disabilities' Disability Mentoring Day Program

http://aapd.com

Middle school high school, college students, and job seekers are all welcome to participate. You must be at least a middle school student to participate in DMD; however, there is no maximum age limit. For more information or for questions, please contact the DMD National Team at (800) 840-8844 or email dmd@aapd.com.

The Case for College

College is not for everyone. You do not have to go. There are other options, and as we've seen the cost of the investment keeps going up without the return on that investment necessarily following suit.

However, the chart below gives you reason to seriously consider college, despite the challenges. In high school, although I did not have this chart or any exact statistics, I knew that a college education would raise my chances of getting higher paying jobs. This fact motivated me to take the high school courses that would enable me to have a good shot at getting into college. It should also motivate you to start planning for as many aspects of college as you can, as early as you can.

US Census As educational attainment goes up; work disability goes down

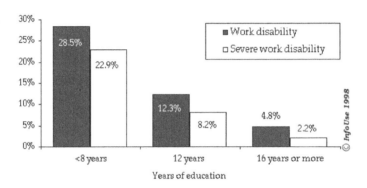

Figure 20: Percentage with work disability and severe work disability, by level of education, 25-64 years
Source: U.S. Bureau of the Census Website

Points to Remember from Chapter 1

✓ Start thinking about your career path early – long before you graduate from high school.

✓ Use Career Clusters to clarify your goals.

✓ Choose reasonable objectives and pursue them aggressively, with the understanding that you will make different career choices throughout your life.

✓ Cultivate mentors and other contacts who can help pull you forward and place you in advantageous positions.

✓ Do job shadowing and informational interviewing.

✓ Use the Internet resources provided in this book and elsewhere.

✓ Not everyone needs to go to college to pursue their chosen career or business path.

✓ If you don't plan to go to college, work part-time in high school and more hours in summer. Show that what you lack in academics, you make up for in hard work!

✓ Attend your IEP meetings; start respectfully participating when you feel comfortable doing so. Look for accommodations and modifications that might serve you. Invite special allies. Keep copies of your written IEPs.

✓ Make smart choices about mobility assistance.

✓ Carefully consider the timing of surgeries.

✓ Do early assessment of ADLs and aim high. Use summers to work on becoming more independent.

✓ Consider assistive technologies that might be of great help to you.

Chapter 2: Selecting a College

There are approximately 7,000 colleges and universities in the United States. How do you pick just one? This might very well be the biggest decision that you have had to make so far in your life. For many of you, that will feel scary at some point in your journey.

But when you start to name all the things that you need or want from a college, the number dwindles very quickly. Soon you will have a college list of five to ten. That list is a lot more manageable. You can't visit hundreds of schools, probably not even dozens. But you can and should visit at least a few before you make your final decisions about where to apply. This chapter will guide you through the process of consciously narrowing your choices.

After you have done your research and created a short list of institutions where you will submit applications, you will be able to celebrate another major milestone. You will have selected several schools that meet most of your requirements.

Know that there are MANY schools out there where you can excel. Also, college is not prison, or a contract to do four seasons of a reality show no matter how bad of an edit you are getting. If, after a semester or two, you feel you made a mistake in your college selection, you can decide if it's best to transfer.

My Mistake

To be quite honest I think my parents and I did a great job picking a college for me, and then another when I decided to transfer. Maybe you're thinking, "If they did such a great job with her college selection, why did Julia have to transfer?" That's a valid question. My answer is, one's needs and ambitions are always changing, so it's okay to choose a "starter school," get used to college, then transfer to a better school, which is what I ended up doing. It is just how my story evolved. Yours will evolve in your own way.

Both schools I attended absolutely fit all my disability-based needs When I was in high school, we set out to find a college that was already set up for me and close enough that I could come home every few weekends. And I wanted the stereotypical pretty campus. We succeeded! Then I felt I needed a bigger school – one that was known for my MIS major – and had more going for it socially. But with these new requirements, as a transfer student, I also needed my new school to fit my disability requirements. We succeeded again! As a student, I could not have been happier with the school that I graduated from in these areas.

As I have described elsewhere in this book, my second school missed the boat with job search assistance. This was a crucial gap, one that I'm hoping to help you address through this book. After all, the main reason most of you are going to college is to be more successful in your chosen field of employment. It impairs your progress in your career path if you have a lot of trouble getting that first job after graduation. It seems to me that many college disability services professionals, strangely enough, lose sight of this. As a student or parent, when you are picking a school you get caught up in the glitz of how nice the campus is, wondering if you can get in, and how you will pay for it. Once you are a student, then you are focused on course work and social life. As a student, you and family are thinking about other things, and assuming that disability services is keeping an eye out for you with regards to career post-graduation. But in my experience the professionals seemed to spend too little time thinking about what will happen after a student graduate.

My parents and I assumed that because I was transferring to one of the top colleges in the country for people with physical disabilities, extensive efforts would have already been made to help graduates find jobs. How wrong we were! We thought we were asking the right questions, but we failed to ask one of the schools I attended if they actually tracked employment outcomes of alumni with disabilities. If so, what are those statistics? Do they have a person within their department whose only job is career counseling and job placement? Does their school take part in the Workforce Recruitment Program (WRP) ? What other efforts are made to facilitate on-campus employer recruitment of students with disabilities? Reflecting back, I transferred to the top school in the country for wheelchair athletics. This would have been great if I was looking for a strong adaptive sports program, but I wasn't. I wanted to make sure the school I picked set me up well for employment in MIS.

"The best school for students with disabilities" will be different for each person with disabilities. What do you need it to mean for you?

The Workforce Recruitment Program: How I *Wish* We Started my College Search

The Workforce Recruitment Program (WRP) is a federal program operated by the US Department of Labor that sends trained recruiters to over 200 college and university campuses to students with disabilities for both internships and jobs after graduation. This program underwent an expansion in 1995 and since then has placed more than 6,000 graduates in positions in both the public and private sector

https://wrp.gov/

This program was the tipping point that led me to write this book! I had an IEP throughout high school, went to two colleges with large disabilities services departments – both of which I was active in – and I had a vocational rehabilitation counselor the last three years of college. Yet no one ever told me about this program!

When I found out about WRP, I wished someone at my high school had told me about it. If they had, I would have had my mom call the federal hotline to get the list of campuses where WRP recruits. That would have been our starting point for my college search. For someone with a significant physical disability, this is as good a starting point as any – and perhaps better than most!

Remember, all idealism aside, you are going to face a much higher unemployment rate than your fellow college graduates will. Don't let this fact *worry* you; instead, use it to *inspire* you to make smarter choices. The first step to doing this is to keep in mind that the main reason you are going to college, if you're like most people (with or without disabilities), is to start a career!

You can request an updated list of schools where the WRP almost always recruits:

Office of Disability Employment Policy

https://www.dol.gov/odep/wrp/

Attn: WRP Coordinator

200 Constitution Ave NW, Rm S-1303
Washington, DC 20210
(202) 693-7880 Voice
(202) 693-7881 TTY
(202) 693-7888 Fax
E-mail: wrp@dol.gov

If I had found out about this program in 1995, I would have had my mother make this call! The vast majority of students who go through the college search/application process have at least one adult who helps. You do not have to be any different!

Once you have the list, start sorting the schools according to the criteria in your chart.

A great many jobs where the WRP places applicants are in government. Don't rule out a government job too quickly just because you'd prefer to work in the private sector. In fact, I devote all of Chapter 12 to getting government jobs!

It's always good to have a backup plan. Working in the private sector is a wonderful goal. It is never too early to start working towards that by making any contacts that you can and getting any work experience you can.

However, the vast majority of recent college graduates start out in a job that isn't their dream position. If the only job offer you get right after graduation is in the public sector, you are best off taking it. You can get some career experience while planning your move for a year (or three) down the road.

Another reason your private sector aspiration should not lead you to rule out the WRP, is that it also places college students into internships. If you have multiple internships on your résumé, you will be a more attractive candidate when interviewing for the position that you most want after graduation.

Finally, one great trick is for you to interview for positions that you are ambivalent about, before interviewing for jobs that you really want. Taking part in the WRP's process will require you to complete several interviews on campus. These can be perfect dress rehearsals for you. Not only will interviewing force you to get your résumé and your interview wardrobe ready while you are still in college, but also it will give you a chance to do your first interviews with an interviewer who has some experience with people who have disabilities. This in turn will allow you to ease into the whole job-hunting process. If the WRP extends you an offer that's attractive to you, great! If you get a better offer elsewhere, that's great too. Worst case, you get practice interviewing and following job interview advice that you can get all over the Internet and in other books, without so much performance anxiety.

Also Consider
The Workforce Recruitment Program is getting more and more competitive. Meaning, if your school has it, or gets it, you need to make sure you have a strong résumé to be selected to interview. Fear not, there are countless ways for you to build a winning résumé in college. In fact, Chapter Seven is devoted to doing just that! So please, read ahead…

No WRP at Your School? Consider Advocating for It
In keeping with a main theme of this book, there is more than one way to do everything. If you end up attending a college where the WRP does not currently recruit, consider starting an effort to bring it to your college.

This program will not work directly with students. It requires that students go through the college's WRP contact or representative. Hence, you need someone on your college's staff. If you have any relationship with your disability's specialist, that person would be good to ask first. If you get a yes, ask for a follow-up call to you after they've been in contact with the WRP to let you know what is going on. Let them know you want to work with them to make this happen. They can help get a group of students together that would be able to participate in the interviews.

If you feel you need to make a more formal presentation to a prospective faculty or staff contact, you might want to take it upon yourself to find a few other students who would both qualify and would like to take part in the interview process. Try to find ten students on your campus and get them to sign a petition. You may also want to ask one or two of them to come with you when you talk to whomever you want to be your sponsor. You have two departments that you can work with, the disability services and career services. Take the information about this program to someone in the department that you chose and ask them to contact them.

An effort like this can-do double duty. Not only might your effort be successful in bringing WRP to your campus, but also, your successful advocacy will look good on your résumé! Make sure the recruiter that comes to your campus from the WRP knows that you were instrumental in bringing them to your school. It can only help you in their hiring process.

Don't start this effort the first couple of weeks of your freshman year in college. You will have enough on your plate. However, don't wait until your senior year either. That would make it tougher to work summer internships while you are still in college.

It will take some time to get the program started at your school. By the time your faculty/staff sponsor contacts WRP, they might already have their schedule set for that academic year and not be able to add a college to it. If you start the process in your sophomore year, then this will not be a huge setback as you and your sponsor can work so it comes to your school in your junior year. If you find this out when you are a senior, about ready to graduate, while you can take part up to a year after graduation, you would need to then be able to travel back to your school.

Again, based on my own experience, it would have been so easy for me to coordinate an effort to get this program at the university where I graduated. I just didn't know about it. And yes, I think some people who I worked with from 10th grade on should have known about it and told me. *But I'm telling you now!* Please refer to page 292 for details about the WRP's interview process.

No School Will Meet All Your Criteria

Having a disability doesn't mean that colleges you'd otherwise like to attend must have everything you could think of in terms of services for people with disabilities. You just need to decide which areas are deal-breakers, which are "nice to have", and which ones don't apply to you. Just because you have hearing loss doesn't mean the college has to have the right kind of alarms installed and working perfectly in every hall of every dorm. Just because you have a service dog doesn't mean you have to rule out all schools that don't have experience with service dogs. Gaps like these might just mean that you'll want to do some extra planning. It might mean giving your school a copy of the law that entitles you to have a service animal, and a copy of the animal's certificate. It might also mean that you'll be a bit more on your own when it comes to knowing how to manage your animal on campus.

One of the dorms where I lived during college had its laundry room in the basement. This beautiful dorm was built in the 1880's and there was no elevator. I loved it because it was in a great location and had a single room with its own bathroom – one of the handful of rooms designated for accessibility throughout the campus. My mobility impairment was such that I was just able to go up and down the stairs with my laundry. Frequently, I would not have had to expend this extra bit of effort, as I was friendly with many of the girls in this small dorm and someone would say, "Let me carry your basket."

If I couldn't walk at all, there were plenty of other dorms with laundry on the main level. Or, the school would have gladly given me permission to use the laundry room of the dorm next to mine. But wheeling far with my laundry on my lap seemed harder than negotiating one flight of stairs. If I'd needed an attendant, of course my attendant could have done my laundry.

It was funny: the first few times the dorm head saw my empty chair right by the stairs, she got scared, wondering if I had fallen down the stairs. She got used to my abilities and my empty wheelchair became a normal sight. Despite my abilities, I felt I needed to have home base easily accessible. I could not imagine being late for class and having to get my chair down two flights just to leave my 'house.'

> ***Key Point:*** You need to decide what you need, as well as what you can make work and how.

How Your Disability Plays into Your Choice of College

Title II of the ADA requires that all post-secondary institutions make their course of study accessible! Furthermore, the ADA explicitly prohibits any school from denying students admission because they do not have experience serving students with disabilities. That means you can go to *any* school you are admitted to regardless of level of disability. I opted to go to schools that are known for catering to those with disabilities because I was tired of fighting for my rights in high school.

During high school, my home life was as good as any teenager could ask for. As with most high schoolers, my meals were cooked for me, my laundry was done, my bathroom was cleaned, my doctor's appointments were made, and my medications were picked up for me. Parents do this stuff for teenagers without disabilities. In my case, my parents made sure they did these things because I did have extra challenges. I knew moving away from home was going be a huge adjustment for me. I just felt I could not handle this if the college didn't really know what to do with me.

Both colleges were great in that they were very glad to give me any accommodation that I needed, both in the classroom and my dorms. Unlike in high school, I did not have to fight for anything! Neither college that I attended supplied PCA services. I do not need PCAs, but at both colleges I knew students who did. They needed assistance twice daily from PCAs. Yet these students lived on campus successfully because they could arrange for their own PCAs.

I am glad I did not decide to go to a school with minimal support for students with disabilities because I hated being classified in high school. Don't let a bad relationship with your high school's IEP team determine the level of service that you pick in college. College is totally different. The disability services department (DSD) does not force anything on you above what that college requires of any other student. They will never contact your parents about anything. The Family Educational Rights and Privacy Act (FERPA) prohibits colleges from contacting a student's parents without the student's permission.

In addition, DSD won't force you to take special classes or meet with them if you don't want to. It is totally your choice whether you register with them, which accommodations you use, and how much you are involved in their department. I have nothing nice to say about my high school's IEP's team. They did a horrible job handling my case. But the staff members of what my college called the Office of Specialized Services were wonderful. I cannot say enough good things about them. It would have been such a mistake if I had not registered with them on the assumption that my experience would be the same as it had been in high school. The experiences were exact opposites.

Your disabilities do not have to play a role at all in the colleges you choose to apply to and attend. But they *can* play the largest role in this choice. How big or small a role that they do play is up to you. For me, it was very helpful to include accessibility and "disabled-friendliness" in my selection criteria.

Otherwise I do not know how I would have chosen from the hundreds of schools that are within a couple hours' drive of my home. When I realized I wanted my college to be almost 100% accessible and to have an active disabilities services department, the choices narrowed fast – down to just two!

Throughout this chapter I will help you decide how much weight to give to your disabilities in picking a college. You don't have to know (and you probably can't know) in advance, which criteria will ultimately be the most important to you. But you can always become one step clearer – about one area at a time.

The first step is to look over the chart one on the next page. It lists the needs that relate to your mix of disabilities as well as considerations for all students. From the 'disabilities side,' check off what you know you're going to need or would be helpful to have. You may only need or want a few features listed on the 'disabilities side.' Or you may check many to most of the items from the 'disabilities side.'

For the, 'questions for all student's side, just answer as best you can. As you advance in your college search, what you both need and want in all categories will become clearer.

After the chart, I will dedicate the next several pages to explaining more in depth what all the items on the chart mean and factors that you may want to consider. The goal of this is to help you decide what you are looking for in a college.

Divide your requirements, from both sides, into *Must Have*'s and *Nice to Have*'s. This entails deciding am I willing to sacrifice this or that, to get something, in a school that is more important to me? Or do I need to be willing to sacrifice something else to get something that I _really_ want?

Questions for Students with Disabilities

- ✓ Building accessibility?
- ✓ Grounds accessibility?
- ✓ Specialty Access?
- ✓ Accessible housing?
- ✓ Disabilities Services Department?
- ✓ Priority class registration?
- ✓ Service Animal-Friendly?
- ✓ PCA or PCA referral?
- ✓ Mobility equipment service and repair?
- ✓ Pharmacy?
- ✓ In class Note-takers?
- ✓ Homework Scribes or Tutors?
- ✓ Alternative testing arrangements?
- ✓ PE / Foreign Language?
- ✓ Accessible Shuttle?
- ✓ WRP?
- ✓ TRIO?
- ✓ Allowance for Weather?
- ✓ Career Services?
- ✓ Library Help?
- ✓ Tray Carrier?
- ✓ Visible Compatriots?

Questions for All Students

- ✓ Strength in Your Academic Major?
- ✓ Big or Small?
- ✓ Same Sex or Co-Ed?
- ✓ Urban/Suburban/Rural?
- ✓ Location?
- ✓ Entrance Requirements?
- ✓ Overall Academic Reputation?
- ✓ Financials?
- ✓ HBCU/PBI?
- ✓ Religious College?
- ✓ Same college as your family member(s) attended?
- ✓ Honors program or honors housing program?
- ✓ How important to you is a strong athletics program?
- ✓ How about a Greek system?
- ✓ Do you need daycare for your child?
- ✓ Do you want a school with an active GLBTQIA+ community and/or gender-neutral housing?
- ✓ Other?

Questions for All Students

Below are the most important questions you'll want answers for, to start evaluating and ranking the colleges and universities on your list. You'll be able to find answers to these questions for any college you are considering online.

✓ **Strength in your academic major?**

If you are pretty sure what you want to major in, how good is that program at each of the schools you're considering? Keep the rankings simple: *1, 2, or 3*, or *Good, Better, Best*. (If you have no clue what you want to major in, that's okay. Mark this one as N/A.)

✓ **Big or Small?**

    o   How many undergraduates attend the institution?

    o   What is the average class size?

    o   What is the faculty-to-student ratio?

    o   How large is the role played by teaching assistants?

    o   What is the male/female ratio?

In my case, I wanted a co-ed college, but I did not get more specific than that. However, if it's important to you to either date a lot or get married straight out of college, this figure can be easily determined, and you might want to give it some weight.

> *Really:* All you really need to decide is: Do I want a small college, something in between, or a big university? Same sex or co-ed? You only need to get more specific if you want to.

✓ **Urban/Suburban/Rural?**

    o   How is the economy near the school? If there are lots of large businesses in the area, that will make it easier to get internships or co-ops while in school. That in turn will make it easier to find your first job after college.

    o   If it is determined in high school that you cannot drive and you have lived in the suburbs you whole life, college could provide you with an easier transition to "city life" where you do not need a car.

✓ **Location?** Is the campus within easy commuting distance from home or another part of the country? Do you want a certain climate, and if so, what type?

✓ **Entrance requirements?** Are the school's requirements for GPA, class rank and test scores within the range of what you have? It does not have to be exact match; if you are close and still want to apply, do it!

✓ **Academic Reputation?** Do you want to go to the most demanding school that you can get into, or is that not important to you? Would you sacrifice prestige for not having to study as hard? Is it worth going into more debt?

✓ **Financials?** Even with financial aid, you'll have expenses. How much can you (assuming you work while in school) and your parents afford? How much debt are you willing to incur?

> Scholarships for students with disabilities are listed in the appendix. Also know that after, graduation if one is unable to work due to disability, their student loans can be forgiven. This is a lengthy and difficult process. You are eligible for medical discharge only **once**, so take this into consideration when considering when and if to go to grad school. If you go straight through, with only one loan, you'll be better off in terms of financial aid.

> Here's what I mean. You can put your undergrad loan into forbearance for a year while you either try to find a job or take time off, then get another loan to go on to get either a master's or a PhD. But if your condition changes, or for whatever reason your doctor certifies that you cannot work, the loan could be dismissed. If you try unsuccessfully to find a job after you have earned an associates or bachelor's degree, and you use your medical condition to get your student loans discharged, you could be forgoing your opportunity to secure future loans. If this happens you would obviously have a harder time advancing your education any further.

Questions for Students with Disabilities

General
✓ **Building Accessibility**

If your mobility is impaired and you use a wheelchair crutches, or a walker, this is a big one.

- Do they have automatic door openers?

- Are all the bathrooms in academic buildings accessible?

- Can you reach all the floors in the academic and general campus buildings that you'll be frequenting?

✓ **Grounds accessibility**

How hilly is the campus? Are sidewalks or other pathways well paved and easy to navigate? This also is best evaluated on a campus visit.

➢ **Specialty access?**

- Are computer and/or science labs accessible? For example, are lab tables available for wheelchair width and height? You can mark this N/A if you plan on bringing your own computer, can easily transfer to a regular computer station, or are not planning to be a science major. I would not rule out a school because it takes a little extra effort to get in one computer lab, or I need to ask someone to hand me what I just printed. I've always found people happy to help with little things!

- The same applies to chemistry labs, most of which are not set up for someone in a wheelchair. However, if you know your major will require lots of lab classes, this is another issue you would want to consider.

- Also consider fieldwork: Will any lack of accessibility to field sites be an issue?

- How helpful will the science department be in working around these challenges?

✓ **Accessible housing (on/off campus)**

Keep in mind, everyone's definition of *accessible* can be different. To some it just means that your room is on the first floor, or there's an elevator. To others it means that door handles, light switches, closets, fire alarms and bathrooms are all designed to with those who have disabilities in mind. What is your definition?

✓ **Is There a Disabilities Services Department?**

If there is a department with "disabilities" in its name, its staff members are probably more accustomed to serving students with disabilities. That could be very helpful to you. On the other hand, if you are directed to the office of student affairs or affirmative action, they are less likely to have all the kinks worked out. That doesn't mean that that school can't accommodate you, but it might take more work or adaptation on your part.

✓ **Priority registration.** To what extent does the school prioritize students with physical disabilities with class registration? Regardless of whether you think you need or deserve this, it's another quick test to see if they have policies in place to serve students with disabilities.

✓ **Service Animal-Friendly.**
   What are the provisions for service animals on campus and in the dorms?

✓ **PCA.** If you need a personal care assistant, does the school know what outside agencies to refer you to?

✓ **Mobility equipment service and repair.** If you need your mobility equipment repaired, where can you get it fixed? Is loaner equipment available to use while yours is being fixed? How fast can the repairs be made?

✓ **Pharmacy.** If there a pharmacy on or near campus? If not, what arrangements can be made to keep this from being an annoyance?

✓ **Scribes and Tutors.** Will the school help you arrange for note-takers, homework scribes, or special tutoring?

✓ **Alternative testing arrangements.** What does the school offer in these areas?

   o   Individually proctored exams

   o   Untimed or extended time

   o   Reader available

   o   Scribe

   o   Computer available

✓ **Shuttle.** Does school have an on-campus shuttle, if so, is it accessible?

✓ **Career Services.** How strong is the career services department? Do they have designated staff to work with students with disabilities? Do they make efforts to sponsor programs geared towards students with disabilities?

✓ **WRP.** Does the school take part in a Workforce Recruitment Program (WRP)? (See above.)

✓ **TRIO Grant Program.** Is school a recipient of the federal TRIO Grant? (See below)

✓ **Adaptive Sports.** Does the school you are looking at offer Intermural sports teams for students with disabilities? How about Paralympic training opportunities or Division 1 scholarships for disabled athletes? Do they offer intermural teams or Paralympic teams? or both? What sports do disabled athletes have to choose from? What programs exist in that school's town or city?

✓ **Allowance for Weather.** If the school is in a cold climate, do they have procedures to help those with mobility impairments when it snows? Do they plow right away? Will they deliver meals to your dorm until you can get out? How sympathetic are the professors likely to be if you miss a class due to weather?

✓ **PE / Foreign Language.** Does the school require students to take physical education (PE) or a foreign language to graduate? Will your disability pose any obstacles in fulfilling these requirements?

> Schools will generally waive these requirements. However, a 1997 court ruling – *Guckenberger vs. Trustees of Boston University* – found that colleges are not legally obligated to do so. Don't let concerns about these areas stop you from applying to a school that is otherwise a good fit for you. Despite no legal obligation to do so, schools normally grant these requests (perhaps with a course substitution rather than a waiver). It is just one more piece of red tape that you will need to handle. This could be a tiebreaker if you are trying to decide between two schools.

✓ **Library Help.** If you need help in the library getting research materials, is that available?

✓ **Tray Carrier.** Is there assistance available in the cafeteria with carrying your tray?

✓ **Visible Compatriots.** Do you see other students with disabilities when you visit the school? Does the school offer any specific organizations or athletic programs for students with disabilities?

This book is targeted towards helping those with physical disabilities navigate their college journey and start on their career paths. In the disability community it is common for people to also have disabilities in more than one area. Given this fact, I've included the following checklists.

Attention Deficit Hyperactivity Disorder (AD/HD) and/or Learning Differences (LD)[1]

✓ What type of documentation is needed to be admitted with accommodations made for AD/HD or LD?

✓ What types of specialized programs and support services do you have for AD/HD or LD?

- o How long has program been established?
- o How many students have been served?

✓ Are note takers available?

- o Is there a charge?
- o How is the scheduling handled?

✓ Is there a service available to proof assignments, etc. for grammar, spelling, etc., if necessary?

✓ If necessary, will there be a scribe?

✓ Are books on tape available?

✓ Can you get your textbooks, etc. recorded on tape? How do you get that done? And what is the lead time required?

✓ Is there a specialized learning center available for AD/HD or LD students?

- o Learning strategies
- o Time management
- o Test taking and study skills
- o Writing skills

✓ Is there an AD/HD and/or LD support group available on campus?

✓ Are there waivers for courses toward degrees, if necessary?

✓ May there be course substitutions in degree programs, if necessary?

✓ Are high school college-prep special education courses accepted as fulfilling college admissions requirements?

✓ Is tutoring available?

- o How do you arrange for it?
- o Who pays for it?

---

[1] This and the next several sections are courtesy of http://www.collegecountdownkit.com, which has since disappeared from the Internet

- o What is the typical cost?
- ✓ If math is your disability, can you use a calculator in math-oriented exams and classes?
- ✓ Will it be possible to take the essay portions of exams orally, if necessary?
- ✓ Are accommodations made for tests and exams taken as a student on campus, if needed?

  - o Individually proctored?
  - o Untimed or extended time?
  - o Reader available?
  - o Scribe available?
  - o Computers available?

- ✓ Is counseling available?

Visually Impaired

- ✓ Are textbooks and supplementary reading materials available in Braille? Are textbooks available on tape?

- ✓ How do I make arrangements to obtain these materials for each of my classes?

- ✓ What is the lead-time needed for this service? (This may be outdated soon due to the advent of technologies such as E-readers.)

- ✓ Are readers available?

- ✓ Who hires, trains, schedules and pays for readers?

- ✓ Are Descriptive Video Services (DVS) (audio description capabilities) available for any visuals used or required for courses?

- ✓ Are Optical Character Recognition (OCR) systems available?

- ✓ Are computers with voice recognition software programs available?

- ✓ Are synthetic speech systems and/or voice synthesizer systems available?

- ✓ Are magnification programs for computer screens available?

- ✓ Are there talking calculators available for your use?

- ✓ Are talking computer terminals available in the computer center, library, and dorm?

- ✓ Are TVs available with Descriptive Video Service (DVS) capabilities in the public areas of the dorms, public buildings such as the student union and in lecture halls and classrooms?

- ✓ How many people will be using these adaptive devices on campus or dorm? Will you

- ✓ Be able to access them when you need them?

- ✓ What types of services and assistants are available to me when doing research in the library for example?

- ✓ What provisions are made for the guide dogs that students use in classrooms, public areas and in the dorms?

- ✓ Are personnel available to assist a visually impaired student get across campus?

- ✓ Are personnel available to give a student orientation to the campus, specific buildings, etc. each semester?

- ✓ How many other blind students or visually impaired students are there on your campus?

- ✓ If you have to cross any streets with stoplights and automatic "walk/do not walk" signs, are the signs set with a long enough time interval that will allow you to safely get across the street?

- ✓ What are the accommodations allowed for tests and exams while a student is in college, if required?

  - o How do I arrange for help with exams?

  - o Individually proctored?

  - o Untimed or extended time?

- Reader available?
- Scribe available?
- Braille test version available?
- Braille answer sheet available?
- ✓ Computer with OCR and voice synthesizer available?

Deaf or Hearing Impaired

- ✓ What types of interpreter are available to the student?
  - o ASL
  - o English signed
  - o Oral
  - o Cued
- ✓ Will student have the same interpreter from class-to-class and semester-to-semester?
- ✓ Do you have a formal interpretation program?
  - o How long has your interpretation program been in place?
  - o How many students have used these services?
- ✓ Are interpreters available for non-class activities?
- ✓ Who makes the arrangements for the interpreters and who will?
  - o Make arrangements?
  - o Do the scheduling?
  - o Pays for their services?
- ✓ Are note takers available:
  - o How do you make arrangements?
  - o Who does the scheduling?
  - o Who pays for their services?
- ✓ How do you arrange for any accommodation you might need for tests and exams?
  - o Individually proctored
  - o Untimed or extended time
  - o Signer available for spoken portions of tests
- ✓ Is closed caption capabilities available not only in classrooms, but in the dorms?
- ✓ How many other deaf or hearing-impaired students are there on your campus?
- ✓ Is there a support group on campus or in the community?
- ✓ Are tutors experienced working with the deaf or hearing impaired available?
  - o How are they arranged and scheduled?
  - o Who pays?
- ✓ Are advisors experienced working with the deaf or hearing impaired available?
- ✓ What is the faculty attitude toward helping hearing impaired students, especially freshmen?
- ✓ Will there be a specialized smoke detector in the dorm room?
- ✓ Will there be a TDD in your dorm room and in the main offices of campus?

Medical or Mental Health

- ✓ If there are heart, asthma or lung-function problems, what services are available on campus for emergency care?

- ✓ When are medical support staff available on campus?
    - o 24/7
    - o 9-5 Monday through Friday?

- ✓ Is there a way to arrange your classes around medication and/or treatment schedules?

- ✓ If walking long distances are issues, can you use special parking places close to your academic and dorm buildings?

- ✓ If rest during the day is prescribed or required, is there some place for you to lie down without having to return to your dorm, if it is far?

- ✓ How long does it take to get into the Student Health Center for a non-life-threatening illness?
    - o Do they accept walk-ins?
    - o Or appointment only?

- ✓ Are there specially trained personnel available in the dorms to assist in medical situations when the health center is closed?

- ✓ How far is the closest hospital with a full-service emergency room?

- ✓ What are the services offered to a student with chronic or serious health problems on campus?

- ✓ What are the policies about attendance, official extensions and support for a student who becomes ill or suffers from a life-threatening illness?

- ✓ If a student becomes or is suffering from a serious illness, does the college allow fewer credit hours and still be considered a full-time student in good standing?

- ✓ If a student needs to take an extended leave due to illnesses, how long is allowed before the student must withdraw?

- ✓ What types of services are offered in support of the recovery of a mental illness?

- ✓ What is the level of psychological professional counseling and/or psychiatric care available?
    - o On campus?
    - o Off-campus for students?

- ✓ What are the support groups available?

- ✓ What is the campus's policy regarding notifying parents/guardians concerning serious mental illness or suicide threats?

TRIO Grants

The Federal TRIO Programs award grant money to certain institutions of higher education to provide services for individuals from certain demographics. They are administered, funded, and implemented by the United States Department of Education.

TRIO includes eight programs targeted to serve and assist low-income individuals, first-generation college students, and individuals with disabilities. This type of grant is awarded to the school itself, not individual students. Only certain colleges and universities receive these grants. These grants enable schools to offer students in these populations increased resources in the areas of financial aid, career mentorship, internships and post-college employment .

The fact that I have a documented disability would have made me eligible for this program regardless of my parent's income or level of education. I cannot stress enough that the best way for you to smooth the rocky employment road that you'll face after college is to pick a college that has strong programs to help you find a job.

For more information contact:

> Student Service
> Higher Education Programs
> Office of Postsecondary Education
> U.S. Department of Education
> 1990 K Street, N.W., Suite 7000
> Washington, DC 20006-8510
> Phone: (202) 502-7600
> Fax: (202) 502-7857 or (202) 219-7074
> Email: OPE_TRIO@ed.gov

Colleges That Offer Adaptive Sports Programs

More and more colleges are recognizing that students with disabilities want to play sports. Taking part in these programs offers several benefits. We all are different. You may or may not want to look for a school that offers programs for disabled athletes. That is because you may or may not be interested in participating. It is a safe assumption that if a school has a disabled sports program, it is probably a school that would be ranked 'Disability-Friendly.' Below is a list of some schools that are known for their disabled athletes. As always, each school will vary in what sports they offer and their level of competitiveness. Some will offer intermural teams, while others have Paralympic training opportunities and Division 1 scholarships. Some schools offer both. If a school, you want to attend isn't on this list ask what does that school offer.

- Edinboro University
- Oklahoma State University
- Penn State University
- University of Arizona
- University of Central Oklahoma
- University of Illinois at Urbana-Champaigne
- University of Missouri
- University of Oregon
- University of Texas at Arlington
- University of Wisconsin at Whitewater

Delta Alpha Pi International Honor Society

When many people think of sororities or fraternities, they think of the stereotypical view of groups who are centered on social functions. However, at colleges and universities throughout the world there are a wide variety of "Greek" organizations that cater to a whole host of interests. The Delta Alpha Pi International Honor Society is a co-ed society dedicated to providing the Greek experience to students with disabilities. Students who pledge this organization have an interest in disability rights, building community and spreading awareness throughout their campuses.

Today there are 150 active chapters of Delta Alpha Pi International Honor Society at colleges and universities. Delta Alpha Pi International Honor Society, the first of its kind in the nation, was established in 2004 at East Stroudsburg University of Pennsylvania specifically to recognize the academic accomplishments of college and university students with disabilities. If you are interested in a career in advocacy for people with disabilities, involvement in Delta Alpha Pi will give you excellent experience and contacts.

For more information contact:

> Delta Alpha Pi International Honor Society
> http://deltaalphapihonorsociety.org/
> Edith F. Miller, President
> 5540 Montauk Lane
> Bethlehem, PA 18017
>
> Email requests or questions to:
> dapihonor@msn.com

At the above contact addresses, you can get a list of schools with Delta Alpha Pi chapters. It is also a reasonable assumption that if a school has a Delta Alpha Pi chapter, it has a significant population of students with disabilities and offers a wider array of services. You can also elect to go to a school without an established chapter and either work to start a chapter, take part in Greek organizations that are not exclusively for students with disabilities, or simply not make Greek life part of your college years.

What Level of Support Do You Need?

To further help you navigate through the maze of college selection and the fact that some schools provide more services than others, I have defined three levels of disability-related services that a school might provide:

- Level I: ADA-Compliant

- Level II: Disability-Friendly

- Level III: PCA Schools

The next few sections will help you decide which level of support you want, then assess the level of support that's provided by each school you are considering. After that, I'll discuss the issues that should be considered by all students, with or without disabilities. Then I'll round out the chapter by covering how to do all of this evaluation.

Level I: ADA-Compliant Schools

Title II of the ADA mandates removal of architectural barriers and that a school must provide accommodations as note takers, extra time on tests, individually proctored exams, reading, dictating, typing, and alternative formats, when the need is properly documented. This means all colleges must accommodate you. However, the ADA does not require any institution of higher learning to aid with what are called "personal needs." For example, in high school if a student needed assistance toileting during school hours or special transportation to and from school, the school is legally obligated to provide that. Not so for college.

Nor does the ADA mandate the *quality* of services. Not all schools do equally well at following the law. And there's even more variation in the extent to which colleges provide services that go *beyond* the law, such as counseling, tutoring, universal design or support groups.

Again, ADA-Compliant schools comply with the ADA but do not go "beyond the call of duty." You should be able to attend these schools no matter how severe your disabilities are, but you might find it a little more difficult – or a lot more difficult – than attending schools in the higher levels described above.

If you have a dream to go to a certain school and are on a ventilator, it *is* doable. If you have a family member who can go with you and take care of your needs full time, and you feel that is the best option, do it! If your family's wealthy and can hire whatever staff you need, do it! Or maybe it would be enough for you to have a family member "on call" from a remote location. This person can regularly help you deal with both Medicaid and home health agencies to make sure things are going smoothly.

Brooke Ellison is an amazing example of making her dream school (Harvard) work for her, even while being a quadriplegic who depended on a ventilator. She was the first student with a disability of this magnitude to attend Harvard. Her tireless mother went with her to act as Brooke's 24-hour care attendant. Brooke went on to graduate magna cum laude and was invited to address her class at commencement.

If you use a wheelchair and a class you register for is scheduled to be taught in a classroom that is not wheelchair-accessible, the ADA requires the school to move the class to an accessible classroom. The school does not have to make every building fully accessible. Buildings built or renovated after June 3, 1977, must comply with the relevant accessibility code required by Section 504 and, after Jan. 26, 1992, the ADA. Buildings constructed before the 1977 date need not be made accessible if the college or school can ensure that its students with disabilities enjoy the full range of its programs through other means such as relocating classes to an accessible building.

This kind of thing is a judgment call on yours and your family's part. How much extra work will you need to put in to get what you need? Are the school's other attractions worth it to you? If it is supremely important to you to go to a small, women-only, values-based school where you will be the first student ever with a physical disability … but you and your family have talked to the president of the school and they are more than willing to make it work … then you should go for it.

Going back to my experience, I seriously considered attending an ADA-compliant school. When as a high school senior, I spoke with students at that school, everyone was extremely friendly. My mom remarked, professors who might have to move their class to accommodate me were coming up to us and saying, "I hope you choose our school." All this told me that that school, despite being "only" a Level I school, would work with my disabilities. Why didn't I decide to enroll there? Because it did not fit my other desires, aside from disability issues. I was apprehensive about going to an urban school, and the tuition was considerably higher.

This is a perfect illustration of how any level of school can work for you, and how your needs/wants outside of your disabilities always come into play.

Level II: Disability-Friendly Schools

Disability-friendly schools have extensive programs to accommodate students with disabilities beyond what the law requires. Their buildings tend to be almost completely accessible, and they offer housing with the needs of students with disabilities in mind. They also are more likely to employ specialists who have experience with working with students with disabilities.

Some disability-friendly schools offer amenities such as special tutoring programs, recreational programs or facilities, equipment repair services, assistive-technology-equipped computer labs and specialized counseling for career and/or independent living. Services and procedures will still vary from school to school. They do not provide personal care, but they can probably give you a referral.

If you fill out the chart and check off several items on the Students with Disabilities side, you probably want to look for at least a Level II (Disability-Friendly) school. You might also want this level of support if you want to make sure the school does a really good job in the areas of accessibility and basic classroom accommodations. Disability-friendly schools are accustomed to serving students with physical disabilities.

So how can you quickly find out whether a college is disability-friendly? After all, the writers of all college guides did not sync up with my brain and start assigning schools to one of my three levels, ADA-compliant, Disability-Friendly or PCA Schools. And if you call a school and ask, of course they will all tell you that they are perfectly disability friendly.

Although college guides do not use my three-level classification system, they do generally contain the information you need to determine how disability-friendly a school is. One way they do this is through telling you what percentage of the campus is accessible.

But use accessibility percentages as a guideline, not gospel. I would give both campuses that I attended 100% in this regard. However, there might have been some buildings that I never needed to access that weren't accessible. Campuses like that can't claim to be 100% accessible, but they might meet your needs perfectly well. Percentages come in handy when deciding where to visit, but you still need to visit to determine if a school meets your particular accessibility needs.

The second way to find out if a school may be disability-friendly is to check their website and see if they have a department with "disability" in the name. Another way is to find out whether a school offers Disability Studies as a major. That's a good sign that the school is used to serving students with disabilities.

An additional way is to check whether they offer students with disabilities priority when registering for classes. Regardless of whether you feel you need that, it's another indicator. I thought it was a nice perk, but I wasn't sure why they were offering me priority. Shouldn't single parents or student athletes get priority? Shouldn't I need to prove that I'm entitled to this – either because of medication, attendants that I need, or some other objective reason?

Regardless of my reaction to this accommodation, it is another fast way for you quickly ascertain whether a school you are looking at has policies in place to serve students with disabilities.

Finally, if you pick a school that offers the Workforce Recruitment Program, you can be pretty sure it is disability-friendly.

Level III: PCA Schools

PCA Schools assume responsibility for providing personal care attendants to students who need them. The students involved in these programs pay an extra fee for this service. As of this writing, and to the best of my knowledge, only four schools in the US offer this as an option. They are:

- ✓ Edinboro University of Pennsylvania
  - o http://www.edinboro.edu/departments/osd/attendant-care.dot

    [Prior to the publication of this book; Edinboro University announced they are majorly re-structuring how the school will handle delivery of attendant care services. The school plans to outsource attendant care to local home health agencies, rather than employ attendants directly. Edinboro University still plans to provide students with a lot of assistance in securing these services.]

- ✓ University of Illinois at Urbana-Champaign
  - o http://www.disability.illinois.edu/living-accommodations/beckwith-residential-support-services-nugent-hall

- ✓ Wright State University
  - o http://www.wright.edu/disability-services/services

- ✓ University of Houston
  - o http://www.uh.edu/healthcenter/services/attendant_care.html

Even if you need attendant care you are *not* limited to these schools. Medicaid pays for attendants so you can hire, train and employ your own wherever you live or decide to go to school. You might feel it is easier to go to one of the few schools that have PCA programs, so you don't have to take total responsibility for managing your own care right away. If you require a lot of skilled nursing care, e.g. you are dependent on a ventilator or need G-tube feeding, you may want to consider a PCA School. Of course, for many of you, this will mean a substantial relocation. For some of you, that will be part of the fun of going to college, while others will want to stay closer to family and the community where you graduated from high school.

If you are transitioning from foster care with high needs for care or feel your family cannot help you with your needs, one of the PCA Schools may be your best option. If you have an involved family, you need to decide whether they can be your "fallback" option, should you want to attend a school closer to home and manage your own attendant care. Or you might decide, because of current circumstances or your long-term goals, that it's better to go to a school that has wrap-around services.

Each of the 'PCA Schools' run their program differently. You should inquire via email into how each run their program to decide which ones you want to attempt to plan a visit to. Since they are spread across the US; it may be hard for you and your family to look at each! If you do a little homework, you may decide you prefer how two out of the four run their PCA programs and then proceed from there as to if you can visit those two schools.

Just because a school provides assistance with ADLs doesn't mean that they offer help with anything and everything. There are limits, both in terms of the time that you get with an aide each day and the kind of help they can give you. I can take a shower by myself, so rather than having the aide help me with that, I would use his or her help writing my math homework. Most schools' personal care programs help you only with direct personal care for anything else you'll need to make other arrangements. Most attendant care programs will refer you to alternate channels to assistance. The college's disability service department may be able to provide a homework scribe.

The kinds of help I needed around my living space was with things like hanging things on the wall, or small fixes such as changing a light bulb or putting paper in my printer. In my situation I was better off going to school where my relatives were just two towns over. My relatives could help me with whatever I needed, regardless of the personal care attendant policies of the college.

Big Universities vs. Small Colleges and Students with Disabilities

Most students prefer either a small or large school. This preference seems to be built into most people's character, just like the way most people are either morning or night people. I would definitely classify myself as a big-school person. You might think that my mobility and speech impairments would make me prefer to attend a smaller college. I have not found this to be the case. My middle school was tiny. When I got to a regional high school, I was much more comfortable. There are advantages either way. In my experience it was easier to deal with my disabilities at a larger school. This opinion may be biased due to my natural preference. I did attend two colleges; the first was a small college and the second was a large university.

The main reason why I thought a larger school was better is that everything is right there! I am not talking about academics or extracurricular activities, but rather life management. The university was its own small city. It offered so much more in the way of dining, entertainment, banking, personal care (haircuts, manicures, tanning, waxing and cleaners), off-campus tutors who "taught to the test," and a wider array of on-campus medical services (including a pharmacy.)

I did not drive, so on a small campus I felt trapped. There was not even a place on campus to buy shampoo. Now, this was about twenty years ago. Since then, I've lost track of how many new residence halls Ramapo has built. Today, there could be considerably more on campus due to the number of students living on campus has substantially increased. Still, there is nothing close to campus that caters to the college crowd. When I got to a larger university, there were nine different places for me to get whatever I needed (I'm not exaggerating). One of those that was hugely useful to me, as a student with a disability, was the copy center.

Lots of students are intimidated by big lecture hall classes. But I loved them! In high school, due to the way the classrooms were set up, I could not get to the back of the classroom in my wheelchair. This led me to always sit in the front row. This did not match my personality, and it annoyed me. Lecture hall classes allowed me to finally sit in the back!

In middle school, there were memos constantly going to all my teachers saying things such as what to do with me if there was a fire drill. I knew the intention behind this was not to make me feel like a freak, but it did. Large lecture hall classes made me feel as though I blended in for the first time in a long time.

Some students feel that accessibility in lecture halls is poor. The challenges they report range from having to sit either in the very front or the very back, to feeling cut off from classmates and instructors, to having trouble seeing or hearing. This is an area where you'll need to consider your needs in addition to your preferences. But it's going to be a bit tricky to do that until you are actually attending classes. Every lecture hall is slightly different, even on the same campus. Look for opportunities on your campus visits to ask students about these issues. Or even try and sit in on a lecture. That can help you see what it would be like for you if you had to sit in that lecture hall two or three times a week for 16 weeks, pay attention to what the professor is saying even if you're not necessarily fully awake, read the PowerPoints, take notes – and maybe even raise your hand and get called on!

Everyone's different. A fellow wheelchair user that I sat near for a lot of lectures one semester commented to me that the lecture hall's design isolated us. He had a different disability, a different educational background – and of course a different personality! When you talk to others with disabilities at a school you are evaluating, don't just get a general thumbs-up or thumbs down. Try to find out *why* they liked or don't like something. What they dislike might be perfect for you.

However, if you cannot see or hear a lecture, that has nothing to do with a preference. It has everything to do with what you need! You need to be able to see and hear (assuming, of course that you do not have a total disability in either of these areas).

Special Concerns

I was more nervous about going to the cafeteria than I was about my classes. I can only eat finger foods or use a fork to stab; using a knife or spoon is out. I had always brought lunch to school through my senior year of high school. I have some "safe foods," but those were the ones my mom packed for me throughout high school! Yes, my mom packed my lunch every day from kindergarten through my high school graduation. This fact both merits my reader making fun of me … and giving huge credit to my parents for doing this!

When I thought about going to college, I knew that it meant I would have to start buying and eating the school's lunch, and for that matter, dinner too. This made me so nervous, I seriously considered not going to college because of it! Fortunately, I overcame that fear. It was not easy; going to eat was definitely more stressful physiologically than my classes.

When I attended a smaller school there was only one cafeteria, so if they weren't serving something I could manage, I was out of luck until the next meal! It was so frustrating when I would wheel myself to dinner, read the menu board, and see that there was nothing I could eat! I would either have to make something in my dorm room – which luckily did have a micro-fridge – or wheel back after 7:00 pm, when we could use the "pay-cafe."

Going to a larger university eliminated this issue. There was not one, but TWO, food courts on campus! So, I could always get something that I could eat. I went from going to lunch at my first school hoping they had a sandwich bar as one of the three choices for the day … to having a full deli open seven day a week for lunch and dinner! I was in paradise.

Mobility-wise, you are probably thinking a smaller school would be easier. For you it might be. However, larger schools may offer "cart-services." This is intended for any student who gets injured and is done through student health. They will pick you up in a golf cart and take you to and from all your classes.

My second school was fully accessible, so they even made the golf-carts wheelchair friendly. For the first couple of days, my second campus felt huge. I thought "What have I done? This was a mistake. I can never wheel around here." But once I figured out where everything was, it was as if the campus shrunk instantly. It was then totally doable for me to push wherever I needed to go.

> ***Key Point:*** At a smaller school, you may have less distance to go, but you might also have no choice as to how to get from point A to B. Example, my first school a campus shuttle only ran at night after classes.

Smaller Can Definitely Be Better

If you determine you are a "small-school person," this will also be fine as far as your disabilities are concerned. There are some real advantages to attending a smaller school for any student; this is just as true if you have a disability. The main advantage is that there is less competition to get leadership roles and be noticed. It's even more important for those with disabilities to start building their résumés as soon as possible in college. Student body president" looks darn good on résumé! It will be easier to get such a position if there are fewer students vying for them.

The same goes for competition for internships and positive attention from faculty and staff. This could especially work in the favor of students with disabilities. Regarding the department of disability services, again, my smaller school did a considerably better job. The university assigned me three different specialists in three different years. This wasn't a big issue for me because, by that time, I barely needed them. I used testing accommodations services only near the end of my college career.

My second school did an adequate job of accommodating my needs when I was a student in the way that was best for me. But there was no serious mentoring or guidance for my future in the working world. This was hard for me to understand. It wasn't as though they were understaffed or otherwise poorly resourced. They had a staff of about fifteen, and they just built a multi-million-dollar building. Yet do not track employment outcomes of their students. While I feel they did a great job in addressing students' needs during school, I feel they fell short in helping students apply their education to their job searches and first few jobs out of college. Nor did they seem to focus on getting the best return on investment on whatever, local, state or federal funding they receive to operate. This is one of the biggest gaps in support for college students with disabilities. It's one of key reasons I decided to write this book!

True-story...

My main disability-related challenge at a small school – my dining related needs – could have been addressed better by my advocating for myself. I could easily have requested that two adaptations be made to my meal plan to accommodate me. This would have probably taken less than a week to accomplish. The school wouldn't have had to spend any money. I was eighteen and too embarrassed to explain my situation to the appropriate people.

And the Lesson Is…

Ask for what you need. If you do that, you might be surprised at how often you can get what you want, regardless of how big or small the school.

College Visits

I can't recommend strongly enough that you visit every college on your short list before making a final decision about which one to attend. You certainly need to visit the one that you think you have settled on.

You should visit at least three campuses. This is the only way to make written descriptions and glowing pictures on these colleges' websites *real to you*. On-site visits are tremendous help in understanding how each campus and institution differs from others in its class. On-site visits will help you better understand what your priorities really are, and how to rate schools based on written descriptions after you've done a visit for two.

What to Do
On each visit you should do at least these three things:

1. Take the standard tour.
2. Eat a meal in a typical dining hall, or the one where you think you might be spending a lot of time.
3. Talk to disability services.

Standard Tour
The standard tour for prospective students is usually guided by an upperclassman. He or she will not know how to answer your disability-related questions. Unless you have a specific reason to assume, they will know something about this area, don't bother asking. However, keep accessibility in mind during the tour, even while the guide is telling you all kinds of other interesting things. Take notice of aspects of accessibility such as sidewalks, curb cuts and building entrances. Does your disability pose any issues when taking the tour? Is there anywhere the guide takes the tour group where you cannot go? For example, because a staircase or a door is too narrow?

Deciding to reject a school doesn't mean the entire tour and visit are now wasted. Use the rest of your time on any particular campus visit to learn more about yourself and what's important to you about your college choice.

The Meal
No, this is not to see how good the food is, unless you really want to make that part of your selection criteria. The main goal is to get a feel for the type of students who go to the school by observing them in their natural habitat. Do you see yourself fitting in? If so, how? If not, why not? A secondary goal could be to further evaluate the accessibility of the entire experience, from entering, choosing food, paying for your food, eating it, and getting out.

Informal Meeting with Disability Services
Part of this evaluation involves trying to schedule the meeting in advance. If you can find the disability services department from the school's main website that is a good sign that it may be a "Level II" (Disability-Friendly) school. If you can't, call the department of student affairs and ask them who would handle disability-related accommodations. Once you reach that person, say something like this:

> "I understand you cannot formally assist me, since I am not admitted as a student and you have nothing to do with admissions. However, I'm

evaluating your campus and I'd like fifteen minutes with someone in your department to discuss your school's policies, in case I am admitted and choose your school.

This is where the "Students with Disabilities" side of your chart comes in. Staff members of the disability services department should handle each of the areas that you identified as priorities for you.

> *Note: This kind of meeting is different from an IEP meeting. At an IEP, you are making a plan specifically for you. Here you are just trying to find out what the school's general disability policies are and what they offer. It is not about your specific case. You just need information to decide if they offer what you need to succeed with your disabilities.*

Ideally, this meeting should be after your tour. That way, if you encounter an issue with accessibility during the tour, you can ask about it. There could be a simple positive explanation, such as temporary construction, or your guide was new and didn't take the mobility-friendly route. Or, the answer might be equally simple but negative: that school does not ideally meet your accessibility needs. You then need to decide whether to apply to that school anyway and just work around the problems.

Another apprehension some students with disabilities may have is how will my professors react to me? Will they be willing to follow the law and accommodate me? It is impossible to meet every professor during a college visit. If this were readily available, I would not want to be professor, who would? The best way you, as a prospective student, can judge how your professors will be, is by the read you get from the school's disability services staff. If they seem, enthusiastic and dedicated to you being able to have as good of an experience as any other student at their school, then the majority of professors will follow their lead.

Finally, you should also ask what they do to help graduates find internships and jobs after graduation. Does their department make efforts that go above and beyond the college's department of career services? Do they work in tandem with that department to best serve their students?

What NOT to Do
- ✓ Don't ask if they can get you special preference with admissions! They cannot, even if they are a "PCA School."

- ✓ Don't ask about course requirement substitutions for college graduation requirements, even if you are sure that you both need and qualify for one. There will be plenty of time later to negotiate such things once you are attending that school. You don't want to provide anyone with any red flags against you.

One Last College Visit-Don't

Don't waste your time visiting colleges during the summer. Most of the student population will be gone. You will not get a full feel of what it is like there. I made this mistake!

You still can apply part of your summers to college planning by doing research. Amazon.com has tons of information. Take notes. Make lists. Look for scholarships.

And of course, don't forget fun and relaxation, after all you are on summer vacation. Enjoy it!

Community Colleges

A common disagreement between parents and their children with disabilities is whether to go away to college or stay home and commute. If this debate gets started in your family, the best solution for all involved is to fully consider both options. You can decide to go to a community college a week before you start. Not so for a four-year school! Deadlines for those are months in advance of the next academic year. If you or your parent wants, you to go away – go ahead and apply! If you get in, meet with the school, fill out the financial aid paperwork, and see if everything can be worked out. You might be surprised. Then if for whatever reason, you are not happy with the proposed plan, you can go to a community college.

As the cost of attending a four-year college continues to skyrocket, community colleges are an ever-more *relatively* affordable option to continue your education. If your career goals only require you to earn an associate degree, (a two-year degree), this is a route you should seriously consider.

If your career goals would be better served by a bachelor's degree, master's degree, or doctorate, starting with a community college with the knowledge that you will need to transfer after two years is another choice you should consider. This gets your general educational requirements out of the way – perhaps with better grades than at a more difficult school – and allows you to get some practice at handling your new level of adult responsibilities. Later when you take more difficult and specialized classes, there is more risk to your transcript. As in anything in life, there are both advantages and disadvantages to either approach. Your disability will impact both the positives and negatives of this option.

Advantages of Community Colleges

Application Process and Admission Requirements
Most community colleges do not have an application deadline or require an application essay. Most community colleges also offer open admission. This means that the only document required is your high school transcript.

Living at Home
Depending on your situation and your personality, this could be either an advantage or disadvantage. Some cannot wait to move out once they hit their teens, while others think "I have it made, why would I want to move out?" I am going to put this in the advantage's column.

Many students – even those without physical disabilities – find it less stressful to live at home with their family for the first year or two of college. The obvious advantage here is that you can adjust to the increased academic demands of college *before* you need to adjust to living on your own! This also can be a huge help in terms of your ADL situation. You have another two years to work it out. The key is to use this gift of an extension to either work on doing things for yourself vigorously, or start to learn how to negotiate and manage PCAs while your parents are still close at hand. They can help you learn the system and be right there should someone you hire make you feel uncomfortable.

Regardless of the level of your disability, you need to start planning for your greater independence from parents. Consider that your family's lives are going to change over time as well. I am not saying you need to start getting ready for your loved ones to die as you go to college! I just mean that, as your parents or other approach the next stage in their lives, they will want to be less tied down. While they will always want to help you, they will need to shift from "daily duty" to being more just "on-call," helping coordinate things but not *doing* everything. If you have siblings, cousins or friends involved in your care, the same will go for them. They will need to move on with their own lives, just as you would in their position. It can be gradual, though.

This issue of personal care is a leading reason that students with disabilities live at home longer. This is okay.

Direct Cost Savings
Community college is cheaper. The credits themselves cost less. And all you must pay for are the credits that you are taking, and books. You save the cost of housing and a meal plan. If you drive, you would also incur the expenses of a car. However, this is usually less than room and board.

If you plan on going straight through to get your master's or a post-graduate degree, starting at a community college could make even better sense! Getting a masters or a PhD is expensive. Any money you can save at the starting end of your academic journey could be used for tuition later when a cheaper option is not available. Community colleges do not offer masters programs. So, once you are at that level, you do not have the option of going to one to save money.

Also, if you do plan on doing graduate work, this will afford you more years to take advantage of all that a traditional college campus offers. Therefore, you do not have to think that you will miss out forever on those advantages. You will be able to make up those years in grad school.

On the other hand, consider the scenario where you only go for a four-year bachelor's degree, and you spend two out of the four years commuting. Then you spend at least your first semester at your traditional college/university just getting used to being there. You might feel as though three semesters is not enough time to get you as ready as possible to get a job and live on your own off campus. This could be compensated for by planning to take five years to get a bachelor's degree. That way you get to take advantage of all on-campus services and advantages for an extra year.

Transferring
Many community colleges have agreements with four-year colleges that enable students who complete one or two years of studies in good standing to transfer easily to a four-year college. Even if there isn't a formal transfer arrangement at the two-year college you attend, you can certainly do so if your grades are good enough.

There are a couple of beautiful loopholes here. If you apply to any college or university as a transfer student – meaning you have been taking college courses for two years – the admissions criteria will be less rigorous than if you apply during high school for admission as a freshman! This will also work if you start at a traditional four-year school and then want to transfer halfway through to a more competitive university to get a better name on both your diploma and résumé.

Now, this will only work if you do well during your first two years of college! Also, do not read this and think "This way I don't have to work hard in high school." Not so. You will need the skills you acquire through working hard in high school to do well in your first two years of college.

Disadvantages of Community Colleges

Transportation

If you don't drive, this can be a problem. You will need to find rides or depend on transportation for those with disabilities, such as Paratransit. These services have drawbacks. The main one it lacks reliability. They might make you deal with up to a half-hour window, meaning they could be 15 minutes early or 15 minutes late from the time you request a pick-up. These services have also been known to strand their passengers.

Transportation difficulties are a leading reason that many students with physical disabilities opt to live on campus. Generally, only traditional four-year schools offer on-campus housing. It is just easier to be able to get to everything without needing a car! Even if your city's Paratransit system works well for you, college is not like high school; there are no set hours of operation. Your schedule will vary more; it will be some hardship to have to predetermine what time you need to be picked up. You might want to stay longer for an impromptu social or academic event, but you cannot because your ride is pre-scheduled. Or you might be in class and decide it's a waste of time today and you want to go home or run errands. When you live in a dorm, there are challenges associated with that, too. But it's a huge advantage to be able to come and go as you please.

If you can drive, will you be able to afford a car or van with whatever modifications you need to get back and forth to school? Your local vocational rehabilitation agency (VR) might assist in paying for one, partially or totally. However, this varies a lot. With continued cutbacks in government services, this is going to happen less and less. If you think the best plan is to try and get VR to pay for vehicle modifications to get to and from school, start early, junior year of high school at the latest. It will take that long to get VR to finance the vehicle modifications that you need to drive back and forth to college! To start this process, find the vocational rehabilitation agency office nearest you and call to request to start the intake process.

Social

At community colleges, people generally come to take their classes and then leave, making it harder to meet people. This may be especially true if you do not have a car to meet up at other locations. If most of your friends from high school leave in August for college, it may feel very lonely. Also, there tends to be a wider demographic at community colleges. You might see that most people in your classes are older than you, or otherwise have less in common with you than at a four-year college. If you chose a four-year college, the student body tends to be more homogeneous and may be less intimidating socially.

Have a Plan

If you are interested in starting out at a community college, first talk to an adviser there right away about what courses will transfer and which will not!

You need to look out for yourself! If you know what school you want to transfer to, do some research as to which credits you've already earned will transfer to the new college.

Difficulty of Classwork

Do not count on the classwork being easier at a community college. It varies. Some professors make the work harder at community college just to counter the stereotype that it is easier.

(On the advantage side, if you do go to a traditional four-year school, you have the option of taking the community college version of a notoriously difficult four-year college class at a community college, even if you are enrolled at a four-year college or university at the same time. Then you transfer that credit to satisfy that degree requirement. This trick involves extra logistics in the areas of transportation and financial aid. Nonetheless it is another option, if you feel that is the only way you can get an "A" or pass a class you need.)

Less Time with the Most-Used Services

College campuses are unique in that no other place has the services that they do, to help you succeed. I wish I had realized this when I was eighteen and planning for college. If you rent an apartment, it will not come with a resident advisor (RA) to quickly and conveniently give you directions or advice. Regardless of whether you get a crappy RA or a wonderful one, most are better than nothing! If your dorm room is assigned to an RA whose skills and – shall we say, dedication to the task – are less than ideal, there is still someone to go to if you must. If you are not in college, it's harder to connect with clubs and organizations to where you can meet people, make connections, and (legitimately) add good things to your résumé! When you have a disability, living on your own can be scary. Doing it for the first time on a campus really is the easiest way.

Some community colleges offer health services, career services, and extracurricular activities. However, these generally won't be as comprehensive, well-advertised, and accessible. College attendance can meet more than just your academic and career needs. Done right, it can help any student prepare for full adulthood, meaning having a better job than otherwise, and paying bills. This is *especially* true if you have a disability. It is easiest to get all this done on a campus. Four years is not a lot of time to do everything to prepare for the rest of your life in such a convenient and exciting way. Do you really want to jump into full adult life without these conveniences and social benefits? Maybe so. It's your choice.

> **Bottom Line:** Community colleges provide an easier transition to college – usually at a substantial cost savings. But in getting set up for life after college, a four-year university will probably be better. Is that tradeoff worth it to you? What do you most need now … and in the long run?

Points to Remember from Chapter 2

- ✓ Your choice of where to attend college is an important one, but it needn't be overwhelming – nor final.

- ✓ Use the list of disability-related and non-disability-related criteria to evaluate each school. No school will meet all your criteria, and that's OK.

- ✓ Rate each school ADA-compliant, disability-friendly, or PCA Schools – and how important its level is to you.

- ✓ Develop a short list of three to five schools to visit and make the most of every visit. Be sure to ask about career placement help, statistics, etc. If outcomes are not measured, they're probably less than excellent.

- ✓ College disability services departments are not IEP teams. You will have increased rights and responsibilities. Feel free to use any or all their services.

- ✓ Having a Workforce Recruitment Program (WRP) in place at a school is a huge plus. If it doesn't recruit at a school that is otherwise great for you, consider advocating to get it to start recruiting there.

- ✓ Look into TRIO grants as this may be an asset in finding employment after college.

- ✓ Consider the pros and cons of attending a community college before a four-year college, in terms of ease of admission, living at home, cost savings, transportation, social life, academic difficulty, and ancillary services.

Success Story: I Grew Up Down an Old Dirt Road

Carla Pease

I grew up down an old dirt road, in a town you wouldn't know. Not much is left of Emmet, North Dakota, but it made me who I am today. For that I will always remember the little town of Emmet.

Elementary school started out rough. I was different and wore a leg brace. I soon learned that if I didn't stand up for myself, no one else would. It was there I learned that I would

be best served having a backbone instead of a wishbone. I had several surgeries during my youth, tendon lengthening they were called. My tendons were cut to open like an accordion to relieve my muscle spasticity. I spent a lot of time at The Shriner's Hospital in Minneapolis, and the nurses there took wonderful care of me. It was then that I decided I wanted to be a nurse. When you are 6 years old, you pretty much think you have the world figured out. Who would have thought I actually did?

As I entered high school, I became cocky and arrogant, wanting to leave my cerebral palsy behind me, forgetting that it would be a lifelong part of me. I lied to my parents repeatedly, told them I was fine when my muscles were killing me, told them I was keeping up with my daily exercises when I wasn't. I walked by swinging my hip forward and throwing my leg ahead of me, not using the muscles I should because they were too spastic. It worked and people believed me, so I went a long time without seeing a doctor. Finally, I couldn't take it anymore and I told my parents I needed to go back to Shriners. By then I was 16 years old and in not the greatest shape. The doctor at Shriners told me I needed to have a tendon lengthening – or a heel cord stretch as it was also called – if I wanted to be able to walk effectively. I decided to have the surgery, but there were complications I didn't count on.

Again, I was not the greatest patient. I had an infection; my leg became swollen and painful in the cast; it swelled up so badly that it cracked the cast. After the cast was removed, I began to feel strange sensations. I was diagnosed with reflex sympathetic dystrophy, a disease that attacks your nervous system after some type of injury or insult to the body. I spent a long time in physical therapy fighting that. By this time, I had become a certified nursing assistant and wanted so badly to become a nurse I couldn't stand it!

After high school I found out that not too many nursing programs were keen on having a student with cerebral palsy. It was not discrimination, it was just about caring for me, because at that time I was not in the greatest shape physically.

So, I spent a long time in physical therapy, while becoming a medical assistant through Minot State University – Bottineau. I got myself ready to show those people I could do this. While I did my practicum to be a medical assistant, I worked with an amazing podiatrist, Dr. Tyson Williams, who mentored me and encouraged me. He wrote me my first letter of recommendation for nursing school.

I received my acceptance letter from The Dakota Nursing Program, a consortium of five colleges in North Dakota. I attended college in New Town, which is 80 miles from where I lived, but I was not going to let anything stop me.

After becoming an RN and working the floor, I began to think I could do more. I learned how to do things despite my cerebral palsy. For example, I used a seatbelt tourniquet to help me draw blood or put in an IV; if I was lifting a patient, I used my strong side and was careful during the pivot. I began to think about graduate school, so I applied and got in!

I started graduate school at the University of Cincinnati in the fall of 2011. When I was ready to start my clinical internship, my site dropped me three days before I was to start. I had three days to find another site or I was done with the program. I called two of my friends that were nurse practitioners with Trinity Health, based in Minot. Both of them said yes, and I filled out the paperwork. It was an amazing time with Jill and Hedy. They taught me so much. They reaffirmed that if I was to be successful, I would need a backbone, not a wishbone. Jill was so patient while she taught me procedures and let me find my own way to work around my disability. Hedy listened to my suggestions about patients with pain, because she knew I had been there. It was a huge boost of confidence. I owe so much to them.

I graduated in the fall of 2013 and passed my boards to become a nurse practitioner. When Trinity Health offered me a position, I was pleasantly surprised.

I had a fear that most could not fathom in my heart. I was finally at the pinnacle of what I had always wanted to be, and all I could think about is…what if I can't do it? As it turned out, I didn't have to worry about that.

So many accommodations were made for me. I went to work with an amazing nurse practitioner and a doctor who mentored me and encouraged me. They taught me that dealing with my cerebral palsy is mind over matter: I don't mind, and my cerebral palsy doesn't matter.

My medical assistants, Cassie and Lexi, can tell when my legs are tired. They save me endless trips by bringing me my prescriptions for patients and anything I need. They are my angels.

There are always horror stories about how rocky it is to start out in healthcare. Mine is a fairytale. A huge fear many nurse practitioners have is that they'll mess up writing a prescription. I have terrible handwriting. We use the computer most of the time, but at times I have needed help. The pharmacy in the medical arts building where I work is huge fan club of mine. They give me nothing but love and encouragement, so I bring them chocolate.

Many nurse practitioners are also scared of reading an X-ray wrong. Let's face it, radiologists go through YEARS of training and they are good, really good. I am not a radiologist and I've had eye surgery as well. My vision is quite poor; that can be a symptom of cerebral palsy, so the radiologists have served as my eyes when I need to examine an X-ray. Dr. Haddon has walked me through X-ray after X-ray, never cross or upset, always quick to encourage, or offer a suggestion.

Sometimes people can be catty in the real world, and then I meet people like Allison Lensman, who was nice to me from the second she met me. She has been a nurse practitioner longer than I, but treats me as a colleague, not the young upstart who is nipping at her heels. I admire her patience and wisdom. Everyone should meet an Allison Lesman the first day on the job.

I also get to work with my hero, Dr. Tyson Williams. I know I am not the greatest nurse practitioner in the world, nor do I claim to be. I don't care about being the best, I care about doing my best. That is what I get to do every day, my best...and it is enough. For Trinity Health, it is enough, for my patients it is enough, for me it is enough! Life is good. Emmet is all but gone now. No more church, no more post office, no more store. I think Emmet is a state of mind now. A place where if you did your best, your chores were done, prayers said, everything would work out how it was supposed to. I wish you all an Emmet.

Chapter 3: Ready, Set, Apply!

Questions and Answers about SAT/ACT Accommodations

Q: Will receiving accommodations on college entrance exams hurt my chances of admission?

A: No. The courts have ruled that *most* test scores cannot be flagged when a student receives disability-related accommodations. This means when schools view your scores there will be no way for them to tell if you had any accommodations during testing. The only exceptions to these rulings are for the LSAT and MCAT, which are for admission to law schools or medical schools respectively. At the time this book was written, those scores could still be flagged. If you are still in high school, you do not need to worry about the LSAT or MCAT yet.

Q: Who should apply for accommodations due to disability?

A: If you have any type of documented disability that directly impacts your ability to take the SAT or ACT or your performance on them, you should apply for testing accommodations.

Q: If I have an IEP or a 504 plan, do I still need to apply for testing accommodations?

A: Yes, Having accommodations at school does not mean you will be granted accommodations during college admissions testing. An IEP or a 504 means you are more likely to get approved for accommodations. But you still need to go through the process of getting approval well before the test date. If you were to receive any accommodations on testing day without getting prior approval, even if you do have an IEP, your scores would be cancelled. You must go through the appropriate channels and get *every* accommodation approved prior to your test date.

Q: If I do not have an IEP or a 504 plan, can I still apply for testing accommodations?

A: Yes, accommodations are approved on a case-by-case basis. It might be harder for you to get approved without an IEP/504 plan. If you have a documented disability, call the numbers below to ask them how to proceed, as well as what documentation you need to submit.

Q: Do I need to get my accommodations approved if I take the same test more than once?

A: No, Once you are approved for an accommodation for a specific test, should you re-take that test, you are automatically approved for that type of accommodation the next time you take that test. When you receive notification the you were approved, you will also get a code that you will then use the next time that you sign up for that test.

You should check to make sure everything is set up for you to receive your approved accommodation(s) every time you take the test beforehand.

If you need an additional or a different type(s) of accommodation(s) than the last time you took the test, you are required to re-apply to get those approved.

If you are taking different types of tests, you need to apply for accommodations for each. In other words, you **cannot** get approval for extra time, and then automatically get another accommodation type because you were approved for extra time. Additionally, you **cannot** get approved for a certain type of accommodation on the SAT and then be granted that same accommodation on the ACT without applying. What you **can** do is get the *same* accommodation on the *same* test without re-applying.

Q: How do I get testing accommodations for the SATs?

A: To receive accommodations on the SATs you must apply to the College Board's Services for Students with Disabilities (SSD). Start the process by going to the following web pages:

- http://student.collegeboard.org/services-for-students-with-disabilities/apply-for-testing-accommodations
- http://sat.collegeboard.org/register/for-students-with-disabilities

Q: How long will it take to get approved for accommodations to take my SAT?

A: About seven weeks. The process of evaluating your request cannot begin until your application for accommodations is complete. An application is not considered complete until ALL requested documents are submitted.

Q: May I register for the SAT before accommodations are approved?

A: Yes. Register for the test just as any other student would. When you are informed that your accommodations have been approved after receiving confirmation of registration, you must call **(609) 771-7137** to make the needed arrangements to use your accommodations on the date you have registered for.

If you receive approval for your accommodations within a week of your test, you must call and inform them of the last-minute approval to ensure that everything is set up for your test.

Q: What accommodations might I be eligible for on the SAT?

A: The most common accommodation is extended time. Other accommodations that test-takers can be approved for because of their disability include:

- **Presentation.** Large print, reader, fewer items on each page, colored paper, use of a highlighter, sign/orally present instructions, visual magnification, auditory amplification, audio cassettes, colored overlays, braille, braille graphs, braille device for written responses.

- **Responding.** Oral, dictated to scribe, tape recorder, computer without spell check/grammar/cut & paste features, record answers in test booklet, large block answer sheet.

- **Timing/scheduling.** Frequent breaks, extended time, multiple day (may or may not include extra time) or specified time of day.

- **Setting.** Small group setting, private room, screens to block out distractions, special lighting, special acoustics, adaptive/special furniture/tools, alternative test site (with proctor present) or preferential seating. [2]

Q: If I get approved for extra time on my SAT, how much extra time will I get?

A: Normally students have 3 hours and 45 minutes to take their SATs. If you get approved for extra time on your SATs you will either be approved for 50% extra time, i.e., a total of 5 hours and 25 minutes. If you are granted 100% extra time, you will test for 7 hours *over two consecutive school days*.

Students must have an IEP or a 504 plan to be granted 100% extra time on the SAT.

The SAT does not afford you flexibility as to how you use your extra time, or let you use more of your extra time on certain sections than others

Q: What accommodations might I be eligible for on the ACT?

A: The ACT offers you these three options:

- **National Standard Time with Accommodations.** You should select this option if you DO NOT need or qualify for extra time; but require another form of accommodation such as a wheelchair accessible room, an extra-large print test booklet, or permission to eat during the test.

- **National Extended Time (50% more time).** Select this option if you need extra time, in substitute or in addition to other types of accommodations, but you **can** test without frequent breaks, therefore, you can test at a national testing site. If you can test with time-and-a-half and paper forms, you should apply for this.

- **Special Testing (at school).** Apply for this if you need testing over multiple days alternative form testing such as Braille, cassettes, DVDs, or a reader; or a computer or scribe for essays, and/or alternate response modes (such as responding orally).[3]

Q: If I get approved for National Extended Time or Special Testing on the ACT, how much time will I get?

A: Normally students receive either 2 hours and 55 minutes if they do not take the writing part, or 3 hours and 30 minutes if they take the writing part. When you are approved for National

---

[2] Adapted From: http://professionals.collegeboard.com/testing/ssd/accommodations/other

[3] Adapted From: http://www.actstudent.org/regist/disab/opt3.html

Extended Time or Special Testing, you will get five hours to take the multiple-choice part, or five hours and 45 minutes on the ACT plus Writing to complete all five sections.

The ACT offers students more flexibility on how the extra time is divided up. With the ACT you can use extra time more or less heavily on different sections.

Q: How do I get testing accommodations for the ACT?

A: To apply for either National Standard Time with Accommodations or National Extended Time, you must complete an Application for ACT Extended Time and have it signed by either your guidance counselor or another qualified school employee. This application will further detail who qualifies, what documentation you need to submit, and deadlines.

If you need to request special testing, do not register either online or by mail. You must ask your school to submit a *Request for ACT Special Testing* on your behalf.

You may call Special Testing at (319) 337-1332 and/or Extended Time Services at (319) 337-1853 to receive additional information or to start the process.

Q: How do I contact the SAT or ACT test administration agencies to get started?

A: See the following pages.

SAT Contact Information

College Board SSD Program
P.O. Box 8060
Mt. Vernon, IL 62864-0060
Phone: (609) 771-7137
Fax: (866) 360-0114
TTY: (609) 882-4118
Email: ssd@info.collegeboard.org

Phones are available between 8 a.m. and 6 p.m. Eastern Time, Monday through Friday.

Additional phone numbers for the SAT:

- The SAT Program Customer Service can be contacted by calling this number: (866) 756-7346

- Services for Students with Disabilities can be contacted by calling this number: (609) 771- 7137

- Students who are deaf or hard of hearing can call this number with questions about the SAT: (888) 857-2477

ACT Contact Information

> ACT Registration
> Extended Time National Testing
> 301 ACT Drive
> PO Box 4068
> Iowa City, IA 52243-4068
>
> Phone: 319/337-1851 (Extended time questions)
> 319/337-1270 (to order materials)
> Fax: 319/339-3032

Additional phone numbers for the ACT:

For extended time on the ACT call (319) 337-1853.

- For special testing on the ACT contact: 1-319-337-1332.
- For student services and ACT registration contact: 319-337-1270.
- To live chat with an ACT representative, goo following link: http://www.act.org/studentforms/chat.html.
- For ID requirements and prohibited calculators contact: 319-337-1510.
- For student services and score report's contact: 319-337-1313.
- For Standard Time National Testing with Accommodations contact: 319-337-1270.
- For Extended Time National Testing contact: 319-337-1851.
- For homebound or confined testing contact: 319-337-1332.

Apply Early

Standardized testing is a common source of anxiety for anyone with college aspirations. When you have a disability, you have the extra opportunity – and responsibility – of registering for the accommodations that you need to make such a test fair. Remember, this is actually not asking for special treatment! This is just asking for a level playing field.

Apply for accommodations early! As I said above, it takes about seven weeks to receive approval. However, it could take longer if you hit a snag, such as the need to submit another form of documentation, or to appeal an adverse decision. These deadlines could mean you are required to register *well before* the registration deadline for the test date.

You will be dealing with a national testing body, which is different from what you are used to with your school district.

Almost every high school student who goes through the process of applying to college gets help from at least one adult. Don't let feeling as if you have to do it yourself, get in the way of letting your parent(s), school, or college admissions coach help you with securing testing accommodations. It is completely normal to have help with this.

One More Thing on the "Day of" Checklist

Most students who are approved for testing accommodations take their tests on Saturday at the same location as all other students taking that exam. If you are taking the test on a Saturday, bring the letter that says you have been approved for accommodations to your testing center. Add this to the checklist of #2 pencils, picture ID, certain type of calculator, and so on that your testing documentation tells you to bring.

Once you are all done with your college entrance exams-yay... You should save any letters saying that you were approved for testing accommodations on these exams, in case you need to take the GRE, LSAT, bar exam or any other test to become state certified in your chosen profession. It will vary greatly, but some testing boards, such as American Bar Association, are reluctant to grant testing accommodations due to disability. The further back that you can produce proof that you had accommodations, the better chance you have at getting future accommodation requests approved.

Request a Meeting

Generally, students take their SATs or ACTs on a Saturday morning. If you require a high level of accommodations, such as doing your SAT over two days, then you'll typically take the test on a normal school day. If you are testing during a school day, I advise you to arrange a meeting ahead of time with your school. This is so that you, your parent(s), and whoever is proctoring/writing your test are on the same page with everything.

Why is this necessary when you take tests all the time in high school? Because the SAT/ACT is so important! You should go over exactly what accommodations you will use, what time(s) you will start and stop, any breaks you will take during testing, what room you will be in, and any issues or questions that your proctor/scribe/reader might have.

If you are used to going into a separate room and dictating your tests, as I was in high school, you know what room you like best for this purpose. Take the meeting as an opportunity to request that room, as well as any other special requests you have. For instance, do you want to be able to have water with you throughout the test, so that your mouth doesn't get dry from dictating? The more issues you can plan for ahead of time, the better!

I was still trying to get an accommodation approved the morning of my test! I was so stressed out. They literally said, "Just go to class while we call the testing board." When they called me back to do the test, I'd been approved for the accommodation I requested. Needless to say, this was far from an ideal way to calmly start my test day! If I'd simply requested that meeting a month earlier, it would have eliminated all that unnecessary stress.

It is not up to your school to determine what accommodations you're granted; it's up to the national testing board.

Again, by requesting this meeting you are not asking for special treatment. You are just making sure you get whatever you are entitled to and that your school can carry that out without any confusion. This test is too important not to do everything reasonable to see that you have everything you need to perform to the best of your ability.

Some students take their SATs or ACTs once and they are done. Others might need to take SAT subject tests, or both the SAT and ACTs to apply to different schools. When this is the case, you do not need a prior meeting for every test. Arrange the meeting before your first college entrance exam.

Get the plan in writing. That way, if there is a para-pro change in between tests, the new person can just look over the plan and in most situations, say "That's fine. I know what the plan is."

Should I State on My College Applications That I Have a Disability?

I get asked this question frequently. Federal law prohibits colleges from asking students if they have a disability on an application for admission. Therefore, you are not required to disclose that you have a disability on your college applications. A common essay topic is, "Discuss some adversity you have experienced and how it has strengthened your character." You could certainly justify talking about your disabilities in such an essay. The goal of course, is to write the best response you can to this and any other essay question. If you feel your disability gives you the best opportunity to do that, then that's what you should write about. If on the other hand you feel writing about how Shakespeare has influenced your life will show off your mental acuity, discipline, ambition, and all the other skills and habits necessary to succeed in college and in life – then forget your disability and write about *that*!

You cannot legally be penalized in the applications process for disclosing. On the other hand, doing so will not automatically get you points.

Should I Include Other Documentation?

You might find yourself in a situation where you meet or exceed every admissions requirement except one. If you feel that your disabilities are the cause of your not fulfilling that one admission requirement, you should write a letter explaining your situation. You may then choose to include a letter with your application that states that you have a disability. This letter should state and briefly describe your disability. It should then go on to describe how you feel your disability hindered you in achieving the admission's requirement. You may then state any additional information you would like considered as to how you might address that requirement. Attaching brief medical documentation of your disability could also help.

> *NOTE: Do not* attach your IEP! This is for three reasons. First, your IEP will contain too much information. The admissions staff will not want to have to weed through all that. Second, there might be information in your IEP that you don't want others to know about. Third, IEP's do not count in college for anything – and you'll look smarter if you make it clear that you know that already.

You also have the option to get a letter from someone on your IEP team, your guidance counselor, your doctor or another medical provider. Any of these people could appropriately draft a brief statement as to why your disability posed a specific challenge in fulfilling an admission's requirement. This letter could either substitute for a personal statement or supplement it.

Who you ask to write this kind of letter depends on your relationships and the nature of your disability. I did not even want my IEP Team knowing what colleges I was applying to! But during that time my medical team was involved in my life and I would have felt comfortable asking my doctor to write a letter if I thought it would help. Again, it's your right to make all these kinds of decisions.

You do not need to enclose a letter stating that you have a disability if you see no reason do so. If you have met all the requirements for admission, then the fact that you have a disability is not relevant in the application process. Once you have been admitted, and you've decided the school that you wish to attend, you can then decide if you want or need to register with their Department of Disability Services.

Will My Disability Influence the Admissions Decision?

Federal law clearly states that colleges or universities are not obligated to **lower** their admission standards due to disability. Nor do they have to give applicants with disabilities any special consideration during application process, other than that the process itself must be accessible. It also clearly states that no institution can deny admission due to disability!

That being said, colleges value student diversity! The admissions panel might decide that they like you for whatever reason. Thus, while you might lack some of what they are looking for, you might meet or exceed all the other criteria. Given the totality of the circumstances, they will be flexible. You need to be close to what they are looking for, for this to have a chance of working.

It stands to reason that more exceptions are made at schools that have more services for students with disabilities. Nonetheless, in the end, the admissions process is largely a mystery. If you ask them, any school will say "No, disability status has no bearing on admissions." In reality, I'm not confident that these disclaimers are always true. Official policy aside, if an institution spends money on staff or facilities to accommodate a certain population, wouldn't they want to make sure that that those accommodations get used to capacity?

Asking for Recommendations: Who?

Every college application package contains a Recommendations section. Generally, schools require you to submit up to two recommendations (check the application instructions to make sure you know how many). It should be obvious that you will want to ask for recommendations from the high school teachers that you like – and that you feel liked by.

Plan Ahead

You need to give these teachers/counselors/administrators plenty of advance notice to write you a letter. Remember, lots of seniors may be asking them for recommendations. Teachers and staff have a life outside of school!

Think Realistically: To Know You Is Not Always to Love You

Of course, the number one criterion for deciding whether to ask any particular teacher for a recommendation should always be, how sure are you that that teacher likes you? My eleventh-grade history teacher sticks out in my mind. I could not get any sense of what he thought of me. I liked how he taught the class, but it was weird being in his class because with all my other teachers, I had at least some idea as to how much they liked me. I decided not to ask him for a reference; it was too much of an unknown.

Number two, how well do they know you? I did not ask my absolute favorite high school teacher for a recommendation, because I had been in her class for only half the year, and the class was not challenging for me. On a personal level, I will always appreciate how she responded to my disability; what she did in terms of encouragement for me was awesome! However, I felt she did not know me or how I responded to challenges as well as some of my other teachers, to the point where it would be worthwhile to get a recommendation from her.

Another consideration is teacher popularity. This book is about telling you like it is. If you are torn between asking one of two teachers for a recommendation, consider how popular they are. One being slightly less popular should give them points when you are deciding who would write the best letter. The more popular the teacher, the more letters they will be asked to write, the more letters that they need to write, the less time they will spend on yours (all other things being equal). This is not good when it comes to college admissions. Admissions staff members tend to be savvy about whether a recommendation letter just got cranked out because it was requested, as opposed to a letter that sincerely expresses something meaningful about an applicant's unique qualities, talents, and abilities. What kind of recommendation letter would you rather be sending off to your colleges' admissions boards?

The teacher who agrees to write the letter obviously bears some responsibility in this too. The right thing for any such person to do is to decide in advance how many quality letters they really have the time and energy to write. If more students ask than that predetermined number, the would-be endorser should turn you down.

I had another teacher who was very well liked. He had a policy where he would write letters of recommendation only for the students who took his elective course. If you just got him "randomly" for ninth grade, he would say "I'm sorry, but I do not know you or your academic abilities well enough." That was partly his way of keeping manageable the number of letters he needed to write. That made total sense to me! But in this world, never count on people to do the right thing or take your life seriously. Some teachers will just say yes to inflate their ego that so many are asking them for a letter of recommendation – and then they will use the same form letter that they downloaded from the Internet for everyone!

Look out for yourself by putting some serious thought into **whom you ask.**

Asking for Recommendations: How?
Asking for a recommendation can feel awkward. You just need to do it! When asking, tell the person you are asking why you picked them. For example, "We got to know each other well last year, and your support meant a lot to me."

Make it easy for others to help you by providing a "fact sheet" about yourself. This should include the colleges which you applying to, what your career goals are, any accomplishments while in high school and what extracurricular activities you participated in. This is NOT bragging!

A word of caution: just leaving one of these fact sheets in your prospective reference's mailbox at school does not count as asking! You need to make your request face to face to make the best possible impression. Putting myself in the shoes of a teacher or staff member, I would not want to write a letter for someone who did not have the moxie to ask me face-to-face, at a time that is good for me. It could also be confusing, as if you think they made an agreement that they have not yet made. Or, even come across as entitled, as if you think it's their job to write you a recommendation.

If you are really on the ball and already have your application essay done for your dream school before you ask for recommendations, give a copy to each person of whom you make the request. By giving each such person the opportunity to read your application essay, you will be providing an even better idea of who you are. That will help them write you a better letter.

It's okay to provide the application essay even if you are still quibbling over minor details such as word choice or that one sentence that's giving you trouble. On the other hand, if the essay is just a rough outline, full of typos, and so on, that's not ready for prime time. Don't offer something that's not likely to inspire confidence in your abilities.

It's far better to ask for your recommendation letters well in advance of the deadline, rather than waiting until the last minute so that you can present your request alongside your application essay.

Another Decision

If your disabilities are visible, let your prospective reference know whether it's okay with you to mention your disability in their letter. This issue will probably cross their mind as they are writing the letter, and it will make it easier for them to handle the issue if they know how you feel about it. You can put it as the last item on your "fact sheet." You could have a generic notice such as the following:

> I, (do/do not plan) on disclosing that I have a disability during the college application process; therefore, (I am/am not OK) with that fact being discussed in my letter of recommendation if you wish to do so.

If you put this last on your "fact sheet," then you don't need to say anything when discussing your letter.

However, you feel about this is okay. Trust your gut and then clarify the issue when someone agrees to write you a reference.

True-story...

This came up when I was applying for college. My Geometry teacher was a truly amazing person and wrote a beautiful letter on my behalf. Then she felt the need to ask if I was OK with her talking about my disability. I said "Of course." I had written about it in my essay, but I hadn't thought to give her a copy of it in advance. When it happened, I felt a little guilty that I had left the door open for her to worry about this. Obviously, this would have been an even bigger deal if I had not wanted my disability mentioned in my application! This teacher had already gone out of her way to help me on several occasions. So, it would have made me feel even worse if I had had to ask her to rewrite the letter.

Tip for Those Not Applying to College

If you are not applying to college in your senior year of high school, it is still a good idea to ask for references from at least two of your favorite teachers, counselors, administrators, or others who know your academic and other work from high school. Ask them to address it "To Whom It May Concern" at the top. This way, you'll have your letters on file if and when you pursue higher education in the future. This will be much easier than trying to contact them later and get them to write the letters then. First, they could change jobs or retire, making it more difficult or maybe even impossible to find them. Second, even if you find them and they remember you, you won't be as fresh in their mind. Remember, you are one of perhaps more than 100 students that they come into contact with every year!

In this situation, wait until April to make your requests. That way, the demand for letters that need to get to colleges by a certain date will have ended and teachers/staff will have had at least a couple weeks' break from writing recommendations. Again, they are only human. Showing consideration for their needs and schedules can only help you get a better reference letter.

One More Recommendation

The last two chapters I have talked a lot about the college selection and admission process for those with physical disabilities. There's a lot more to these subjects that applies to you, that have nothing to do with being disabled. That is because this book is focused on how to navigate issues that relate to college, career *and* disability.

I highly suggest that you consult at least one college selection guide that was not written for those with disabilities. You still need information on topics such as how to study for admissions tests, write excellent application essays, and complete the common application.

May I suggest *Step by Step College Admission Counseling: A Guide for High School Students and Families,* by Jeff Vernamonti. It is an excellent guide to use in tandem with this book. If you get both, you will be covered from all angles!

Points to Remember from Chapter 3

✓ Testing accommodations are not special treatment, they are just what you need to play on a level field with others.

✓ The most common accommodations are in the areas of time management, presentation, your responses, and setting.

✓ It is "safe" to request accommodations, in terms of the school not being informed of it (except on the LSAT and MCAT).

✓ Request accommodations at least seven weeks in advance. On the SAT, you must call to arrange to use your approved accommodations.

✓ Having an IEP or 504 plan makes it easier to get accommodations, but you still need to apply for them.

✓ Getting accommodations on one test doesn't automatically get you accommodations on another, except for a retake of the same test.

✓ It's okay to ask for help from family members and school officials to navigate your way through the maze of information.

✓ If your accommodations allow you to take tests on a school day when others take them on a Saturday, meet with the appropriate school officials in advance to make sure everyone understands the plan. Get the plan in writing.

✓ If possible, spend at least a few minutes visiting the place where you will be taking the test and mentally rehearse the steps you will be going through. Will you be able to get water easily and quickly enough if you need it, or do you need an accommodation to allow you to have water with you?

✓ You don't need to disclose your disability on your college applications, but if you do, do not include a copy of your IEP. Your disability might be worth talking about if it posed a specific challenge in fulfilling an admission requirement or some experience you have had in dealing with your disability is highly relevant to your qualifications for admission (such as how it relates to your career aspirations).

✓ Ask for letters of reference face-to-face. Only make the request of teachers that you think like you. Be careful about asking teachers who are super-popular. They might feel obligated to write your letter even though they have been overwhelmed by requests. Admissions board members can sniff out letters written out of obligation.

✓ Provide plenty of advance notice with your requests. If you are nervous about asking for letters of reference, think ahead about why you want a letter from each particular person that you want it from. Mentally rehearse your request with that reason in mind. It might also help to remember that letters of reference are a routine request for high school teachers, so there's nothing to be nervous about. If one teacher says no, just go to the next one that you have already placed on your request list.

✓ You get extra points for providing a copy of your application essay to the teachers from whom you are requesting letters of reference.

✓ Let your reference letter writers know whether it's okay to mention your disability.

Success Story: My Path to Independence and Successful Employment

Ann Marie Geiger

I was born in 1958 with a very rare bone disorder caused by a collagen defect called Osteogenesis Imperfecta, also known as "brittle bones". I cannot imagine what it was like for my parents to find out their child was born with multiple broken bones of the arms, legs and skull. And at that time, unlike today, very little information or support was available on either my disorder or how to raise a child with a disability. Fortunately for me, my parents, particularly my mom, were strong and resourceful and they pursued whatever they needed to do to assure that I would thrive and later become as independent as possible. The first thing they did was to ignore doctor's advice to keep me immobile and to put me in an institution.

There are several varying types of Osteogenesis Imperfecta. I have the most severe type that survives the first few weeks after birth. In addition to causing brittle bones, it usually causes extreme short stature (as an adult, I am only 3 feet tall) and skeletal abnormalities of the spine, ribs and long bones, leading to one requiring the use of a wheelchair for mobility. As an infant, just rolling over or having my diaper changed could cause a fracture. But my mother sensed how to best care for me and even learned how to set some of my broken bones as an infant, so I did not have to spend my childhood in the hospital. I was encouraged to move in between fractures so I would build muscle and bone strength. Although my early childhood involved broken bones every few months, about the time of puberty, thankfully, the fractures were occurring much further apart.

As was customary at that time, my parents first enrolled me in a school for children with disabilities. Within a few months, they realized this was not in my best interest, as the school was focusing on my disability and not my ability. The school was not developing my mind. I was moved to a Catholic school for two years, but the school was not totally accessible, and the nuns had to carry me up and down a flight of stairs. This clearly was not in my best interest either! In third grade, I was mainstreamed into public school even before mainstream was a word. This began my life in the "normal" world, where I had little exposure to others with disabilities until later in life. I do not think there were any options those days for transportation, so my parents hired several people to drive me to and from school.

At this point in life, I was still periodically suffering from broken bones, which would cause me to miss a few days of class. And there were many times, when I was forced to be side-lined from the typical activities of children, either because I had a fracture or because I wanted to avoid one. Yet, I managed to have lots of friends during this time, partly because I was fairly outgoing, but also because I was sort of a unique attraction being the only child in a wheelchair through grade school. Still, there was plenty of ignorance around me. I clearly remember the time when the mother of one of my friends came to our front door to tell my mom that her child could not play with me anymore because she might catch what I had!

While in grade school, my parents sometimes had to fight for things for me such as getting a ramp built so I could go out for recess like everyone else and then paradoxically, also being excused from having to go to gym class. Little did I know that them fighting for my rights back then was actually teaching me to be my own advocate later on.

High school was an extremely difficult time for me, especially emotionally. It was when I first realized that my disability was going to affect my whole life. Friends were getting into the dating scene and I was not. People were talking about careers that I wanted but knew were not physically possible for me. In addition, the sometimes-violent world in high schools was terrifying for someone with fragile bones and I dreaded the occasional scuffles that would break out in the hallways. But somehow, I got through it all.

Since I was being raised to be as independent as possible, I was expected to go to college just as my siblings did. We began the challenging hunt for a college that was wheelchair accessible where I could live on campus and learn to be independent, but also still be within an easy drive if I needed help. We settled on Widener University about an hour away and where I could also pursue my interest in Biology. Widener had two apartment buildings on campus where each building had one ADA accessible unit. With 2 bedrooms, each unit had the potential of housing 4 individuals. This is where I would once again be exposed to others with disabilities. Happily, the living quarters were far superior to an average dorm environment. One funny rather ironic glitch though in the beginning - they had never thought about making a curb cut for someone in a wheelchair to cross the street to class! This was quickly fixed of course, and I soon learned that I loved living on my own and making my own decisions. I thrived on college life and graduated 4 years later with a bachelor's degree in biology.

While in college and at the late age of 21, I learned to drive a car using hand controls, thanks to help from the Bureau of Vocational of Rehabilitation. I received financial assistance from them for a new wheelchair, some college tuition assistance and a driving instructor from a local rehabilitation center having a specially equipped car that I could drive with my arms instead of my legs. As nervous as I was about driving and the potential for serious injury, the feeling of power and control while driving helped me put these fears aside. I also realized that being able to drive would both increase my independence and open up more employment possibilities. I managed to buy an old but functional used Dodge Dart – my first car! With my own car came an even bigger challenge. But with the help of two friends who also had disabilities and a lot of creative thinking, I finally figured out a way to pull my wheelchair into the car. Now I could drive independently. I will never forget that feeling the first time that I drove myself home from college one weekend!

Getting a college education and learning to drive were the most powerful things that I ever did to help me reach my potential. But the journey would not be easy. As I began the process of job searching, the not-so-open-minded world reared its ugly head. In submitting my résumé and cover letters, I alternated between disclosing and not disclosing my disability. It seemed that when I mentioned it, I never even got an interview. When I did not disclose my disability, my interviews would usually be quick and awkward and it was often obvious just from the look on people's faces when I wheeled in, that they had made up their mind as soon as they saw me – a decision unfortunately based solely on looks rather than facts. It was a very difficult and discouraging time for me. I piled up the incoming rejection letters and started losing self-confidence.

It was a long year and a half later when I got an interview with a large well-known pharmaceutical company Merck, where they had a strong affirmative action program. It was apparent from my first interview that they were looking at my abilities and qualifications rather than my disability. In addition, they were offering to provide me with accommodations. For example, since the plant site was so large and just getting to my desk would be nearly impossible for me, they gave me in-plant parking privileges with a designated parking spot just outside the building I would work in.

I was hired as a lab technician for a position involving the testing of water samples in a laboratory and the collecting of air and water samples throughout the plant site. This second part of the job involved lugging carts with testing equipment from building to building and occasionally even climbing a ladder, neither feasible for a small woman in a wheelchair with fragile bones. So, the job was modified for me to be entirely laboratory work. In the laboratory, I was provided with a ramp to enable me to wheel into a large walk-in refrigerator used to store their water samples, and custom-made smaller lab gowns to wear. I soon felt that I was valued as part of a team. I did not have any problems performing all of the lab duties and in fact, ended up being the fastest water filterer in the lab unit. At first, I remember being worried that my slightly different technique might compromise sterility in the lab, but my testing results proved this was not an issue.

Unfortunately, my entry position was a union position and indeed six months later, there was a small company layoff resulting in me being bumped out of a job. I was on unemployment for the next year, but then was called in to interview at the same company for several open non-union salaried positions. Again, I found the company very encouraging and willing to take me in where I qualified. This time, I obtained a technical support desk job where all of my work would be computer and paperwork, so no major job accommodations were needed.

Getting a salary job at a major pharmaceutical was just what I needed to make the big move away from home. Now, more secure emotionally and financially, I found an apartment both 20 minutes from home and 20 minutes from work. This brought me an incredible feeling of power and independence. I loved slowly acquiring my own things in my very own place! I am sure it was hard on my parents letting go, but my family always fully supported my independence.

Somewhere along this time, I was able to ditch my second used car and buy a brand new one, a Buick Century. I took advantage of the General Motors program to subsidize buying a chair top carrier, a wonderful contraption which would fold and load my wheelchair onto the top of my car. This would save a lot of wear and tear on my body, something that would become even more important later in life, whether I wanted to admit it or not.

Another 10 years went by, when continued financial security and good health allowed me to purchase a condominium. It was a bit scary at first and a real commitment, but one that allowed me even more freedom and enjoyment in life.

During the 32 years I worked at Merck, the company has provided me with many accommodations as needed each time my job has changed or moved me to a different building. In addition to my parking space moving along with me, there have been modifications to restrooms, installation of automatic doors and my favorite accommodation of all, the purchase of a special motorized desk which can be lowered to a comfortable height for me. Some of these modifications were things I requested, but many were done automatically. Sometimes it was just a very simple thing, like moving files to a more accessible location for me. Other times, I have been allowed to work from home on an occasional icy or snowy day, when it would have been extra risky for me to drive with my bone condition. Once, I worked from home for about 10 weeks while I recovered from a hip fracture. Regardless, all of these things have allowed me to focus completely on my job rather than spending energy elsewhere and helped me achieve my maximum potential on my job.

There have been challenges during my working career, like having to work full-time with a body that does not always want to let me and sometimes, feeling exhausted trying to explain what I might need with the increasing workloads. But in all, I have felt respected by my co-workers and part of the team that makes the company so successful.

And there have been occasional perks where I work that I never would have expected, like having the shop mechanics available for an occasional wheelchair adjustment or repair. Once, they actually built me a custom footrest for my new wheelchair, when I otherwise would have had to wait months to get.

I feel very fortunate…. fortunate to have been born into a supportive family ahead of their time as far as what was the norm if you were born with a disability. Some people might have thought my parents were cruel in pushing me, but that helped me to become as independent as possible despite having a major disability. Later I followed my parents' examples to advocate for myself in the sometimes not-too-understanding world I was growing up in. That, combined with a decent education, enabled me to have the tools I needed to qualify for a good job. With some tenacity and a little good luck, I have managed to achieve my independence and success in the working world.

Chapter 4: You're IN! Now the Countdown Begins

Yay! You got those much-deserved letters of acceptance! Congratulations!

You either have just decided – or are about to decide – which college or university you will grace with your presence. The second semester of your senior year in high school should be about two things: celebrating and planning.

This might mean you need to miss some classes in your senior year to best prepare for college. That's what I did, and I don't regret it. Every couple of weeks I would miss school because there was something, I needed to do to start college in the fall. I had already been accepted into the college of my choice, Ramapo College of New Jersey. As finals approached, I made sure I had not missed so much that it would endanger my chances of graduating. The things I needed to do to be ready for college were of more benefit to me than a perfect attendance record in high school.

Disability-Related Accommodations: High School vs. College

To plan, you need some idea of what to expect. College and high school are more different than alike in how they handle disability accommodations. This is simply because legal requirements are tighter at the primary and secondary levels. Institutions of higher learning are not required to provide a Free Appropriate Public Education (FAPE) under the Individuals with Disabilities Education Act (IDEA). This means that colleges and universities are not obligated to provide special education or related services.

Special education means "specially designed instruction at no cost to the parents, to meet the unique needs of the child with a disability..." Related services are provided if students require them in order to benefit from specially designed instruction.[4] Related services can include transportation, assistance in carrying out personal needs such as eating or toileting during school hours, purchasing special equipment, or providing diagnostic or therapeutic services in order to support students' academic success.

Again, these are all things that by law colleges do not have to provide. And because IDEA does not apply to postsecondary institutions, there are no IEPs in college, either.

Basically, colleges do not have to offer any "special education services." They *do* have to offer services that help you access their normal course of study. This means that if you need special physical help to take a test, your college is required to provide a reader, scribe, or other assistive technology to take that test. This is because your need directly relates to an academic requirement.

Colleges do not have to offer services such as physical therapy (PT), occupational therapy (OT), or special transportation to and from school because they do not directly relate to academic requirements.

Another crucial difference is that in college you need to *register* for academic accommodations. Colleges are not required by law to identify students in need of services.

The Difference between ADA and 504
The two federal laws *do* mandate that all postsecondary institutions be *accessible* to persons with disabilities: are the Americans with Disabilities Act (ADA) and Section 504 of the Rehabilitation Act of 1973 ("504"). The ADA requires all postsecondary educational institutions to "remove any barriers impeding the student – whether these are architectural, communication related, or transportation – or to provide reasonable modifications to rules, policies, or practices. The school may provide aids or services such as readers, interpreters, note takers, adaptive equipment, relocation of classes to accessible environments, audio recordings, computer programs, early enrollment, rescheduling of classes, allowance of service animals, alteration of materials, or substitution of certain courses in programs."[5] This works together with 504, which states that an "appropriate" education means an education comparable to that provided to students without disabilities. This gives you some "protection" in college.

---

[4] See Disability Rights Education and Defense Fund, "A COMPARISON of ADA, IDEA, and Section 504," http://www.dredf.org/advocacy/comparison.html.

[5] See College Parents of America, "How the Americans with Disabilities Act Might Affect Your College Student"

There's not much difference between the ADA and 504. They both pretty much do the same thing. There is a very small minority of schools who are not legally obligated to follow 504. If a school does not receive *any* federal funding, they are not required to comply with 504 regulations. The vast majority of post-secondary institutions do receive federal funding. They still are required to comply with Title II of the ADA, but maybe to a lesser extent. The law presumes schools not receiving government funds have fewer resources, therefore, are required to provide less than schools that do receive monies either from the federal or state level. This being said, all schools are required to accommodate students with disabilities.

Most schools are required to follow both the ADA and 504!

What's the Good News?
Some say these differences make the transition to college harder for students with a disability. They report that they find this new responsibility confusing or burdensome. I felt just the opposite: college finally had a model that suited me! Do not let people tell you that college services for those with disabilities don't exist or are too hard to obtain. Not so! You just need to realize that you must take more responsibility for getting your needs met. If you accept this and plan for it, you can still succeed in getting your degree and being on a great career track just like anybody else!

Do I Have to Register with Disability Services?

No, you do not have to disclose that you have a disability to anyone at your school. It is both the student's choice and responsibility to register.

Conversely, the college is under no legal burden to identify students with disabilities and refer them to services. If you want to exercise your right to any of the accommodations, you will probably need to register. If you can get by as long as everything is basically accessible, you can choose not to register. But if there's any chance you'll need testing accommodations, go ahead and register.

It is the right of any professor to require that you be registered with your school's department of disability services to receive any academic accommodations in their class.

I always laughed that membership has its privileges. These include priority registrations, access to another computer lab, or more people to go to should you encounter a problem. Because of this, I recommend that you do register if you're eligible. You don't have to use any particular service even if you are registered. Unlike in high school, I saw *no* downside in college to being identified as having a disability.

Furthermore, at the college level the specialists are trained to be discreet and non-intrusive. One of my accommodations specialists told me, "If I see one of my students outside my office, I won't say 'hi.' If they talk to me, of course I then respond. But every one of my students is entitled confidentiality." Having such an obvious disability, I had never thought about it. Up until then, everyone knew I would need some accommodations. It was one of the many ways in which college was different from high school.

There is no additional cost to register with disability services so that you can receive academic accommodations and the other amenities offered under that name. There *is* an extra cost if you qualify for and take part in a comprehensive tutoring program for students with learning differences. An example of this is the SALT program at University of Arizona. Most schools do charge extra cost to participate in a school's personal care program, such as at Berkeley or Edinboro. You can register at any time, but it's best to do so at the beginning of the semester or before your first semester.

Towards the end of college, I used the disability resource center (DRC) only for testing accommodations. It was "on the books" that I needed to take my tests at the testing center. My professors automatically got a list of the students who signed up for this, so they would know how many tests they needed to send over to the testing center. All I needed to do was let the testing center know I had a test. For me, it was very easy. I don't think I met with the DRC specialist even once during my last semester. By then I had everything down. However, I liked the peace of mind of knowing that, if an issue were to arise, I would have someone to go to.

For those of you who do decide to register, it will not be noted on your college transcripts, so you don't have to worry about future employers or grad schools finding out if you do not choose to disclose.

You Will Need to Prove your Disability

Another key difference between high school and college in terms of disabilities is that colleges require students to submit documentation or proof of their disabilities to qualify for services. Not to worry, this won't be as hard as it sounds! You can always ask when arranging the first meeting.

Most schools use seven elements established by the Association on Higher Education and Disability (AHEAD) to evaluate what documentation they request and what they will accept. These elements were put in place to establish consistency for postsecondary staff, parents and students. Your school's policy is probably at least influenced by these seven elements:

- The credentials of the evaluator(s).

- A diagnostic statement identifying the disability.

- A description of the diagnostic methodology used.

- A description of the current functional limitations.

- A description of the expected progression or stability of the disability.

- A description of current and past accommodations, services and/or medications.

- Recommendations for accommodations, adaptive devices, assistive services, compensatory strategies, and/or collateral support services.[6]

Frankly, if you have a physical disability, this process will be easier for you than students needing accommodations due to other types of disabilities. Individual situations will vary. In some cases, students will need to undergo professional evaluations for the purpose of obtaining the documents to be eligible to receive academic accommodations at the college level. Should this situation arise for you, your high school is not responsible for paying for such evaluations, and neither is the college. You'll either need to pay through insurance or out of pocket. In populations with physical disabilities, though, this is rare. You probably will not need to undergo any further evaluation to secure the documentation you'll need.

---

[6] From: http://www.creighton.edu/disabilitysupportservices/documentationandguidelines/index.php

College Visits After You've Been Accepted

If your first visit to a prospective college is like kicking the tires of the used car, now it's time to look under the hood and go for a test drive. That's right: I'm recommending that you do a second round of college visits after you are accepted. Don't just show up on move-in day. A second visit allows you to go deeper into issues you were left wondering about from before, or just to visit places and ask questions that time didn't allow on the previous tour. Plus, it will be more real to you now.

This can mean you only go to the school that you definitely decided to attend, as I did, to make firm plans for when you start in the fall. You may want to combine trips and do this during new student orientation in the early summer. But if you've been accepted to two or three institutions and are still trying to decide among them, make separate trips in March or April. Spend two or three days at each school to really get a feel for what your life might be like as a student on that campus!

Schools that have accepted you will be willing to spend more time with you, talk to you in more detail, give you "insider" tours, and so on. After all, they accepted you; they *want* you to go there. They might arrange for you to sit in on a class or two. This will help you evaluate the physical access to at least one or two lecture halls. Campus representatives might arrange for you to be hosted by a student who knows their way around on and off campus.

If you still have to decide whether to attend a given institution, try to make the simulation of college life as realistic as you can! Actually, use the library. Visit the dorms you have to choose from.

And actually, eat in the cafeteria. I spoke earlier of the challenges I have with eating because of my lack of fine motor skills. At my second school, the cafeterias all had disposable cups with lids. Had I spent a day or two living as a college student in my senior year of high school at both a small and a big school, I might have realized how much better the larger school would be for me. The system at the first school was all-you-can-eat, so they didn't provide any disposables. I just assumed a cafeteria is a cafeteria. Don't make that mistake.

For you, your big challenge might not be the cafeteria; it might be a totally different area of campus life, but you get my point.

Most important, talk to as many people as possible! The more people you talk to at a school, the better sense you will get as to what is the best fit for you.

Attention: Future Science Scholar's
Many students with disabilities want to major in a science or engineering discipline. If this is you and you have a visual impairment, a mobility and/or motor disability, I recommend you meet with the head of your major department to discuss how accessible their labs are. Also, ask if they are willing to work with you in terms of accommodations for field work. Are there any accommodations you'll need that they are not used to providing? How open do they seem to work with you?

You can still manage if they seem reluctant or if there are issues with the facility that you'll just have to deal with. But obviously it is a lot easier if your facility is supportive.

Remember, a Holistic View

All this focus on disability-related issues when checking out schools on your short list doesn't mean you should make your final decision only about which school is the best in this one area. You might find that the Department of Disability services of all the institutions on your short list offer pretty much the same thing.

The same might be true of the departments of career services and residence life. One school might be a little more accessible, but overall both schools would work for you. Accessibility-wise, and for whatever other reasons, you might both like and feel more comfortable at the slightly less accessible campus. Just think it through from all angles and make the decision that is right for *you*! Wanting to go to the same school as your boyfriend/girlfriend, friends, with a chapter of a Greek organization or that a family member graduated from, is no more or less legitimate than your accessibility and other disability-related needs.

I do not mean to neglect academics! After all, it is the main reason you are going to college. If one school is stronger, either generally or in your chosen field, then of course that needs to be a major consideration.

In my second semester of college I called my mom and told her, "I think I want to transfer to the state school closer to home. A bunch of people I know from high school go there so I just feel it would be easier to make friends through people I already know. I knew no one up here when I started in the fall. It is not getting any easier to make friends. Everyone up here is still in their high school cliques!"

My mom replied, "I don't think that is a good answer. The other state school doesn't have as much experience in dealing with people with disabilities. The professors will probably be just like your middle school and high school teachers, thinking a student with a disability at a regular school is odd. That campus is not as accessible."

"But Mom, who am I going to hang out with? I can't hang out with my professors. And that other school is accessible enough. It just doesn't have automatic door openers. I still have the upper body strength to handle that!"

I'll never know who was right; maybe we both were. I never transferred to the other school. After two rocky years of feeling Ramapo was a great match for my disability but not for me overall; I ultimately decided to transfer to the University of Arizona. This was due to my family's plans to relocate to Tucson. I was very happy with that decision.

College Placement Tests

One of the very first things you will have to do freshman year of college is take a math and reading skills test. All freshmen need to take these to determine which classes they will be placed in. If you need accommodations, set them up as early as possible. Get in touch with your disabilities services specialist and ask whether they would be able to send the test forms to your high school and let you do them at the end of senior year. This way you will be taking them in an atmosphere you are used to. For example, if you need to dictate these, as I did, you will be used to the scribe or parapro that you are working with. I did it that way, and it was a huge help!

It will be an advantage to get these done: one less thing that you need to worry about the first week of college! Also, if you do not pass when you take them at the end of high school, you can take them again the first week of college, and then you will know more about what's on them. These tests are important because they will give you an opportunity to test out of courses, if you do not need to take them. You need to advocate for yourself in this process.

Do You Want a Roommate?

Most people who live on campus have a roommate. You may want one like any other freshman. Or perhaps, like me, due to disability, you might think a private room is best for you.

Remember, your roommate will at first be a stranger, so they will not have the same mindset as your family, who loves you. My family usually seemed to just automatically do whatever I needed, most of the time without even thinking about what they were sacrificing. My mom never complained about the extra space my equipment took up, the extra cleaning needed because I would drop my food, or the plain old extra understanding I needed to help deal with the frustration of having a disability on top of all the normal teenage challenges.

I felt; it was not realistic to expect a random eighteen-year-old to be there for you in that way. I thought it wouldn't even be fair to expect my two good years-long friends to share a dorm room with me because of the various challenges they would have had to put up with. Success in life requires you to be honest about your limitations. I feel that am not neat enough to share a tiny space.

For me, sharing a room would have been really hard! Disability accommodation is intended to help people with disabilities not work any harder than their peers without disabilities to accomplish the same thing. During most of the writing of this book, I was sharing a house with a roommate. We typically got along great. However, I think that if we had needed to share a dorm-sized room, there would have been major tension between us. Roommate conflicts can add greatly to your stress. You'll appreciate having an emotionally safe "home base" where you can retreat when things are tough in class, or elsewhere outside of your new home.

Consider things also from the roommate's point of view. If you have to bring a service dog home with all the time, or getting daily or twice-daily PCA care, your roommate is forced to have a guest whether they want them then or not.

I'm not saying having a roommate is an automatic disaster. And even if there are "incidents," you will either make lifelong friends or have some really awful roommate stories to laugh about with your friends throughout your life.

If you're concerned about feeling isolated, don't worry! You are still living on campus. There are plenty of ways to find people to hang out with. For one thing many colleges offer a dorm option with suites, in which several rooms share a bathroom and common area. This was perfect for me, as I could have a single room but be near other students. This was especially important to me since I didn't know anyone from my high school who was going to my college. My disability would not interfere with sharing a bathroom. I would have to change a little. All college students need to change to acclimate to dorm life. Living in a dorm will never be exactly like living in your family home.

Meeting with Disability Services

The best time to think further about the accommodations you'll need in college is right after you've been accepted. The less you need to handle the first week of your freshman year, the better! Most Disability Services Departments will be happy to work with you as soon as you are admitted. Not only are you entitled to this help but seeking it early cuts down on their first week-of-the-semester rush!

The first task is to figure out whom you need to contact, using your school's website. If your school has a department for disabilities services, that's who you need to contact. Do so right after acceptance and work out a plan. Again, this process will be way less formal than an IEP meeting. No legal document will be drafted. In contrast to your meetings with DSD's when you were visiting prospective schools, your objective now should go beyond understanding the school's policies: it should be to get a plan in place for your first semester.

If you can meet with Disability Services in person, that's best. If you're still deciding which college to attend, contact them via phone or email to relay you've been accepted to their school and you want to make sure it's the right school for you. See what they say.

You might also want to ask about PE and/or foreign language graduation requirements (if you did not already get that information). Each institution is different. At my first school, neither PE nor foreign language was required to graduate. My second school also had no PE requirement, which thrilled me. I suffered through four semesters of Adaptive PE in high school, and I was so glad I did not have to deal with another semester like that in college! But my second school had a foreign-language requirement for graduation.

Do not start the fight for course substitutions during this first meeting! You do not want to run the risk of alienating them. Just ask them what's required and see what their answer is. Do they simply say "Yes," or do they go on to say, "But we have had students who both do the requirement with accommodations and we also have had students who have gotten course substitutions approved?" The more information you gather, the easier it will be to choose a school.

The only other step I will remind you of from Chapter 2 is about the Workforce Recruitment Program. If a given campus does not already participate, ask if they would be open to working with you to bring WRP there. What does *their* department do to help *their* students get jobs? Again, if you are still choosing, this should be a top priority for you!

Meeting with the Department of Residence Life

Another key objective of any post-acceptance visit is to select the right place to live. Residence Life is the department that runs all campus housing. If you plan to live on campus, schedule an appointment with the director to discuss your options. If mobility is an issue for you, make sure he or she knows that. Ask which freshman dorms are closest to what you will need to access on campus.

Do they have designated rooms in which they normally place students with disabilities? Why so? Ask for a tour of the hall you will be assigned to.

Also, talk with them about any specific needs you might have. In my case these included a fold-down shower bench in the bathroom and a special lock on my door. These two things were not a problem to get, all I needed to do was ask! It was so nice that when I arrived on campus to move in, these things were already in place for me!

If you are bringing a service dog or require PCAs to have easy access to you in your dorm, you need to alert Residence Life as soon as possible so you can work any issues out before you move in. For instance, if you are hiring a PCA to help you get out of bed every morning, Residence Life needs to know so they can work out how to grant that person access to the building. The last thing you want the first week is to have security say you need to get out of bed to escort the person who is there to get you out of bed!

My first school had a policy that students who used wheelchairs had to live on the first floor of a residence hall, in case of fire. My second school had no such policy. Do you feel as if you need to be on the first floor in case there is a fire? Or, do you feel that the way most dorms are built, it is unlikely that there would be a major fire, and if one were to happen you could do whatever you needed to get down three or four flights?

Mobility Trial

The third thing you should do in your post-admission visit to your school(s) is "walk around" the same distances you will need to during a typical day on campus. This is to make sure that it is doable with your current mobility aids. My advice is to go with "one size bigger" thinking. For example, if you are only a little tired after doing it, you will probably "grow into it" easily. This is what happened for me. The first week I was a little tired pushing around campus. But by the second week, I was used to it and I was fine.

Should you find yourself not even being close to able to cover the distance, use the summer to get yourself one or more mobility aids. This can mean anything on the spectrum, from a cane, to a power chair or scooter. The earlier you make this decision the better! If you need a wheelchair, it will take time to get insurance approval and receive the equipment. Plus, you'll need at least a couple of weeks to get used to a new device before you take it to school and depend on it to get yourself to class on time.

Even if you do get a wheelchair, it doesn't mean you have to use it all the time! It could just be a backup. However, it is way better to have something and not need it... The worst thing would be to struggle in school because you cannot get around easily. College is a time of many challenges. Walking everywhere when you have a disability in this area doesn't have to be one of them.

Another difference between college and high school is that in college you will not have to carry your books around all the time. Factor this in when making your mobility plan. In college most of your studying will take place outside of class. This means that you will normally be able to leave most or all your textbooks in your residence hall when you go to class. In college, plan on carrying your notes, some kind of binder or folder for handouts, a laptop/tablet and maybe one book. More and more students are required to bring a laptop or tablet to class in college, so plan for that, not books, to be the thing you need to carry around campus.

Attention, Manual Chair Users

If you use a manual chair, I *highly recommend* that you also bring gloves for pushing at least for the first couple weeks. When I started college, I was used to pushing wherever I needed to go, and never wore gloves. The first few weeks of college, I needed to push my chair further than I was used to. My arms did fine with this; my hands did not. I got blisters: not fun! The solution is easy: wear gloves, at least while you are still getting used to your campus. If it were my arms that were rebelling, I'd just have to sentence myself to a summer of upper body exercises. To me, that wouldn't be fun. Maybe it would be to you.

It is easy to throw a pair of bike gloves in your bags. If you settle into not wearing gloves, as did I, put them with your dorm first-aid kit. Do this just in case you are like me and cut your palm doing something stupid. (I treat you to that story in Chapter Six.) If your hand(s) get a cut, you will want to wear gloves to keep it clean and dry.

Meet with Vocational Rehabilitation

Another meeting I suggest you have in preparing to go to college is with the Department of Vocational Rehabilitation (VR) in either your home community or the community where you will be attending college. Vocational rehabilitation departments are federal government agencies whose goal is to help people with all types of disabilities become employable. If they decide that a degree or other education will make you employable, then they will pay for *some* of the costs. In the eyes of VR, whatever they pay for must be part of an effort to get their client employed.

This visit does not need to take place during your trip to your college. However, it should be part of your planning.

This might or might not be facilitated by your high school. As of 2004, a representative from VR should be at your IEP once you are 16.[7] If someone from VR does make an appearance at your IEP, it will be a perfect opportunity for you to find out what you might qualify for and how to start the process of getting an Individual Plan of Employment (IPE) in place with their agency. You'll need an IPE to receive VR funding. If you do not have an IEP, or no VR rep shows up, schedule an appointment to go meet with them at your local office.

They *could* pay for:

- ✓ Help with tuition expenses.
- ✓ Room and board.
- ✓ Transportation/commuting expenses.
- ✓ Books and supplies.
- ✓ Out of class reader services for people who are blind or who have learning disabilities; interpreter services for people who are hearing impaired; and/or individually prescribed aids and devices.
- ✓ Telecommunications, sensory, and other technological aids and devices.
- ✓ Other goods and services that help an individual with a disability become employed.

Your Mileage May Vary
Every state is different in what they will pay for. A "free-ride" from VR is either non-existent or very rare. Normally they pay either the whole cost or partial cost of one or two items on your "college bill." As a student you will have at least some costs that they will not cover. The state of Arizona paid for books and part of my tuition. It would not pay for on-campus housing or any living expenses or tutoring that I needed more because of my inability to write.

Should you need VR to buy you something such as adaptive driving equipment, assistive technology or a mobility aid, then I suggest you meet with them earlier: sophomore or junior year of high school. This is because VR processing for purchasing equipment for clients can

---

[7] From: The Heath Guide

take a very long time. You will have to go through evaluations using their specialists and so on.

In many cases this meeting will be about as fun as a visit to your least-favorite relatives. For those of you who like all your relatives, substitute something you find un-fun in the above statement (reading this book? I hope not). But, hey, if you get your books paid for, that will save you a ton of moner! That is sure worth sitting through a boring meeting or two, signing some paperwork, and agreeing to keep in touch with your counselor. You will only need to do this a couple of times a year. You might even be able to just send a short email.

> ***Pre-College VR Tip:*** When you meet with VR tell them about **ALL** expenses that are in any way related to your disability. You will never know what they will cover unless you ask. As long as you are there, you might as well try. Every state is different, and it probably also varies year by year. If you need PCAs to assist you with basic ADLs, also inform VR of this. Their agency probably will *not* pay for ADLs, but they will be able to tell you how to start the process to get funding through your state's Medicaid program.

Financial Aid Resources for Those with Disabilities

Please check out the appendix of this book, as there may be one or more scholarships you decide to apply for. In addition, here are some other financial aid resource for those with disabilities;

College Funding for Students with Disabilities
http://www.washington.edu/doit/Brochures/Academics/financial-aid.html

This web site contains a six-page document about financial aid for students with disabilities. It is published by the University of Washington. Like the Heath document, it provides a good list of scholarships and resources for students with disabilities.

DO-IT
University of Washington
Box 354842
Seattle, WA 98195-4842
doit@uw.edu

Phone/TTY: 206-685-DOIT (3648)
Phone/TTY: 888-972-DOIT (3648) (voice/TTY)
Fax: 206-221-4171
Phone/TTY: 509-328-9331 Spanish

DSSHE-L

DSSHE-L is a mailing list discussion of issues relevant to students with disabilities in higher education. Topics include: the legal responsibilities of institutions under the ADA; how to meet the physical and academic needs of disabled students; and how to fund such services. To subscribe to the list, write to listserv@listserv.buffalo.edu with subscribe DSSHE-L in the message body.

Submissions may be sent to dsshe-l@listserv.buffalo.edu.

Financial Aid for Persons with Disabilities and Their Families
Gail A. Schlachter and R. David Weber, Reference Service Press A listing of scholarships, fellowships, grants-in-aid, and other sources of free money available primarily or exclusively to persons with disabilities or members of their families, plus a set of six indexes: Program Title, Sponsoring Organization, Residency, Tenability, Subject, and Deadline Date. In its 13th edition at the time of this writing.

Grants & Scholarships for Disabled Women
https://www.scholarshipsforwomen.net/disabilities/

We help women find financial aid to help pay for college. If you have any questions, please email webmaster@scholarshipsforwomen.net

HEATH Resource Center's Financial Aid for Students with Disabilities
http://heath.gwu.edu/financial-aid

The HEATH Resource Center of the American Council on Education operates a national clearinghouse on postsecondary education for individuals with disabilities. Their Financial Aid for Students with Disabilities publication is updated annually and provides information on US federal student aid programs and other financial aid programs for students with disabilities. It also includes a list of 29 sponsors of scholarships specifically designated for students with disabilities. Disabled students may also wish to request a copy of Vocational Rehabilitation Services -- A Postsecondary Student Consumer's Guide.

HEATH
One Dupont Circle, Suite 800
Washington, DC 20036-1193
Phone: 1-800-544-3284 or 1-202-939-9320 (both numbers voice/TTY)
Fax: 1-202-833-4760

National Directory of Financial Assistance Programs for Post-Secondary Students with Disabilities

http://www.neads.ca/en/about/

Since its founding in 1986, the National Educational Association of Disabled Students (NEADS), has had the mandate to support full access to education and employment for post-secondary students and graduates with disabilities across Canada.

National Educational Association of Disabled Students
Rm. 426, Unicentre
1125 Colonel Bay Drive
Carleton University
Ottawa, Ontario, K1S 5B6 Canada

Phone: 1-877-670-1256
Fax: 613-369-4391
Email: info@neads.ca

Scholarship and Award Opportunities for Visually Impaired Students

https://lavellefund.org/scholarship-and-award-opportunities-for-visually-impaired-students/

Courtesy of the Lighthouse Guild and the American Foundation for the Blind

You Need to Buy Your Own Equipment

When you are a K-12 student, the school is responsible for providing whatever equipment you need to learn or function in school. Colleges are not. An easy to grasp example of this is books. In high school they are provided for you; in college you must buy them. This fact comes into play more when you are a student with disabilities. You might have been using either computer equipment or mobility equipment provided by your high school. When you go to college, you will need to supply these for yourself. During your senior year of high school, you need to think about what special equipment you need, if any, and how you will pay for it.

In my senior year my mom and I knew I needed a chair for college. My mom said, "Let's go to the Abilities Expo to compare power wheelchairs with scooters."

I knew I wanted a manual chair. In my mind, fine, anything to get a day off school! When I got there, I saw the chair I wanted and decided to start lobbying for it. I would recommend going to an Abilities Expo if one is in your area and need to buy DMEs. It worked well for us, because I got to use the chair for a couple hours to make sure it was what I wanted. My mom got to see that I looked comfortable and did amazing in the chair before she bought it. That day was very productive for us!

Abilities Expo Tip: These events are usually held over a Friday, Saturday and Sunday. Go on a Friday! I have gone twice, both on Fridays, and both times it was already crowded. I could only imagine how crazy it would be on a Saturday or Sunday. This is especially important if you are going to look at wheelchairs. If it is really crowded, you will not really get to move around enough to see how well the chair really works for you in a less crowded situation. Also, for such a major purchasing decision, you'll want the product reps to have more time to talk with you and answer questions.

Options for Funding Your Equipment

✓ **Centers for Independent Living**
   http://www.virtualcil.net/cils/

✓ **Department of Vocational Rehabilitation**
   https://askjan.org/concerns/State-Vocational-Rehabilitation-Agencies.cfm

✓ **Diagnosis Related Associations**

✓ **Health Insurance**
   If the equipment is considered medically necessary, such as a wheelchair or even augmentative communication devices, your insurance might cover it. To start this process, ask your doctor to submit a letter of medical necessity to your insurer.

✓ **Local Lion's Club**
   Might have funds to grant or help in organizing fundraising efforts.

✓ **Out of Pocket**
   Depending on your needs and your family's means.

✓ **Your high school and/or college**
   They are *not obligated* to buy equipment for you, but they might know of local funding sources. Your college might even have loaner equipment for a trial or until you get your own equipment. This happened for me at my first college. Or, your high school might be able to sell you what you have been using for a reduced price.

Funding Resources for Assistive Technologies, Mobility Aids and Medical Equipment

Adaptive Equipment Rebate Programs

https://www.discountramps.com/info/mobility/auto-modification-reimbursement-programs/a/B57/

These programs were established to help disabled people pay for the vehicle modifications they need to be able to drive, such as hand controls.

Assistive Technology Law Center

http://aacfundinghelp.com

People with very different backgrounds and wide range of experience need information about SGD funding. This web page will help SLPs, advocates, people with severe disabilities and their family members, funding program staff, and decision makers. It is designed to be of benefit to those who are confronting SGD funding questions for the first time, as well as those with prior funding experience. AACFUNDINGHELP.COM provides information useful to each of these diverse populations interested in SGD funding.

300 Gateway Center
401 East State Street
Ithaca, New York 14850
United States
Phone: 607-277-7286
Fax: 607-277-5239
Email: lewis.golinker@aacfundinghelp.com

Association of Blind Citizens

http://www.blindcitizens.org

The mission of the Association of Blind Citizens (ABC) is to advance relevant causes, increase opportunities in education, employment, cultural, recreational and other life activities, as well as enhance the social, political, and economic well-being for all people who are blind or visually impaired.

The ABC supports, argues in favor of, and defends the rights of individuals who are blind or visually impaired. The ABC is a membership organization of blind/visually impaired persons, their friends and families, and other interested individuals who recognize the needs and issues effecting the blind community.

PO Box 246
Holbrook, Massachusetts 02343
United States
Phone: 781-654-2000 or 781-961-1023
Fax: 781-961-0004
Email: president@assocofblindcitizens.org

GiveTech

http://givetech.org

GiveTech plans to solve this problem for many financially disadvantaged people with severe physical disabilities.

Phone: 415-750-2576
Fax: 415-387-1516
Email: info@givetech.org

National Christina Foundation

http://www.cristina.org/

Through the Cristina Network, we provide free donation management system software and solutions for use by nonprofits, schools and public agencies in their local communities to manage their own reuse agendas to benefit people with disabilities, students at risk and persons who are economically disadvantaged.

The National Cristina Foundation and our grassroots partners are bound by the collective belief that technology re-use helps Link Life to its Promise.

500 West Putnam Avenue
Greenwich, Connecticut 06830
Phone: 203/863-9100

Pass It on Center / National AT Reuse Center

http://passitoncenter.org/

The Pass It On Center is creating national and state resources to foster the appropriate reuse of AT so that people with disabilities can get the affordable AT they need in order to live, learn, work and play more independently.

C/o Georgia Department of Labor, Tools for Life
1700 Century Circle, Suite 300
Atlanta, Georgia 30345-3020
United States

Phone: 800-497-8665 or 404-638-0390
TTY: 866-373-7778
Email: info@passitoncenter.org

State List of Financial Loan Programs for Adaptive Equipment

https://www.gogrit.us/news/2016/2/9/the-complete-list-of-financial-loan-programs

Telecommunications Equipment Distribution Program Association

http://www.tedpa.org

The mission of TEDPA is to convene for the purpose of information exchange and to assist one another with the administration of specialized telecommunication equipment distribution programs for persons with disabilities.

Email: cphelps@mt.gov

The Foundation for Science and Disability

http://www.stemd.org

The Student Award Program of FSD helps to increase opportunities in science, engineering, mathematics, technology, and pre-medical/dental areas for graduate or professional students with disabilities. FSD has established a Science Graduate Student Grant Fund, which is available to fourth year undergraduates (who have a disability and have been accepted to a graduate or professional school in the sciences) and graduate science students who have a disability. Awards of $1000 each are made to qualified college or university students in any field of Mathematics, Science, Medicine, Technology, or Engineering. Awards are given for an assistive device or instrument, or for some other special need.

Requests for further information or membership should be addressed to:

> Dr. Richard Mankin
> USDA-ARS CMAVE
> 1700 SW 23rd Dr
> Gainesville FL 32608
> Phone: 352-374-5774
> Fax: 352-374-5781

Wheelchair Foundation

http://wheelchairfoundation.org

The Wheelchair Foundation, a division of Global Health and Education Foundation, a 501(c)3 charitable foundation, has a goal to provide a free wheelchair to every child, teen and adult worldwide who needs one but has no means to acquire one.

3820 Blackhawk Road
Danville, California 94506
United States
Phone: 877-378-3839 or 925-791-2340
Fax: 925-791-2346
Email: info@wheelchairfoundation.org

Wheelchair Recycling Program (WRP)

http://www.wrp.org

Too often, persons with disabilities, of all ages, are unable to participate to their fullest potential in their communities due to equipment limitations. For some, insurance does not cover the necessary equipment. For others, they need backups in case their equipment needs repair or is not suited to every need. Or, they remain on waiting lists for months or years, before they can get assistance through governmental programs.

2554 Advance Road
Madison, Wisconsin 53718
Phone: 608-243-1785
Fax: 608-243-1787

True-story...

Earlier in this chapter I spoke about having Roommates or suitemates if you live on campus. You will probably get notice in the summer before freshman year of who you are going to be living with. I recommend that you tell them up front about your disability

When I went through this process, all I got was a letter in the mail with my suitemates' phone numbers. No email was provided, and this was way before social networking and texting existed. I was excited to read the names, but did not feel ready to call, since my speech was very hard to understand on the phone.

Later that day, my brother answered our landline. Again, this was before everyone had a cell with caller ID. He asked the caller to wait a second. I got on the phone and it was one of my suitemates. She introduced herself, but when I replied, she could not understand me at all! After a minute she just said "Well, bye." I got so upset, I locked myself in my room and started crying! I was thinking, "Nobody prepared either of us for this call!" Of course, she couldn't have known that I would be harder to understand because of my CP. Why would she even know what that was? It's not like when I meet someone in person. Then they can see that I use a wheelchair or I'm not steady on my feet; it's obvious that I have some type of disability.

What an awful way to make my first impression on my suitemate-to-be! I thought maybe she was now on the phone with our other suitemates telling them, I didn't even know what. Then I got really freaked out, thinking "If I can't even manage the first phone call, how am I going to get through college?!"

When my mom came home, she helped me calm down. She called my suitemate to explain. Mom then handed me the phone, and as with everyone else, we were gradually able to talk more and more over the phone. That first phone call ended up having *zero* effect on our relationship!

And the Lesson Is...

Going to college is daunting for everyone. Everyone has moments where they feel they can't handle everything. These moments will pass, no matter what, and you will push on.

Points to Remember from Chapter 4

✓ Visit the colleges where you've been accepted, even if you already visited once. This will help you finalize your decision or simply be less anxious on move-in day. Ask to be shown around as an accepted new student. Use the library, eat in the dorm, visit a science lab, and talk to lots of people. Talk to disability related services staff and ask about WRP.

✓ Schedule a meeting with your local department of vocational rehabilitation to see if the government will cover any part of your college costs.

✓ Know the difference in disability accommodation laws in terms of what your high school verse what your college was required to do. Colleges have to comply with the ADA and Section 504; anything else is icing on the cake. They are not required to identify you as having a disability; you are free to identify yourself as such. This can get you some accommodations to level the playing field, such as extra time for tests. Plan for the impact on how you'll function in the classroom in college.

✓ Decide whether you want to register with disability services. If so, find out what documentation you need to submit. Most schools use the AHEAD guidelines to evaluate documentation you submit to prove that you have a disability. Then follow up to ensure that it was received and is adequate to get you registered for accommodations.

✓ Decide which residence hall and room type you want.

✓ Plan a trip to the college that you will be attending to get everything set up:

   o Meet with the department of disability services to get your accommodation plan in place.

   o Meet with the Department of Residence Life to find more out about all the campus housing options and ensure that you get placed in the one that most fits your needs. Inform them about anything you'll need in place on your move-in date, such as a flip-down shower bench, combination lock, or building access for your PCA(s).

   o Do an on-campus mobility trial and decide on the option that best enables you to get around on campus, be it your own two feet or a mobility aid.

✓ List all the equipment you'll need to purchase and/or bring to campus.

✓ Make a plan for how you will fund anything that you need to purchase and start working the plan.

✓ Inquire if you can take college placement tests at your high school, especially if you need a scribe to write your responses.

✓ Contact future roommates or suitemates.

✓ RELAX! If you prepare, you'll do great! Your college accepted you for a reason.

Chapter 5: Managing PCAs, Service Dogs, and Wheelchair Maintenance in College and Beyond

This chapter might seem to represent a deviation from the main purpose of this book, which is to position yourself to be strong in the job market. I am including this material because the issues in this chapter discourage many people with disabilities from attending four-year colleges. This chapter will help you take over many of the daily tasks that your parents or other family members have been managing for you.

Whether you end up at a college a few towns over from your parents' house or at a university across the country, your parents will not always be there to do everything. This chapter will help you plan for handling more of your own needs Your plan can include provisions for getting your needs met by any combination of PCAs, school staff, family and friends, and of course yourself.

When I was in college, I moved several times. This is not uncommon even if you stay at the same college throughout your undergrad years – and beyond. Your needs and the available support might change even if you don't move. But I say *change*, not *mount*! When one thing got harder for me, another would get easier. For example, when I transferred to my second college, I no longer had to deal with fire alarms going off at all hours where I was expected to go outside. But then the laundry was further from my room, making it harder for me to manage. This is life: you'll like the way some changes work out and not others!

Starting the Transition from Family to PCAs

Going to away to college is challenging enough. When you have been relying on family to get you from your bed to your chair all of your life, it might seem daunting. But you can handle it! Plenty of students before you have successfully transitioned to college with help from a PCA and graduated. It's just another thing you will have to plan for.

As I've mentioned, unlike in high school, your college is under no legal obligation to provide you with help with self-care. So, unless you choose to attend one of the few colleges that do have attendant care programs, it will be your responsibility to fund, hire, and manage your own PCAs.

Even if you don't go away to college, at some point you will need to get used to people outside your family providing your care. It will come at a different point for everyone, yet it is inevitable for almost everyone with a major physical disability. Whatever challenges you encounter with this, it generally gets easier as you get used to it, and you and each new caregiver get to know each other. Also realize that there is an immediate upside: since your new non-familial caregivers will be getting paid, you won't be tempted to worry as much about their feelings about helping you, as I tended to do when my family was helping me. Since your new caregivers will be getting paid, you'll be free to tell them when they didn't do a good job!

Suggestions for getting started

When starting out on the journey of how to get used to this, I suggest baby steps. One way to do this is to ask someone that you are already talked with, but who is not currently your caregiver, to start doing some personal care tasks for you. This can help you get more used to the idea that of new people doing these things for you.

With this new caregiver, practice telling them how you want things done. For example, it's important for me that non-family caregivers keep up a certain level of chatter with me to help keep my mind off what's going on. We talk, we laugh, and before we know it, the shower is done!

Next, take it up a notch. Practice giving your "acquaintance caregiver" as much instruction as possible when doing the task. This will also start you on thinking what kinds of people you will want to hire as PCAs? How will you train them? If you find it particularly difficult to give them instructions by talking, how will you work around that? More about training later.

Obtaining Funding for Personal Care

Those who need personal care assistants fall into two groups, those who receive funds through their state and those who pay out of pocket. Generally, your needs have to be greater to qualify for state funding.

If you are starting college and do not qualify for state funds, you might feel the need to hire someone to be at your disposal once or twice a week, as a "catch-all" person. Make this known to both your college's financial aid office and your state's vocational rehab agency. It is more likely that your financial aid department would be able to give you extra student loan monies to cover this out-of-pocket expense; however, check with VR also, just in case they can help.

Medicaid is the largest payer of personal assistance. For comprehensive personal assistance, this is probably your best bet. Medicaid is a state/federal partnership that is uniquely designed and administered by each state. The federal government matches at least 50% and up to 83% of what the state appropriates according to federal guidelines. There are two basic types of Medicaid funded PAS: Waivers and Personal Care Option. To qualify for a Waiver, nursing facility or institutional levels of need, both financial and functional, must be met. This means that a person must typically be very poor and have a significant disability in order to qualify for assistance.

Assessing Your Needs

On the next few pages are worksheets that are designed for you to assess what daily activities you really need help with. Everything listed below is intended solely to be an assessment of your physical ability to perform each task. I assume that you are *mentally* able to carry out the processes needed for each of these activities. It is my experience that a lot of people talk about "teaching life skills" or "independent living skills" in a way that includes a cognitive component. That turns me off. I do not want to give you that same feeling.

You may determine that you can get along fine without personal care. I recall one social worker who was my case manager in school. I can picture her filling out this kind of work sheet with me and concluding that I need help with daily tasks that I don't think I need. She would deem it unsafe for me to take out the trash, but I have never had any sense of risk doing that. "You cannot get the mail out of the mailbox," she'd say. Well, I do not need to get my mail that often. I either ask my family/friends to get it when they are visiting, or I hang out by the mailbox for a couple minutes until another student gets his or her mail. This is what I did frequently in college for mail, getting drinks in the café or using vending machines. This social worker would say I wasn't capable of doing laundry because I do one step slightly differently. I have been doing laundry for years; my pouring soap directly into the machine instead of into the measuring lid has never caused a disaster. The worse thing is that maybe over the years I've had to buy detergent more often.

My point is it is okay to get input, but ultimately it is your choice which tasks you decide you need help with.

If you are fine with your mom changing your sheets once a month when she visits, that works for you! If you are a stickler for the once-a-week rule and feel you need help with housekeeping, then put that on your task list for your PCA.

Finally, your needs as a college student may differ from your needs as a working adult. I cannot cook. In college that did not matter as much, because I could go to the cafeteria. When I worked, I was not required to hand in math homework, so I did not need to worry about hiring scribes.

Bottom line: Make the plan that is right for you!

ADL Assessment Charts

Use this section to decide if you need PCA care. If you do need care, use it to plan what you need, how long, how often and when.

Self-Care

ADL	Independent or Not Applicable	Need Advance Help to do Independently	Require a PCA	How Often & When Do I Need a PCA
Respiration				
Dressing/Undressing				
Toileting				
Showering				
Hair Care				
✓ Washing Hair				
✓ Brushing/combing or styling				
✓ Making Haircut/Dye Appointments				
✓ Treating Pressure Sores				
Taking Medications				
Nail Care				
Shaving				
Applying Make-up				
Menstrual care				
Dental Care				
✓ Brusshing/flossing				
✓ Making Dental appointments				
✓ Getting to Dental Appointments				

Self-Care (continued)

ADL	Independent or Not Applicable	Need Advance Help to do Independently	Require a PCA	How Often & When Do I Need a PCA
Bowel Care				
✓ Digital Stimulation				
✓ Suppositories				
✓ Enema				
✓ Laxative				
✓ Colostomy				
Skin Care				
✓ Preventing Pressure Sores				
✓ Treating Pressure Sores				
Taking Medications				
✓ Opening Bottles				
✓ Getting Pills to Mouth				
✓ Calling in Refills				
✓ Picking up Refills				
Injections				

Mobility

ADL	Independent or Not Applicable	Need Advance Help to do Independently	Require a PCA	How Often & When Do I Need a PCA
Transfers and Lifts				
✓ Wheelchair				
✓ Shower/tub				
✓ Toilet				
✓ Car				
✓ Transfers and Lifts				
Driving or Transportation				
✓ School/work				
✓ Social events				
✓ Medical appointments				
Care of Equipment				
✓ Wheelchair charging				
✓ Cleaning				
✓ Maintenance				
Exercise				
Sexual Activity				

Dining

ADL	Independent or Not Applicable	Need Advance Help to do Independently	Require a PCA	How Often & When Do I Need a PCA
Cooking				
Serving				
Putting food away				
Cleaning up				
Eating				
Breakfast				
Lunch				
Dinner				
Snacks				
G-tube or other feeding pumps				

Housekeeping

ADL	Independent or Not Applicable	Need Advance Help to do Independently	Require a PCA	How Often & When Do I Need a PCA
Laundry				
Changing sheets				
Shopping				
Sweeping				
Mopping				
Vacuuming				
Taking out the trash				
Bedroom				
Kitchen				
Bathroom				
✓ Toilet				
✓ Tub/shower				
✓ Sink/mirrors				

Miscellaneous

ADL	Independent or Not Applicable	Need Advance Help to do Independently	Require a PCA	How Often & When Do I Need a PCA
Care of service animals				
Filling out paperwork				
Getting mail				
Making phone calls				
Charging Phone/Tablet				
Paying bills				
Banking				
Using ATM				
College life				
✓ Buying Books				
✓ Typing papers or assignments				
✓ Assignments (writing, building projects, doing lab work)				
✓ Moving in/out of residence halls				

Where to Find PCA Candidates

- ✓ Your school's department of disability services
- ✓ Your school's career services office
- ✓ Grocery stores bulletin boards (I would try Trader Joes, Whole Foods, Wegmans first; in other words, higher-end grocery stores)
- ✓ Local Center for Independent Living
- ✓ Home health agencies
- ✓ Other students who use PCAs
- ✓ Medical colleges (If I was able to hire a physical therapy student, I'd feel more likely that they would work out. I've never met a PT/OT that was totally awful!)
- ✓ Any organization or place of worship that you would join. It's more likely to be a good match if you share some of the same values or passion for the same cause.

Planning to Interview PCAs

Interviewing prospective PCAs is a crucial part of the process! You might want to use the phone or email in the beginning to communicate with applicants. During the phone or email stage you may assess whether they meet your basic requirements. Are they strong enough to lift you? How good is their English? How are they with your kind of pets? However, if this person is really going to be vital to your routine, you should meet them before you hire them. On the phone you can learn only so much about them.

Try to meet in a public place. If you want to have a parent with you, that is fine. Again, when you are new to this process, it is okay to have help! However, do not be passive. You should be the one doing the interview! Your parent or other relative should be there mainly for input after you are finished with the interviews. If your parent has a question or two, that is fine, but you should be the one conducting the interview.

> *Caution*: If the candidate talks only to the person you are with, that's a big red flag! You never want a caregiver who treats you like a child.

Interview Questions

The material on the next three pages is adapted from MAKING THE MOVE TO MANAGING YOUR OWN PERSONAL ASSISTANCE SERVICES (PAS) [8]

✓ *Tell me about your experiences with persons with disabilities:*

There are pros and cons to hiring someone with experience. While someone who has worked as a personal assistant before may require less training, they may also come with preconceived ideas about how things should be done.

✓ *Tell me about your other work experiences:*

Has the candidate moved from job to job? If so, ask why. This could be an indication you'll be training someone who won't be around for long. What are things they liked or didn't like about their other jobs? Will some of the same skills be required here (e.g., getting up early, working on weekends)? Did they like working with people?

✓ *Why are you interested in this job?*

You want to pay close attention to not only what they say, but also how they say it. Are their first and only concerns/questions related to money? This could be a red flag. In any job interview, issues of money/salary should be some of the last questions. Besides, if it was mentioned in the ad, the applicant should have some idea of what to expect.

✓ *What is your current schedule, and how would this work fit into it?*

If the candidate has other commitments, will they interfere with providing you with the services you require? How far will they have to travel to get to you? If a person has only a little bit of flexibility in their schedule, this may impact the flexibility you have in getting their assistance.

✓ *Do you have reliable transportation?*

If they are relying on others for transportation, this could present problems in the long run. Will the personal assistant's driver wait outside or inside your home if s/he arrives before the personal assistant is ready to leave? Are you willing to have individuals in your home unsupervised?

✓ *Do you have any questions about the job that haven't been answered?*

In any job interview, it's seen as appropriate and beneficial to ask at least one question, even if there is very little that has been left unsaid. Asking questions demonstrates a genuine interest in the position.

✓ *Have you ever worked as a personal assistant before? Where? How long?*

A person doesn't necessarily need previous experience to be a good personal assistant. In fact, some people prefer to hire individuals that have no prior experience working with people with disabilities, so they come with no preconceived ideas about what will work best. If they have served as a personal assistant before, it's useful to determine how long they were in the position and their reasons for leaving.

---

[8]From: http://www.ncwd-youth.info/PAS-Toolkit.

- *Why are you interested in being a personal assistant?*

This question serves as a good indicator of whether the person has realistic expectations of the job. If they are looking for a position that will help them pay their way through school and you are only able to give them 10 hours of work, being a personal assistant should probably not be the primary job for them. Be wary of someone who quickly agrees to take on as many hours as possible. Sometimes people are so interested in helping that they fail to look realistically at their own limitations to fulfill the job duties. In cases like this, urge the applicant to take several days to consider what s/he can handle, given his/her other responsibilities.

- *Are you looking for temporary or permanent work?*

You should consider how often you want to be looking for personal assistants. Are you interested in hiring someone only for a few months? Or, are you looking for someone to help you longer term?

- *What other jobs have you had?*

Asking for a résumé may not be a bad idea. It will give you an opportunity to look at the individual's work history and ask questions. For example, has the applicant moved often between jobs, staying no more than a couple of months at a time? Does the individual have previous work experience that required a moderate or significant level of responsibility?

- *What did you like or dislike about those jobs?*

Are there aspects of being a personal assistant that are similar to the dislikes s/he has had related to other jobs? For example, s/he is not a morning person, and you're searching for someone to fill several morning slots.

- *Why did you leave those jobs?*

Knowing why an individual left a job can provide great insight as to whether they are willing and able to work through small issues/ big concerns. It can also indicate how dedicated the person is to stay in a particular job situation, even when there are challenges/difficulties.

- *[Discuss in detail the duties the assistant would perform.] Do any of these tasks make you uncomfortable? Why?*

It's important for your personal assistants to feel comfortable with the required tasks. If they are not, it may be best to consider other applicants for the job. Remember that you are hiring individuals to help you with your daily activities. While it's important to be flexible at times, you should not compromise your health or general well-being to accommodate others.

- *Do you prefer a job that is highly structured or one that is more flexible?*

Consider your own needs and preferences. Do you function best when your schedule is highly structured or more flexible? Do the applicant's preferences match your own?

- *How do you like to receive feedback from your employer?*

Does the applicant do better with oral or written instructions/feedback? It's best to determine that sooner rather than later. This will give you a better understanding of the best way to train an applicant, either through written instruction or by watching another assistant.

- *What would you do during "down time" on the job?*

Avoid having to pay someone for being with you when s/he is not doing anything. There may be times an assistant will have to wait for you (as you finish dinner or are running late to meet him/her). Is the applicant a self-starter? In either case, it may be helpful to leave a to-do list in plain sight.

✓ *What is the biggest mistake you made in your last job? How did you correct the problem?*

Does the applicant readily share an instance when they made a mistake? It's important that the individual be able to take instruction/correction from you, especially as s/he learns what works best. A good personal assistant is usually confident enough to try new things, but not overconfident/overbearing.

After Interview: Choosing

Consider:

- ✓ Did the person respond in a timely manner?

- ✓ Did s/he provide all the requested information?

- ✓ Did s/he show up for the interview on time?

- ✓ Was s/he actively engaged in the interview (not checking their watch, cell phone, or looking around the room)?

- ✓ Did s/he seem interested in what you had to say, and did s/he ask appropriate questions?

- ✓ Is the candidate open and willing to share some personal information without sharing too much?

- ✓ Does the candidate seem to treat you the same way s/he would anyone else your age—i.e., not talking down to you?

- ✓ Does the interviewee seem ready and willing to help in the short time you interact—i.e., willing to assist when needed?

Always Have a Plan B

My limited experience with hiring scribes in college or driver's post-college has taught me one thing: have a backup! These people very frequently quit or do not show up! My first driver quit without notice, saying that he had found a better job I could not really blame him; everyone has to take care of themselves first. And this is not high-paying work.

If I were to relive this, I would have had the sense to save the contact information for everyone who responded to every ad that I ran. I kicked myself for not saving everyone's number, so I could have made calls that night. As it happened, I had to wait a week for the local paper to run another ad. (This was just before Craigslist started up.)

Now, my scribes quit, and my drivers quit. Maybe I am just unpleasant to work for. However, I do not think that's the case. I think life is just complex for everyone! Stuff happens; plan for it!

Checking References

The kind of help you need also will dictate how thoroughly you screen your applicants. I have had tutors and scribes in both high school and college for math. I think it would have been overkill to run background checks on any of them! In fact, not much of an interview process took place! However, if I was reliant on someone for my most basic needs and they were vital to my routine, I would want to screen people more carefully. I am annoyed that adults with disabilities are thought of as more vulnerable across the board. It is different for each of us; that should be obvious. But I have seen a lot of stereotyping by people both within government agencies and generally within society.

It is totally OK to have your parent(s) help you in checking references. Most of you who are reading this book have a substantial physical disability. Getting help in college and elsewhere is just going to be a fact of life in many areas. But by the time you are 25 or 30, most of you would be able to do this yourself.

That being said, do not just hand off this task to your parents without discussing it. You need to have more input than anyone else into who gets hired! You also should have the final say about what you are looking for in a person. My grandma said I should hire a retired person for a driver. Nope, I was sure I wanted a younger person. I felt both more comfortable and safer with someone under forty. If you know you want either the same sex as you, or the opposite sex, stick to that. It is *YOUR* life!

I felt more comfortable with my dad being present when I interviewed drivers. We both agreed on what I wanted. It helped me that he met them, and he was another person to get a "vibe" on this person who I would be getting into a car with. Reading people is part of his job, so that made me feel safer. Dad and I even agreed on who the best person was.

If I were hiring an au pair for a newborn, you'd bet your life, I'd want fingerprints, an FBI background check – the whole nine yards. Thus, I feel it should be up to you. What do *you* feel comfortable with, for what kind of helper?

Questions to Ask Employment References

- ✓ How long did [Applicant's Name] work for you?
- ✓ Was [Applicant's Name] dependable?
- ✓ Do you consider [Applicant's Name] to be honest?
- ✓ How does [Applicant's Name] respond to directions being given by a supervisor?
- ✓ Would you hire [Applicant's Name] again?[9]

---

[9] The above questions are taken from "Making The Move to Managing Your Own Personal Assistance Services (PAS), published by the national Collaborative on Workforce and Disability for Youth (NCWD/Youth)

Drafting a Personal Preference Statement

Look over the topics below and fill in any that apply to you. You might want to delete some items because they are not applicable to you, or substitute items that do apply to your preferences or job description.

Sample Topics for PCA Selection Guidelines

1. Deal breakers: actions that will always result in firing
2. Smoking or non-smoking home. How do you feel about them smoking before they arrive; are you sensitive to smelling smoke on people's clothes?
3. Cell phone use
4. Religious preferences
5. Using or borrowing of items
6. Downtime
7. Swearing
8. Housecleaning
9. Bringing children
10. Interaction with any children in home
11. Interaction/instructions about household pet(s)
12. Temperature control
13. Visitors during shift
14. Privacy

True-story...

My driver kept forgetting which days he was supposed to come over to pick me up. After a week of him 'forgetting what day it was' I did what I am telling you to do: I spent ten minutes typing up a basic schedule/information sheet that really helped him. I was shocked that something so basic was needed.

This is an example of how everyone is different. I thought he'd politely thank me for it while thinking, "I so do not need a stupid schedule," and throw it away after he dropped me off. Instead, he said that it really helped him keep track of which days he drove for me and which days my dad drove.

I recommend carrying this a lot further, and not only about a schedule but also personal preferences. If I did this again, not only would I include a schedule and phone numbers he needed; I would also include situational preferences, as follows.

Situational Preferences (true-story continued)

- **Schedule.** As above.

- **Phone numbers.** Whatever might be needed.

- **Radio.** I do not want to listen to right-wing talk radio on the way to and from work. I feel it is fairer to find a channel we both agree on. I like a variety of music, so it should not be hard to find something we both like.

- **Seatbelt usage.** I prefer not to wear one. However, as the driver, you *always* have the final say. I can buckle myself in, it just takes me longer. I do not like it when people jump to help me with my belt.

- **Cellphone use while driving.** I trust your judgment as an adult whether you can talk and drive. I do not feel safe with you texting, emailing, or using other apps while driving.

- **Your Errands.** It is usually fine for you to stop on the way home from work to run into the store and pick up something.

- **My Errands.** Sometimes on the way home I will request that we either drive through somewhere to get me dinner or run into Wawa (a popular convenience store chain in New Jersey). You can say no if that doesn't fit your schedule that day. I also could add to my job description that on certain days it is expected that we run certain errands on the way home. I need you to carry items from your car to my front room. From there, they are my problem.

Everyone has different preferences. You might be fine with listening to talk radio. Or you'll pop in your own ear buds anyway, so it doesn't matter. On the flip side, you may be really annoyed if your driver stops to pick up something for his wife and you're stuck waiting in the car for ten minutes. The main idea is to make your expectatio1ns known in advance so there is no confusion!

It also shows how situational these matters are. I did not feel my driver needed to know if I was on any medications or had allergies. If you are hiring a driver, you may feel they need to know that. If you are hiring someone to help with your morning/evening routine, it would make more sense to let them know what medications you take.

Adopt an Employer Mindset
In keeping with the idea that you are now an employer is that you now need to plan for how to train your new employee. Of course, you want to be friendly with those who work for you, but you want them to recognize you are in charge. You need to decide what is OK and what isn't.

Special Issue: The PCA's Children
Big considerations can arise if your PCA has kid(s). How do you feel about them kids being brought to work? Is it never OK? Is it OK only in emergencies, or on alternate Saturdays? If you are in a situation where your health could be compromised if you catch a cold or the flu, you might need to have a "no child policy" when it comes to your PCAs, even if you like kids.

I try to be realistic here. If my PCA is earning only the minimum wage from the state, if she has to pay for childcare out of that, how is she going to clear anything? If the child is "low maintenance" and you like how your PCA does his parenting, then what's the harm? They can watch a DVD while their mom is doing what I need her to do for me. On the other hand, if the child frequently disrupts our work or bothers other people, or I'm constantly witnessing my PCA scream at or hit their child... You get the idea.

Living in a dorm tends to argue against bringing kids into the equation. I know my first dorm would have been a really strange place for kids to visit. Even my later dorm, a way better environment, still didn't have much space to both 'get me dressed' and let the kid watch DVD. But in an apartment, it would have worked fine.

I always have a right, as do you, not to have unacceptable behavior occurring in *my* home. This is true whether children are involved or not! It is *your* home; whatever behavior you consider to be unacceptable, you have a right not to have it go on in *your* home. Whatever the issue is, you need to communicate how you feel. The sooner you "iron out" such things, the more the PCA will respect you as the person in charge. Speak respectfully but with authority.

Preparing to Work with Your PCA

Prepare your school. Again, when you live on campus, you must let the Department of Residence Life know you need PCA services in your dorm. Schools could have policies regarding this, and you need to ensure the appropriate people have access to your residence hall.

Prepare a 'Manual on You.' It is a good idea to give a prospective employee a 'manual on you.' This should always include their schedule with you, how much and when they will be paid, and your Personal Preference Statement. This could simply be two pages stapled, or it could be a small binder telling them how you need everything done, where you keep things in your home, a list of your medications, and medical/emergency contact information.

Everyone's manual will be different depending on their situation and the level of organization and detail they either prefer or feel they need to be in place. Students who start college with a PCA might want to have your parents help you put this together. When making the transition from having family caregivers to hired staff, this manual could make it easier. As you get into your twenties, thirties, and forties you will have all this down. All you will need to do is type up a schedule for your new employee and print out the same document.

Prepare to Ask for Feedback. Ask them if they have anything, they want to tell you. Ask if they have any suggestions or ways, they like to do things that might work better. You can be open to suggestions without giving up control! Part of being a good leader is making people feel as though you hear what they have to say. If you are okay with any changes they propose, okay it. If not, say "This way works best for me because...." It is the PCA's job to respect you!

Prepare to Offer Feedback. Everyone likes to be told that they are doing a good job! In instances where they are doing something wrong on the job, most people like to be told so that they can readjust. You want your PCAs to like working for you! How you give feedback, both good and bad, will be a major way to achieve likeability – and not have to find a new PCA.

Prepare to Evaluate. Having a PCA is just like everything else in life in the sense that you need to pay attention to how things are going every so often. If something is going wrong, how can it be fixed? The answer could be anything from making a minor adjustment in the schedule to giving more instruction to replacing that person.

On to Training

When working with anyone new, if you need them to show up and do their work before you can go to class, work, or another commitment, it is a good idea to expect this work together to take longer than you expect. It will take longer at first for them to follow your instructions. Also, everyone has a different pace at which they do various things. Some may be able to get your hair and makeup done in ten minutes, while with others it will take twenty minutes. Finally, different people have different ideas about what arriving 'on time' means. Some people if they are 'on time' they think they are late; others will get there five or ten minutes late and think nothing of it You have no way of knowing what type of person your new hire will be until you deal with these situations and give them your 'manual.'

Because of these factors when you are starting someone new, *overestimate how long everything will take*. If you are consistently getting through the routine quicker than needed, then you can say "You can get here (specify how much time) later in the mornings."

The first couple of times someone works for you, you need to take the responsibility of training them to work as you want and need. There are several ways to train people. There is no right or wrong way. You just need to figure out what works for you. The most common way is just to tell them how you need everything done.

- This is how I like to be lifted...
- My (whatever) is in the (wherever)... (You might want to label certain cabinets or drawers, so items are easier for your PCA to find them.)
- This is how I like my bath/shower water...
- This how I like my food cut...

And so on.

It will not be long before your new hire gets used to you and you will not have to tell her every little thing. Saying every little thing is annoying but needed at first. Be patient, no one will know exactly how to do your care the first day. You need to have the attitude that you are in this *with* your new hire and *together* you will accomplish what you need to get done!

Sometimes, you may have your new hire observe or be trained by someone who is already used to doing your care. Another strategy: make lots of lists to make it clear what you need your new hire to do!

If I were going to college for the first time and needed twice-daily care from a PCA, I would try and have my mom come and stay around me for the first couple of days, or a week. Ideally, you will already have hired people. But I would want my mom there for each person's first shift so she could make sure I felt safe and we could train them together. Starting college is a lot for any freshman! This is a huge added adjustment for you. It is OK to get help!

Your mom does not have to bunk in the dorm with you, marking you to your dorm-mates. She can stay in a hotel and come and go. My mom did this for me when I went to school out of state and I did not even need PCAs. She just wanted to be there for the initial adjustment, to make sure it went OK. Some of your dorm-mates might notice it's the first week and your parent is still coming and going after all the others have left. You can just be honest. Say, "I need help and am going to have people coming and going to do my care, so my mom/dad/whoever is staying a little longer to get that set up. But they are leaving soon – after we make sure no one we hired is totally scary and everything is at least kind of in place." They will understand! Most freshmen cannot imagine having extra challenges, so they will think it is natural to get a little more help. If you have your mom/dad/whoever meet your PCAs, it will be easier for them to be involved from a remote location throughout your first year. This will mean you can share the burden of managing your care! The best way to transition is gradually.

Training for the first time will be hard no matter how old you are. And you will not know exactly how to do it! If it is your first-time training, go ahead and admit it: "This is the first time that I am doing this, so bear with me; we'll figure this out together." As in everything else in life, the more you do it the better you get at it!

You Deserve to Always Be Respected and Feel Comfortable

People are not perfect! There is no such thing as the parent, child, spouse, friend, and so on. There is also no such thing as a perfect PCA. People are only human! They are going to have bad days, they are going to need to cancel on occasion, and finally everyone is going to be different than you are in some way! In the honest and touching documentary *Little Man*, a doctor talks about the experience of parents needing to find in-home caregivers for their medically fragile baby. This situation is a little different from yours, but the doctor said, "it very often comes down to hiring the person you dislike the least."

This stuck with me, because I know my personality. Because of this, if I had to find PCAs to cover two or three shifts a day, every day, I know that I would come to thinking, "OK, who can I tolerate the easiest?" Realistically, I know maybe one or two, I would *like*. As for the rest, if they show up, do their job, and do not cause me *any* harm, I would feel that would be the best that I could hope for!

I would like to address the phrase "do not cause me *any* harm," further. We all know that extreme acts of hitting, screaming, not letting you be mobile, stealing, breaking your things because they are mad, handling you in a rough matter physically or being sexually inappropriate are unacceptable. If someone hits us, steals from us, or does any unwanted touching, we get away from them, simple.

However, sometimes it is harder to deal with the situation where they just make you uncomfortable. Or they keep saying or doing things that upset you. Even though you need to find someone to do your care and that is no easy feat, you still should not be uncomfortable! Everyone has a different tolerance, and like all other relationships everyone has things when they say "Do I love this about them? No! But I am willing to deal with it." Other things are deal breakers in relationships. For everyone these things are different; one person may tolerate one thing in their child or spouse where another would not. Again, having PCAs is the same way!

A good rule is to trust your feelings. If you get a feeling something is wrong, it probably is! Life has taught me that unaddressed problems with people do not go away, they get worse. I am all for trying to talk to people! If you express a concern and the PCA comes from a place of "How can we resolve it?" that's good. That means it is viable and you can resolve it! But if react in any other way, you need to think seriously about replacing them!

Another good indicator is how you feel when you think it is their shift tonight or tomorrow. If that gives you a lot of anxiety, that is not good! You cannot live like that. The sooner you recognize that and are honest with yourself, the better. It is better to identify a problem before it becomes a crisis! That way, if things don't improve quickly, you can find a replacement and fire your current PCA before things reach the point where you dread the time you will have to spend with him or her.

One year, I had two individuals around. One had, shall we say, some interesting views on life. This person would say something, and I would just think "okkkay." But they were a very hard worker and would never hurt anyone or me. So, if she had been my PCA, I would have kept her! I am hiring these people to do a job and therefore they do not need to have that much in common with me. I am not marrying them; I am not going to be making my way through life with them. They do not have to be someone I would go to for advice. We do not even need to like the same movies, TV or music. They just need to reliably do the job.

But there was this other person in my life, and when I saw her in the parking lot, I would want to throw up with anticipatory anxiety. That was certainly a huge red flag. I would get so anxious because I never knew how they would act toward me that day. Thus, if that individual were my PCA, I would have had to seriously consider firing them!

The way someone treats you doesn't have to meet a criminal standard for those actions to be not OK! My advice is that you should replace any PCA that you have such strong instinctive reactions against.

Firing Your Personal Assistant

You don't want to fire someone impulsively or unfairly! But you don't want to tolerate unacceptable behavior, because it's too hard to find a good replacement for that person, either. Your challenge is to find the 'right balance' for you.

Most people are a little uncomfortable when they need to fire anyone, especially someone who has been working physically closely with them. Here are a few pointers for getting through it without crying:

(If at all possible) Have a clear reason. It is important that you have taken the time and effort to articulate your reasons, and not just have a bad feeling. This way you will not second-guess yourself or get talked out of it by the PCA. If you need to talk through the issues with someone to make the decision, do that with friends/family, not the employee!

Always give a reason. This does not have to be the real or full reason. Giving either too little or too much explanation can just open you up to fighting or the PCA saying "Come on, give me another chance."

Wait till they are about to leave anyway. Deliver the news do it at the end of the shift, for both of your benefits.

Plan ahead for assistance if you need it. If you feel at all in danger, either have someone else there, or have someone else call on your behalf to say that you do not want them showing up to your home again.

Get back keys. Consider changing the locks. This is expensive and may be an inconvenience if you have multiple people working for you. It boils down to doing whatever you feel is needed to be safe. Although it's rare, these situations can sometimes mirror break-ups. Sometimes, it just does not work out, but you know they would not do anything to hurt you. Other times are more unpleasant, and you need to do what you need to do!

Consider a white lie. Tell the person you're firing that you've found a replacement even if you haven't and family/other staff are filling in until you find a replacement. The PCA does not need to know that. This way the decision sounds more final, so they don't see any opportunity to argue or try and change your mind.

Never feel bad for doing what is right for YOU!!!

Again: It Is OK to Get Help

If this situation occurs in college, especially your first year away, I say it is fine to have your parent (or whoever acts as your parent) deliver the news. You are dealing with a lot – give yourself a break! Again, in your first couple years of managing PCAs, it's OK to have family help.

What is *not* OK is that you complain about something to a family member and then that person automatically calls the PCA to either lecture them or fire them without you saying that is what you want. You need your parents to know how much you value their support/input, but you need to make all the major or final decisions.

Taking a Service Animal to College

Service animals are crucial to the independence and quality of life of lots of people with disabilities. Your service or guide dog might be just as much an extension of you as my wheelchair was of me when I went to college. It would have been practically impossible for me to have left my wheelchair at home when I went to college.

Going to college with a service dog is just like everything else associated with a disability and going to college: it is doable, it just takes more planning.

Is it right for YOU to use a dog on campus?

Some service dog organizations give dogs to children starting at the age of seven. Most admit clients starting at the age of twelve. I started using a computer to do schoolwork at seven and a wheelchair at twelve. If someone had said to me "You can't bring either of those things to campus," I would have replied "I have to; that is how I am independent and live my daily life." If your life has been intertwined in that way with a service animal since you were little, then the answer is clearly yes, take it to school. But to do so you need a plan!

On the flip side, the major transition of living away from home the first time, is not a good time to suddenly decide to get a service dog. You will just be adding to the trauma of your adjustment. You need to learn to work with a dog and the dog needs to learn to work with you, whatever the quality of its training. I would not have been able to get a chair one day and then the next be able to wheel myself all over campus. My first few days in a chair, I could barely push a few feet down the hospital hall! After I got *that* down, I got used to using a wheelchair at my very small middle school. Then it was on to a bigger high school and around town.

Using a service animal is much more complicated; it's a living thing with needs of its own! While you do not have to have had a service dog from age seven to be able to function with one in the community, you do need *some* time! I would say you that you should take over care of your dog at least a year before you leave for college. If you reach eighteen and really feel a service/mobility animal is right for you, then consider delaying going off to college for a year to work with your dog. Or start at a community college so that you only have to manage the dog in class, not also in cafeterias, in the dorm, etc.

Inform the School That You Will Be Bringing a Service Animal

As soon as you reply to the school that you will be attending there, inform them that you have a service animal and will be bringing them to school. Let them know whether the animal will be working only in the residence hall or will also be brought to class and other campus buildings. Your school will probably need to see documentation that your animal has been certified. You should have that documentation ready; it is no different than your transcript.

If you are going to school without a lot of experience serving students with disabilities, you might need to submit a copy of the law that allows you to bring a service animal to campus! For students with a physical disability or have epilepsy this will probably be an easier process than those who rely on Emotional Support Animal or ESAs. If you need to bring an ESA onto campus you might need further documentation from either a doctor or another medical professional.

Once you get the ruber stamp from the school to bring your service dog on campus, you'll need to work with Residence Life to consider you and your dog's needs when your campus residence is selected. Most college dorms are not designed for pets. Ask whether there a hall or set of apartments with easily accessible outdoor space for your animal to be able to do his business without either of you having to walk too far. Residence Life should know you need to be placed in a dorm with the biggest rooms. At my first residence hall, the rooms were tiny. It would have been better for me to have been placed in a different dorm that had larger rooms. The school could have removed the second bed to give us more space. There were two closets: one for me and one for pet supplies.

Again, you must notify your school well in advance that you are coming with a dog, to give them a chance to make arrangements. If I had notified my school in March that I had a service dog, appropriately trained staff members rather than my resident assistant (RA) would have worked with us so that on move-in day everything would have been set up. To just show up with your animal and paperwork that you think someone should accept, will not fly – even if you are blind and it is a guide dog. The RA will not know what to do. It will just be a mess.

The only situation where you don't need to notify your school is if you are living off-campus and you don't plan to use the dog on campus.

Notify Roommates/Suitemates

When living on campus, if you are going to have suitemates, they should be notified the summer before you move in, either by you or the school. Some people are not animal people; they deserve a chance to be re-assigned if they fear dogs! Your dog deserves to be around animal lovers. Trust me, you the department of Residence Life will be able to find plenty of people who love dogs and can handle people who are different from them. There are no guarantees, but if people like your dog, you are more likely to hit it off with them as well.

If you are living with people off-campus, common sense says that you need to tell them up front and discuss how it would impact them. Again, why would you want to live with a non-"animal person" if you have an animal?

Plan for Costs

Duh! Your service animal has needs. You will need to budget extra for food and other supplies, grooming, possibly someone to care for the animal when you can't, and occasional (or possibly more than occasional!) vet bills. Who will be responsible for these costs? Your parents? A job? Do you need extra student loan money? Should you perhaps seek advice from vocational rehab, the Center for Independent Living, or where you got your service animal, as to where you might seek financial assistance for your dog's needs? These also may be of help:

- Alumni associations
- Chamber of Commerce
- Diagnosis-related associations
- Elks
- Lions Club

Pack for Two
Make a list of everything your dog needs. You will not only go college shopping for yourself but also your dog. Stock up and pack up. Make sure you get an ample supply of medication for your dog. Almost anyone will think of food, a dish, a leash and a toy. But also consider grooming, medications, and other supplies. Also consider either purchasing or putting together a canine first aid kit.

Plan to transport your dog safely to school. If you do not already have an appropriate crate, that is another thing you need to buy. If you need to fly to school, plan on preparing for this. Find out the requirements for the airline that you are using.

Also bring a folder with a copy of your certification, vet records and lists of emergency numbers, microchip information (if any), and a photo of the dog.

Go to Your Vet
Get your dog a checkup within a month of leaving for school from the vet who knows you and your dog. Tell the vet you are planning to take your dog to school to continue its duties as a service dog. Talk to the vet about how you plan to care for your dog on campus. See if the vet can think of anything that you didn't think of or might want to be aware of as the dog adapts to new surroundings.

Before you leave for school, find a reputable vet where you are going to college. Go online to read reviews, if you do not know any pet owners in your new area. Call the local Humane Society or Center for Independent Living for a recommendation. Contact that vet to explain your situation. Plan how you will transport you animal to the vet's if it needs care.

Prepare for Your Commitment as a Service Dog Owner
If you were old enough to participate fully during service dog training, they told you that you were making a commitment to take care of an animal in exchange for greater independence. Maybe when you were a kid your parents cared for the animal that helped their child. Now, when you are at college, it is on you to either care for all your animal's needs or make sure that someone else does! As a college student, you will need to schedule this into your routine. You'll need to set aside time EVERY SINGLE DAY to devote to your dog. Make sure he isn't alone for too long, he gets properly exercised, and of course fed, watered, let out, and groomed. You also need to plan on extra cleaning of your living environment!

Take over all care at least six months prior to leaving with your dog to make sure you are physically able to do it and know all that is involved.

Chick (and Dude) Magnet: Students Will Pay a Lot of Attention to Your Dog
This is a positive. Your dog will help you meet people on and around campus. For those of you who took your dog to high school, this will not be new. Whether this is new for you or not, you

should plan on this, as well as answering questions about your dog. While all dogs like some attention, you need to make sure they do not get too much. Like humans, dogs do not like people always petting or trying to play with us. Dogs also need down time.

As a service dog owner, you are probably aware of "service dog etiquette." Students at your school will mostly not be aware of this. It is up to you to respectfully teach strangers about this as the need arises. You need to be able to explain to people how to be perceived by the dog as friendly while informing people about appropriate boundaries at the same time. You, your dog, and your friends may regularly have fun together; however, you need to know when to say *when*. Also, some "calm time" should regularly be spent just between you and your dog. This is when the dog is not working.

Plan for how you want to deal with public or semi-public gatherings with your dog. Can you remain in control of how people interact with your animal at these events? Can you, again, make sure the dog is enjoying his time playing with others? Can you leave with your dog if people are getting out of control, being disrespectful, or bothering your dog? Are there occasions when it might be better to leave your dog at home? If you are playing beer pong all night with tons of people, would your dog be happier sleeping in his bed?

Have a Team in Place
You need a vet, but hopefully not all that often. You also need people on standby for when less severe issues arise. Ideally this should include both people you have known for a long time, and people at your school who can help you with things like a thorn getting stuck in your dog's paw. Or maybe you can't nail down the problem, but you can tell that your dog is not acting normal. Your dog might need a trip to the vet right away, but family isn't due to visit for a week. Or, you are sick with the flu and are unable to get your dog out to go potty. *Line up this kind of support before you need it!*

As you make friends, those friends will be available to help if you need an occasional favor. In fact, you might find that being "the neighbor in need" provides the occasion for you to become friends with someone that you had not yet spoken to.

Still, when you first start school, ask your RA whether she or another student support staffer could be your "just in case" person for these kinds of nonprofessional but urgent tasks? If not them, how about a security guard?

If your school is not helpful, contact animal organizations in the area. Many people volunteer to help animals; maybe someone would be willing to give you their number just in case. The same may be true of local churches, synagogues, or mosques.

For some of you, like me, it is very hard to ask for help. However, if you want the benefits of a service dog, you need to do what you need to do. Everything is a tradeoff.

Wheelchair Maintenance

Caring for your wheelchair, should you use one, is another thing that you need to be involved in when you move out. In reality, cleaning will probably be the most common wheelchair maintenance activity you will need to do. However, you should check the following periodically. Any issues or problems should be addressed properly.[10]

Keep tires inflated at the proper pressure. The pressure is always stamped on the tire. Use a hand pump or a small electric pump with a gauge. Do not use a gas station air hose. Wheelchair tires have very small volume and it is very easy to explode a tire. Keeping the tires inflated will increase tire life, decrease rolling resistance, and keep the wheel locks effective.

Replace worn tires promptly. Don't wait until the black cords of the tire show. Tires are much less prone to flats if they have adequate tread. Wheel locks will work better with good tires.

Check your tires regularly. Sometimes a puncture will cause a slow leak that is not obvious. If you do find a small nail in the tire, leave it in place to seal the leak and get the flat fixed.

> *Tip:* I really prefer solid wheelchair tires. One less thing I need to worry about, keeping air in my tires! To me this is a huge advantage. The downsides are they are heavier and do not ride as smoothly. But I personally have never noticed these downsides.

✓ **Batteries.** Wheelchair batteries are different from car batteries because they are used in a different way. A car battery's main function is to start the engine. At other times, it is loafing along, constantly being charged by the alternator. A wheelchair battery is usually charged once a day and must supply large amounts of electricity while it is running. So, wheelchair batteries must be a special type called deep cycle. This means that the battery can be almost completely discharged without damage to the battery. If a car battery is used for a wheelchair, it will soon fail.

Wheelchair batteries will last longer if they are kept as close to full charge as practical. They are unlike the small nickel-cadmium batteries that need to be run down occasionally to preserve their full capacity. Most users need to charge the batteries every night to keep a full charge. Modern battery chargers are automatic so there is no problem of overcharging. If a wheelchair is used only occasionally, the battery needs to be charged at least once a month and should be charged whenever it is used during a day.

The life of wheelchair batteries depends on how he0avily they are used. Most last about a year. Compare this with the life of most car batteries, which last about 4-5

---

[10] From: http://members.cruzio.com/~yogi/whchair.htm#maint.
My comments are indented and introduced with italic text.

years. The difference is due to the deep cycling of the wheelchair batteries. Some users who travel mostly indoors can use a battery for 2 years. Anything beyond 2 years of life is rare. The best way to tell whether a battery is getting old is to notice if the wheelchair is getting weak at end of trips that were no problem when the battery was new.

New batteries require about 5 cycles of use and recharging before they reach their full capacity Don't push a new battery for a few days.

There are two types of batteries for wheelchairs: wet and gel. Wet batteries require adding distilled water about every two months. Wet batteries can be damaged permanently if the water level falls below the level of the battery plates. Adding water is often quite difficult, even for someone with training and no disability. The batteries are heavy and difficult to reach. Adding water is usually impossible for wheelchair users. If you do it yourself, follow these precautions:

- o Use only distilled water. Tap water has minerals that will damage the battery.

- o Don't overfill the battery. If the outside of the battery is wet, the battery has been overfilled. Fill only to about 1/8" below the ring in the hole. Use a flashlight to see the level clearly. Overfilling the battery will result in leakage of battery acid, which will quickly ruin battery connections. The water level will rise as the battery is charged, so a weak battery with low water level should be filled less than normal.

- o Be careful not to short-circuit the battery terminal with any metal. The sparks can ignite the gas in the battery and cause an explosion. Don't smoke. Be careful not to get battery acid on skin and in your eyes -- use gloves and eye protection.

- o Wipe up any spills and replace the caps tightly.

Gel batteries avoid many of the problems of wet batteries. They never need water. They eliminate corrosion problems. They are much easier to take on an airplane trip because airlines require wet batteries to be removed from the wheelchair and placed in a sealed container. The main disadvantage of gel batteries is that they have about 10 to 20% less capacity than comparable wet batteries. This is usually important only for users who travel long distances. They cost more and most insurance will not reimburse us for the full price, but this is not the user's problem. If you want to switch battery types, make sure that the battery charger is suitable for the type of battery. Many old chargers will not charge a gel battery properly. Most new chargers have a switch to select either type of battery.

Many chargers will not charge a completely dead battery. Some have a button that will allow manually starting the charge cycle. In other cases, a different charger must be used. Charging a battery that has been dead for several months is very difficult and requires several days of charging. The battery may be permanently damaged. So, it is best to keep batteries charged, even if they are not being used.

> *Personal experience warning:* You need to keep the battery charged even on a chair that you are **not** using! I got stuck being responsible for a power chair that I was not going to ever use in college, just because Mom wanted me to have one. I would stash the thing somewhere for a while. Then someone would inform me that I needed to move it. The thing would not charge. It would not start! It was a major problem.

Whenever you plug in the charger, always check that the battery is charging, as indicated by a meter or light. The charger plug is subject to a lot of stress, so be sure that the cord and plug are in good condition.

> *Tip:* Get *at least* one spare charger cord! If you are like me, you can plug things in for yourself, but it is harder for you. This means your cords can wear out quicker. Your chair is vital! Avoid a situation where you cannot charge it. Remember, you cannot just pick up a charging cord for your chair anywhere. It has to be ordered. What are going to do in the meantime if you can't charge your chair?

✓ Front casters wheels and forks

> Check that the caster wheels spin freely. If not, the problem may be due to hair and other debris caught in the bearing. The wheel usually must be removed to clean the bearing. Check for noises coming from the bearing; a good bearing should be silent. Caster bearings take a beating because they are so close to the ground and pick up dirt and water. The caster stem bearing that supports the fork pivot should turn easily but should not be so loose that the caster wheel flutters from side to side at high speed. Check that the stem bearing barrel is perpendicular to the floor. If not, the caster will have difficulty turning. Check that the stem caps are in place; they keep water and dirt out. Check that the forks are not bent.

✓ Glide test for manual wheelchairs

> Find a smooth level floor such as in a supermarket. Push the chair and let it glide. It should go a long way in a straight line. If not, bearings may be bad, or the wheels and casters may be out of alignment. Listen for noisy bearings. If the rear wheels are cambered with a connecting axle, the axle needs to be adjusted so that the wheels are parallel. Otherwise the wheels will have excessive friction."

✓ Wheel locks and electric brakes

> Check manual wheel locks for slippage with tires inflated to the correct pressure. The locks should operate easily. If not, the pivots may need lubrication. The pivots need to be tight enough that the wheel lock stays in place when released. If not, the wheel lock will drag against the tire,

resulting in wear and wasted effort. Electric brakes for power wheelchairs need to be checked to ensure that they stop the wheelchair without veering and that they hold on a slope.

> *Option:* My brother and I took off my brakes. This is because I never used them, and they just got "perma-dirty." I am not advocating this. I am advocating you customizing your chair to fit your lifestyle!

✓ Footrests

Check that the footrests are not bent and are at the proper height. Check that the latches hold securely.

✓ Seating

Check that the seat cushion is not bottoming out. The air level in inflatable cushions needs to be checked frequently. Gel cushions need to be massaged periodically to keep the gel from settling into hard lumps. Check cushion covers, especially on-air cushions since air cushions will not work without a proper cover. Check sling seats and backs for tears and sags.

✓ Rear Wheels

Check that rear wheels on manual chairs spin freely without wobble. Check for loose and broken spokes. Check quick release axle pins. They should release easily. The axle pins should be adjusted so that they are slightly loose when in place to ensure that the locking mechanism is fully engaged. Always check that the wheel is locked firmly in place after mounting a wheel.

✓ Electrical problems on power wheelchairs

If you have electrical problems, note which side it affects. If the lights on the joystick box are flashing, note carefully the pattern; they signify an error code, usually by the number of lights or the number of blinks.

✓ Drive Motors

Listen for unusual noises coming from the motor or gearbox. Check drive belts for slippage and wear. Check for jerking motion of the chair; this indicates serious problems.

✓ Joystick control

Check that the joystick returns freely to neutral without binding. Check that the seal on the joystick is intact; it keeps dirt and water out. Check that all switches and controls are tightly in place. Check that the joystick clamp holds the joystick firmly in place.

Wheelchair Care Kit

✓ **Cleaning items.** You can use wet paper towels or bathroom cleaning wipes. But if you prefer to use a cloth or a certain type of cleaner, toss them in your kit.

✓ **Owner's Manual.** For some of you this will be vital; others will find it useless. Make the choice for yourself.

✓ **Dealer information.** If something breaks you can call the dealer and ask them where to take your wheelchair to be repaired. For this you should be sure to write down your exact model number.

✓ **Repair shop number.** Should you have pre-located one.

✓ **Duct tape.** Can be used for short-term fixes, particularly for torn upholstery. You can shop online and find duct tape in almost every color and pattern under the sun.

✓ **Zip ties.** These can be used to attach items to the back of your chair. They can also sometimes be used as a temporary screw or bolt until you can get a real fix.

✓ **Nuts and bolts.** Any nuts or bolts on your chair can come loose. Have spares that you store either in a zip lock bag or a small Tupperware container.

✓ **Phillips and flat screwdrivers.**

✓ **Slip-joint pliers.**

✓ **Tire pump.** If you have pneumatic (air-filled) tires this is a must. You can find one both cheap and compact.

✓ **Tire inner tube.** Only for pneumatic (air-filled) tires. You can order these from medical supply companies. Or you can go to a bike shop and ask them if they carry both the size you need and if they'd recommend a tire repair kit. Getting tire repair supplies at bike shops will probably be cheaper than from medical supply companies.

✓ **Hex key wrench set.**

✓ **Spoke wrench set.**

Points to Remember from Chapter 5

✓ You'll probably have to hire your own PCA if you need one. You'll have to train them to understand your personal needs and preferences. It's okay to start small.

✓ Check with Vocational Rehabilitation and Medicaid about funding.

✓ Use the checklists to evaluate your needs.

✓ If you are faced with hiring and managing your own attendants, it will probably feel like the most challenging aspect of going away to college. Relax, many college students have done the exact task you are facing. If they can do it, so can you!

✓ When hiring or working with attendants, if you get an instinct about someone, trust it. It is probably right.

✓ You are now an employer, those who you hire should treat you with respect. They do not need to wear a uniform or call you Mr. /Ms. They do need to make you feel as you are always safe around them, not just physically but also emotionally.

✓ People are just people. They are going to quit on you with little or notice. Prepare for this by making sure you keep the contact info of anyone who responded to your add for help.

✓ For those of you taking service dog to school, it will be something you need to plan for.

✓ Go to your vet, who knows both you and your dog and talk with them about the transition.

✓ Find a vet with good recommendations near your campus. Inform your school you will have your dog with you, as soon as you tell them you will be attending.

✓ Make sure you pack everything your dog will need as well as a copies of their service dog certification and medical records

✓ Before you go whatever equipment that you rely on, be it a walker or a wheelchair, or other assistive technology to do your schoolwork, and should be in full working order!! Anything that can get serviced the summer before college, should! Pack any spare or replacement parts that are needed to keep equipment running optimally throughout the school year. Should any equipment break, have an advance plan as to how you will handle it.

Part II: Getting the Most Out of College

Chapter 6: Welcome to College

We are finally here! After all the shopping for extra-long bed sheets, packing too much, and moving in, your first week of college has started!

What should you expect? An adventure that you will certainly remember for a lifetime! DO NOT expect everything to be perfect, it won't be. Adjustment to campus life takes time. How much time and the degree of difficulty (or ease) of adjusting will be different for everyone. For some it may be days or weeks; others report it taking months, or even 'til they are into their sophomore year. Be kind to yourself and understand that whatever you are feeling or experiencing during this adjustment is fine. While the beginning of your college years will not be instant paradise, it is also unlikely to be awful. The typical freshman mishaps are not the end of the world. If you look at them right, they will just become part of your life's history, no more, no less.

During my first week of college, with every little mistake, I thought "Ooh no, I am doomed." Really, the first week – or month –you are going to make mistakes, but they're *usually* no big deal! When I first transferred, I was using the bike lane to wheel around campus. The University of Arizona is a big school for riding bikes around campus. Well, I was a major annoyance to the cyclist who shouted, "Wrong way!" at me as they whizzed by. I just laughed to myself. "First week! I won't make that mistake again."

My main regret as a person with disabilities who has had struggles with finding employment after college, is that I now wish I had done more in college to help me avoid this! Some things that I thought were important at the time seem trivial now. One was having grown completely sick of living in my dorm by March of my second semester. Another was picking some "wrong people" as friends. These sufferings and mistakes don't bother me in the slightest now. But my failure to use those years to do everything I could to prepare myself for the job market – that's been painful! That is why I wrote this book: to help you, my amazing reader, to steer around at least some of the icebergs that I ran into.

Don't get scared about this, get excited! You've been given the special gift of the opportunity to attend college, where there are so many things you can do to lay a foundation for the kind of life you want. College provides a perfect opportunity to make yourself so strong that you will be able to get that job!

But before we get you a job, we need to get you settled into your dorm, co-op, or apartment. Read on!

> ***It's All About Attitude:*** From the first day your mission is to adjust and have fun! Once you have "adjusted," or have done all the adjusting that you can do, your mission is to have fun and prepare for life after college!

First Semester Course Plan

It is my opinion that all first-semester college students should take one class less than a 'full' course load. Usually a full load is four or five classes per semester. I say you should take three or four classes your first semester! You could think of the "extra" class that you are taking as "Getting Used to College Life 101." Your goal is to build as strong a foundation as you can, both in terms of your academic habits and your general well-being. No matter who you are, this will take time and effort, and should be in place of a fifth class.

Make it your first-semester twin goals to (a) make the Dean's List and (b) plug into a healthy social scene. By doing do both of these things, you will be off to a very strong start. You will create the kind of momentum that will keep you growing right on through college and help you establish your post-college life, whether you are graduating with a job or gaining admission to graduate school.

In my first semester, I had no clue which classes to take; I just let my mom make the selections for me. I was also daunted by the process of buying my books, so my mom also went and did that for me before she returned home from helping me get set up. I am a little embarrassed to tell you all that, but my point is that by second year, I was able to pick which classes to take and buy books for myself – no big deal! No matter how clueless you feel at first, you will soon move past that. Here's is what I say you should take first semester:

- **English "101" (or whatever they call it at your school).** No matter what you major in, you'll need at least one English class to graduate. Taking this class and working hard at it will help teach you how to read and write at a higher level, and in less time. Another advantage is that almost all your classmates will be first-semester freshmen, so this class is a great way to make new friends!

   It is a good idea to take a few night courses for 'networking' purposes. I would take English during the day, if you are a 'traditional student.' Try to make it right before a mealtime so you can naturally go with some classmates to grab something to eat. Networking is vital. My suggestion is that you take lower-level or "Gen Ed" courses, during the day whenever you can, then a few of your electives for your major at night. This will both maximize your opportunity to make new friends your age and as they used to say, to start your business Rolodex!

- **Your major requirement's first math class.** This probably seems unappealing . Many people report math is their most challenging subject. I say get going with it in the first semester, while whatever you retained from your high school math classes is still somewhat fresh! Even if you only retained ten percent of what was taught to you in high school, if you wait until senior year that ten percent will have dwindled to five or less! That's a 50% to 80% reduction in what you remember! (See how fun math can be?)

   The second reason I want you to get the jump on math is that, if you're like me, you'll use your school's tutoring center to get through it. The trend with such "supplemental" service areas, however, is that their budgets are getting cut more and more all the time. Whatever tutoring services your school offers when you start as a freshman could very well be the most extensive of those services offered while you're attending that school. By your senior year, those resources might not be (as) available. Also, if you are not a math or business major, you can celebrate by completing your math requirement your first semester.

- **One other basic requirement OR one elective.** Take an introductory course in your major – or at least what you think your major will be (many people change their mind about that). If you are undecided, that's OK too. You will have a myriad of classes to choose from to fulfill one or two 'Gen Ed's.' Choose any that sound at least somewhat interesting, and not too hard – because your math and English will take more work.

What Makes College So Great?

One of the best things about college is that, most of time, you can choose class times that fit for you! If you are a night owl, you get to take afternoon classes. I loved that about college!

Another thing to consider is tests or projects. Try to schedule your classes so you don't have them all on one or two days, because that means you will also have *tests* back to back: not a good thing. In Chapter 8 I recommend a book by Lauren Berger that suggests students schedule courses all on two days so that they can intern the other days. I think that is a great suggestion – for upperclassmen (juniors and seniors – students in their third and fourth years)! But as a freshman, if you have a job, you should schedule your job around your classes. Most of you will find that you've got plenty of new things to learn to manage without concentrating your classes back-to-back like that right away.

Also take it easy at first with working at a job. Work on campus just a few hours a week. Then, as you approach graduation, you might want to switch the emphasis, scheduling your classes around your job. Or maybe not. Even as a senior, you might want to be primarily a student. That is your choice. But I say, first year, focus on your education. That's what you are therefore; that's why you are (probably) borrowing so much money and working on top of that. Don't structure your course schedule around a job unless you absolutely must.

My first semester, despite having a rough time adjusting to living away from home, I made Dean's List. I even got an A in College Algebra; I was so proud of myself! A regret of mine is signing up for five classes my second semester, getting a little in over my head, and not dropping one of my electives that was a "Gen Ed." I do not regret trying to take five classes; I regret not dropping one of them when things were not going well.

I was stressed out for multiple reasons. One was that the 24/7 hustle and bustle in the dorms really got to me by February. Moving out was an option, but that thought just added to my stress. I also had a health setback. It would have made so much sense to just drop a class! That would have been the easiest change to make my life easier, enabling me to both do better in my other four classes and focus on self-care.

Fast forward two years: I was taking *six* classes with way more ease than the five my second semester! My major's program was highly structured, and all MIS students were required to take the same six classes their first semester of advanced standing. Many undergrad programs are not that rigid. I was able to excel in such a program because I was in a better place in so many ways. All college students go through good semesters and bad semesters. If you have a semester with too much going on, consider dropping one class.

College Survival 101

Here's a short list of some resources and techniques that I found most helpful in college.

Used Books. Always buy used books. They are cheaper, and you can usually find some that are already intelligently highlighted. This is one trick that I used to compensate for my disability in college. Since I could not highlight any better than a two-year-old, buying books already highlighted was an easy answer.

Copy Center. I used my second school's copy center to compensate for my disability in two ways. First, I printed out a whole semester's worth of notes and/or handouts at once, then took them right over to the copy center to get them spiral-bound. This eliminated the need to keep organized or handle a couple hundred pieces of loose paper. Because of my motor disability that would have been very difficult. Second, I used the copy center to make overheads when an assignment required them. At my smaller school, I had to pay a friend to write them out for me.

Department of Disability Services. As I said in Chapter 4, it's up to you how often you meet with your specialist. However, during the first semester, plan to check in with them at least once after a couple of weeks. Make sure you know any perks that they offer to their students, such as free printing, priority registration, career guidance or social events.

Tutoring Center: In some ways I used my campus's tutoring center to do some things that my mom did for me in high school. I needed someone to write my responses to math problems. I was not really allowed to have the tutor write my homework, but it was the only solution I had to get my needs met. The head of the center threatened to kick me out because I was using the center for something other than what it was designed for. Fortunately, the tutor did not mind helping me with my situation. When I earned an "A" in the class, I bought her a gift card to the bookstore as a thank-you.

This is an example of doing what you need to do to work around your limitations to succeed. It also illustrates that a key survival strategy of finding those who will help you – and how important it can be to stay on their good side.

Another way I used the tutoring center is to get my papers proofread. I am not super-confident in my proofreading, spelling, or grammar. (Ironic, right, since I'm now writing a book!) Being a procrastinator, I sometimes did not get my papers done in time to do this, but I tried. Why get a lower grade on something that you spent time on, simply due to a spelling or grammar booboo, or even a typo?

Drop/Add Period: This goes on for the first week or two of each semester. First, it is important because it is a way to get into a class that is full. Often professors will sign you in. Secondly, this is a good way to try out classes to see if they will work for you. I would sign up for six classes during registration, knowing after I go to, then I'll drop the one that's the most work or I get bad vibes from. Now, sometimes you must take a class and sometimes you need to take it *that* semester, and only one person teaches it. Other times, you will have more flexibility, where you can say "I know that I need another science class to graduate, but I have two more years to find another class which will fulfill that requirement. I'm going to wait and see if there's one that looks easier or seems to have a nicer/better professor. Or maybe I'll just be better able to handle it next semester."

Even though I had priority registration, I recall a lot of drop/add forms going through my hands. I would frequently change my mind or something else would change, so I would change my plan. In my freshman year, I went to an elective class that sounded interesting. The professor required 14 books! This was before VR paid for my books. I thought, "Even if I have time to do all that work, I couldn't afford to buy 14 books, so I didn't even ask the prof to sign my add slip. It was not the class for me!

Your School's Staff. I will discuss how to work with professors later in this chapter. However, professors are only one of several types of employees that will be at your school. It is quite possible that being friendly with another type will get you more of what you need than getting to know all your professors! You will have lots of needs/issues in college. If you need help in the cafeteria, get to know the staff. The same goes for the library or the bookstore. If people are starting to bother you, make friends with the security guards (or better still, don't wait until then).

Have a computer lab monitor that you are friendly with, in case you ever need help producing a project. Get friendly with your department's administrative assistants; they are the gatekeepers to your professors. They can also help you get the classes you need. There are going to be times where you will be racing to turn in an assignment minutes before it is due. You will rest easier if you know that the admin knows you and will get that all-important take-home final into the correct mailbox. If you are rushing in with your paper at 5:03 and it was due at 5:00, again you will have more luck if the admin likes you, either letting you drop it in the box or giving it a time stamp that you need. Most other college books will lecture you on time-management. That's great advice too, but the more allies you have on campus, the better!

Of course, in the real world, not everyone at your school is going to be able to be won over. Even, when you try and try, some people just aren't going to respond as you'd like. Accept this and move on. Learn to sense who you can probably get "on your team" with reasonable effort, and who isn't worth it. If you win over just one out of five people, you're doing well.

> ***Tip about RAs:*** You should have a "go-to" person in your dorm to help you work out issues. In theory this is supposed to be your *Resident Advisor*, However, it does not matter if it is your RA, another RA, a desk person or your dorm director. If you get two or three, *go, you*!

The last point on how to network informally with staff members at your college has to do with specialist in both your career and Disability Services departments. Again, it does not have to be the staff member that an assigned to you. Try to meet all of them, then decide which one(s) you are going to draft for your team. In the case of your disability services department, you need a "go-to" person for issues during that semester. However, more important, you need to make connections that could land you a *job!*

Career Services. I saved the most important for last! You *must* visit this place at least once a year starting in your freshman year. Visit your school's career center and talk to a counselor. The goal of this visit is to figure out what they can do for you. Tell them straight out that you know what they know if they are competent at their job: because of your disability you face a much higher unemployment rate after you graduate. Tell them "I don't want my education to be for nothing. How can you help me be proactive to form a plan so that I can "be the best I can be" when I hit the job market?"

Ask about internships, co-ops and other campus networking events. If they offer you anything, follow up! If not, email whomever you met with the next day to thank them for their time. Say that you look forward to an ongoing partnership with them as you progress in your career preparations. Go in at least once a year to ask what they can do for you now, at this point in your education, with the challenges that you have faced, regardless of which of them you have overcome. The squeaky wheel gets the grease!

Wellness in College and Beyond

All basic books on college life tell you how to take care of yourself in college. I will not repeat the same old "eat right and exercise." In keeping with the message of this book, I'll emphasize using the resources available to you. Colleges offer facilities to help you stay healthy. I say use them for everything they're worth! Not only will doing so help you while you are in college, but even after you graduate.

Counseling Center. I really regret not taking advantage of this in college. It is FREE THERAPY! At no other time in your life will you have this. Insurance companies often don't offer mental health benefits. When such services are covered, they are usually limited. If/when you end up full-time – maybe at more than one job to make ends meet – you might have a hard time juggling your schedule to get to your appointments, should you have coverage or be able to pay out of pocket. If you're not working, you could be stuck at home without transportation to get to your appointments. It is easiest to access these services when you are right there on campus. At my first school, all I would have needed to do is wheel down the hall and I would have been able to bend an objective ear. This also may be helpful with dealing with the mere fact you are living away from home for the first time. Most students experience homesickness to some extent. Many students with disabilities report having an even harder time. It's okay to get some extra help, and it is always confidential.

I am talking about this because no matter who you are, life is going to take its toll. Everyone will have something *less than great* happen to them at some point. Most people will have something less than great happen before their eighteenth birthday. That is just life. Whatever happens will have an effect on you. Do not let such happenings produce baggage that you need to carry throughout college and then have it affect your career or your relationships.

For me, that *less than great* thing was being born with a disability. This may also be your less than great thing. Or yours could have nothing to do with your disability. I've met plenty of individuals with disabilities who have had no problems with having a disability. Most adults I know who were born with a disability say "It's who I am." If someone suddenly cured me of my disability, I would not be me; why would I want that? I feel everyone is different! For me, it has been an emotional struggle and I regret not taking advantage of the counseling services that were available to me on campus.

Health Center. This offers many of the same benefits as the counseling center, but from a physical angle. Even aside from your ability to move around and get through your day, how you look can have a great impact on your ability to get and keep a job. Right or wrong, this is how it is. If any health issues come up for you in college, get them treated while you are there. If you move home after college and are trying to find a job from your parents' house, it's not a good time to be scrambling to resolve health issues at the same time. Some medications make issues worse before they get better. When you are trying to get interviews, it's not a good time to have your acne break out worse because you are just starting a medication.

Another reason concerns transportation. How easy will it be for you to get to a medical appointment once you are back home? If you are living with your parents, or just one, they will probably be both working and having social lives. They will try to help you, but they'll only be able to do so much. That has been a post-college trap I have fallen into. This has taught me a key lesson I want to impart to you: *Get as much taken care of in college as you possibly can!*

This way, if you do need to move home or pay rent from SSI while you are still trying to find a job, you can use your resources (which are *always* limited, aren't they?), whether it is rides from your support team or paying for rides, to get to interviews and networking functions. Don't worry about this too much in your freshman year. Rather, as you get into Year 2 or 3 where you feel your campus is your home, start asking yourself "What issues can I take care of now?"

Be Prepared

Because of my disability, when I catch a cold or the flu, it hits me harder. My body gets really sore and weak. You are likely to get sick in your freshman year and your mommy will not be there. When you do get sick, because you have a disability it may be a little harder to deal with. So, it's even more important to be prepared by having tissues, cold/flu medicine, coconut water, and other helpful supplies on hand. This way you do not have to go out when you are weak to get them! Like a lot of the advice in this book, this is smart even if you don't have a disability. Who feels like going to the store when you have a cold or flu?

You should also keep a basic first aid kit ready; this is a good idea for anyone. However, it's even more important if you wheel all the time. You need to be able to properly clean and bandage a cut on your hand. If you don't like to wear gloves, keep a pair near your first aid items anyway, in case you get a bad cut or other hand injury and you need to wear gloves to help keep a bandage on and the wound clean.

I had this experience at college. I saw this ramp and thought it would be a blast to go down it fast. I have been in a wheelchair since I was twelve, and I still get a childish joy from ramps. However, this one was too steep, and my hand got all torn up trying to steer my chair. Not one of my smarter ideas. The student center was halfway between the site of the incident my home. So, I stopped in and got bandages, then cleaned up in the basement bathroom. The next day, I awoke to find that my hand was still in bad shape. I had a zillion things to get done; staying home was not an option. I bought a pair of gloves at a bike shop that was conveniently located just off campus. If I had been on a smaller campus and those shops hadn't been right there, I don't know what I would have done.

The lesson here is not to stop having fun on ramps. I still do that! But I learned that (1) some ramps are too much for me, and (2) be prepared. Things happen. You can't always see what's around the next corner – or control things even when you see something coming.

What About the Social Scene?

Most incoming freshmen are concerned with what kind of social life they will have. It is a huge part of going to college. If you are not taking care of yourself by having fun, you will not be happy. If you are not happy, you are not going to have an easy time earning good grades. Nor will you have the energy to pursue all the activities that are healthy at this time in your life. My experience taught me this. Semesters when I spent enough time out with friends, I also studied harder and made better grades. It seemed natural that if I had more to do; I had to manage my time better. The semesters when I had nothing to do but go to class and study, I had too much time on my hands. Therefore, I did not maximize my time.

It takes time for most people to make friends in a new environment such as a college campus. It may take you some time; just know that it will happen. As a freshman, I expected that living tin a freshman dorm would make it easy to make friends. I also looked forward to people being more mature. We were in college, not high school anymore. For some, their social life gets intertwined with those who they live around and attend classes with. I expected people to be more accepting of me in college, not less. Like a lot of people when they leave high school, they feel they will be given a new start in college. No one will know me (I thought) as that girl who had a Para-pro throughout middle and most of high school. When people still not only saw my CP but also were rude to me about it, I went through a social low.

During the second semester, freshman year, I wasn't really clicking with anyone. The fact that someone made fun of me really did not bother me. The fact that I was lonely, did! Like a lot of freshmen, I missed the people who I went to high school with, but not high school itself. That time was hard on me, but the main take-away is I got through it! As *you will too*!

Yes, my disability impacted this struggle, but it is a freshman struggle that is certainly not unique or exclusive to freshman with disabilities.

When I got into my major, then I started having classes with the same people and that's where I found my group of friends. It is different for everyone! Know it will happen; hope that it does right away but do not expect too much too soon.

Pre-think, what do you want your social life to revolve around: partying, religious activities, academic work, or maybe on-campus involvement/advocacy – either regarding people with disabilities or not? Attend the events that make sense with your schedule and abilities. If you are not clicking with any of the students in your dorm, that's more reason to join in activities to meet a wider variety of people. This will help both socially and with your résumé!

Don't overlook the obvious: make friends in class! Start or join a study group, have pizza, cram, then go out and dance off the pizza – whatever dancing might look like for you! The more you show that you are comfortable with your disability and you don't let it stop you from having fun, the more fun and healthy-*minded* people you will draw.

True-story...

A common theme in my life, and maybe yours, has been trying to get my wheelchair into people's cars.

One time I'd been at a tutoring session, right off campus, at eleven at night. The tutor said, "I really don't want you wheeling home this late." I think I was planning to have him call Safe Ride, a service run by campus police, which would pick you up within a certain radius of campus after a certain hour. He said, "I want to give you a ride home, but I drive a two-door Corvette. How will the chair fit?"

I said, "I'll bet you half off on my next tutoring session, it will fit." He laughed, "OK, I so want to see this." Sure enough, my chair fit! I got a ride home but didn't take the half off. The guy was helping me enough.

In my third year of college I went out to hear a local band with my best friend "Sally." Her red sports car was insanely small, so it took quite an effort to fit my wheelchair into the back. But the band was in fine form and we had a great time. The bar kicked everyone out at 1:00 AM. We weren't ready to go home yet, but I couldn't blame them for wanting to close on time. We drove back to my dorm, which wasn't far. Sally was getting my chair out and then asked, "Where's your wheel?" Turns out that somehow, my wheel either never got loaded or fell out, I'm still not sure which.

"Oh no, what am I going to do?" Sally put what we did have of my chair back in her tiny car and said, "Let's go find the wheel."

Now that I know how this ended it's funny. We drove back to the bar slowly, with her high beams on. I am thinking, if we don't find it, I am in trouble. Luckily, we were not pulled over for suspicious driving. She was sober. But that would have only added to our stress.

We reached the bar's parking lot. Still no wheel. I was thinking "This is not good!" We drove past the bar, looked across the street, and saw a couple of guys playing with my wheel! I can still hear her breaks slam. In five seconds, she's in their face saying, "That's our wheel!" She grabs it from the guy who has it, gets back in the car, and we drive off. I think they were too stunned to say anything.

Sally was a true friend that night. You will find friends like that, too. It just might take some time.

Professor 101

The "bell curve" principle, in which there are a few people at either extreme of the spectrum and a whole bunch of people in the middle, applies to everyone you meet. This includes teachers and professors. There is a small percentage at either end of the bell curve that will either inspire you to strive to be your best self – or cause you to count down the days until you never have to look at their face again. Most will fall in the middle, and typically you will forget all about them. This was my experience with professors during my college years.

We all have our own way of dealing with people. I knew some students with disabilities who emailed their professors before their semester starts to introduce themselves and explain they have a disability. I don't know why or how they did that. I would not have known how to get in touch with my professors before the first day of class. In retrospect I guess they got help from the department office. I had some one-on-one conversations with nine out of ten of my professors, but those didn't happen until classes started.

If you are registered with the department of disability services, they'll usually give you letters of documentation to present to your professors at the beginning of the semester. These letters are given to you by your access specialist. I remember doing this one semester. I was just doing what I was told to do. After that, I found no practical reason to do this. Additionally, it just was not my style. I did not go in to get the letters.

I took the tack of waiting until something came up to talk to a professor about my disability. Pop quizzes are a good example. If they were mentioned in the syllabus or in class, I would approach the professor after class and explain the logistical challenges that pop quizzes present for me. I would then ask how they wanted to work this. Different profs each have their own way of handling it.

Basically, I treated professors the same as I did anyone else. If I got a positive vibe, I would interact more, otherwise less. This worked well for me; I just wish I had carried this thinking further, to apply the "5 out of 40" rule for networking purposes. Below are a few considerations when working with professors.

The "Five out of 40" Rule

You will have roughly 40 professors during your undergrad career. Five years later you will not remember half of them. It is crucial to start networking in college! A good way to do this is to start building your network through your professors.

When you start college, go with the mission of establishing a lasting relationship with five of your professors in the four or five years that you are there! You can start doing this freshman year if the opportunity presents itself. If you have a class where you feel the professor is great and could be helpful in your internship/job search, just go up and tell him or her that you like the way they lecture or something about the way they run the class. If nothing about that stands out, make a point about the material itself, how interesting something was that they said or that was in one of the readings. Be real about this. If you don't have something real to say, don't try to fake it. Most people in positions of authority have learned to tell when someone is just trying to suck up to them. It won't hurt your prospects all that much if they incorrectly come to that conclusion about you, but it won't help either.

Office hours are a great way to start this. Use the paper trick that I spoke of above, if it makes you feel more comfortable to have an excuse. Or, you can go in and get right to it with an opener like this: "Through taking your class, I have come to be impressed by you. I want to talk to you about my career planning in this field. People with disabilities face such a high unemployment rate. Do you have any suggestions for how I might get a leg up on the competition?" You can expect suggestions in one or more of the following areas:

- On-campus experience
- Internships/co-ops
- Contacts for informational interviews
- Contacts for actual job interviews
- References for same
- Suggestions for supplementary training in your field while you are still in school
- Someone to contact after graduation

Don't go in and list off these things, just have them in your mind as what you want to gain from these relationships.

Another way to get your "five" is to do well in class! Sit towards the front, be engaged. Not all five of the professors in your network must be in your major. You never know who will know someone. However, try to get to know the head of your department. If you try this and they are not receptive, you tried, you lost nothing. However, if it works, you could have hit gold. If this person seems student-friendly, go to their office hours seeking their opinion on your résumé. The goal of this is to engage them in your job hunt, even if it's naturally at a very preliminary level because of where you are in your college track. Ask them if they know of any internships that are not posted on the department bulletin board. If you know of a company that you are interested in, ask if this professor has a contact for an informational interview.

I had a professor second semester of my first year who would have been a fabulous person to network with. She was very passionate about women succeeding in business. I very much regret not having tried – and I believe I squandered the great opportunity of being in her class.

I could not have called her up five years later, when I really needed a job. Why would she remember me? I did not do anything to make myself known.

Office Hours

Use them! Unless a prof gives you a seriously bad impression in class or lecture, office hours are a great way to get to know each other better. Professors are required to hold office hours, and lots of times nobody shows up. So of course, they have learned to plan on getting work done during office hours between student visits, but I've never had one look annoyed when I would show up.

Use them when there's trouble. If you are having trouble with a course, go talk to the professor. I was having a great deal of trouble in Accounting. It was by far my hardest course – and the biggest hurdle to earning my degree (for which it was required). I saved myself by going to the professor's office hours. I said "Look, I don't know what I am going to do. Can you recommend a tutor? I'm in a lot of trouble." The professor said, "It is not my policy to recommend tutors. What I would do is go see the TA in his office hours before every class. Hardly anyone comes to that hour. You should go over the material with him before each class."

I did this, and it was brilliant! It was free tutoring! At one point I told the TA, "I feel as if I should be paying you for working with me before every class." But of course, he pointed out that he is already being paid to be there. This is another reason I keep saying that you should take advantage of everything that is available at your college. You don't necessarily have to pay extra to have a tutor!

Another use of office hours is to help if you missed an exam or too many classes. Go to apologize and explain – especially if attendance counts for part of your grade. You have nothing to lose by trying to get the prof to be sympathetic to your plight. It will be much easier if you do this before they assign a final grade than after!

I learned this the hard way my first year. I got a B in the class despite getting A's on all the assignments, because I had missed too many classes. I contacted my professor to inquire. She replied, I docked you because I never saw you after October. After I explained why I had missed so many classes, she agreed to raise my grade. She told me, "Learn a lesson from this: keep in contact with your professors."

TA's ROCK. Teaching assistants can be as helpful to your learning process as professors, or even more so, depending on how your school and any given course are structured. Large courses at universities often have two teaching assistants for the same class. So, between them and the professor you might have three chances to find someone responsible for the class that you really click with.

Visit the prof or TA during office hours when things are going *right*. Be proactive and build relationships. Let's say you identify a class as 'an easy A.' Use office hours to "seal the deal." Go in with a close to final draft and ask, "How I can improve this before it is due?" Do not do this to get it proofread for spelling and such, but rather to show your professor that you are really working at their class! Most profs will be glad to read a draft and offer feedback. Some will not, but if they say no, you haven't lost anything. When you are there, compliment them on the course and say one or two things you are getting from it. Usually if a professor knows you are trying and engaged, it will pay off in at least your grade, if not recommendations and networking.

What If a Professor Will Not Accommodate Me?

It is the professor's right to require that you be registered with your school's department of disability services to receive any academic accommodations in their class.

All my professors were accommodating; most were *extremely* so. I had a minor incident where one of my professors wanted me to write a 15-page paper instead of writing a ten-page paper and doing an oral presentation. She told me this was because she could not understand my speech. While some would have gladly taken this offer, I felt it was not fair because I preferred presenting to writing extra. I talked to my disability services specialist and the issue was easily resolved. This professor would not have been one of the five I would have tried to network with. However, it was no big deal. My accommodation's specialist and my professor agreed I could do the presentation if my specialist agreed to attend class, discreetly, that day. I did my presentation and earned an 'A' on it!

Should you have an issue where a professor will not accommodate you, you have two options for how to try to resolve the issue at the first "level." One is to visit the prof during her office hours. The other is to discuss it with your disability services specialists. If the staff are as professional and resourceful as mine were, they'll immediately be able to lay out your options for you. Your issue will more than likely be resolved through this conversation. Should it not be, you could escalate the issue through your school's channels, or (if it's not too late) drop the course.

If your school doesn't have a disability services department, you don't get along with them, or you feel they are not adequately handling the situation, every school has some channels for both support of diversity and to handle complaints. Go to either the counseling center or the women's center to get referred to the right department. Just know that taking either of the two options *may* escalate it. It is completely your call how far you want to pursue it.

Another example was, when I asked another professor a question about how an assignment needed to be handed in. When he replied, "Whatever," I knew he did not understand me. The next class, I tried to hand it to him. He said "No, drop it at the office." This led me to have to wheel back to a building that I just came from in really hot weather.

I could have complained to DRC, but I felt as if everyone has professors, they don't like due to minor issues. Having a disability does not exempt me from likes and dislikes. A lot of life has nothing to do with disability! All students are annoyed by their professors at some point during college.

In some situations, the best option is to drop the class. If it's required to graduate, retake it with a different professor. During college, I had to do this once. At the time it was very stressful. But, once that semester was over, it was over! Ultimately, I was glad that I re-took the course.

Final Recourse

If you are consistently being denied accommodations by your school, you've worked with disability services, have gone through your school's channels for student grievances, and are still not receiving what you think they are legally obligated to provide, then you can contact the federal Office for Civil Rights:

> U.S. Department of Education
> Office for Civil Rights
> Lyndon Baines Johnson Department of Education Bldg.
> 400 Maryland Avenue, SW
> Washington, DC 20202-1100
>
> Telephone: 800-421-3481
> FAX: 202-453-6012; TDD: 877-521-2172
> Email: OCR@ed.gov

The best time to use this resource is after you have (1) repeatedly tried to work through the issues with your disability services department without success, and (2) called the hotline to be certain of your legal rights prior to your hearing before the university's grievance board. Only after if you are still not happy with the outcome should you file a complaint. This is not for complaining about a grade on one essay! This is for ongoing, serious issues of non-accommodation or discrimination.

Before starting or continuing a legal battle, consider cutting your losses by transferring to a school that seems more promising – especially if the other school was already on your short list and they already accepted you.

As always when you're having a conflict with a bureaucracy, you have a choice to pursue the grievance or to just leave. Neither choice is right or wrong. It is only what feels right for your life.

As you might remember from earlier in this book, I transferred to another school, but that choice had nothing to do with the quality of the accommodations at my first school. I thought both schools were fair, and I never felt any need to fight for anything; everything I needed was automatically granted. Disability services were hugely helpful, and I never needed to escalate anything beyond them.

Course Substitutions

A course substitution is gaining permission from your school to take another course in lieu of a required course to obtain your degree. This is often granted when one's disability prohibits taking the required course or would make it exceptionally more difficult.[11] As in most disability-related matters, you should start this process by inquiring at the disability services department. Every school has its own procedure for determining who is eligible for this. Schools are not going to waive GPA requirements or prerequisites.

If you are a foreign language major, you will have a much harder time getting a foreign language course substitution, while it might not be such a big deal if you are majoring in business. If you are a business major, the foreign language is purely a general education requirement. This scenario is where you would have the best shot in being allowed a substitution. The same goes for a lab science-intensive class for non-science majors, or a PE requirement.

To get a course substitution, you will probably need to submit documentation to support your contention that the requirement constitutes an exceptional hardship for you. Evidence that a language requirement was waived in high school, or documentation from a medical professional might qualify. You might need a letter from a doctor indicating that you are not able to do physical education, take a test to establish that your disability prohibits certain functions, or a medical professional's correspondence with your previous school. The school is not required to pay for copies or other expenses connected with your desire to get this documentation into the school's hands.

Follow your school's procedures to apply for the substitution. If you are turned down, there might be a defined avenue for appealing the decision. I suggest that you consider at the beginning of your sophomore year whether any of your school's major requirements raise any concerns for you. Approach Disability Services then; don't wait till you are a semester or two away from graduating. But also, don't bring it up when you first arrive at the school. Asking for this kind of exception to early could start things off on the wrong foot with disability services by making you look like you think you are a special case even more than your disability really justifies. This issue is likely to be the most adversarial that you will encounter with this department. You do want these folks in your corner throughout most if not all your time at the school – and beyond!

As Richard Lewis says, "put some good stuff in the bank first, before withdrawing." This is not to say, because they know you better, they will automatically grant your request. It's just about picking the time and place of your battles. It is all about managing their image of you while you get what you need, both while you are in college and post-graduation.

If you start this process in your sophomore year, it will in most cases be resolved long before your senior year is over. Your graduation date will not have to be moved back because of the issue.

When I requested a course substitution, my specialist told me that I would not get approved. He said, "No one's ever been approved due to a physical disability." I said, "I understand, and I don't want to have a confrontational relationship with your office; however, I would still like

---

[11] However, as noted in chapter Two; schools are not legally *required* to grant course substitutions or waivers.

to submit a request." My request was denied. I appealed. To appeal, I had my medical professional contact the director of disability services, had the head of advising for the business college contact the director of disability services to say he did not object to the course substitution, he just needed a "rubber stamp" from them. I then met with the director and my request was granted! Despite initially being told not to bother applying, I ultimately did get what I needed. It took only about a month or so to get through the red tape.

When I was going through this, I wasn't aware of the Guckenberger vs. Trustees decision. I just got lucky that my university did not use that to deny my appeal. My university's Department of Disabled Resources was (and is) more influenced by social justice than just "What does the law force us to do?" That attitude is why the University of Arizona's Department of Disability Services is among the top in the country.

GPA

Your undergraduate GPA matters, even if you don't plan to go to grad school. A lot of employers use your GPA to quickly decide which résumés will get a more extensive review and which go into the recycle bin.

This is not to say you need to spend all your time studying. If you are preparing for the job market rather than grad school, you will be better off with a 3.4 GPA, plus work experience and ample on-campus leadership, as opposed to a 4.0 GPA and nothing else. Employers want the full package.

Choosing a Major

This is an issue all college students grapple with at some point. It is okay to change your mind. On average, students change their major three times during their college career.

There are lots of resources to help you make a decision that fits for you now even if you don't stick to it. (Remember, many people change *careers* several times during their working lives.) This is, as with your college choice, after you have thought through this-what your plan is, is more important than what your major is. The harder you work whatever your choice, the better it will be. Sometimes it will be easy; you want to teach at the primary or secondary level; therefore, you need to be an education major (for example). Others of you just need more time. Most colleges don't force students to pick a major in their first two years, only the general area of concentration to guide their choices of classes. Majors are all about building skills, these skills can be gained through any major. Below is a chart of skills employers look for. You should be able to fill this out no matter what your major is.

Skill	Course/Extracurricular Activity/Work Experience where it's Acquired	Specific Example
Speaking		
Writing		
Teamwork		
Influencing People		
Research		
Critical Thinking		

This table is designed to take some of the pressure off choosing "the right" major. It is also to get you to plan to be a marketable job applicant regardless of your major. If you enter college with the goal of having this kind of skill table amply filled out upon graduation, you will be prepared to answer the prospective employer's question "What can you do for me?" Employers are happy to hire applicants who answer that question with the way they carry themselves as well as with what they say. A well-rounded college student can easily prepare for interviews in which they will have great examples to show off their skills in the areas above without having to make up anything!

Back to Reality
You will still need to choose a major eventually. If you are clueless, there are also ample books and websites on this subject. Type "choosing a major" into Amazon or Google. If you want to be a history major, don't rule it out just because you've heard there are no jobs for history graduates. Research and develop a plan. If you are a parent reading this book on behalf of your child, get beyond the stereotypes of marketable and non-marketable majors! Instead, challenge your child to present you with a proposal for what they intend to major in:

- What kind of work do you want to do with a history major?
- How do you intend to fill in the above chart while pursuing that major?
- What work experience – major-related and otherwise– will you get while in school?
- How do you plan on maximizing your chances for getting hired for the type of position that you are seeking?

If your parents are no longer holding you accountable, make up a proposal for yourself!

Even if you have been sure of what you wanted to do with your life since you were five years old, explore all your options. Colleges provide resources such as major fairs. Don't be shy about approaching professors to ask questions about majors that you are interested in. Attend follow-up presentations for those that interest you. After the presentation start networking with the faculty there. Find out what procedures you need to go through to either declare or get admitted into that major. This may be as simple as filing a form or be a lengthier process.

This is how I decided to be an 'MIS major.' Prior to college I was debating a couple of different paths. One October day my first semester, I was having a day wondering why I was there "I do not know what I am doing, I miss my friends from home…" Most freshmen go through this to some extent at some point. I was in the bookstore and literally started reading some funny greeting cards to try to help myself snap out of it. When I came out, I heard something going on in the large assembly room by the bookstore. It turned out that it was a major fair. Great, I think, maybe I will get some direction that makes sense. *And I did!* I got a free T-shirt from the head of the MIS department. I kid you not, that led me to do some research and decide "Hey, this is probably the best major for me. I want a lucrative career and something that I can do with my disability. Yup, sounds like a plan!"

If you are still struggling, talk to someone at career services. It's their job to help guide students through this. I want to hammer home, you are paying for these services when you pay tuition, make sure to use them as much as possible.

Your Choice of Major and Your Disability

With a disability, you must decide how much of a role you want your disability to play in choosing a major. The way I see it is some are practical – what can get me a job – whereas others approach this by asking *"What is my passion?"* Some are more driven by financial rewards, while others are more attracted to either helping others or doing what they enjoy. This is a spectrum, not an either/or. Where you naturally fall on the spectrum will probably correlate to how much you consider your disability in this choice. That is, if you are more practical and financially motivated, the more apt you are to consider your disability in choosing a major. There are no right or wrong answers in terms of this. How you naturally are, is right for you!

Another consideration is that different majors require different amounts of writing and math. Some are more writing-intensive; others are more math-intensive. Which one are you better at? Does your disability impact either? One thinks physical disability does not affect one's academic ability. This is not entirely true. I cannot write, meaning use a pen and paper; this makes math harder. How do I write practice problems when I live alone? This led me to not be a math major. I got through all my basic math courses to complete a major in business. But I decided it didn't make sense to major in accounting or finance because I had so much trouble writing (figures or anything else).

As always, there would have been a way around this if I really had the drive. My school had a separate program for students with learning differences. This program offered comprehensive tutoring. I asked once whether I could I get tutoring because of my inability to write. They said no, that's a separate program. I would have had to document that I have a learning differences and go through their procedures to register with them. If it was my passion to study mathematics, I could have gone to that program and found out their documentation requirements. I could have obtained documentation that not being able to physically write was tantamount to having a learning difference. That way I would have had more access to tutors and been able to let them write out my answers to the homework problems.

My friend was an architecture major. I looked at the kind of assignments that she would need to regularly turn in. I would not have been able to make the kind of models he made by myself, again due to my fine motor issues. Again, if I had really wanted to become an architect, I could have hired people to "be my hands" in completing my assignments, but I would've eventually had to find and acquire some technology to make a career in that field realistic. If you know or are pretty sure that you will get a job and be able to pay the loans back, go for it. Do not let your disability stop you. Unfortunately, the grant sources I was able to find did not deem making architectural models necessary for survival. Don't expect Medicaid to grant a PCA or VR to pay for this. You can try. More power to you, for attempting to get what you need. However, expect to be denied, and expect to need to rely on your family's funds, credit, or personal labor to support your dream.

Warning: Do not Fall for Your 'Major's Hype'

No matter how "in demand" some people might say your major is, no matter how difficult it is to get into your major because everyone wants to get in – don't let yourself become overconfident or complacent about getting a job in your chosen field. Majoring in a high-demand field is never enough – because high-demand majors attract competition! You must fill out the "chart" and become a well-rounded, well-networked applicant. This is crucial for every college student. It is exponentially more important for students with disabilities! Choose whatever you want, then work the program. Fill out the chart. Make the proposal and always be working to fulfill it.

The Worst Mistake I Made in College

The worst mistake I made during college was being too confident in my major! At my university the major of Management Information Systems was super-competitive. When I told people my major, everyone said, "Wow." This lulled me into a false sense of security. I thought, I am majoring in something marketable and practical, and I had to work hard to get into that major. I'm involved in a couple of clubs, I interned the summer before senior year, and started my job hunt in my last semester. *How can I go wrong?*

There was so much more that I could have done! I could've gone out for president of the MIS student organization, instead of just being a member who went to some meetings. I could have run for a position in student government to gain access to the board of regents, not just be the president of my dorm. I could have taken a little better care of my GPA. I could have asked my parents for $400 to pay the dues at the business fraternity for networking. I didn't want to ask for money, but in the long run that $400 might have saved my parents money!

The list goes on. I could have gotten an on-campus job or volunteered from second semester on. Even if it had meant giving up SSI and living off about the same income, it probably would have been worth it for the extra experience and "go-getter" quality it would have given my résumé. I could have used some of my student loan money to attend a conference on employment of those with disabilities in my senior year. And I could have spent more time and effort connecting with students from higher-achieving families to make more connections.

And that internship did that I thought was so good compared to my friends who did not do one? I worked designing a database for a small pharmaceutical marketer. In hindsight, that internship would have been fine had I done it the summer after freshman or sophomore year. That should have been my "starter" internship which I then used to gain an internship such as at Entry Point, Google, Emerging Leaders or an internship in DC that was specifically set up for people with disabilities. I say this because I now think that participating in an internship program for those with disabilities would have more likely led to my being offered a position after graduation. Working for a small business owner, nice as she was, just didn't carry the gravitas of some of these other opportunities.

The above paragraphs describe what I did WRONG. In the next few sections I will tell you how to do things "right" Or, at least think about how you can do college better than I did?

If you are a parent of a college student with a disability, one of the best things you can do for your child is to encourage them to both get involved on campus and do something each college summer to be more employable. I do not mean taking another class unless it is an extra certification in the summer. I mean study abroad, volunteer or intern each summer. Now, I know your student is going to call you in October, saying "I am sick, I am upset about this thing with a boy and I do not know if I even want to be here." That is not the time to start nagging, "Did you get a job? Which clubs did you go to this week?" I get it, I have been there from the student's perspective-anyway. But ask about those things on winter break, after your kid is finally been able to catch up with a week's worth of overdue sleep and benefit from your TLC. Talk to your son or daughter what they plan to do next semester, what they feel their options are for summer. Try to *pull* (not push) the kid into doing something, even if it is just volunteering online, by talking about the benefits about what the kid wants for his or her future. If your student is not a morning person, he or she can still volunteer lying in bed at 3 am. Whatever they are able to do with their break that will help them add something else meaningful to their résumé, encourage it.

Why I Believe College Should Take You Five or Six Years

I've already asked you to do a lot during college besides take classes. In the next chapter, I am going to suggest that you do even more! College courses are not easy. But I want you to achieve higher than a 3.0, have a part-time job, have a social life, find something to do each summer, network, and be a campus leader. I am recommending all this even know you have a disability. If you are like me, that means everything is harder, from brushing your teeth, to talking, to typing, to managing your care or health situation. You may say "I can't do all that without flunking out." I have a solution to this. Reduce the pace of your coursework and stay in college longer! Like a lot of adults, I wish I had done that. College is the best place to get yourself together and prepare to live the rest of your life!

According to a 2009 study conducted by *USA Today* 53% of students take six years to graduate from four-year universities. The myth that college takes four years is becoming increasingly outdated. This is for many reasons, including economics, increased graduation requirements, and changing student populations. It is also an example of how the one-size-fits-all educational model in the United States is dissipating. Unfortunately, this is not going to change from the top down. You as a student must change it for yourself by strategically customizing your own plan.

Also, repayment of undergrad student loans can get deferred if you go into grad school. If you feel as you need to graduate with your bachelor's but feel unprepared to go to work, talk to your school's financial aid department about how to keep the loans coming for grad school. Find out if you can get a six-month or a year period to try and seek employment and if you cannot find a job, roll the loan into your graduate education?

As I said in chapter two, you can get a medical discharge for only one loan. If you discharge your undergrad loan, you're stuck with the grad school loan (even if you can get) forever. Remember, student loans are *not* dischargeable in bankruptcy court. The smartest way to do it is to have it all be one loan. Upon graduating from either grad school or completing post-grad work, you will have a grace period should you still be seeking employment. Hopefully you will have found employment and be able to begin making payments after your grace period. If not, defer a couple times while you pursue your job hunt. Should you not be able to work, you can then apply for discharge the loan. Give yourself the best chance to have the life that you want.

In addition to student loans, apply for work-study. This is a double plus because it will lower your education costs while giving you work experience! I was ignorant in that I thought the only kind of work-study was work in the cafeteria, which I could not do. However, there are tons of on-campus jobs in all areas that I could have been placed in.

My first semester, I took one less course and said my fifth course was adjusting to college. My last semester, I took one less course and said my fifth course was finding a job. I wish I had that mindset all the way through school. Your fifth class should be preparing for after college! That could encompass anything I touch on in this book: self-care through counseling or other treatment from health services, your social life, working on campus, doing extracurriculars in a leadership capacity, applying for internships or study-abroad programs and funding for such, getting to know your five professors, doing informational interviews, or just studying enough to keep your GPA above a 3.0.

I was worried that if I took too long to get a "four-year degree" it would be a turn-off to employers. This is not so. As the statistic above says, it is becoming the norm. Employers want a well-rounded applicant. When they ask about your college career, you can say straight out I took longer because I—and then brag about everything you did! If it takes you seven years but you end up with a fabulous résumé with a higher GPA and lots of work experience, you will be snapped up faster … by better employers.

Points to Remember from Chapter 6

✓ Take four classes your first semester. Going off to college is challenging for almost everyone. Your very first semester shouldn't be about your 'killer workload,' it should be about you and your holistic well-being.

✓ College is a major adjustment for just about everyone. Some books advise you not to go home for the weekend too much or stay overly connected to your high school friends. I've never been a "just throw yourself in and swim" kind of person. If going home for weekends is an option and that feels right to you, then it probably is right for you! Same with talking to your friends from your previous life, if you want to text every day. What does it take, five minutes to text someone from home? Then that is what you need to do! Of course, if frequent visits home or contact with your old friends just add to your stress, then do not force yourself to do it.

✓ Give yourself time to adjust and make what just may be lifelong friends. If it does not happen your first week, first semester, or even your first year, know you will. Do you know how I know? You are you, and you will make your way.

✓ College usually affords you choice as to what you take and more so when you take it. Professors are not robots. They will differ in how they teach and grade – and how much work they assign. Decide what you want from a professor, and then try to find out who's who. Sometimes you will want to do more work, if it means laying a good foundation for your career.

✓ Expect that things will go smoothly in terms of your professor's ability to accommodate you. Should any hiccups arise, know that there are avenues to get such issues resolved. Most of the time, you should talk to you specialist at disability resources and they will help you work with your professor to come up with a solution.

✓ Professors are vital and can be an extraordinary resource. In the course of your undergraduate career you will have 40 professors. As an incoming freshman, make it your goal to really know five out of those forty, for networking purposes.

✓ Did you ever see the movie *Casino*? It came out before many of you were born. But it is an impressive film. Make it your goal to be like Ginger's character: she always knew who to go to, to get stuff done! Your campus is both your new home and where you will lay the groundwork for lifelong career success. Make as many allies as you can in as many areas of campus life as you can. Find out how life on campus really works and use it to your advantage.

Success Story: All People Must Work

Neil Jacobson

Every person needs to be needed. This has always been one of my strongest beliefs. The need to be needed may be as important as the need for food, clothing and shelter. The need to be needed may be even greater than our need for love. For many people, work is the primary way we get to feel needed. Work brings meaning to life, provides a social connection, can be a pleasurable and fun experience and, of course, pays the rent. Yet most people with disabilities do not work. We do not work not because of physical, mental or emotional constraints but because we are literally not allowed to work.

To understand my passion for work it's important to know that my parents are Holocaust survivors. During the war, people with disabilities in ghettos and concentration camps who were unable to work were instantly killed. Work was the only remotely possible way to survive. As a child with Cerebral Palsy, my parents were fearful for my life and did all they could to foster my self-reliance. My Mom would wake me at 5:30 each morning insisting I dress myself, even though it took 2 hours to do so. At night, I'd get 2 dinners. One dinner I had to feed myself. I'd spend so much energy feeding myself that dinner, I'd be hungrier afterwards than before, so my Mom fed me the 2nd dinner. I was not allowed to use a wheelchair until high school which forced me to walk - a slow, difficult process. These events may seem extreme today. Today I know that a key to independent living is knowing when and how to get assistance. However, these tasks taught me the rewards of hard work. I learned that anything is achievable through determination and perseverance.

Throughout my work career, work has been the way I defined myself. Regardless of whether it was my 1st job as a pool-hall cashier at my alma-mater (Hofstra University), or my last job as a Senior Vice President at Wells Fargo, work is one of the main ways that I felt I contributed something to this world. Whether I was a security guard on graveyard shift at the dorms at Hofstra, or the Executive Director at the Computer Technologies Program (CTP), a computer training program for people with disabilities which I founded in 1979, working always made me proud of myself.

Working is also one of the best ways to feel and be accepted. My disability is very obvious. I can't sit upright in my powered wheelchair. I have involuntary movements and my speech impairment is significant. At Wells Fargo, I loved rolling into meetings where people did not know me. The tension was apparent. Usually no one made eye contact and the air could be cut with a knife. As we began talking and as we focused on the business at hand, it was great to see how people relaxed and got comfortable with me. My disability faded into the background. Not everyone could understand what I was saying, but there was always someone who could. That someone would naturally interpret for me. Inevitably, by the end of the meeting, I always found myself chatting with folks and feeling like part of the team.

Having people with disabilities at work often results in innovation, creativity and an overall better work environment. As a teacher at CTP, my students gained something from having to help each other understand my speech. At Wells Fargo, I often marveled at how quickly computer operators learned to ask good yes or no questions when they called me in the middle of the night. I still remember how, in the early

'80's, before online computing, Wells Fargo dispatched an armored truck at 2am to bring me and my in-collapsible wheelchair to the data center to fix a system's problem.

Work is also critically important to the economics of disability. Perhaps the biggest disadvantage of having a disability is that it is very expensive! We are aware of the high cost of health care. We often forget about the high cost of Personal Assistant Services. Imagine the cost of needing a personal assistant a couple of hours a day, or 4 hours or 8 hours or 7x24. Costs add up quickly! For a person with a "high-cost" disability who is unemployed, the government pays for the cost of the personal assistant along with other disability benefits and subsidized housing services.

After 29 years of working for Wells Fargo as an IT professional, I retired to start a disability-focused employment company that specializes in staffing and placement. Abilicorp was founded to try to improve employment for people with disabilities in a business-like fashion rather than through charitable and government agencies. Since my childhood in the 1950's, the unemployment rate for people with disabilities has always been above 70%. Laws including the Rehabilitation Act of 1973 and the Americans with Disabilities Act (ADA) of 1990 that have made this country much more accessible and accepting has done nothing to improve employment. Billions of dollars have been spent by many government and non-profit agencies on trying, unsuccessfully, to improve employment opportunities for people with disabilities. Unfortunately, Abilicorp was unsuccessful too.

As a result of my experience with Abilicorp, I now believe, more than ever before that there are systemic problems inhibiting people with disabilities from working and being productive. Our society's low-expectations and the work disincentives imposed by our government must change before economic growth for people with -disabilities can be achieved. I am dedicating the rest of my retirement from Wells Fargo to see that this happens. Towards that goal, in 2011 I helped start The World Institute on Disability Center on Economic Growth (CEG).

WID's CEG measures success as creating a level playing field where people with disabilities have the same employment rate, earning power and asset-building opportunities as their non-disabled peers. Those of us representing the CEG believe that until government invests in the success of people with disabilities rather than continuing programs and practices that relegate people with disabilities to a poverty position, people with disabilities will remain unemployed, unfulfilled and undervalued. We believe that now is the time to change the paradigm of how we think about economic growth for people with disabilities. As entitlements continue to be questioned and their funding becomes more tenuous, we must embrace the belief and create the reality that people with disabilities are equal members in our society and full economic partners. We must change our mindset from providing disability benefits and safety-nets to providing what it takes to enable people to successfully fulfill their role in the economic growth of themselves, their family and their extended community. Economic success for people with disabilities should be defined exactly the same way it is for everyone. Economic success is taking full advantage of opportunities one can find or create that uses one's abilities to be as productive as one can be and as prosperous as one wants to be. The return on investment of this paradigm shift is both significant and measurable.

The Disability Movement has historically been about changing paradigms. Growing up in the 50's and 60's, the predominant paradigm regarding disability was that people with disabilities had to 'adjust to their environment'. Our goal was to look and sound and act as 'normal' as possible. It wasn't until the paradigm changed and we realized that 'society should be accessible to all people' that true progress began to occur. Surprisingly, the predominant paradigm in regard to employment of people with disabilities has not changed. We still hear 'hire people with disabilities', and 'people with disabilities can work.' In this global economy, when employers know they can hire very qualified and experienced people anywhere in the world, expecting them to hire people with disabilities will only get harder. As a retired senior vice president of Wells Fargo Bank, hearing that 'people with disabilities can work', is demeaning and patronizing. I submit to you that the crux of the problem behind the employment of people with disabilities lies in these antiquated constructs. I submit to you that the paradigm for the 21st century should be that everyone must be productive. Now is the time to raise expectations, to determine how we will be productive, and determine how we will create our own prosperity.

WID has been collaborating with the National Council on Independent Living (NCIL) in developing the ACCESS Program (Adult Coaching, Counseling, and Employment Support Services). We will soon be working on getting Congress to pass legislature enabling us to demonstrate how the Access Program can replace the current Supplemental Security Income (SSI) and Social Security Disability Insurance (SSDI) programs for young adults with disabilities, ages 18 to 30, in 5 states. The Access Program is being designed to promote employment and to expect participants to be as productive as they can be. Instead of a check compensating them for their inability to work, participants will receive a stipend to offset their high cost of disability. Every participant will be expected to develop and follow an Individual Career Plan (ICP). Tasks on the ICP may include activities such as;

- being employed
- attending school
- attending training programs
- internships
- volunteering
- attending rehabilitation programs
- attending day programs
- pursuing personal enrichment goals
- understanding what supports and accommodations are available

The Access Program will also coordinate all services the young adults with disabilities need to successfully perform their ICP. For me, the Access Program represents the greatest chance I have of completing the number one thing I have on my bucket list – to see the unemployment rate for people with disabilities drop below 50%.

Chapter 7: College is Golden

As an 18-year-old college freshman attending Ramapo College of New Jersey, when I let myself be totally honest with myself, I was scared that even after I proved my value by graduating, no one would hire me. Instead of fully acknowledging that fear and talking about it with the people in my life who were the most supportive, I thought that I had to just try to suppress my fear, as if with brute force... just pretend it wasn't there … put on the best act I could to convince everyone, mostly myself, that I had everything handled.

When my fears got the better of me, my grades would temporarily dip. I would recover by pushing my fears into the back of my mind and working extra hard to pull my grades back up. This pattern started when I was in middle school and it persisted through college. The difference was that, by the time I was in college, no one except me noticed when I was slipping in my grades. I would just go through the low part of my cycle, then pull myself together. When I was in the down part of the cycle, the future seemed scary. At the time, that strategy worked, more or less. However, a much better strategy would have been to take actions reasonably calculated to help me attain my goals!

Cultivate a Friendly Inner Dialogue
Many of you have heard the expression "get your game head on." This has to do with what you are telling yourself some key truths about your abilities, and what it would REALLY mean (as opposed to what you FEAR it would mean) if you were to lose a game or experience some other loss or failure. For me to "get my game head on" in college looked something like this:

Yes, I have a disability. That might make it harder to find a job. It might also make it harder to do the job once I get it. But that doesn't mean I won't find a job that I can even enjoy and excel at. Many people with disabilities have done exactly that!

I am going to do what I can do to increase my chances of getting hired and of getting into a job that I will enjoy. I am choosing to be proactive by doing either some of the ideas in this book or using Lindsey Pollak's book to create my own plan during college. I will confide in my support team when I need to. I will remind myself that resources are available, and will continue to be available, to help me." By focusing on the areas where you do have control, and by taking constructive action, you WILL feel better!

News Flash: Discrimination Still Exists
Despite strong laws against it, discrimination is one factor that keeps unemployment and poverty rates higher for the disabled population. I am not saying this to discourage you, but just to let you know of another one of the obstacles that you might encounter. You already are on track to beating these statistics by choosing to go to college – and reading this book!

Your Troubles Are Not All About Your Disability
Everyone who pays any attention to the news is aware that knows that the economy has not been soaring in the past 10 years or so. Even people without disabilities have trouble getting and keeping decent jobs, or any job at all. Dozens or even *hundreds* of applicants pounce on the best jobs as soon as the opening is posted. Accordingly, many of the suggestions that I make in this chapter I would recommend to *any* college student – to help you look better than your competition.

The economy is changing; a college degree is no longer the golden ticket to employment that it once was. So, the "tricks of the trade" for being selected for a job interview – and then getting the job – are even more important for people with disabilities.

How to "Do It All" in College

College is overwhelming at some point for nearly everyone. I may have said this before. But it bears repeating. Right now, when I say that, I mean that you will get busy! There will be times where you will either think or panic to yourself. "However, will I get this all done? There are not enough hours in the day. Fear not…

The number one thing that helped me through the times where, 'I just had too much to do,' was asking myself, "What needs to get done right now?" (This I learned from my extraordinarily ambitious mother. She was the first woman in her medical school's history to graduate with three children.) Then I'd devote all my attention to that one task. Once I got it done, I'd re-ask myself, that simple question. Rinse, and repeat, you get the idea. Sometimes I would accomplish several goals in a day by just checking assignments off one by one. Other times, I would either several weeks or several months working on one task. I did this to get all 'A's in summer pre-session and impress my supervisors at my summer internship.

Taking the Lesson Deeper: Being Fully Present Doesn't Mean Doing Everything
Just because you are signed up for a class does not mean that you need to attend every lecture. Just because you are in a club does not mean you need to attend all its events or agreed to be its new leader. Your job in college is to figure out how best to spend your time.

If you have a hard exam to study for or a project due the next day – skip the club meeting. Even if you are an officer – delegate. If your club is having a major event and you need to do a lot for it, it is okay to skip a class provided that the class is under control that day. Plan to make up for it later so that you can still get the grade want or need in that class.

Employers what well rounded workers. If you can to learn how to manage your time by prioritizing this skill will make you both a stronger job applicant and a better employee!

Tweak your plan to your specific post college goal. If it is an advanced degree, you might want to spend less time on extracurricular activities so that you can focus more on keeping your grades up to help ensure that you can attend the graduate school of your choice. If your goal is to go straight into the workforce after you get your bachelor's degree, it might be more important to ensure that you can present a résumé that shows you as well-rounded in addition to having a degree. College is the time to build a strong foundation for the rest of your life. Use it wisely – even while you are, of course, having fun being away from home for the first time!

Recommended Reading

I know as a college student that you have a lot of reading and at some points the last thing you want is more! I also find it annoying when buy I book, and I feel as if it is just advertisements for other books. Despite all that, I suggest you read *Getting from College to Career* by Lindsey Pollak. I recommend you do this after high school, not college, graduation. Ms. Pollak's ideas are in line with my beliefs that all throughout college is the golden time for any student to start building their résumé! I wish someone had given me this book or required me to read it. She goes more in depth on topics such as networking, informational interviews and job search preparation as they apply to everyone. Get it and use it!

Get a JOB on Campus

It has been my experience that college campuses are some of the most open-minded places out there. What better place to start gaining experience? Employers want to hire applicants with an employment history-even if they are straight out of college. If you work on campus at least some of the time, you will have an edge when you are trying to land your first job after college.

 Probably a lot of you are thinking "I don't have time to work when I'm in school." I say "Yes, you do! Other people do it, why not you?" By using the principles of time management, taking fewer classes, and giving yourself time to adjust first, you can do it. Again, I am not telling you that you need to get a job the first week or even the first year of college. I do feel that at some point, working on campus is a must.

I really get where you are. You don't have to try and work on top of going to school before you are ready. But, also believe me, at some point, you will feel "I've got this campus life thing down." For some, that may come within a few weeks, while for others it may take into your second year. Trust me, it will come for you. That is the point where I want you to get a job!

Also, if you apply to summer internships, an on-campus job will help you. For one thing, campus jobs will potentially give you references (assuming you do a good job!). You should aim for having at least two work experiences to list on your résumé by the time you graduate. An on-campus job would be an excellent first work experience. If you get a couple of them under your belt during college, then if one of them is less than excellent you'll have an alternate. What if they're great but after knowing them for a year, something unforeseen goes wrong? Then you are stuck. Can you imagine if you only had one teacher in high school, and that one teacher had to write your college recommendation? That could very well had been a disaster. *Work from abundance.*

You want the same thing when it is time to apply for your first position after college. You should plan for three types of references:

- Academic (professors)
- Personal/Character
- Professional

Of these, the last will be the hardest to get. In the academic category, the same principle will apply as it did in high school: you'll have 40 professors to choose from. In the personal arena, you can use almost anyone who doesn't share your same last name. The professional references are the hardest to get due your relative lack of work experience. This is one of many reasons why the more work experience you get the better!

What Kind of Job?

There are lots of campus jobs that can do more for you than help pay the bills. Don't worry about whether they pay well or not. Almost no one's first few jobs come with a high salary! Your goals at this point are experience and networking. I thought to myself, I cannot work in the cafeteria. And even if, despite my speech issues, they would give me an RA position, that doesn't suit me at all. What else could I do? My thinking was faulty. There were so many administrative jobs on campus that I could have done. And being an RA is a great way to gain *leadership experience* (which employers love to see).

One advantage to working as an RA is fewer set shifts. Even when you are "on call," you'll be in your room, able to study or relax unless your cell rings. Contrast this to a desk job, where you would have to be at work more hours and your time there might not be your own. Desk jobs vary; with some of them you can do homework, but with some you cannot.

In doing the research for this book, I read Ms. Pollak's book. She tells her readers to become campus tour operators. A light bulb went off in my brain: What a great job for students with disabilities!

Colleges love to show that they are diverse. What better way to show this, than to have someone with a visible disability leading their tours? You might be thinking "I am too shy to do that." If you are, that is the reason why you need this job! Train the shyness right out of yourself! Shyness will hinder you with networking functions and interviews. This kind of job will help you get more comfortable interacting with lots of people and answering questions –a key interviewing skill! Your first tour probably won't go perfectly. That's okay! You'll get better with every tour. Before long you will be a master! This will give you an opportunity to practice skills when it is not crucial that you perform perfectly (or at least darn close!) the first time – as it will be when on an interview for your dream job. Depending on your school's structure, a job as a campus tour guide might give you opportunities to make connections with student government and the president's office.

This will be especially good to have as a person with a disability to prove to employers that you are capable! It is a fact of life that most people underestimate us. In my own life, I have had many experiences where I just scratch my head. This person knows I went to college, yet they are acting as if I cannot get from point A to point B by myself. Hmm, how strange! The more experiences that you get to hammer home that you are able to do what anyone else can do, the better! If you use an augmentative and alternative communication device, this is a great way to show prospective employers that you are an expert at using it to get things done! The more reassurance you give those who are interviewing you that they don't have to worry about your disability, the more likely that you will get them to see past your disability and give you the job.

How Will Having a Job as a Student Affect my SSI?

Another concern that you might have about getting a job in college is "I cannot work while I am on SSI and SSI is my sole income while I am in school." Won't working students lose SSI eligibility and their Medicaid benefits because they are now earning a paycheck? The answer is **NO**. While Social Security will count *some* of the income they earn, a great deal of it is not counted, and by working, they will come out ahead financially. There are several work incentives that SSI recipients can utilize to lower their countable earned income, thereby reducing the impact that wages have on their SSI check.

The following material is from: [12]

WHAT IS THE STUDENT EARNED INCOME EXCLUSION?

This provision allows a person who is under age 22 and regularly attending school to exclude earnings from income.

- In January 2013 the amounts we could exclude were $1,730 monthly up to a yearly maximum of $6,960.
- In January 2014 the amounts increased to $1,750 monthly up to a yearly maximum of $7,060.
- We usually adjust the monthly amount and the yearly limit annually, based on any increases in the cost–of–living index. We apply this exclusion before any other exclusion.

WHAT DOES "REGULARLY ATTENDING SCHOOL" MEAN?

"Regularly attending school" means that the person takes one or more courses of study and attends classes:

- in a college or university, for at least 8 hours a week; or
- in grades 7–12, for at least 12 hours a week; or
- in a training course to prepare for employment, for at least 12 hours a week (15 hours a week if the course involves shop practice)

Example

Jim is a student who earns $1,800 a month in June, July and August of 2013. In September, he returns to school and continues working part-time. He earns $900 a month in September through December 2013.

---

[12]From: http://www.socialsecurity.gov/ssi/spotlights/spot-student-earned-income.htm.

Using the student earned income exclusion; Jim can exclude $1,730 of his earnings in June, July and August, and can exclude all of his $900 earnings in September. Through September, Jim will use up $6,090 of his $6,960 yearly limit. Excluding $870 from his October earnings will use up his yearly limit. His remaining wages, after deducting monthly and yearly limits, will still be subject to the earned income exclusion of $65 per month and one-half of the remaining earned income.

ARE THERE ANY OTHER RULES WHICH MAY HELP?

Other SSI work incentives such as Plan to Achieve Self-Support, work expense exclusions, and continued Medicaid coverage may help an SSI beneficiary while working.

Think Logically About This

Even if you did lose some SSI money, I know from experience that SSI is not a lot. If you work on campus, you will not make a lot; if you collect SSI you will not make a lot. Working may give you a salary comparable to your SSI. If you must sacrifice SSI to work, you'll be getting a salary plus experience! Your sacrifice could increase the chances dramatically that you will be able to get a job and pull in a much higher income after college … as opposed to having to live on the very limited income of SSI after college. I wish I had made this choice.

Some of you who are reading this are still thinking "I don't have time." Many on-campus jobs are designed specifically for students. This means, among other things, that your supervisor will be cognizant of the fact that you are in school! They will know that your classes take a lot of your time. She will not expect you to work full-time and might even be flexible with you around finals. If you try a certain job and just cannot do it, it's no big deal. You will just need to give proper notice, explaining that you're falling too far behind in your classes. Give your employer the chance to start looking for a replacement.

Or, you can decide the job stays, and you are dropping one class to keep things manageable. College affords you tons of flexibility. Another way you can use this flexibility is to stay on campus to both work and take a class. I am not for college students exclusively taking classes all summer. However, if you are also working part-time, that may be a good way to ease into work/study/fun balance by starting a job when you have only one class to handle.

If you are a disability services specialist, please talk to your students about this. Again, I wish someone had told me to do this. My ideal would be that the disabled services department at colleges work with their school to place their students in jobs around campus. In my experience, disability services departments need to be more aware of the obstacles to employment that face those who they serve.

I know of no laws that make transition planning mandatory for college staff. This contrasts with high schools. I also know there are many incredible people out there who do not need a law to force them to care, or to be innovative! You can change student's lives simply by caring about this issue and speaking up about it.

Two Myths about Internships

Myth #1: "Internships are only for upperclassmen."

"Internships are only for upperclassmen." Not so at all! There are internships open to all college students. In fact, it is smart to get a "starter internship" as a freshman or sophomore. By doing this you will give yourself a better chance at getting selected for more competitive internships later on in college. Getting a more competitive internship will up your chances of getting that job you want after college/grad school.

Myth #2: "I don't need experience to get a good internship."

Common sense tells you this is not true. When deciding who will get an internship, hiring managers don't just pick names out of a hat; they look for applicants whose résumés are impressive for a student. How do you get this "impressive résumé?" You do some of the things I cover in this chapter.

Now that I have brought up internships, I suggest you read the next chapter as a freshman and start thinking about a plan.

The Case for Studying Abroad

Studying abroad is an excellent thing to be able to put on your résumé. The reason? Again, to prove to employers that you are as capable of day-to-day activities as the next guy.

You would think that people would see that you went to college and assume this. It has been my experience that many people don't connect the two. You need to help them. Employers who lack experience with those with disabilities will be impressed by your experience studying abroad. They are likely to think if you can manage living in a foreign country with your disabilities, then you are tough, ambitious, and look forward to challenges.

In addition, overseas experiences give you opportunities for personal growth. Any such experience will likely be one that you will cherish throughout your life. It will help build not only your confidence in yourself, but your appreciation for what life has to offer. Transitioning to the working world is daunting for any new college grad. If you are like me, almost any new situation is made more intimidating by my disability. If you have lived in another country and were able to problem-solve to make it a successful experience, you will feel that much stronger when it comes time to graduate to the next phase of life at home!

Starting Your Study-Abroad Journey

Starting the process of studying abroad will to a large extent mirror the steps you took to select and prepare for college. Having to plan for studying abroad might seem to inundate you with details. You find yourself questioning whether it's worth all the planning, I say resoundingly *Yes!* All good things require work and tenacity.

Just as with picking a college, you first need to narrow down where you want to go. This, again, might feel overwhelming. So many countries, so little time! For many of you, if you are open to the idea of studying abroad at all, your gut probably already has some suggestions for where to go. Factors such as having to learn the rudiments of another language, what fits in with your major, and romantic ideas about places you've always wanted to visit, will all come into play. For me, my speech is strongly impaired. That makes me want to visit an English-speaking country. This goes with my not being particularly adventurous made it quite fortunate for me that both my schools offered programs in England. Unfortunately, due to my lack of persistence, my plans fell through. I so regret not seizing the opportunity to visit a foreign country before I was out of college. I do not want you to have the same regret.

Your first step should be to talk to your school's study abroad office to see what they offer. Also, ask your department of disability services; they might have advice or guidance. My first week at Ramapo, my disability services specialist said, "I want to send you to England for your junior year." I thought *Okay, maybe, let's just get through one transition at a time.* Orientation was literally yesterday; I am still trying to get into a math class … let's not get ahead of ourselves.

Even if your disability is particularly with speech, keep in mind that there are people with disabilities in every country on the globe. Therefore, theoretically, you could go anywhere. Just like figuring out what college you wanted to attend, some options might be easier with your disability. Some options may require you to do more work and planning. You just must judge what can you do, and how badly you want to travel to a certain destination. You might decide that taking it a little easier on yourself in terms of physical and other challenges, might allow you to enjoy the aspects of the trip that are the real reasons.

Another factor you may want to consider when picking a host country is whether your target country has ratified the UN Convention on the Rights of Persons with Disabilities. At the time this book was written the UN was trying to get this treaty passed. Researching which countries might be easier from this angle may give you some insight. But again, there is no perfect country. I am sure you can think of a time when America was less than perfect for you, in terms of accessibility, attitude, or both. You found a way to make it work … as you will in your temporary host country.

When evaluating study abroad programs in terms of how disability-friendly they are, consider the following questions from the University of Exeter.[13]

- o   What accommodations do I anticipate that I will need on a study abroad experience?
- o   Do I have special housing or dietary needs? How will these be met?
- o   Do I need classroom accommodations, such as extended time on tests or note takers?

---

[13] From: http://www.exeter.ac.uk/fch/abroad/study_abroad_good_practice.pdf

- Is the program I am considering equipped to provide the academic accommodations that I need?
- Do I need specialized equipment in order to access the curriculum of the program? Will my current equipment work abroad?
- Are there physical accessibility issues that need to be worked out? How likely is it that I will be able to participate in the group activities of this program?
- How physically demanding will this program be? What if I can't meet the demands of this program?
- If you use a service animal, investigate the policies of the host country regarding the allowance of service animals into the country. Will the host country make allowances for service animals?
- Do I take medications that are illegal in my host country?
- How accessible will the transportation into and around my host country be?

Preparing for Your Adventure

After you've decided where you'd like to go, it's time to start checking off logistics from your trip countdown "to do" list. In addition to getting the appropriate visas and attire, you also need to prepare to manage your disability when abroad. In some respects, this will also feel like preparing to leave for college.

Learn Host Countries' Laws and Cultural Mores Around Disabilities

The United States is a world leader in terms of accommodating those with disabilities. The rest of the world is different. Some countries are keeping up with us, while others are lagging. I do not say this to dissuade you, but you need to know what you are in for, and how best to prepare.

You must find out what laws support you when you are in your host country. This can be done primarily through Internet research. It should be obvious that different countries have different laws. It might not be as obvious that different cultures have different mores or ideas about those with disabilities. Those differences are best ascertained by talking to those from the country you are going to. The more prepared you are, the less susceptible you will be to culture shock.

Put Together a Network of Support

As soon as you are accepted into your study abroad program, notify the program representative of specific accommodations that you anticipate needing. The more notice that they have, the better they will be able to accommodate you. Find out how your academic accommodation needs will be met and what documentation, if any, is needed for them. How do you need to go about setting up exam or notetaking accommodations once classes start?

Also, make contact with disability-related organizations in your host country in advance. They will probably be able to provide you with a wealth of information regarding laws, accessibility, mores, as well as pre-locating your "go to" people in case of challenges. If your program includes a sightseeing trip to another city, as is frequently the case, ask if they can provide you with maps of accessibility for your tourist destinations. Ask if they have or know where you could find maps of accessible bathrooms. Ask about the bathrooms so you can first finally know is this doable for you, and then what to expect. You may need to get creative, no matter how good your advance preps, but knowledge is power!

Prepare to Stay in Touch

If you go to a college in the US with a good disability services department, they will probably be helpful when you are studying abroad. Ask them if you can contact them with any concerns while abroad. As with any exchange or study abroad student, your family back at home can be a huge support, depending on the nature of the problem. Make sure you have the appropriate cell phone plan so that you are sure you can call the US from the other country and can do so without getting slammed with overages. In some instances, a pre-paid phone or calling card could be useful. With any plan or card, be sure to inquire about not only the per-minute rate, but also any connection fees.

Plan for Medical Issues

If you were to have a medical issue, it's helpful to already know where you would go to seek treatment, both for emergencies and non-emergencies. Will there be staff at your program to assist you?

Visit your primary care doctor in the States and ask for a letter describing your disability, how it impacts your health, and any other information that will help health care providers treat you when you're traveling. Have that letter translated into your host country's language. Don't just pack it; make sure it is always easily accessible to you. You might even want to write the letter for the doctor and send it via e-mail. That way the doctor could just transfer the text onto his or her own letterhead but won't have to spend time composing a letter.

Contact your insurance provider and find out what your options are to be covered during your trip. You might need to purchase a different plan or be prepared to pay for medical services with that country's currency up front, then file for reimbursement upon returning home. Your school's study abroad office/coordinator should also be able to help you resolve health insurance issues. All students should plan for such contingencies.

Medication and Other Supplies

Some medications that you take might be illegal in your host country. Find out whether that's the case in the country where you'll be studying. If your medication is illegal, will you be able to obtain an equivalent, or is it best to work with your doctor at home to switch meds way in advance of your departure?

Ideally you should bring with you enough medication for the duration of your studies. Your insurance company might balk at this. If so, ask your doctor to contact them to try to get it approved due to special circumstances. If you cannot leave with the number of meds you need to last 'til you get back, then look into receiving your medications through the mail in the country you are going to. Every country is different.

Medication should be packed in both carry-ons and (maybe) also in checked luggage, in case one or the other gets lost or damaged. Depending on your length of your program, you might want to split up supplies to guard against losing everything. If it's a shorter program, it might make sense to keep all vital medications and other supplies with you in your carry-on, the same as you would for any domestic trip. All medications need to be transported in their original, correctly labeled bottles, so that you do not run into trouble with customs or any other authorities. To be safe, you should have a letter from your doctor saying you were prescribed the exact medications that you are flying with, the exact dosages and why. Keep this letter with your medications while traveling. Again, make sure the labels all match what your letter says.

Most airlines allow passengers with disabilities to have an extra carry-on bag, provided medical supplies are in that bag. Check this with the airline in advance. Don't just take my word for it!

If you use catheters, bring whatever you need with you. Don't count on being able to buy such crucial supplies in the country you are going to. Additionally, bring vitamin C to try and lessen your chance of getting either a bladder or urinary tract infection. Consider asking your doctor for a prescription for an antibiotic in case you get one. This will depend highly on who your doctor is and your medical situation. Finally, if you are going where there's no clean running water, bring plenty of sterilization and sanitation supplies.

Preparing to Fly

International flights tend to be LONG, even if they are not nonstop. First, if you are mobility challenged, you may find it easier to make sure you have an aisle seat. Only you can make that determination, but pre-think what will be easiest for you, and reserve your seats accordingly.

For those who are concerned with pressure sores, what is your sitting plan for the flight(s)? Some flyers prefer to put their wheelchair cushion on their seat. This way they have the seating that is already designed for their needs. Others find it too bulky to sit comfortably that way for long periods of time, especially if there's turbulence and you end up being told to keep your seatbelt on for longer than usual. You might find it better to use an egg crate pad or another solution. If you really want to go all out, test this at home spending as much time in the same seat as you can, while you watch four movies back to back! Trust me, this will be much easier than what you end up with on the plane, unless you have the funds to sit in first class!

You need to plan to fly with your mobility equipment. Contact your air carrier to find out their policies, especially if you are flying with a power chair. Chairs usually must be taken apart, whether they go in the overhead bin or have to be checked and placed in the cargo compartment. You should tag each piece of your chair that will be separated with your name and contact information.

You can get a lot of great additional information at http://barrierfreetravel.net/sample.php.

Selecting Equipment

Put some thought into what mobility equipment you want to take overseas. For those who use a crutch, cane or walker, this is obviously not as serious a consideration. But there still could be an option that's either more durable or portable. Do some research. If walking long distances is difficult for you, consider bringing, shipping, or finding out where you can rent a lightweight manual wheelchair. If you are just using the chair for sightseeing, the easier it is to transport, the better. Do not miss out on the richness of the experience because you are too tired to walk!

Those who are more reliant on their wheelchairs face a tougher decision: power or manual. Here are three things to consider:

o   Is it easy to take the chair apart? If not, it could be difficult to load on and off transportation when you are traveling in your host country. Remember, the ADA is specific to America; public transit in many other countries are not required to have lifts.

- o Where are you going? Industrialized nations are much more likely to be able to accommodate your chair in terms of both accessibility and charging. If you are going somewhere more remote, a lighter chair with push handles might be more functional.

- o Are there repairs and loaner options? Again, plan for what you'll do if something goes wrong with the chair in your host country.

Once you have decided what type of chair you're taking, consider getting tires with extra tread. Again, these will be more durable. Also consider replacing your plain casters with "Frog Legs" casters; this will make it easier to navigate more difficult terrain.

Finally, just as when going to a US college, pack a wheelchair repair kit with your destination country in mind.

Charging Your Chair

Most countries of the world use electricity at 220 volts / 50 hertz. This is different than North America, Central America and parts of Japan, which use 110 volts / 60 hertz. This means many electronic devices that we use in America won't work in other parts of the world. A common complaint I hear is "Italy was fabulous, but we couldn't get our hair dryer to work anywhere." No matter how obsessed you might be with your hair, your chair is more important. Trying to charge it at the wrong voltage is almost certain to damage your chair and would probably create a fire hazard. Electrical plugs are designed to work only with an outlet of the correct voltage. NEVER try to force a plug into an outlet that it doesn't easily fit into! And if your hair dryer can handle multiple voltages, be sure that the switch is on the right setting – especially if you are traveling from country to country!

You need to plan for this by purchasing the proper voltage converter or transformer. These will allow the electricity that comes from your lodging to safely charge your chair. If your chair says it requires 110/240 volts, then it's set up to handle all the usual household voltages. In that case a converter/transformer is not needed. If the chair requires one voltage or a voltage different from 110/240, then a converter/transformer is a must!! If you are like me and are starting at this like, huh, show your dad or uncle and ask, what do I need and where do I get it!

Converters and transformers are two completely different things. Converters are generally used for appliances that are used for a shorter period. Most of the time power chairs need a transformer to charge. However, you should familiarize yourself with both and make sure you get the exact one you need!

For more information visit: http://www.miusa.org/resource/tipsheet/electricityconversion.

In order to choose the right transformer or converter, you will need to know the wattage of your equipment. Wattage refers to the amount of electricity used by a device, and this information is usually included on the label.

Another thing you should bring to make sure you have what you need to charge your chair, is a plug adapter. This has nothing to do with the type of electricity; it just will enable you to plug a three prong 110 V plug into a two-pronged 110 V outlet, if necessary. I keep one of these so-called "three into two" adapters (also known as grounding adapters) in my laptop bag because my laptop uses a three-prong plug. (Note, you will not actually get the benefits of grounding if you don't connect the little grounding tab to a grounded screw somewhere near the outlet.)

It bears repeating, do not think an adapter will work if you do not have the right voltage; it will not. Adapters, convertors and transformers are not interchangeable; do not attempt to use them as if they are.

If any of this is the least bit unclear to you, consult with an electrical expert in your area. I cannot possibly explain all the variations to all of this. I'm just letting you know that it's an issue. It's easy to deal with IF you give yourself enough time in advance before you leave for your trip abroad! One last reason to do it in advance is that you will probably find that it's much less expensive to buy what you need in the United States. Overseas vendors who sell these items know that you are up a creek without them, so they are priced accordingly!

Prepare to Mail Your Service Animal (Just Kidding – Mostly!)

Different countries have different laws regarding dogs in general, and the use of service animals. Some breeds are banned in some countries. Contact the embassy or consulate of your host country to find out what their laws or policies are. If you are visiting multiple countries, consider getting your dog certified under the Pet Passport Scheme. These can take a while to get. You may or may not need this, investigate it.

You need to bring a letter explaining that your dog is a service animal, the very basics of why you need it, and your right to have one. This letter should be on official letterhead, such as that of a doctor, and be translated into your host nation's language. This should be with you when you are out and about, so you can show any business owners that may be resistant to letting your dog in. You may also consider having your dog wear a vest that says, "Guide Dog" or "Service Dog," in order to lessen resistance from people when traveling.

It would also be very smart to get a letter from your vet stating that your dog is in good health and does not have rabies. Some countries stipulate that the veterinarian must be on an approved list of veterinarians to provide this type of documentation. Contact service animal organizations in your host country to find this out. This letter needs to be easily accessible when traveling through airports, although you probably don't need to carry it with you everywhere you go in the host country. You also need to find out if there are any re-entry requirements for your dog upon return to the US. Know what to expect in terms of going through customs.

Talk about the whole trip with your vet. Let him or her know where you are going and how long the flight is. Ask what your dog's needs might be on the trip. If the doc thinks tranquilizers will make the flight easier on your animal, consider it. Talk through whether you should take any medications with you just so that you won't have to deal with that in a foreign country.

If you are going to a warmer climate, consider shaving your dog's coat, if possible. Also brush the coat more frequently. For some dogs' booties should be used to protect their paws on hot surfaces. You also need to pack freezer packs to keep them cool. Also consider what type of collar they will wear.

If you are going to go to a colder climate, consider purchasing vests and booties that are designed to keep your dog warmer.

Again, contact your airline way in advance to find out their policies and procedures for flying with a service animal on an international flight.

Once You Get Home

There are two ways to extend your study abroad experience to make yourself a better job applicant. The first is to become truly fluent in the language of your host country (or at least as much so as you can in the time you have before and during your study abroad stay). Many students take foreign language classes and even go abroad, but do not immerse themselves enough to become fluent and able to retain the skill. Being fluent in another language can be hugely valuable when it comes to getting a job, at least if the language has anything to do with the job. Should you decide that this is a goal, look for a program that is designed for language immersion.

Two, mentor others who are preparing to go abroad. This probably will just involve emailing back and forth with them but will be both rewarding and great for your résumé.

Study Abroad Resources

Aviation Consumer Protection Division

https://www.transportation.gov/airconsumer

The toll-free hotline provides general information to consumers about the rights of air travelers with disabilities, responds to requests for printed consumer information, and assists air travelers with time-sensitive disability-related issues that need to be addressed in "real time." The line is staffed from 7 a.m. to 11 p.m. Eastern time, seven days a week. Air travelers who experience disability-related air travel service problems may call the hotline to obtain assistance. Air travelers who would like DOT to investigate a complaint about a disability issue must submit their complaint in writing or via e-mail.

Aviation Consumer Protection Division
400 7th St. SW
Washington, D.C. 20590
United States
Phone: 800-778-4838
TTY: 800-455-9880
Email: airconsumer@ost.dot.gov

Benjamin A. Gilman International Scholarship Program

http://www.iie.org/Programs/Gilman-Scholarship-Program

Provides scholarships for U.S. citizen undergraduate students of limited financial means and diverse backgrounds to pursue academic studies in non-traditional study abroad destinations. American students can receive up to $5,000 to pursue overseas study for college credit. Students studying critical need languages are eligible for up to $3,000 in additional funding as part of the Gilman Critical Need Language Supplement program.

Gilman Scholarship Program
Institute of International Education
1800 West Loop South, Suite 250
Houston, TX 77027

Critical Language Scholarship (CLS) Program

https://www.clscholarship.org/

The CLS program provides overseas foreign language instruction and cultural enrichment experiences in 13 critical need languages for U.S. students in higher education. Undergraduate, master's and doctoral-level students of diverse disciplines and majors are encouraged to apply.

Critical Language Scholarship Program
American Councils for International Education
1828 L Street N.W., Suite 1200
Washington, D.C. 20036

Phone: 202-833-7522
Email: advisors@clscholarship.org

Fulbright U.S. Student Program

http://www.iie.org

The Fulbright U.S. Student Program provides grants for individually designed study/research projects or English Teaching Assistantships in a country outside the U.S. Applicants for the Fulbright U.S. Student Program include recent graduates, masters and doctoral candidates, and young professionals.

U.S. Student Programs Division
809 United Nations Plaza
New York, NY 10017-3580
Phone: 212-984-5525

Fulbright-Fogarty Fellowships

(See above)

The Fulbright-Fogarty Fellowships provide medical students and graduate students interested in global health the opportunity to conduct research in public health and clinical research in resource-limited settings. Fellows spend nine months in one of twelve countries in Sub-Saharan Africa, Asia or South America.

Fulbright Canada Science, Technology, Engineering and Math (STEM) Award

(See above)

The Fulbright Canada STEM Award offers U.S. students support for three years of doctoral study at one of six leading Canadian research universities.

National Clearinghouse on Disability and Exchange

http://www.miusa.org/ncde

A comprehensive one-stop resource for people with disabilities, exchange and disability staff interested in study, work, intern, volunteer, research or teach abroad programs, a project sponsored by the U.S. Department of State.

Join, Join, Join

Joining clubs in college is a must! The more you do this, the more you will get out of college.

There is a recurring theme in this chapter: *résumé*. Just as you needed to join clubs in high school to stand out, the same is true during college. The more clubs and organizations you participate in, the more contacts you'll make! You never know when one of these relationships will end up helping you.

It should be your goal to be involved in multiple activities each year that you are in college. Naturally you won't be equally committed to all of them. With some groups, you will be a casual attendee where you only go to events that interest you, but you know what is going on. In other groups you will choose to become an active member, where you put in efforts to advance the group at least a couple of times a year. Just because you join something does not mean that you need to attend everything they sponsor. It is all about figuring out which activity would benefit you most in that time space (even if it is *sleeping*).

You should join everything affiliated with both your major department and its college (if you are going to a university with multiple colleges). I majored in Management Information Systems (MIS), which was part of the College of Business at my university. I joined the MIS club; however, I was merely a casual attendee. If I had it to do over again, I would have become an officer in the club, showing that I'm not afraid to be of service to others.

Be a Leader

Don't be shy, run for office in one or two of your active attendee clubs. You have nothing to lose! If you don't get elected, there are plenty of worse things in that could happen in life. Then try out again with another organization or position in student government.

Have confidence that you will be able to work around your disability to be just like any other well-intentioned campus leader working as best they can. Employers look for "can do" people, being a leader exemplifies that you are one of those people. Refer to the chart in the previous chapter on what skills are most sought after in recent college graduates. Most or all of them you will need to both use and improve by being a leader! When employers see a leadership tittle on your résumé, they will begin to assume that you have these skills. This will get you an interview. At the interview, you can then talk positively about your leadership to further convince them that you are able to meet their needs.

Again, as with many of the suggestions in this book, think about the timing. You do not want to rush into anything the second week of school. Yet, waiting 'til senior year is not optimal either. If you get a position in your last semester of senior year, you will not have much time to make an impact that you can boast about. Also, in your final semester of school you may be busy with both jobs hunting as well as extra work for your capstone classes.

When deciding which clubs to prioritize and go for being an officer, consider three things in this order of importance:

- How high a priority is the area in which this organization works?

- Is the structure of the organization conducive to you being your effective?

- How much networking potential will the position really offer you?

Spend your first year analyzing potential opportunities using these questions. If you "click" with the other officers and the advisor, if they are actively involved, and the club has good attendance, you will get the most out of your service because these factors will make it easier for you to get things done.

Also, serving as an advisor of a club that you worked well with for two or three years can then transition into a great personal reference. After you first year, start running for positions! Should you not get the first one that you run for, no big deal. You will have about two full years to rack up some achievements in this area without it interfering with getting acclimatized to school or wrapping up your graduation requirements.

Not everything has to go perfectly for you to reap the rewards of your efforts. Let's say you are doing the best you can in a club, but you are challenged by low attendance rates and an advisor who lets you know in subtle ways that he is not thrilled by having a president with disabilities. This happened to me in college. It was still a positive experience overall! I got lots out of my service as president of my residence hall. I got to list it on my résumé and talk positively about what I accomplished on interviews.

Leading Will Be a Dry Run

Equally important, as "resident president" I gained confidence that I could be an effective leader with my disability. I saw two challenges when I started the position. First, I could not make large posters with markers. This issue was easily resolved: when I asked who wanted to run for vice president elections, I specifically stated that making signs would be among the duties. I then checked to make sure signs were out when they needed to be. When they were, I always thanked or complimented the VP. Once they were not, and I nicely reminded the VP. Problem solved.

I also faced the issue of running meetings with a speech impairment. Again, I confronted this head-on at the first meeting. I said, "If you have trouble understanding me, raise your hand. I'll be happy to repeat myself. If the flow of the meeting gets slowed too much, then next time we'll have a PowerPoint so you can read along." Then I injected some humor, asking them to repeat what I just said. "Okay, mike check, I mean speech check, completed, and we are good."

By getting this experience and successfully doing oral presentations in my courses, I gained assurance that I could communicate effectively during both job interviews and work meetings. No matter what your disability is, being a leader will give you practice on how to compensate for it to get the job done! You need this. When you report to a job, there won't be any a teacher or therapist to figure out how best to get you to achieve your goals. Your employer is required to grant you reasonable accommodations to perform the essential functions of your job. I will cover this in later chapters. But it is going to be solely on you to figure out what you need to effectively do your job and make that arrangement work for your supervisor. Put yourself in the supervisor's position. You got work that must get done. You would not appreciate being hamstrung, stuck with someone who can't do the job, would you? No matter how sympathetic you might be to the person's plight, if they can't get the job done, eventually you are going to have to let them go. This is the same as with anyone else!

Ideally, I would have gotten a reference as an additional perk for serving in the role I described above. As I said before, you very rarely get everything you set out for. The position is listed on my résumé; when asked about it, I leave out the detail that the advisor didn't treat me well. If asked, I can simply say "I do not have her current contact information. Here is my reference sheet which has up-to-date contact information for people whom I have either worked with or know me." This is the truth; I did not bother to stay in touch with someone who I did not think would give me a good reference. Having to work with all different types of people is part of life. You will run into people who you do not click with, are rude or sometimes downright mean.

The key is, when you are a leader, to accomplish something. If you have "president" listed for a bunch of organizations on your résumé, some prospective employers will see through this. Try and get just three such positions and give them everything you've got!

If you are still too shy or time-pressed to run for an officer position in a club, that's okay! You can still get some leadership experience by simply volunteering to lead a project or two that you are assigned in your courses. Serving as leader of a group project during the final year of your major will look more impressive than taking some class unrelated to the types of jobs you plan on applying for. However, anything is better than nothing!

Think About Doing Something "Disability-Related"

This is for two reasons. The first is about you. It might be extraordinarily helpful for you to network with both older professionals with disabilities and "disability champions." The main reason is that it's not what you know, it's who you know, when it comes to getting your first internship or job. Older folks with disabilities might very well have faced the same challenges, or even worse ones, when entering the workforce. They may be the best source of advice.

The second reason has to do with your future potential employers. If you have an invisible disability, the wisdom is not to put anything disability-related on your résumé. When one has a visible disability, I say ignore that wisdom. If they are going to be able to see you using a chair or whatever other manifestation applies to you, you are going to need to do what you can to make them comfortable with that. During an interview you are frequently asked to expand on what is on your résumé. By having one disability-related activity on your résumé, you are creating a chance to talk with an employer *positively* about your having a disability. This will help the employer become comfortable with your disability. This can only help *you* get the job that you are qualified for.

If you do not join a club, you cannot list it on a résumé; so, join up. Join whatever is the closest match for your career interests!

Start a Club

This will show employers that you possess initiative and leadership skills. All schools have procedures in place, should any student want to start a new club on campus. Start this endeavor by either going to your student affairs office or online to find out what your school's procedures are. It can be anything you are interested in, if you want to start a Finding Bigfoot club – do it!

One exception: if you are a hard-core activist with anything that might turn off future employers, or makes you come off as angry, *leave it off your résumé*. Now, you can certainly BE a hard-core activist who starts a grassroots organization and angry about the opposition to your cause. You just cannot list it, or you need to be very careful about how you list it, on your résumé.

Not everything you are going to achieve during college belongs on your résumé. It's okay to be involved in clubs and organizations for your own reasons. You'll need to decide whether résumé-building or feeding your passion is your goal about an organization. There is no right answer; the ideal compromise is something that fulfills both!

Whether the club that you start relates to a disability issue is your call. There is no right or wrong answer or way of feeling. One advantage to being involved in a disability-related club is that you can open the door to conversation about it on an interview. The law forbids prospective employers from asking about your disability in an interview. This is good for those with "invisible disabilities." This is not good for me. My disability is very visible. I know people wonder about it when they see me. It has been my experience that I can do more than people think I can do. If they would just ask me, I could explain.

In all aspects of my life I strive to put people at ease with my disability. Why should an interview be any different? Because of this I wish the law were less stringent. However, like everyone else, I cannot write my own laws. I just try to raise the issue in a way that I feel will serve my goal of getting them to see past it!

If you are living on campus and are dependent on PCA care, a great way to serve is to start a mentor program on campus for those who are coming to campus who also need such services. This will involve you asking your Disability Services Department to refer newly admitted freshmen with PCA needs to you, giving them your email address or phone number. Talk them through using a PCA on campus and let them know that when they get to campus you will be available to counsel them on how it is going. Make it known that the program only provides resources, advice and peer counseling; it is not a backup PCA, should one's scheduled attendant not show up, or quit. Tell them you can listen and make suggestions, but you cannot send someone over to do their care. This probably will not take up much of your time as you will probably only get one or two people at a time. If you get a greater number of students, you could set things up so that going into their freshman and sophomore years, people who need a mentor get one, but then they need to serve as a mentor in their junior and senior years.

If you want to expand this to other schools in your area, great! When you are getting close to graduation, hand the program off to another student who you feel can keep it going. Another key aspect of leading is being able to hand off what you've started.

This would be an invaluable asset to this population on most campuses. I also feel that if you list it on your résumé, it will open the door for your prospective employer to ask you "I see that you founded (name of program), tell me about that." *Boom*, the door is open for you to talk about how you are in complete control of managing your needs – so much so that you have taught others how to do it!

It's not fair, but some hiring managers will wonder "Can she really get to work every day?" If you need assistance in the morning in your home, will you be calling in sick if your attendant can't make it? By talking about this issue, you can overtly put the manager at ease, letting him or her know that you basically have things under control, and your disability will not cause frequent absences. It is also a way to say that you've gained management skills in a non-traditional way, by managing others who provide your care for however many years.

As in my last suggestion illustrates, you might or might not start a traditional club. You might start a service or a campaign for campus change. Please refer to page 51 to read about the Workforce Recruitment Program and starting one on your campus.

You could even start a group that will work on the principles in this book regarding preparing for life after college. Meet once a month to discuss how the members can incorporate some ideas from this book into their lives. The members can discuss what has worked for them, and brainstorm as a group to find solutions to challenges people are having. Make it informal and fun; if it goes off-topic for a while, that's okay! Most parenting groups do not talk about *only* parenting. However, they are a group of people supporting each other in the same goal of raising kids. If you start this group it would be an excellent project to work towards bringing the WRP to your campus together.

Attention Departments of Disability Services

If you work in disability services, I think it will be a great help to your students to start monthly meetings with the primary focus of career planning and job hunting. I attended a large university with a fairly large population of students with disabilities. Yet, the only group for us on campus was geared more toward disability studies. This was not anything I cared about or found relevant in my own life. I would go to try to network yet did not feel I got anything out of it. Unemployment is rampant amongst adults with disabilities. Why aren't colleges doing more about it? When the AIDS crisis was at its peak, colleges and universities sprang into action, rightfully so, to emphasize prevention to their students. I feel this is "our" crisis and it is not being addressed at the collegiate level.

Spring Break

You are going to get only four or maybe five spring breaks. Think ahead about how you really want to use them. You basically have three choices, relaxation, active partying, or service. I suggest you use one for service. The program at my first school was called "alternative spring break." A lot of schools have programs where they offer their students the chance to go somewhere and volunteer. Now, you do not have to do this all four or five years! I know my first spring break, my mom walked in, and I said, "Mom, I am sick of everything, can we hit the mall and go home?" She replied, "That was the plan: retail therapy and then a week break, you'll feel better."

If you are having a spring semester where all you want is your own bed, to go to sleep, and know the fire alarm will not go off because someone dared someone else to set it off, that is okay! In fact, it is good if you are using the break as you most need it. And if you opt to go home, you can still make good use of your time without working more than an hour a day.

In my second year of college, I'd been more able to go somewhere other than home. My third year, again I wanted to go home despite things on campus going remarkably better. Since I transferred, I had not been home or seen family. At that point, that was the longest period I had ever been gone. My fourth and fifth spring break, I could have and should have done volunteer work! My fourth year, instead of moping around my empty dorm thinking "Poor me, I can't afford to go anywhere," I should have investigated how I could get a free trip somewhere, help others, and get the experience onto my résumé. You just need to decide when it makes the most sense to do what. For more information go to: http://www.alternativebreaks.org/

Regardless of when you take a break, it can be a wonderful time for you to either research opportunities such as internships, study abroad programs or scholarships that you plan on pursuing in the next year or two – or apply for the ones you've already found.

Spring Break Is Not the Only Time to Volunteer

Almost any work or volunteer experience looks good on your résumé, so if you have a chance to volunteer on or off campus, take it. The nice things about volunteer jobs are that you can always get one, and you are able to work as much or as little as you want. It will be a bonus if you can get volunteer work that will build your skills in the area where you want a career. Sometimes, volunteering with something that relates to your field, where you are making connections, is a better use of your time and effort than paid work! You need to consider all factors and pick the opportunities which will give you the most of what you value.

You can even volunteer from home in a wide array of areas. If you have a summer in college where you are battling health problems or dealing with family issues or just feeling burned out, as I said in the last chapter, it is okay to do less, and it is not okay to not do anything. Go to

http://www.volunteermatch.org/.

Some schools give you a long winter break in that you get off mid-December and do not go back until the beginning of February. Take from the end of the finals through New Year's to enjoy yourself. This is a longer break than you got in high school. Then during January spend just a few hours a week online volunteering, researching summer plans. If you do that then you are doing awesome!

Apply, Apply, Apply

Scholarships are great because they reduce or eliminate the cost of your education. However, winning awards also have other benefits that are less thought off. One, they will look good listed on your résumé. Employers want to hire top students! If they see a scholarship, academic award on your résumé, it will make them think you did well in school. By applying for and winning scholarships you are not only helping pay for school; you are increasing your chance of getting a (good) job.

Some scholarship programs such as Google or TRIO do not only give money; they also offer internships to their recipients. This is great! The earlier you get hooked into an arrangement such as this, the better. Seek this out! If you know you want to work for a company, see if they have a scholarship program. If a company gives you money for school, they are more likely to hire you! They will want return on their investment.

Network, Network, Network

When it comes to getting interviews, the old saying is true: *It's not _what_ you know, it's _who_ you know.* Studies show that more people find jobs by networking than any other method.

As in anything else in life, do not wait until you need to job hunt to start networking. The earlier you start the better! Anyone that you know could lead you to the contact that lands you that all-important first job that launches your career... And I mean everyone, try and involve your whole family, friends or co-workers of your parents/siblings, neighbors, your friends' families, your doctors, etc. Don't be shy about trying to explain your situation and ask for advice! One rule of networking is, ask for advice and introductions, not for a job! Another rule: talk to as many people as you can, whether it is at a career-related event or in your daily life.

The idea of networking may be counterintuitive. Many people with disabilities have experienced instances throughout their lives where those around them act as if they need more help than they do. If this has happened to you, you might have developed a hyperactive sense of independence. If this describes you, it is my suggestion that you change how you look at it. It is not wise for anyone to go through the process of getting a job alone.

Why would you be any different? Again, more jobs are found through networking than any other method. You need to apply a litmus test of what your peers without disabilities are receiving help with to decide if you are being reasonable or not in wanting to "do it yourself." You better believe that all successful people have received assistance with their career goals. Be it having someone look over your résumé before it goes out or getting an internship through their dad's neighbor. Everyone gets help to navigate through life!

It's a numbers game. For every ten conversations you have about this, maybe nine will go nowhere … but then that tenth person will give you that golden contact!

If you have a relative who works anywhere in a field of interest to you, enlist their help ASAP! Ask for an unpaid internship. If you don't ask, they probably won't think to ask you out of the blue whether you are interested. They might not even know of internships available at their workplace. I wish I had done this my first year of college! Said, "anything you can do for me is great! Of course, at this point, I do not expect to be paid."

While you are in school it is never too early to start finding out about your classmates and their families. The more people you know, the better! As shallow as it sounds, I wish someone had told me to try and seek out friends from higher-achieving families. I would not limit your contacts exclusively to such people, but it stands to reason that they are the ones who will usually be able to connect you with better jobs than people outside such circles. Even if it doesn't work out that way, it never hurts to have more (quality) friends.

 From time to time your professors will bring in a guest speaker. If you feel a connection to the speaker or at least the topic, go up after class and introduce yourself. Ask for their business card, and then follow up with an email within 48 hours. Re-introduce yourself, express gratitude for the lecture, and ask if you can keep touch with them as you progress from student to professional.

Previously I said you should try to form professional relationships with at least five of your professors during your college years. Do not limit yourself to professors whose courses you take. I blew an opportunity by not accepting an invitation to dinner with my dorm faculty fellow. There was a sign-up sheet at the front desk. I should have signed up. My reason for not doing so was stupid. If the dinner had led nowhere, so what? Nothing lost except an hour.

Another way you should start networking in college is by joining professional organizations. This can be invaluable not just for networking but also gaining extra skills that could help give you the edge you need to get the job that you want. Go to meetings both to network and acquire extra skills. These are going to be organizations that are targeted toward experienced professionals, so your role as a student will probably be to learn rather than lead. However, being involved will often prove to be no less valuable than with on-campus activities. When you go to a meeting or an event, dress and act like a professional, not a college student. These organizations can be networking gold mines!

Keep in touch with all contacts and never throw away your contact list. When you do land your first job, contact everyone your list to let them know the good news. You will never know when you will need or want to find another job, hence you will never stop needing your network. And you never know when you might be called upon to return a favor someone has done you. They need to know where you are working now, otherwise they won't know that you might be just the person that their nephew needs to get a leg up.

Networking Resources

General

Delphi Forums

http://www.delphiforums.com/

With more than 10 million registered members and more than a million new messages posted per week, Delphi is one of the leading networks of member-managed online communities. Delphi's services enable individuals to build, manage and grow their own online communities.

LinkedIn

http://www.linkedin.com/

Strives to make your existing network connections more powerful. LinkedIn lets you see the whole network of people you can reach through your trusted friends, and search for the contacts you need to get business done. If your 20 connections each connected with 20 more of their own, you would be able to make contact with more than 150,000 professionals. LinkedIn enables users to make deals, as well as find employees, industry experts, jobs, and contracts by making contact with the right professionals. Your friends introduce you to their friends, and they introduce you to the people you want to contact.

MeetUp Groups

http://www.meetup.com/

Helps people get together with a group of neighbors who share a common interest (46,315 groups and 4.7 million are part of Meet up). The site helps users self-organize global, monthly "Meet up Days" -- local group gatherings on the same day everywhere -- for almost any interest group. Meatus take place in up to 3,600+ cities at local cafés, restaurants, bookstores, and other local establishments.

Net Party

https://www.linkedin.com/company/netparty---the-worldwide-young-professionals-network

Net party functions as the entry point for a network of parties held in 17 U.S. cities, aimed at professionals in their 20s and 30s. The events, held at stylish clubs, are designed to combine business networking with social fun.

Professional Organizations and Associations for Networking

Since thousands of professional organizations are available, the best resources in this area are tools that help you find professional organizations and associations in your field that you can attend/join for successful career networking.

Power Lunch!
[No known website]

> Seeks to enhance networking capabilities by matching an individual seeking a specific type of information with an expert in that field. Capitalizes on the concept "it is not what you know, but who you know." Activities are currently limited to the Washington, DC area; plans to expand nationally.

> Ellie Wegener, Executive Officer
> c/o The Employment Support Center
> 900 Massachusetts Ave. NW, No. 444
> Washington, DC 20001
> Phone: 202-783-4747

Quintessential Careers
http://www.quintcareers.com/professional_organizations.html

> This webpage provides a list of still *other* lists of professional organizations. The website provides a treasure trove of job resources.

Student Mentor
http://StudentMentor.org

> Through StudentMentor.org's innovative national mentoring program based on its pioneering technology platform, college students can conveniently find and collaborate with mentors from diverse industries and professions to achieve their academic and career goals.

Toastmasters International
https://www.toastmasters.org/

> While not strictly a networking organization, Toastmasters enables members to build confidence by speaking to groups and working with others in a supportive environment.

> Toastmasters International
> PO Box 9052
> Mission Viejo, CA 92690
> Phone: 949-858-8255
> FAX: 949-858-1207

U.S. Junior Chamber of Commerce (JAYCEES)
http://jciusa.org/

The Jaycees describe themselves as "the organization of choice for men and women 21-39 years of age who want the best opportunities for leadership development, volunteerism and community service."

4 West 21st Street
Tulsa, OK 74114-1116
Phone: 918-584-2481
Fax: 918-584-4422
Phone: 800-JAY-CEES

Points to Remember from Chapter 7

✓ Whether it is joining, leading, working on campus or studying abroad, just do it!! Do not be intimidated; if something doesn't work out, no big deal. All you need to do is keep putting yourself out there and then that brilliant résumé or grad school application will all but write itself!

✓ It really does come down to who you know in the end. College is a vital opportunity to NETWORK! Do not waste it.

✓ The approach that this book takes to college is good for any student, regardless of what their disability status happens to be. Good jobs are getting harder and harder to get, especially for new grads. Anything that can be done to build a strong résumé, you should do. The advice is in these chapter is even more important for you as a person with disabilities!

✓ Discrimination still does exist. Even more prevalent than blatant discrimination is the 'Oh gosh, I just don't know,' thinking. Do you know how you beat the 'Oh gosh, I just don't know,' and get the job? By having the strongest résumé. It is really that simple. If you want something, go after it. Same for your counterparts without disabilities.

Chapter 8: Internships Are THE Pathway to Jobs!

Top Ten Reasons to Intern Your Way to Success

10) Expand your network: every contact you make could be that one who helps you out upon graduation!

9) Possible way to earn college credit!

8) Possible way to earn some money!

7) The best way to gain new skills!

6) Test-drive your career plans. If you hate your original idea, there's still time to change your major!

5) Gain motivation. A great internship will give you fuel to keep going hard in school!

4) Nothing looks better on your résumé!

3) Nothing will give you more confidence.

2) Possible in at a company: A 2008 study conducted by the National Association of Colleges and Employers (NACE) found that, "Not only does participation in an internship make the student a more attractive candidate," says NACE Executive Director Marilyn Macke, "but it can also be an avenue to a job." NACE's 2008 Experiential Education Survey shows that hiring from the intern program is growing."

1) Employers increasingly want to see experience in the new college grads they hire. A staggering 95% of employers said candidate experience is a factor in hiring decisions, according to an annual survey by the National Association of Colleges and Employers (NACE) nearly half of surveyed employers wanted new-grad experience to come from internships or co-op programs. If you have completed internships, you will clearly have an edge over your classmates who haven't. [14]

---

[14] Adapted From: http://www.quintcareers.com/internship_importance.html

What's Better Than an Internship? Two or Three Internships!

If you do multiple internships in college, they can either be with the same company or different companies. There are pluses and minuses either way. If you intern somewhere during the summer after your sophomore year and the employer invites you back the next summer, that means there is a good chance they'll extend a job offer to you upon graduation. Considering this, do not be afraid to do internships with the same company.

On the other hand, having varied experiences will offer you a chance to find out what you want, extend your skillset, and meet more people. The more people that you meet, the more networking connections that you will have.

Internships for Those with Disabilities?

Just as with scholarships, there are internship programs specifically designed for students with disabilities. I list these later in this chapter. I regret not doing an internship for people with disabilities. The company where I did my first internship was small; it did not have a full internship program, in the sense that support after the internship was not available from them.

Internships with larger organizations such as Entry Point or Emerging Leaders offer more support afterwards in finding a job. Participating in a program that's designed to transition students with disabilities from being interns into being employees gives you a better shot at getting a good job after college.

I had vaguely heard of Entry Point and I knew there was something in Washington for "disabled college kids." However, I did not bother to investigate to find out the particulars. I made the mistake of throwing the baby out with the bath water. I did not want anything to do with anything for those with disabilities. When I was in college, I resented my past because so much stuff "for the disabled" was forced on me and I always hated it! I was in college now, I was grown, no one could force me to do "that stuff" anymore.

I did not realize that it's not all the same. If there is a program that helps you get what you value from life, use it! Using it does not mean you need to take part in anything else that does not give you what you value. Sounds obvious, but I wish that I came to that realization earlier. I should had found out more prior to deciding whether I wanted to apply to some of internships targeting students with disabilities!

With all that said, you are in no way limited to internships for students with disabilities. Investigate and find every opportunity that interests you. Apply to all of them!

Completing each application process takes time. That is one of the reasons that I suggest that you to take one less class than what is considered a full load – and use your "breaks" wisely. Ideally, just as with college, you will have your choice of internship to attend, because you've applied to several that would be acceptable.

My Journey

Both of my parents found me internships for the same summer. I had been working with my father to get our first choice of an internship for me. I didn't get it. My mom also talked to people she worked with and they offered to have me as an unpaid intern for the summer. Then one morning I was getting ready for class; my phone rang. It was dad saying, "Plan B worked! My neighbor said she'll hire you for the summer and it pays ten dollars an hour."

I considered several factors and chose to work for my dad's neighbor. I had a gut feeling that it would work out better. This was mainly because the company did the same type of work that I wanted to do after college (management consulting). Additionally, being able to walk (okay, wheel) to work, seemed like a bigger perk than my salary! I wasn't looking forward to having to having to try and drive to work every day with a stressed-out parent. I was right to consider what was going on in my life and my parents' lives, and factor all that into my decision.

Paid vs. For-Credit

Approximately half of internships in the US are unpaid. Some for-credit internships do offer a small stipend for either housing or transportation. For-credit internships are frequently arranged by your school, but you must apply. Just as with jobs, there are only so many slots and the best ones fill up first.

If you want credit for your internship, you need to arrange this with your school before your first day as an intern. Schools do let students find their own internships and if various conditions are met, receive credit for them. However, the intern site and/or supervisor will need to be approved beforehand. In addition, there will need to be a faculty contact and probably a paper to write, regular meetings with the faculty member to discuss progress toward your learning objectives, or both.

For me, I had no need to get academic credit for my internship. I already had enough credits to graduate. I was still enrolled in college because I had not completed all the required courses for my degree. I knew my program was not going to say, "Do an internship instead of the courses you still need." Hence, there would have been no point in doing extra work to get credits from my internship. I did the internship because I needed work experience, new skills, and contacts for after graduation.

Start with the End in Mind

You need to define what you most want out of your internship. Out of all considerations, I say that salary should rank last. Ask yourself these questions:

> ➤ Do I know what I want to do after college? Do I want my internship to help me discover that? Or do I already have a defined career goal which I want my internship to give me a pathway towards?

> ➤ What do I want the rewards of my internship to be? Work experience, credit, some money or a job offer?

> ➤ Do I want a full- or part-time internship? Do I want it to be during my school year while I am also taking classes? Do I want to take a semester where I do a co-op full time and then return to campus next semester to finish my degree requirements? (Some schools and companies have programs structured this way; ask your school.) Do I want to do a summer internship? Summer internships are the most common, but don't rule anything out without knowing all of your options.

> ➤ Do you need your internship to either be by your school or your home during the summer or can you temporally relocate? Most internships don't offer relocation help.

> ➤ Do you want a program for students with disabilities or not? Do you feel a program geared to student with disabilities better will help you get a job post-graduation?

Ways to Find an Internship

Through Your School

No matter what internship you end up doing, one of the first stops on your journey needs to be your school's career services department. I have lost count of how many times in the last few chapters that I told you to go to your school's career services department. Point made; I hope! You pay for these services every semester through your tuition; get your money's worth. You don't have to accept every piece of advice offered, but it is vital to find out what it is that you are saying yes or no to.

Your professors are also a potentially great resource; use them! The great thing about college professors is that at least half of them have worked in the profession that now they are teaching. This means they have lots of contacts. If you have identified a certain workplace that you hope will pick you up after college, ask those professors that you have identified as knowledgeable if they have any contacts or information that could get you an internship there. This is an excellent way to both use and further the "five out of forty" rule that I spoke of in Chapter Six. It's time to start leveraging the relationships that you have been building with your professors.

The last department that you need to talk to at your school regarding internships is, you guessed it, your department of disabilities services. Another mistake I made was never making an appointment with the staff member that I knew had something to do with promoting Entry Point. If I could go back and do college over again, I would have made an appointment with her and asked for her advice. I might still have ended up doing the internship that I did. Who knows? But at least I would have better explored my options.

To be fair, the Disability Resource Center could have also done a better job. They could have held an information session once a semester on this topic and make sure that it was well-publicized. I think that if I had gone into the DRC and seen a flyer or a sign or received an e-mail after having signed up to get such notices, just as so many other college events are advertised, I would have attended one of those sessions. I am saying this because I am trying to inspire college professionals who work with students with disabilities to promote employment readiness! Again, I take responsibility for my choices; I should not have needed a flyer or an email. I should have been more proactive and thought to make an appointment. However, I feel it would be such a positive change if colleges start offering information to their student.

My cousin's experience helps further illustrate that asking around and being involved with your major's faculty works when it comes to getting an internship. She asked during sophomore year but did not get anything career related. She ended up lifeguarding again. In her junior year, she asked again; that time she got an internship in her field that summer. After she graduated, she got a job offer in her field! Although she is younger than me, I truly wish I had been as on top of everything as she was.

It's the Network

This is the way I got both of my internships. Both of my internships came from my network. Actually, they both came from my dad's business connections. Yes, your parents are part of your network! Do not forget it! Do not be above using their help! After all, in many cases they have been your biggest supporters since birth. It's natural for parents to want to help their adult kids with whatever comes up, to the extent that they can. When getting help from your parents, you also need to act as an adult. For example, if your dad says you need to fax your résumé somewhere, do it. Don't make him nag you.

It is perfectly fine to do an internship where one of your parents works, if you feel that is your best option. Should it work for you to ride to work with them, that's fine too. Not all college students can afford a car. Not all people with disabilities are able to drive. But, set your own alarm for in the morning! Your parents should not be making you get out of bed and get in the car with them because they need to get to work, the way they did when you were in grade school. Whatever issues come up at your internship, leave mom or dad out of it. Don't pull rank; it will sour the relationship and defeat the purpose of your doing the internship. (This of course is unless you are working directly for one of your parents, or you are dealing with a truly irrational situation.)

Email Blasts

A lot of us do not have parents who can get us internships. This is why, by the time you are in college, your network should already extend way beyond your parents and family. This is where you employ the blast email technique. It should go something like this:

"Dear Friends and Family *or* Dear Team of Allies."

The second salutation might be preferable. After all, and the list of recipients can include professors, guest speakers who spoke in your courses that you were smart enough to save their contact info, your favorite teachers or other staff from high school, people you met at networking events, neighbors/ex neighbors, medical professionals that you've gotten to know, your hairdresser or if you attend any place of worship, people you know from there. These might not all be in the category of friends or family for you. But they are in your network and you should send all of them your blast email. So, either start the email with "Dear Team of Allies" or just "Hello."

As many of you know I am graduating from _____ with a degree in _____ next <spring, fall, whatever> of _____ . I am currently looking to do an internship in—this upcoming summer. My ideal internship would meet the following criteria:

- Paid/unpaid/don't care

- Geographic area

- Specific skill(s) you want to use/learn further or are looking to work in any specific area of your field, e.g., K-2 education, social work with those recovering from addiction, or supply chain management.

I am emailing you because I know each of you have varied experiences and may have either advice or know of someone who is looking for a hard-working intern. If you have any leads, I would very much appreciate hearing back from you. Thank you for your time and your thoughts.

Sincerely,

<Your Name>

The idea is to send this to as many people that you can think of! I feel that it is ok to do it as a blast email, meaning send the same email to lots people at the same time.

Should You Include a Résumé?

I believe that at this stage, it's too early to send out your résumé. People who have a serious lead for you will reply and request your résumé. This is good, because you want to know who is actively helping you. If they just forward your résumé on without talking to you about it, you won't know that they did that.

Obviously, when you send out your blast email, you should have a résumé ready to send to anyone who asks for it. Do not send this e-mail blast thinking you'll throw together a résumé real fast if you need to. Take things in the right order. You're going to want at least two good proofreaders to go over your résumé before you consider it ready to send out. I know I sound like a broken record but plan ahead with this. Otherwise you are wasting some of your efforts – as well as the efforts of some of those in your network who are trying to help you!

It has been my experience that it is not possible to throw together a quality résumé quickly, especially if you've never done one before. In my first year of college I had an assignment in a computer class to create a résumé using Microsoft Word templates. The data could all be made up. I thought to myself, "This'll be easy." I grew up using a computer; I know how to use Word. I figured it would take an hour or two. Six hours later, I wanted to throw my computer through the window. It can be tricky to work with résumé templates, and it will probably take some time.

When you are creating your first résumé, it's natural to be concerned about the shortness of your work history. Your career services office can help you with your details.

The point here is that you need to give yourself time to figure out both the content and the mechanics of a good résumé. Have it ready and reviewed by several trustworthy people before you send out your e-mail blast.

A good response rate on your e-mail blast is 40%. Do the math: if you want to be sure of getting two or three good offers, you probably need about a dozen responses. This means you need to send your e-mail blast to 30 people. It will take time to reply to every reply; but make time for this as well.

This is a good activity to take on in late January. If you are still off in late January, perfect. If not, do your résumé during winter break. Start your new semester, then a couple weeks in, you will have a lull in your workload. This will be after the new semester rush but before you need to study hard for midterms. I think spring break is a bit late to be doing this. You'll miss out on some opportunities, for the upcoming summer, if you wait that long.

Internship Success 101

Your Mission: Produce

This starts with you reading a job description of what is expected of you. Ask if they can give you one when they offer you an internship. Let's say your job as an intern is to design a prototype for a department's internal website so those in that department will use the website to accomplish daily tasks. From this you can make a goal by the end of your internship you want to have documented, what was wrong with the existing website from the employer's point of view. You can do this by surveying to find out what the problems are causing the site not to be used. Save these, design a prototype that specifically fixes the most common reasons why it is not being used. Upon submitting or implementing your prototype, get feedback and find a way to measure that you've increased site usage? Print out all changes. If you increased visitors to site daily; that is also a measurable goal that you achieved.

By looking at your job description, and then setting your goals, you can make it more likely that the goals you set are within your power to reach. Keep goals specific to your job. Don't try to make large changes to the company; it won't work, and in the attempt, you will annoy people who have been there for far longer than you!

Meet with Supervisor(s)

On your first day as an intern your supervisor will introduce themselves. They will need to show you around and give you something to do. If you're lucky, you'll get a tour and some type of orientation.

If the supervisor doesn't tell you when you will be expected to meet with them to review your work and get new assignments, it's a good idea to ask. In most workplaces this kind of conversation will be informal, but you want to be prepared by always having a pad of paper and a pen that works ready for such conversations whenever they might occur.

Again, if the supervisor does not point out such a resource, it's okay to ask if there are any employee manuals or reference books you should read, to familiarize yourself with policies and procedures around the office. Unfortunately, however, it can look bad if you spend the first two or three work sessions doing nothing but reading. Find something you can do to help get work done around the office or make something better for someone there within the scope of your duties every time you go to that workplace. Strike a balance between getting nothing done, versus doing too many things the wrong way.

During your check-in's your main objective is to be sure you know what is expected of you, not only the "what" but the "how." Take your lead from them! If they want to keep things brief, don't dillydally. However, if they want to be chatty about topics either work or non-work related, do stay and chat.

It's okay to ask questions about the job. Your bosses won't expect you to know everything. They do expect you to *know* that you don't know everything.

Another absolute benefit is they will not forget you are there. Or put another way: You want your work to go so smoothly, from your supervisors and co-workers' point of view that they DO forget you are there. Imagine what it would be like for them if the work started to just magically get done after they brought you in. They don't want to have to think about you during the routine of the daily grind. They want to know that they can trust that the work they've assigned to you will get done fast and well, with a minimum of explanation and correction.

One benefit of having regular meetings with your supervisor is that they can get to know you better. If people with authority over you ever ask you to go anywhere with them, your answer should probably be yes. They can excuse you from what you would normally be doing. Of course, when I say you better say yes, I am talking only about things that would be considered "normal" – things you would not think twice about mentioning to your grandma. Going out to eat where they serve alcohol is considered within the norm.

Ask What You Should Do with Spare Time

Another excellent question to ask is "If I finish everything you've asked me to do but you're too busy to give me a new assignment, is there a long-term 'background task' that I can always be turning to?" This is a suggestion made in Lindsey Pollak's book, and my experience it is a good one. In both my internships there were times when I would run out of work. I did not want to be seen surfing the web or emailing my friends. Yet, I also did not want to bother my supervisor all the time. Be proactive in handling the situation before it comes up. Also, ask if they know of anyone else in that could use some extra help if you have free time.

Finally, towards the beginning of your internship, ask your supervisor "Is there anyone here you would recommend that I talk to or spend some time with to learn more about _____ (your field)?" This will let her know that you really want to learn and use every opportunity to build experience. This could mean an informational interview, if so, you should prepare. Or, it could mean observing or assisting.

Be Everyone's Friend

You are an intern. Being friendly is one part of being pleasant. Another part is not complaining. Photocopying, stapling, stuffing envelopes, filing and data-entry come with the territory of being either an intern or an entry-level hire. Do these tasks them with enthusiasm and consciousness.

Make Yourself Known

One goal of being an intern is to meet and talk to as many people as you can. A good way to think of it is not that you only work for your supervisor. Think of it as your role is to support your whole department, if it is a large company or the whole company if it is a smaller company. By this I mean try and help as many of the employees as possible. Do not have anything to do because you have done everything you have been assigned. Ask your co-workers if they need any help. Another way to get to become known is to join anything sponsored by where you are interning.

Finally, you should get to know your other interns. Lunch is probably a better way to do this than through excessive checking when you are supposed to be working. If they invite you out after work, go. You might be able to start a weekly after-work dinner for all the interns during the period that you are there. Make it a goal to be able to keep in touch with as many people as you can after the internship is over. You cannot *keep* in touch with someone if you don't form a connection with them first. This is what networking is all about and it is a crucial part of any internship.

Ask Questions

If you do not know what you are doing, ask; it is that simple. Do not waste half a day struggling to figure out how to do something. Your supervisor would rather spare two minutes to explain than have you be non-productive for an entire day. I learned this the hard way.

Be Open to Questions

If you are in a wheelchair or have an obvious disability; be open to questions. Most people are curious; this is natural. I do not get consider questions such as, "Did you have an accident?" or "Are you able to do most stuff for yourself at home?" as invasive.

My supervisor was merely curious. I had the sense he had not been around a lot of people with disabilities. Whether or not it was legal for him to ask such questions was irrelevant to me. It is no big deal for me to answer those types of questions in a way that is brief, matter of fact and natural. I do not go on and on, acting like "poor me" or Miss Disability Pride. To me these questions are no more personal than where did you go to high school or what town do you live in? In the same way, one could go on for twenty minutes about negatives or positives, but that's not usually helpful. In a work environment it is best just to give short answers. It's the same way with your disabilities. If you're comfortable answering reasonable questions, they will be comfortable having asked them, and everyone will move forward.

I do wish I had offered him more support when he said, "I need an evacuation plan for you in case there's a fire." Tersely, I said "I can walk down three flights of stairs if the elevators aren't working." In hindsight, I wish I'd gone to JAN's website, printed an emergency evacuation form, filled it out, and left it on his desk. I missed an opportunity to follow advice I had gotten from a successful businessperson, "How do you get promoted?" Answer: make your boss's job easier."

Another reflection from a work experience of mine: I was at my desk working. My supervisor walked up and I reflexively startled. The supervisor saw my reaction and said, "Sorry to scare you." I denied that he had startled me, saying "Oh no you didn't, it's fine." I wish I had said "I startle easily that's a common symptom of cp," and left it at that. One sentence would have done the trick.

Look for a Mentor

If you find a mentor at an internship, what an excellent gift! Be open to any opportunities that may lead to this.

Leave with Souvenirs

No, I do not mean steal as many office supplies as you can. Think of your portfolio. What can you print an extra copy of to stick in your own file, to impress future employers? Print out only one extra to keep. If you want more copies of something, make them on your own time/expense. Emailing yourself what you are about to "turn in" is also an excellent and nonchalant way to archive your achievements for future job-hunting endeavors (provided your work is not confidential; and even then, with some kinds of work, you can save a redacted version).

Towards the end of your internship, ask your supervisor for a letter of recommendation. You can skip the brag sheet that I told you to do for your teacher recommendations. This is because the letter is only going to be about your performance as an intern.

Do Keep in Touch

Within a month of your internship ending you should shoot out an individual e-mail to everyone you worked with and thank anyone who had any part in your getting an internship. To the co-workers you met during your time there, say how nice it was to work with them. Look for specifics that they taught you or gave you additional experience with; specifics make expressions of gratitude more genuine, which is good for both of you! These thank-you notes need to be individualized to everyone you think of. Try and make each person's a little different, tailored to them. For your fellow interns, try to use social networking to keep track of them. Holidays and graduations are another great opportunity to send another message.

You Are Not in School Anymore

When I was on the phone with my mom during my second internship, I said, "I do not know how I got through high school the way I did!" In high school I would stay up till 11:00, but now I get up an hour and a half later, yet I go to bed most nights by 9:30. In high school I didn't really care what my homeroom teacher thought of me. All I needed to do was show up. If my speech was not clearly understood by homeroom teacher, did I care? No. I now care what my supervisor thinks of me; I need him to be able to understand at 8:55 AM as well as he does at 4:55 PM. I valued my future with that company way more than any TV show I'd miss by going to bed! I realized it was my choice to be here in the internship, as opposed to being a child who was required to do so many things. You can make the most of things regardless, but it does seem easier when you realize that you are there by your own choice!

Expect a Great Experience

My internship in college was such a wonderful experience, in that my disability did not get in the way of it. That is rare for me! I was in such a positive place after, my motivation to grab the career that I wanted was at an all-time high. I wish I had worked at my internship a year earlier. If I had, I think it would've made it easier for me to be enthusiastic about trying to get an even better internship the following summer. Even if that hadn't worked out, and I had returned to my first internship site for a second summer – my last one prior to graduation – that, too, would have been positive for me for several reasons.

My internship the summer before I graduated college was one of the best experiences of my life. I both learned so much, for starters how to send a fax! I was so excited, simple, I know, but when you've never done it. It was a real welcome to the world of work moment. That was just the beginning of what I learned about database architecture and the world of marketing. I met so meant great people who were not only co-workers but also friends. I left that experience with so much confidence, both in myself to perform my given job, and that people would generally accept me, so that I could perform my job. That confidence had been all but shattered nearly a decade before. This confidence gave me such a strong foundation to start my last semester of college. I truly was motivated to conquer the world the semester leading up to graduation.

As Always: Evaluate if your Disability was an Issue

Internships are important for anyone. They are even more important for you because you have a disability! They not only give you an edge for your first job after college over your "non-disabled" peers. Internships can also serve as, yet another trial run to help you see how your disability might affect you on the job and how to adjust and adapt. By interning before the summer before your last year of college, if there is anything that comes up, you will have more time to address it when you go back to college. Most times, you will not have any problems.

Most problems that you do have can be solved by finding a simple way to work around the issue. Talk to whoever you feel is the greatest problem-solver in your life about what you experienced. See if they can help you find an angle you might've missed. Of course, if the issue is not *too* personal, and you've made a connection with one or more people at the internship site, you might be able to discuss it fruitfully with them.

If Not: Question One

A minority of you will feel that your disability caused major problems in meeting your responsibilities during your internship. If this is so, you need to ask yourself some questions, and you might have some decisions to make. The good news is you have time to make them.

You need to do a mental audit of your experience. Did you have a bad or unreceptive boss? This happens to us all! Just because I had many teachers who were, in my opinion, not good at working with students with disabilities didn't mean I was incapable of doing grade-level work. Bad teachers or bosses happen to everyone. If you get a bad teacher, all you can generally do is get through the year as best you can and move on. The same can be said of internships. If your supervisor or co-workers were the problem, you are lucky. You did your internship, you got whatever you could out of it. When it comes time to either find your next internship or find a job, you will look elsewhere.

Question Two

A bad boss is the first thing you need to rule out if your disability posed any issues which hindered you from doing the job. The next is, did you have the proper accommodations? Just as in school, you are entitled to accommodations at work. The major difference is that in the work world, the accommodations must enable you to produce the same work as any other employee that would hold the job. Whereas, in schools all students are entitled to an education, but that education could be very similar or vastly different from another student at the same grade level. In the work world the ADA is the law that ensures this, using the term *reasonable accommodation*:[15]

> Reasonable accommodation is any modification or adjustment to a job or the work environment that will enable a qualified applicant or employee with a disability to participate in the application process or to perform essential job functions. Reasonable accommodation also includes adjustments to assure that a qualified individual with a

Ask JAN

A good place to start to answer this is JAN's website. A list of disabilities can be found at: http://askjan.org/soar/disabilities.html. Click on your disability and explore; you'll find a list of 'Accommodation Examples.' Would any of these address the obstacles that you

---

[15] From: http://www.ada.gov/qandaeng.html

encountered? You can also search for 'Accommodation Examples' by occupation on JAN's website, by going to:

http://askjan.org/media/occind.html

Once you have explored JAN's website, you will have either found something that you think will work, or you are still looking for a solution. Either way your next step is to talk to someone about this. A person with experience with working with clients with disabilities will be useful. Bounce your issue and potential solution off them. You need to figure out if it is a piece of equipment you're going to buy, or is your employer obligated to provide it? Again, your local department of vocational rehab would know whether you or your future employer should purchase the equipment. If they agree that you need something to compensate for your disability to be able to work, they will pay for it. An augmentative communication device is a great example.

If none of the 'Accommodation Examples' seem to fit, you can submit a question and a consultant will get back to you by the next business day. They'll do their best to make suggestions for how to obtain the accommodation and put you in touch with vocational rehab or other organizations if needed. Here is their contact information:

Submit a Question to JAN on Demand: http://askjan.org
Phone: (800) 526-7234
TTY: (877) 781-9403
Email: jan@askjan.org

Whenever possible, try to integrate the new accommodation in either your life on campus or, even better, another work experience before you graduate. This will help you be confident when looking for a job after college.

And, Finally...
In the unlikely event that you've ruled out "bad boss" and have looked hard but failed to find ways to work around your disability to do your dream job, you will be faced with a difficult decision.

Most of those who do internships most will find their disability did not hold them back in a way that couldn't be overcome. But if you do feel that way after working it through with several qualified people, you will need to consider changing your college major and your career goals.

You must ask yourself. "How passionately do I feel about doing what I am trying to do? Would I almost be as happy doing something else that is easier with my disability? Would settling for a second choice of career be made up by the confidence I would have about doing it, and not having it be a constant uphill battle? Or, can I bring enough passion to my first choice that I will work this out somehow?"

Do you have the financial resources to live even if it is considerably harder for you to get steady work in your chosen field?

For example, if you are in a wheelchair with a speech disability, is your passion for acting or modeling strong enough to motivate you to keep going even though it will be a lot harder to get parts or jobs? Do you have a trust fund to live off, if the paychecks are not steady, or are you a single parent who needs a paycheck every two weeks to live?

Can you shift what you want just a little to make a compromise between your dream and being disability-friendly in your plans? For example, maybe you could work with a different population such as in teaching; switching from early childhood education to high school, or from special education to regular education cause it's less physically demanding, from or regular Ed to special Ed, because with special Ed you always have a para-pro. Again, no answers are right or wrong! Talk to someone about it and do what is right for you!

Changing DOES NOT Mean You Failed

If you do change your major or focus within your major, don't feel bad! About eighty percent of college students change their major at least once. It is perfectly normal! Even if changing majors means it takes longer to graduate, we have already seen that the idea of college only taking four years is becoming more outdated by the year. It is well worth it to find what is right for you, so you are not stuck with a degree that does not fit you in as many ways as possible.

Finally, *many* students do internships and then realized that the field in which they did the internship really isn't right for them after all. This has nothing to do with disability and everything to do with the fact that you are in college. A huge part of being in college is figuring out what you want before you are locked into anything. That is another reason that internships are so important!

Intern Abroad

Doing two internships and then studying abroad is a great go-getter alternative to doing three internships. You might run into the challenge of having only three or four summers of college and wanting to do five or six things. There are many ways of solving this! Using spring break, working during the traditional school year and extending your graduation date are all valid options.

Interning abroad is a way of combining the two. For me personally, that would have been too much for me to do. We all have different limits; knowing when to push yourself and when to let an option go is a real asset! While I feel it would not have been right for me to intern abroad; I knew several people with disabilities who would be able to handle it by the time they were nineteen or twenty. They are just different than I. We all have our strengths and our challenges. Should you decide to try it and it turns out to be a disaster, it will at least be a short one

This is how I look at many things in my life. No matter how college goes, the semester will end, and I will come home. I will try to push to the store; if make it, great. If I get tired, I'll just wheel home without goodies, no big deal. Life is an adventure! If you intern abroad and prepare properly, you will probably have a great experience. If it doesn't work out that way, remember that being in another country adds a whole extra level of challenges on top of working with a disability.

Recommended Reading

All Work, No Pay: Finding an Internship, Building Your Résumé, Making Connections, and Gaining Job Experience, by Lauren Berger. Ms. Berger had 15 internships in college! Clearly, she is passionate about their value.

Internships for Those with Disabilities

AAPD Summer Internships for College Students with Disabilities

https://www.aapd.com/summer-internship-program/

AAPD administers two prestigious internships. One is funded by the Mitsubishi Electric America Foundation and places students in congressional offices in Washington, DC. The second, funded by Microsoft, is for students majoring in information technology and accepted candidates will work in various agencies in the executive branch of the federal government.

Email: internship@aapd.com

Adaptive Sports Center (ASC) Internships

http://www.adaptivesports.org/page.cfm?pageid=16964

ASC offers two different internship programs one in the winter season and one in the summer season. The winter internship begins mid-December and ends in early April, with the summer internship beginning in late May and ending in mid-September. We require a season-long commitment during these times. The Adaptive Sports center offers housing to the interns along with a season ski pass in the winter and a modest stipend in the summer. The Application deadline is March 15th for summer interns and September 25th for winter interns.

Adaptive Sports Center
PO Box 1639
Crested Butte, CO 81224

Phone: (866) 349-2296

American Bar Association Internships

http://www.americanbar.org/groups/disabilityrights/resources/employment/cdr_internship.html

The American Bar Association Commission on Mental and Physical Disability Law has paid, volunteer, and for-credit internships during the fall, spring, and summer semesters. Undergraduate and law students are welcome to apply. Duties include using Westlaw to research disability law issues, cite-checking cases and legislation, and assisting with various Commission projects.

Email: amy.allbright@americanbar.org

Brown, Goldstein & Levy Disability Rights Fellowship

http://www.browngold.com/fellowship

Brown, Goldstein & Levy, is now accepting applications for next year's Disability Rights fellowship. The Fellowship offers a recent law-school graduate or judicial clerk with a disability the opportunity to participate in all phases of disability rights litigation at our firm in Baltimore, Maryland. The Fellowship is available to recent law school graduates (0-3 years out) with a disability. The term of the Fellowship is one year. Salary and benefits will be commensurate with the salaries and benefits paid and provided to non-Fellowship BG&L attorneys of equivalent experience. The Fellow should be a member of a state bar or planning to sit for a state bar.

Brown Goldstein & Levy, LLP
120 East Baltimore Street, Suite 1700
Baltimore MD 21202

Phone: (410) 962-1030
Fax: (410) 385-0869
Email: info@browngold.com

Burton Blatt Institute Summer Law and Policy Internship
http://bbi.syr.edu/about/scholarships_and_programs.html

BBI [a division of Syracuse University] employs a team of second- and third-year law students during the general academic year. These Law Research Assistants (Law RAs) work closely with BBI's legal research team in examining the latest developments in disability law and policy, and extensively writing on these developments for a variety of BBI projects and target audiences. The RAs also work with diverse BBI social scientists to gather relevant research that informs grant proposals and deliverables.

Law RAs receive regular guidance for improving their legal research and writing skills, and have gone on to work in private practice, public interest law, and law and policy research. During the summer, BBI typically employs two or three Law RAs for more time intense work weeks.

The Law RA program is directed by William Myhill and Kelly Bunch.

Syracuse Office
900 S. Crouse Avenue
Crouse-Hinds Hall, Suite 300
Syracuse, NY 13244
Phone: (315) 443-2863
Email: wmyhill@syr.edu or kjbunch@law.syr.edu

CanWest Internships for Canadian Students with Disabilities
https://www.neads.ca/en/about/media/index.php?id=359

The CanWest Internships for Students with Disabilities are a series of five (5) internships awarded each year for the next seven (7) years designed to encourage and aid Canadian talent in establishing or furthering a career in the Canadian broadcast industry. These annual internships, valued at approximately $10,000 each, are offered to Canadian students with permanent disabilities. The recipients will receive a challenging opportunity to work in private television in pursuit of a career in broadcasting. The students will be placed in three- or four-month paid internships at one of our Global or E! Television stations, or our Specialty television facility.

Canwest Television Limited Partnership
121 Bloor Street East, Suite 1500
Toronto, ON M4W 3M5
Fax: 416-386-2779

Career Opportunities for Students with Disabilities (COSD)
http://www.cosdonline.org/home

An exciting tool for both employers and students. Career Gateway is the first nationwide online job posting and college student résumé database system. It is a primary tool for employers to reach this population while students use this as a tool for identifying employment opportunities and employers who are committed to including disability as part of their diversity efforts.

Disability Rights Education and Defense Fund (DREDF) Fellowships

https://dredf.org/jobs-and-internships/

The Disability Rights Education and Defense Fund, Inc. (DREDF) located in Berkeley, California seeks candidates for collaboration on Sadden, Equal Justice Works, and other public interest fellowship applications for the two-year period beginning fall 2012. If awarded, such fellowships offer recent law graduates an invaluable opportunity for entry–level training in impact disability civil rights litigation, as well as many other aspects of a public interest practice. DREDF is particularly interested in candidates who want to collaborate on more than one fellowship application, and particularly interested in sponsoring candidates to work on a disability civil rights project in website access and health care access. Individuals with disabilities, minority, and women candidates are especially encouraged to apply.

DREDF
3075 Adeline Street, Suite 210
Berkeley CA 94703
Phone: (510) 644-2555
Fax/TTY: (510) 841-8645
Email: hmin@dredf.org

Disabled Sports USA

https://www.disabledsportsusa.org/get-involved/jobs/

Disabled Sports offers winter and summer internships for college students, graduates, or people interested in entering the field of therapeutic and adaptive recreation.

Michael Hunter
Disabled Sports USA Far West
PO Box 8339
Truckee, CA 96162
Phone: (530) 581-4161
Fax: (530) 581- 3127
Email: Michael@disabledsports.net

Eileen Sweeney Graduate Internship in Disability Policy

http://www.nasi.org/studentopps/eileen-sweeney-graduate-internship-disability-policy

The National Academy of Social Insurance (NASI), in partnership with the Children's Defense Fund (CDF) and the Center on Budget and Policy Priorities (CBPP) is establishing the Eileen Sweeney Graduate Internship in honor and memory of Eileen. Graduate students aspiring to a career in social policy with a focus on disability are urged to apply for this 12-week summer semester internship. A student will be awarded the internship based on nationwide recruitment and a competitive selection process. The internship provides an honorarium of $3,000.

Internship Programs
National Academy of Social Insurance
1776 Massachusetts Ave., NW, Suite 400
Washington, DC 20036-1904

Emerging Leaders Internships

http://www.emerging-leaders.com/

This program launched and funded by the international consulting firm, Booz Allen Hamilton, is administered by the National Business & Disability Council and provides internships for college students with disabilities. These internships are in several geographic locations and with a wide range of companies.

The Viscardi Center
201 I.U. Willets Road
Albertson, NY 11507
Phone: (516) 465-1400
Email: info@viscardicenter.org

Entry Point's Advancement of Science Internships

http://ehrweb.aaas.org/entrypoint/

Entry Point! offers outstanding paid, 10-week internships and semester co-ops in major companies throughout the United States including NASA, IBM and Merck. Qualifying students must be full-time undergraduate or graduate students; be it Science, Mathematics, Engineering, Business, or Computer Science major. At these summer internships for college students with disabilities, you will benefit from a mentor and receive competitive pay.

Project on Science, Technology, and Disability – AAAS
1200 New York Avenue NW
Washington, DC 20005
Phone: (202) 326-6649
Email: entrypoint@aaas.org

Google Building Opportunities for Leadership & Development Internship

https://www.google.com/about/careers/students/bold.html

Google's Building Opportunities for Leadership & Development (BOLD) Diversity Internship Program is designed to provide exposure into the technology industry for students who are historically under-represented in this field. Google invites you to come join us for a unique summer experience, including an 11-week paid internship and professional development workshops.

Email: bebold@google.com

International Disability Alliance

https://www.internationaldisabilityalliance.org/content/opportunities

The International Disability Alliance (IDA) has just launched paid and unpaid internship programs to give people with disabilities and family members the opportunity to work with the IDA Secretariat in Geneva in the area of the Human Rights Council. Preference will be given to people from poorer regions and staff or volunteer leaders can also apply.

International Disability Alliance (New York)
245 Park Avenue, 39th Floor
New York, NY 10167
Phone: (212) 672-1614
Fax: (212) 792-4001
Email: info@ida-secretariat.org

Kennedy Center Internships

http://www.kennedy-center.org/accessibility/#hsc

The Kennedy Center for the Arts organizes two different internship programs for students with disabilities. The Experiential Education Initiative (EEI) Internship is an innovative program designed to offer meaningful instruction and cultural arts experiences to individuals with intellectual disabilities, providing hands-on internships and opportunities to explore today's complex performing arts environment to six motivated individuals each year. The HSC Foundation Internship Program has been established to provide opportunities for individuals with disabilities to participate in internships at cultural arts institutions around the Washington, D.C. Metropolitan area. Internships are designed to build skills that will enhance participants' potential for future competitive employment in a career in the arts.

The John F. Kennedy Center for the Performing Arts
2700 F Street, NW Washington, DC 20566
Phone: (202) 416-8727
TTY: (202) 416-8728

Leadership Alliance Summer Research Early Identification Program (SR-EIP)

https://www.theleadershipalliance.org/programs/summer-research

SR-EIP offers undergraduates, interested in pursuing a PhD or MD/PhD, the opportunity to work for eight to ten weeks under the guidance of a faculty or research mentor at a participating Alliance institution. Through this one-on-one collaboration, students gain theoretical knowledge and practical training in academic research and scientific experimentation. The SR-EIP is designed to encourage students from groups traditionally underrepresented in the sciences, social sciences and humanities to consider research careers in the academic, public or private sectors. Students are required to present a written report and/or abstract at the end of their summer research activity and complete a program evaluation. All participants are expected to make oral or poster presentations of their research at the Leadership Alliance's annual, national symposium. This all-expense paid summer internship provides students with a competitive stipend, travel and housing.

133 Waterman Street
Providence RI 02912
Phone: (401) 863-1474
Fax: (401) 863-2244

Lime Connect Fellowship Program

https://www.limeconnect.com/programs/page/the-lime-connect-fellowship-program

This program helps college students make long-term connections that will lead to employment after graduation. It includes participation in an all-expense paid Leadership & Development Symposium in New York City, access to Lime Connects partner companies via networking events, mentorship programs and career workshops, continued support and coaching through the recruitment process via a year-long post-symposium leadership development program, networking with other Lime Connect Fellows and Alums from around the country, and a $1,000 "Lime Fellows Award" You must be a college sophomore in order to apply.

590 Madison Avenue, 21st Floor
New York, New York 10022
Phone: (212) 521-4469
Fax: (212) 521-4099

Mobility International USA

https://www.miusa.org/exchange-type/internships

Mobility International USA (MIUSA) is a US-based nonprofit organization with the mission to empower people with disabilities around the world through international exchange and international development. MIUSA sponsors internships for undergraduates and graduates year-round, and internships typically last 3-6 months. Opportunities currently available depend on program needs. Interns must be able to commit to at least 10 hours per week.

Internships at Mobility International USA
132 E. Broadway, Suite 343
Eugene, Oregon USA 97401
Phone: (541) 343-1284
Fax: (541) 343-6812

Paid Internships in Pittsburgh, PA

https://www.benderconsult.com/partnerships/college-partnership-program

College juniors, seniors and master's degree students with disabilities (US citizens) with majors in Internet Technology, Finance, Accounting, Communications, Political Science, Business Administration, Liberal Arts, and Engineering are invited to apply for 3 month (40 hours/week) or 6 month (20 hours/week) paid ($10/hour) internships.

Reeve Foundation

https://www.christopherreeve.org/about-us/careers/student-internships

The Reeve Foundation says: "We are looking for amazing interns... Our interns love us here. There is more food around this place than any five college students can eat. So, if you are a college student in the New Jersey/New York area apply online."

Required Hours: 12 - 21 hours per week
Length: a semester (fall, spring, or summer)
Unpaid Internship: for class credit and possibility of travel stipend

Christopher & Dana Reeve Foundation
636 Morris Turnpike, Suite 3A
Short Hills, NJ 07078

Smithsonian Internship Program for People with Disabilities

https://www.smithsonianofi.com/minority-internship-program/

Access to Opportunities is the paid internship program of the Smithsonian for people with disabilities. It provides four paid internship opportunities annually to applicants who are in college or graduate school, or who have graduated within the last 6 months are invited to apply. While applicant pools and recruitment efforts will be based in the greater Washington, D.C., metropolitan area, interns can be from anywhere in the U.S. and must have United States citizenship.

Phone: (202) 633-4340
Email: floresk@si.edu

The National Leadership Program at RespectAbility

https://www.respectability.org/about-us/fellowship/

The National Leadership Program is for young leaders who are committed to disability issues and plan to go into careers in public policy, advocacy, communications, fundraising, nonprofit management or faith-based inclusion. The program enables participants to gain skills and contacts while making a positive difference for people with disabilities. We are seeking creative, results-driven individuals who want to achieve breakthrough results while getting hands-on experience. The Fellowship is for college and graduate students, as well as recent graduates.

RespectAbility
11333 Woodglen Drive, #102
Rockville, MD 20852
Office Number: 202-517-6272
Email: info@respectability.org

Washington Center's Public Service Internship Program for Students with Disabilities

http://www.twc.edu/prospective

The Washington Center for Internships and Academic Seminars (TWC) is working to help students with disabilities develop leadership skills and gain valuable work experience in public service. The Washington Center compliments students' professional experience with solid academic training for credit from highly qualified instructors. In addition, students will be exposed to community, national and international leaders through workshops, seminars, lectures, embassy visits and networking events held throughout the course of each semester. Interns are offered a fully inclusive program, including accessible housing.

1333 16th Street, NW
Washington, DC 20036-2205

WrightChoice Intern Program

http://www.wrightchoice.org/

WrightChoice's mission is "Building a bridge between resource & opportunity for minority students & students with disabilities." As such, WrightChoice has an internship program with openings to which you can apply year-round.

911 Robinwood Ave, Suite G,
Whitehall, Ohio 43213

Points to Remember from Chapter 8

✓ If you're considering doing an internship for those with disabilities, carefully consider whether it will increase your chances of getting long-term employment after graduation. The main ways these internships lead to jobs is through networking and establishing support among alumni for their internship program. The answer does not have to be yes. It could very well be no, leading you to do an internship (or two or three) with a firm that did not set out to hire a student with a disability.

✓ When you get the title of Intern, do not blow anything off, or tick anyone off. Even if you are positive that you hate the entire industry (now), hate the entire geographic area and would rather die than ever work there full-time... Just ask yourself what you can get out of the role for however many weeks you'll be there. You truly never know where something might lead. Let's say you never end up in a full-time job. Life goes in some crazy directions sometimes. Who was it who said, "Life happens when you're making other plans?" Let's say you become a stay-at-home parent (the world's noblest profession and the hardest job on earth). Someone you met as an intern and have stayed in touch with, might end up helping you get your kid into the perfect pre-school.

✓ Those who you have met an internship cannot help you if you don't stay in touch. Keeping in periodic contact with your connections *even when you don't need anything* is a vital part of career success!

Chapter 9: As College Comes to an End

Step One: The Résumé

Your résumé is the most important job search tool that you will use. Its purpose is to get you an interview, *not to get you the job*. It is a marketing document, not a written interview. Perfection is expected on this document, so you will need to spend a great deal of time ensuring that there are absolutely no errors! There are many resources available that go greater in depth into this subject than this book. There are entire books just on how to write and distribute a résumé (that's how important it is). And of course, a great deal of information and examples are available on the Internet.

A general rule for résumés is not to include any personal information other than your name and contact information To a lay person, disability status is considered both personal and health-related. If you have an invisible disability and decide not to disclose during your interview process, that's your call. Just make sure nothing that you include on your résumé or in your cover letter leads the reader to believe that you have a disability if you do not want this.

Even if you are totally open about your disability, be it by choice or of necessity, I still feel it has no place in your professional email address. It is fine if you want your family and friends to email you at *CPDude* or *Texaswheels*. But please get a neutral, professional-sounding email address to put on your resume! I talk lots about disclosure of disability in the workplace; do not use your email address to disclose to potential employers.

My current résumé states that I have CP. I put it in my Education section, because I wanted to point to my personal achievement of being the first person with CP to complete my school's nationally ranked MIS program. I did this because I took stock of my situation and, although unorthodox, it seemed like the right thing for a couple of reasons. (Just because there is a rule does not mean you have to slavishly follow it. It does mean whatever you do must be well thought-out.)

Step Two: The Cover Letter

The goal of a cover letter is to request an interview, by reference to an accompanying résumé. Each cover letter should be concise and specifically targeted to the organization in question, the available position(s), and to the person who you are hoping will read it.

Again, you are never required to disclose your disability, whether it be during the hiring process or during your employment. Yet, if you have a specific reason for wanting a hiring manager to know that you have a disability, your cover letter is the first opportunity to do so.

According to JAN's website, you should state that you have a disability in a cover letter if:

- You are applying for a job with a state or federal agency that must comply with affirmative action policies

- The job you are applying for directly relates to your experience as a person with a disability, such as rehabilitation counselor; or

- Your disability is a qualification for the position.

Your cover letter should never solely focus on your disability. It should summarize your qualifications and express measured enthusiasm for the position.

Do not use the cover letter to request an accommodation during the interview process. The ADA grants job applicants the right to accommodations while interviewing. Should you need an accommodation for an upcoming interview, wait until after the interview is scheduled to inform whomever you scheduled it with that you need one or more accommodations. Review Chapter 11 for more information.

Step Three: The Portfolio

When you hear the word *portfolio*, you might think of an artist or someone in the fashion industry. In fact, every serious job seeker should have a portfolio ready regardless of their industry.

Your portfolio needs to be impeccably neat: free of grammar and spelling errors, well organized, and with everything in it clearly relevant to the job for which you are applying. The next step is to write a personal statement. Your personal statement, like a cover letter, will go first in whatever you use to present your portfolio. Next will be your résumé: The remainder of your portfolio should be divided into sections, such as: academic achievements, leadership, work history and references. For further explanation on these sections consult *Getting from College to Career* by Lindsey Pollak or other resources online.

Disability Section (Optional)

Whether it's smart to include a disability section can also depend on who is sponsoring the recruiting effort. If you are attending events specifically designed for those with disabilities, as I will talk about later in this chapter, you might not need to include it. An example of this is taking part in the WRP. Whether you are taking part in general campus interviewing, going to an interview set up by a networking contact, or interviewing in response to a job posting, include it if you feel best served by having one.

Should you decide to include a disability section it *always* needs to be last and could include the following:

- Disability MythBusters Sheet (See Chapter Eleven)

- An emergency evacuation form (See Chapter Eleven)

- Service animal on the job: only if you have such an animal and plan on taking it to work

- Accommodations you need to accomplish the essential job functions

- An article about someone with your disability, or a disability like yours succeeding in the type of job that you are interviewing for. It has to be this specific, otherwise it's not going to make the point.

Don't Do This...

There are some definite no-no's if you decide to include a disability section. DON'T:

- Write out your medical history or list current medications. This is the same for all applicants; it has no place in information which you are going to present while interviewing. (*Possible exception:* You might need to disclose any meds that you are taking if you are required to take a drug test.)

- Provide any extraneous information, good or bad, about your disability in any other area other than employment.

- Include your IEP.

- Refer to the ADA in any manner that implies you are demanding or threatening anything. The goal is to present the employer with information in context that the ADA is on their side and not anything to be nervous about.

- Assert any rights regarding medical leave nor bring up the topic.

Reproducing Your Portfolio

When you have finished assembling your portfolio, you'll need to decide how much money you want to spend on presenting it. Your portfolio goes with you to a job fair or an interview. It is something that you present in person, not something that you email. When you plan to go to a career event you need to decide how many copies that you want to distribute and how much you want to spend per copy. Glossy paper, spiral binding and color printing all cost money. One solution is to bring a copy that has all these elements but make it clear that you need it back. At the opposite end of the spectrum is to print out many copies at home and staple them in order to be able to hand them out. It is common sense that the more potential that you feel an event holds for you getting a job, the more expense you should invest in producing these. The same goes for an interview for a position in which you know that you feel confident that you won't get. Why would you even interview for such a position? You would go for both practice interviewing, and to make another contact. If you have an interview for either your dream job, or a company that you really want to work for, then head on over to the print shop and invest some money. Make your portfolio look as good as possible. Get multiple copies so that you can give them out and leave them with whomever you talk to. You could still ask for them back, but if you don't get them back, it won't be such a big loss if you are only putting out your best copies for the best jobs.

Regardless of how many portfolios you bring, you also need to bring a folder with ample copies of both your résumé and reference sheets. These need to be printed on good quality paper. Whoever is interviewing you might not want anything thicker than a few pages, because they will be collecting dozens or hundreds of whatever the hopefuls are giving them. You need to be prepared and go with the flow. They might accept both the "light" version to give to their assistant to enter into their résumé tracking system and the "heavy" version to review at their leisure. They might even toss the portfolio and use only your résumé when they make their final hiring decision. This doesn't mean you wasted time making a portfolio for them! It still can't help but make an impression – and will give them plenty to talk about with you on your interview. Everyone has their own way of hiring; respect that by giving them options.

On the front cover of your portfolio put your name and contact information. Your personal statement could also be on the outside. If you are an artist or a designer, put a sample of your work on the front page and then then personal statement on page one. If you're going for a teaching job, put a photo of yourself teaching on the front. If you want to go more conservative, just make a cover with your name and contact information. Have the first page be a personal statement, followed by your résumé. Then introduce color as well as a little gloss factor in your other sections.

> *Tip:* You can make different portfolios for each company you want to hit at a career fair. The main differences would be that your personal statement and career objective could be tailored to each of them. Just make sure you don't get them mixed up! Each company gets either a different color spiral binding or a differently colored cover. When assembling your portfolios, memorize which color is for which company. If you are doing it this way, why not try to give each company a color that is their company color? While this will not get you the job, it can't hurt. Either way, this will make it easier to remember which is which!

Create a Website

It is always more empowering to ask for what you want than to wait to be asked. To do a professional website, what you are essentially doing is putting your portfolio online. Your personal statement goes on the home page along with a professional photo of yourself. Then each section of your portfolio becomes a link on your menu bar.

I put together my own website. This gave me another opportunity to sell myself. It gave me the chance to explain my disability to potential employers, helping put prospective employers at ease with my disability. I accomplished this by giving them some information about my cerebral palsy. At the time, I did not see a way to make that fit on my résumé; having my own website was the answer.

I hyperlinked "Cerebral Palsy" in my personal statement, so if someone clicked on the link it would take them to a page with just basic facts about my condition. I picked a page from the NIH's website. I did not want anything cutesy or "inspiring," just the facts. I did not care if anyone cared what cp was! If they didn't want to click on it, fine.

If you have an invisible disability, you can certainly create your webpage with no mention of your disability. All the other sections of the portfolio will go on the website.

Get a professional-sounding URL, of course. When posting your résumé, leave off your address and any addresses/phone numbers of either previous employers or references. Should an employer be serious about you as an applicant, there will be opportunities for them to get this information later in the process.

Another great way to use the website is to start a blog about your industry on it. Keep the blog about your profession. Talk about new trends and what they mean to you. Review professional literature. Discuss anything you are doing in the field or anything new you learn about that interests you. Print the best of your blog to include in your portfolio.

Don't Invite the Boss into Your Room

More and more employers are Googling the names of applicants to look for any issues that might pose a concern. If you have a personal blog where you take any controversial positions on anything, or even if you discuss anything that you would not want a prospective employer to know that you think about and write about, keep your name off the blog (or go through every page and replace it with some other name). You can have multiple websites and blogs just as you have multiple email addresses.

Prospective employers might even Google the email address that you have put on your résumé. This is another reason that you should have a separate email address just for prospective employers. Do not use the same email address on your résumé as you did for some chat room name.

In fact, I strongly recommend that you never use your email address as a chat room ID. I made that mistake. I joined a chat room seeking advice about an ADL issue that would make me more employable. When I was signing up, I used the first part of my email address as my username. I regret that choice. If you form a friendship with somebody through a chat room or email distribution list, you can THEN tell them your name and whatever else you want about yourself!

All this goes even more strongly for social media. As I was writing this book Facebook was a daily part of many young people's lives in the United States and around the world. Who knows, in technology things change so fast, maybe Facebook won't be around in 10 years, but I can't really imagine a world where people aren't doing social networking somehow!

> ***Key Point***: You can't force a forum or other website that you don't control, to remove things you've posted. Once it's out there, by and large, it's out there. This is just a brief introduction to the issues. Become informed of what to do and what not to do to both protect yourself, as well as how to use current technology to enhance you networking possibilities.

Mock Interviews

Mock interviews are simply practice interviews. These can be extremely helpful for you to prepare for the real thing. Start doing them in your junior or senior year of college. Most colleges and universities offer this service through their career services department. If your school does, go do at least one.

When you go on a real job interviews, the result will basically be one of three things:

1. You'll be offered the job;

2. You won't hear anything, which will eventually mean they gave the job to someone else; or

3. They will do you the unusual courtesy of letting you know that they hired someone else.

What will never happen is that they will offer you feedback about how you performed during the interview. Filling this gap is what mock interviews are for! This feedback can be incredibly valuable to you. No matter how gifted you are (or aren't) at interviewing, you can always improve. After all, there's a lot going on in an interview. Even after some years in the workforce, most people don't interview often enough to become or stay all that good at it. (In fact, sadly, many hiring managers are not that good at conducting interviews. You can really shine if you are so confident in your role that you can end up helping a nervous hiring manager feel at ease!) Taking advantage of yet another college resource to raise your skill levels will just give you one more crucial area in which you'll be ahead of the pack.

It is certainly helpful to read about interviewing online or in books. Yet your reading material cannot offer you feedback. You need to rehearse. Schools will vary on the quality of their interview coaching, but they can all be of at least some help. This makes them better for you to practice with than a parent, friend, girlfriend/boyfriend or a pet.

What If a Disability-Related Issue Comes Up?

If during an interview or other discussions with a prospective employer while you are at college, you get the "vibe" that there is an issue related to your disability, this is a good thing! You still have time to address it near the beginning of your work experience. Talk to your disability services staff. If you aren't satisfied with their assistance, contact the appropriate kind of therapist. Since becoming an adult, I have not received PT, OT, or speech therapy. Despite this, I still have people who I would be able to talk to, should I have a question in this area. This is thanks to both keeping in touch with a few of the many therapists that I worked with during my childhood and the luck of having a parent who works in this field.

If you do not have anyone to contact, go online. Reach out to organizations that target employment issues among those with disabilities. I list some of those later in this chapter. Also consider whether some of the assistive technologies described in Chapter 1 might help you.

It has been my experience that most Internet forums meant to help people with disabilities are not that helpful in resolving specific issues. Usually I know more than any of the other participants. Often, I find that they give me more moral support than practical advice.

You can also seek help from vocational rehab regarding interviewing. It has also been my experience that VR professionals are not that knowledgeable or effective at what they say they are going to try to do for you. VR tends to be better a funding a solution that you have found rather than finding you a solution.

I hope that your mock interviewer has twenty years in career coaching and is good at what she does. You'll get something out of it, regardless. The more times that you go to your campus career services office with the mindset of "What can they do for me?" the better! When you are there to do a résumé review or a mock interview, you could see a flyer that leads to your first job! You have nothing to lose and everything to gain by using their services.

Look and Act the Part

Your appearance at any professional event matters. This is a simple fact. Whenever you get an interview, make sure that you show up looking your best. I suggest that you always try to have at least two interview outfits pressed and hanging in your closet complete with pristine shoes and accessories. This will take one key element of stress off you if an interview comes up at the last moment. A good rule of thumb is to dress one level above the normal dress of the workplace where you are interviewing. If you must take out a couple extra hundred in student loans senior year to buy what you need, do it.

If you use a wheelchair or other mobility aid, it is an extension of yourself. People won't just look at you, they will also look at your equipment. Always make sure your equipment is clean before you go for an interview! You would not go in wearing dirty shoes, so why would you go in with a dirty wheelchair or cushion? If you have any "flair" or other decorations on your chair, take it off! You would not go in wearing a shirt with a message on it, or wearing Mardi Gras beads, or a button saying something goofy. Having anything like that on your chair is just as unprofessional and off-putting.

Before I went to my college's career fair, I pulled (yep) my Mardi Gras beads off my chair. I also cleaned out the cargo net, which was like the Bermuda Triangle during my college days. All that belongs in the cargo net is your portfolio(s), your folder with résumés and reference sheets, and water. If you need other items with you, you need a briefcase (not a purse) on your lap or on the back of your chair. If you wheel in with a briefcase on your lap, the first thing you need to do is put it down either on the floor or preferably on a chair next to you. It's best to avoid making changes to your chair or other mobility aids right before an interview.

True-story...

I prefer to use a chair with rubber-coated rims. I attended a fair, I was in the waiting process to get a new chair. My rubber rims were torn. On the assumption that my chair is an extension of myself, I felt it was unacceptable to go in a "ratty" chair. After all, I would not go with torn clothing. I decided to cut all the rubber off my rims. I thought that that would look better. That's what I did the night before. The next day as soon as I started wheeling around the expo, my hands turned black! The bare metal caused my hands to become instantly dirty when I wheeled. This affected the whole event I had planned so hard for!

I went to the restroom to wash my hands between every booth visit, but my hands would still get filthy going from the bathroom to the booth! I was in trouble! As soon as I touched a résumé – which I had gone to the trouble of printing on nice paper – it would get my dirty fingerprints on it. Not good!

I should have had gloves in my bag or modified my chair sooner so I could have tested it for any issues.

Work Career Fairs

At some point in your job search you should certainly attend a career fair. All college campuses have one. You should go with the goal of generating leads for either internships or post-graduation employment. You should also venture off-campus to fairs that may be more specialized to your field.

The first key to making job fairs worthwhile is to get your mindset right. If you plan to simply drop off your résumé at each booth without really trying to connect with anyone in the booth, and grabbing as much free stuff as you can, you might as well not go. If you really want a job or to make connections in an industry, you are going to have to work harder than that. WORK the fair. Get yourself into go-getter mode!

Here are some steps to get the most out of a career fair.

Ten-Step Career Fair Action Plan

1. **RSVP.** If you are serious about an event, you should RSVP for it, meaning pre-register. This will hopefully give you at least two benefits. First, some career fairs put applicants' résumés on a CD that is distributed to all recruiters who attend the fair. The more people who see your résumé the better. The more times they *see* your résumé the better. Second, name tags. If the career fair is structured so that attendees sign in and get a name tag, you better have one. What an easy way for employers to scan and see who planned ahead!

2. **Know who's going to be there.** Go online to see which companies are going to be there. For every company that interests you, go to their website to find out the basics of their company and what they are hiring for. Ideally you should be able to identify where you would fit in for each organization that you are planning on approaching. After you do this, Google them to see any new developments for that company. New product launch, school district just got recognized, hospital just got a major donation or named best in the region for _____. Mention this when you are talking to recruiters. Of course, do not mention anything that got the company in hot water! "Hope you overcome that insider-trading scandal soon!" just won't come off well no matter how you say it.

   The last step in prepping is to Google the phrase "common interview questions" and practice in your head.

3. **Have an intro speech ready.** Be ready to introduce yourself without fumbling for words. If you are not wearing a nametag; start with "Hi, I am _____," or "Hi," and then say the name that's on their name tag. If it is a full name use "Mr." or "Ms." "I am so glad your company is here today because I will be graduating/I just graduated from _____ with a degree in _____. I would love to find out more about (company's name/position or opportunity that you identified in # 2).

   I feel your company is a good fit for because…" (mention a skill you have as well as one news item you found out in #2). Could I give you my résumé?"

   Then wait, let them look it over. Hopefully they will respond! Ask if they have any questions. Ask a question or two yourself. One might be, "What can you tell me about your hiring process?" Ask for a business card and say, "Nice to meet/chat with you."

4. **Show respect for everyone around you.** If there are lots of people in line, do not monopolize the recruiters' time! If a line is forming behind you, you need to wrap it up.

Do not crowd whomever they are talking to. If they are talking to someone but there is not a line, hover nearby 'til they are free. If there is a line, go ahead and get in it. If you are number five or below in the line, network with your fellows. Be positive; never make fun of the event. If you are more towards the front of the line be quieter, spend your time reviewing literature for that company. You never want the recruiter's first impression to be that you were more focused on having a good time then on connecting with someone at his company. Cell phones off/no gum!

5. **Be on your best behavior.** From the moment you reach the parking lot to the moment you leave the lot, act as if you are being watched! I already covered this some with the previous tip. Hair gets brushed in one of two places, the car or the bathroom, not on the open floor. Also, some recruiters will notice if you are hitting every single booth; it can give the impression that you are not really that interested in them. If you run into your long-lost "BFF," act professional and keep the greeting brief. Get a business card from your old acquaintance so you can catch up with them later, but don't scream with excitement and spend the next hour glued to each other.

6. **Time Management.** Arrive early! If you have no interest in a company, don't visit the booth. While you can deviate from who you want to pitch to, have a plan to deviate *from*. If you have not had time to plan properly, don't just start handing out résumés; get a map. Plot out which booths you want to go to.

7. **Come Prepared.** Since your planning will have told you approximately how many companies you want to connect with, print out three résumés for each. Not every company will need three résumés, so this will give you extras should you decide to hit a company that you did not plan on. It is better to have too many résumés than to run out.

   If the career fair seems especially promising, then have some portfolios available. As stated earlier, order a multi-color pack of plastic covers so that you can more easily keep track of which customized portfolio to give to which recruiter. If you go to this much trouble, give the recruiter your portfolio instead of a résumé. Should you make a portfolio for each, you still need to bring a folder of résumés. Remember, you never know what form a recruiter will want or need items submitted in. If the event is less promising, give out résumés and have only one portfolio that you can show if you get into a conversation.

8. **Network with everyone.** Don't just talk to recruiters, connect with fellow job-seekers, and even with those who are holding the event.

9. **Limit Swag.** Taking *some* swag is good; it shows interest as well as politeness. Taking too much is bad. Don't act like this is trick-or-treat! Carrying around massive amounts of stuff will distract you and make you look tacky. Another strategy that you can employ is to do two "laps." On the first lap you make the rounds grabbing both swag and literature, but not giving any résumés out. Pull over and review the literature, and get the swag contained. Then on a second lap, you are sure who you want to talk to, and you go in with some information about the company at each booth you are talking to. This is a good strategy to make up for it, if for whatever reason you didn't plan properly for the fair. Sometimes life happens. The trick is to still "work it" and at least appear prepared.

10. **Be the First to Follow Up.** Some suggest that right after you leave the event, you call each recruiter who has their phone number on their card. Leave them a voicemail such as "Hello (whatever you addressed him or her as, I just wanted to thank you again for the time you spent with me. I will be in touch in within a couple days, after I ... (whatever they instructed you to do when you asked what the next step is). That phone call is

optional. What is not optional is an email. Send one within three days (better still the next day). A great subject line "I just applied online" (or did whatever they told you to do). That is better than "Nice to meet you." Address the message to the specific recruiter; never send a blast email to everyone you met. You need to do each one individually. Begin with "I met you at <name of fair>. Then thank them again for their time. Let them know again what position you want and why you are qualified. Then state that you hope to be given the opportunity to interview. Attach another copy of your résumé.

Follow up is a MUST!

Recruiters get so many résumés; you need to make sure you stand out. This is only the beginning of your relationship. If you apply for a position down the line for that company, make sure you email them as well to let them know. Do whatever you can to make a relationship out of that contact.

Two other ideas are to send them an email wishing them a Happy New Year and if they hear of any new openings you would really appreciate it if they would keep you in mind.

Another idea is connecting to them on LinkedIn. I attended an event where several HR people spoke. One said she requested to add the people she met at an event to her LinkedIn, and only one responded. That was my cue; the next day I requested that she add me to her network. Work at it from whatever angle you can!

Industry-Related Associations for Professionals with Disabilities

Organizations listed below are geared towards advancing the careers of people with disabilities within a specific industry. This can mean mentorship, accommodation ideas, and job fairs, networking functions, fellowships or help preparing for grad programs. These are not general employment resources or job placement services for those with disabilities. If you want to go into any of the fields listed, look at the organization listed to see what they have to offer.

All Professions

Career Expo for People with Disabilities

http://www.eop.com/expo

Welcome to CAREERS & the disABLED Magazine's Career Expo for People with Disabilities that brings industry and government together with people with disabilities who are entry level and professionals in all career disciplines.

Annette Maldonado-Cora
Phone: (631) 421-9421 ext.10
Email: acora@eop.com

Arts/Acting

VSA (Very Special Arts / Department of VSA and Accessibility)

http://vsarts.org/

VSA, the international organization on arts and disability, was founded more than 35 years ago by Ambassador Jean Kennedy Smith to provide arts and education opportunities for people with disabilities and increase access to the arts for all.

The John F. Kennedy Center for the Performing Arts
2700 F Street, NW Washington, DC 20566
Phone: (800) 444-1324 or (202) 467-4600

Coalition for Disabled Musicians

http://disabled-musicians.org

CDM would like to assist and collaborate with disabled musicians nationwide and worldwide in concrete ways. For example, if you have original songs you would like to submit for performance consideration or would like advice in setting up your own groups, or if you would like to broadcast or distribute our music, please contact us. The purpose of CDM joining the World Wide Web is to forge links that would have been impossible otherwise.

Coalition for Disabled Musicians, Inc.
P.O. Box 1002M
Bay Shore, New York 11706

Phone: (631) 586-0366
Email: CDMNews@aol.com

Damon Brooks Associates

http://www.damonbrooks.com

Damon Brooks Associates is the only speaker's bureau that exclusively represents those with a disability." The website includes a list of the performers they represent as well as their clientele. Contact them directly for information about joining their roster.

Damon Brooks Associates
1601 Holly Avenue
Channel Islands Beach, CA 93036

Phone: (805) 604-9017
Email: marc@damonbrooks.com

National Resource Center for Blind Musicians

http://www.blindmusicstudent.org/

Welcome to The National Resource Center for Blind Musicians, A division of Neighborhood Studios of Fairfield County in Bridgeport, Connecticut. (This is the new name for the school of the arts in which we are located, formerly the Music and Arts Center for Humanity.) The resource center provides information and referral services for visually impaired students of all ages, their parents and teachers, learning opportunities for blind students headed to college, and maintains a network of visually impaired musicians willing to share their expertise in braille music, technology and coping strategies. The Resource Center is best known for its Summer Institute for Blind College-bound Musicians, a residential program which brings together students from several states, who are studying music at the college level.

National Resource Center for Blind Musicians
Neighborhood Studios of Fairfield County, Inc.
391 East Washington Avenue
Bridgeport, Connecticut, 06608

Phone: (203) 366-3300
Fax: (203) 368-2847
Email: info@blindmusicstudent.org

Business

COSD FULL ACCESS Student Summits

http://www.cosdonline.org/Full-Access-Students

This exclusive event brings together up to sixty college students or recent alumni with disabilities and ten select national and regional employers for a networking and education summit. FULL ACCESS is not a career fair. It is not an opportunity to interview one-on-one with individual students and there should be NO expectation to extend a job offer at the Summit. FULL ACCESS is a golden opportunity for employers to meet up to 60 prospective employees with disabilities.

Alan Muir, Executive Director
100 Dunford Hall
Knoxville, TN 37996-4010

Phone: 865-974-7148
Fax: 865-974-6497
Email: amuir@cosdonline.org

Tatiana Leavitt, Graduate Assistant
100 Dunford Hall
Knoxville, TN 37996-4010

Phone: (865) 974-5549
Email: tleavitt@vols.utk.edu

Lime Connect

http://www.limeconnect.com/

Lime Connect is leading the way as the premier resource for top talent in the disability space by rebranding disability through achievement – attracting, preparing and connecting highly accomplished individuals with disabilities for careers with the world's leading corporations.

> *Important*: If you want a career in a business-related field, definitely check out Lime! They sponsor fellowships, scholarships, recruiting events as well as list job openings.

Lime Connect, Inc.
590 Madison Avenue, 21st Floor
New York, New York 10022

Phone: (212) 521-4469
Fax: (212) 521-4099

Email: info@limeconnect.com

Lime Connect Canada, Inc.
2 Bloor Street, West, Suite 700
Toronto, Ontario M4W 3R1

Phone: (416) 323-5770

US Business Leadership Network Overview (USBLN)

https://www.ncil.org/usbln/

The US Business Leadership Network is the national disability organization that serves as the collective voice of over 60 Business Leadership Network affiliates across North America, representing over 5,000 employers. The USBLN® helps build workplaces, marketplaces, and supply chains where people with disabilities are respected for their talents, while supporting the development and expansion of its BLN affiliates. The USBLN® recognizes and supports best practices in the employment and advancement of people with disabilities; the preparedness for work of youth and students with disabilities; marketing to consumers with disabilities; and contracting with vendors with disabilities through the development and certification of disability-owned businesses.

US Business Leadership Network (USBLN®)
1310 Braddock Place, Suite 101
Alexandria, VA 22314

Phone: (800) 706-2710
Fax: (800) 706-1335
Email: info@usbln.org

> *Tip:* This website has member names and email addresses listed under the Affiliates section. These would be great people to network with by sending them an email introducing yourself and asking for what you need. If it is a job or an internship, attach your résumé. If it is a question about how to manage your disability while interviewing or on the job, ask.
>
> They also sponsor an annual conference. Some years they hold a career fair in tandem to this. If they do so when you are a college senior and are looking to start a career in corporate America upon graduation, you should consider going.

Education/Teaching

Annual National Minority Careers in Education Expo
http://deptofed.org

Join elementary, high school, K-12, & the US Dept. of Defense Dependents Schools worldwide! This fair is open to all teachers, not just minorities or teachers with disabilities. If you feel you are experiencing discrimination in applying to districts, why not go to where employers are looking to hire a diverse staff?

Case Studies on Teaching
http://www.skill.org.uk/page.aspx?c=267&p=386

Read case studies that feature disabled teachers sharing their experience of why they chose teaching as a career and their journey to achieve their goal. Site is based in the UK.

Educators with Disabilities Caucus (EDC)
http://www.educatorswithdisabilities.org/home

A national network of pre-service students, teachers, researchers, and administrators with disabilities and others interested in the topic of educators with disabilities. Established more than 10 years ago, EDC is a continuing and vital forum for exchanging information on recruiting, hiring, and supporting teachers or related services personnel who have disabilities. They sponsor a mentorship program for Students who have a disability (learning disability, physical disability, deaf and hard of hearing, etc.) and are in a teacher education program are eligible. Students are paired with a professional mentor with a similar disability, when possible. Novice teachers with disabilities or teachers with disabilities who wish to seek a mentor also may apply to this program.

Email: khaselden@fmarion.edu

National Association of Blind Teachers
http://blindteachers.net/

Welcome to The National Association of Blind Teachers. This site is intended to assist blind and visually impaired teachers in their work, to help students make more effective use of the Internet in their classes, to aid school administrators in understanding the capacities of visually impaired teachers, and enable parents of blind and visually impaired children to better help their child.

Phone: (865) 692-4888
Email: johnbuckley25@hotmail.com

The Advantage of Disadvantage: Teachers with Disabilities Are Not a Handicap
http://www.edutopia.org/disabled-teachers#comment-83003

Excellent article that makes the points out that teachers with disabilities can not only succeed in the classroom but can bring unique qualities to the job. You may want to print and bring to job interviews.

Healthcare/Nursing

Association of Medical Professionals with Hearing Losses (AMPHL)

http://www.amphl.org

Association of Medical Professionals with Hearing Losses, abbreviated as "AMPHL," provides information, promotes advocacy and mentorship, and creates a network for individuals with hearing loss interested in or working in health care fields.

Association of Medical Professionals with Hearing Losses
10708 Nestling Drive
Miamisburg OH 45342

Exceptional Nurse

http://www.exceptionalnurse.com

Welcome! If you are a student with a disability considering a nursing career, this is the place for you. If you are a nursing student with a disability, this is the place for you. If you are a nurse with a disability, this is the place for you. If you are a nursing educator or a guidance counselor working with a student with a disability, this is the place for you. Exceptionalnurse is committed to inclusion of more people with disabilities in the nursing profession. By sharing information and resources, Exceptionalnurse hopes to facilitate inclusion of students with disabilities in nursing education programs and foster resilience and continued practice for nurses who are, or become, disabled.

13019 Coastal Circle
Palm Beach Gardens, FL 33410
(561) 627-9872
(561) 776-9254 (fax)
(561) 776-9442 (TTY)
Email: ExceptionalNurse@aol.com

Medical H.E.L.P.

http://www.marshall.edu/medhelp/

The Marshall University Medical H.E.L.P. Program began in 1986 with a vision of helping medical students and physicians with learning disabilities and/or ADHD succeed academically. Since that time, Marshall Medical H.E.L.P. has worked with approximately 600 students from across the United States and several foreign countries. A five-week intensive course is held four times each year in January, March, June, and September, with individual one on one sessions available the rest of the year. Throughout the intensive program topics such as reading and comprehension, reading rate, learning strategies, memorization techniques, test-taking skills, error analysis, and self-esteem are targeted for improvement. Over the years, the medical H.E.L.P. Program has remained dedicated to the belief that many individuals with learning differences can in fact become competent, skilled physicians. Our team of learning disability specialists involved with the program have greatly enjoyed being an integral part in helping so many achieve their dreams.

Law

ABA National Mentor Program for Lawyers and Law Students with Disabilities

https://www.americanbar.org/groups/diversity/disabilityrights/resources/mentor_program_ment
ee_information/

The American Bar Association's Commission on Mental and Physical Disability Law established the national Mentor Program for:

- law students with disabilities
- prospective law students with disabilities, and
- recent law school graduates with disabilities

The Program's purpose is to give members of these groups the opportunity to learn from an experienced attorney.

Service Hotline
Phone: 800-285-2221 / 312-988-5000
Monday-Friday 9:00 AM - 6:00 PM ET

Chicago Headquarters
321 North Clark Street
Chicago, IL 60654
Phone: 312-988-5000

Washington DC Office
1050 Connecticut Ave. N.W., Suite 400
Washington, D.C. 20036
Phone: 202-662-1000

Bar Information for Applicants with Disabilities (BIAD)

http://www.americanbar.org/groups/public_services/mental_physical_disability/resources/biad.
html

Provides information from state, territorial, and federal jurisdictions that grant licenses to practice law.

(See above for contact information.)

Impact Career Fair for Law Students with Disabilities

http://www.law.arizona.edu/impact/

An annual career fair for law students with disabilities to interview with public and private employers in Washington, D.C.

University of Arizona
James E. Rogers College of Law
1201 E. Speedway
Tucson AZ 85721

Phone: (520) 621-1373
Fax: (520) 621-9140

Lawyers, Lead On: Lawyers with Disabilities Share Their Insights

Rebecca S. Williford (Editor), Carrie A. Basas (Editor), Stephanie L. Enyart (Editor)

This inspiring book contains letters of encouragement and advice from lawyers with disabilities to law students and new lawyers with disabilities. The writers share their perspectives on work and disability, based on their own experiences of success and setbacks.

National Association of Law Students with Disabilities

http://www.nalswd.org/

NALSWD is a coalition of law students dedicated to disability advocacy and the achievement of equal access, inclusion, diversity and non-discrimination in legal education and in the legal profession. NALSWD aims to support the growing number of law students with disabilities by providing a safe and supportive community to connect with other students with disabilities from across the country, networking with lawyers with disabilities, information about career opportunities, and advice on succeeding in law school and the legal profession. The success of NALSWD as an organization depends on the active participation of law students with disabilities.

Email: president@nalswd.org

TRIALS

http://trials.atfoundation.org/program/index

Trials is a unique partnership of NYU School of Law, Harvard Law School, and the Advantage Testing Foundation. It is a fully subsidized summer study program for students of modest means whose backgrounds are currently underrepresented at the nation's top law schools....

Having a disability qualifies you to apply to this program. Regardless of your ethnicity or economic status, you are a minority who is underrepresented in the legal community.

Trials
c/o the Advantage Testing Foundation
210 East 86th Street, Suite 601
New York, New York, 10028

Phone: 212-744-8800
Fax: 212-439-9602
Email: trials@at-ny.com

WrightChoice Pre-Professional Law Program (PPLP)

http://www.wcprelawprogram.com

WrightChoice Pre-Professional Law Program (PPLP) offers an elite and unforgettable experience for undergraduate minority college students and student with disabilities who are interested in the legal profession. The eight-week rotation is designed to expose minority college students to various legal careers. The PPLP connects students to large and small law firms, private and public sector legal experiences, in-house corporate, non-profit, and exposure to working with sitting Judges. The selected participants are college sophomores and juniors with strong academic and leadership résumés. Most are preparing for the LSAT and making decisions on where to attend law school…. This program is poised to serve as a pipeline program for law schools and firms committed to diversity. The goals of our program are both education and experience based.

WC Pre-Professional Law Program
911 Robinwood Ave, Suite G
Whitehall, OH 43213
Email: pplp@wrightchoice.org

Science, Technology, Engineering and Mathematics (STEM)

EOP's STEM Diversity Career Expo

http://www.eop.com/expo

Welcome to EOP's STEM Diversity Career Expo that brings industry and government together with members of minority groups, women and people with disabilities in the SCIENCE, TECHNOLOGY, ENGINEERING, and MATHEMATICS (STEM) career disciplines.

Annette Maldonado-Cora
Phone: (631) 421-9421 ext.10
Email: acora@eop.com

How the Workforce Recruitment Program Works

I have mentioned the Workforce Recruitment Program many times. If your school has it, use it! Ask disability services about it. Here is what the process typically entails:[16]

- By early August, the schedule of recruitment visits to schools is posted.

- From September through November, recruitment visits, which include 30-minute personal interviews with individual candidates, are conducted.

- By early December, a database composed of student applications and profiles are made available to employers in the public and private sectors.

Once the database is released, interested employers make direct contact with students about temporary and permanent job offers. The database is active for one year.

More About WRPs: The Interview Process

WRP offers a candidate the opportunity to be placed in a database that both government agencies and private sector employers can access when hiring. You must apply to interview in the fall semester. After your interview, the recruiter that visited your campus will enter a rating into a database. Recruiters will rate you using a 1-5 scale in three categories:

- **Qualifications.** Mostly accessed by items you will have submitted prior to your interview, these may include your transcripts, references and résumé. Of course, being good at interviewing will not hurt this rating.

- **Communication.** Mostly accessed by how well you interview. However, how well your résumé is put together will also factor in.

- **Direction.** In assessing you, the recruiter will be looking to see if you have strong goals that are also realistic. Again, a high score will mostly be won during your interview. However, supporting documents may also help.

Using these three ratings the recruiter will give you an overall rating. You must receive an overall rating of 3 or higher in order to be entered into the database. A rating lower than 3 in a single category won't prevent you from being entered. Your recruiter will write "interview notes" that will be visible to employers reviewing the database. Documents such as transcripts or résumés will also be part of this profile. Employers will review profiles in this database and will contact you directly if they are interested in offering you a position.

---

[16] Taken from the Department of Labor webpage: http://www.dol.gov/odep/pubs/brochures/wrp1.html, which has since been replaced with a redirect to http://www.dol.gov/odep/wrp, which does not contain the material above. Similar material is now available at http://mycareeratva.va.gov/library/internships/workforce-recruitment-program-wrp.

Use Your Student Loans

- Dress for Success
- Attend Job Fairs
- Plan for Life After College

Dress for Success

There are expenses associated with looking for a job. People are commonly faced with the situation of having lost their job, their income has decreased yet at the same time they need to spend money on finding a job. A wardrobe is one expense you will have. As a college student, you might not have professional clothes. Why spend money on suits and formal shoes when that's not how students dress? But this choice not only hurt my chances of getting the best jobs during college; it also drove me away from professional fraternities and sororities.

The dress code at my internship was business casual at best. Again, I had enough to get by without buying a lot of stuff. But as graduation neared, I realized that I needed a suit. My mom bought me one as part of my graduation present. We went shopping together a couple months before the graduation ceremony in case I needed the suit for on-campus interviews.

A couple of months after graduation, I went to live with my dad with my job hunting a focus in both of our lives. He too bought me a couple of nicer tops to start building my professional wardrobe. If you don't have money saved up to buy yourself a wardrobe, or family to fall back on as I did, plan for this. Figure out how you are going to pay for what you are going to need for interviews. It's OK to use some of your student loan money to buy at least two complete professional outfits. Remember, if you are doing this right, there will be events that you will need to attend in professional attire even before you kiss campus life goodbye.

Attend Job Fairs

Another way I wished I had applied student loan money for things other than tuition and daily necessities, is for travel to career fairs that specialize in recruiting those with disabilities for corporate jobs. When I would run into the head of my university's Disability Resource Center and he would greet me with "Hey, future donor." He would say this because at my school, my major was very hard to get into because it was known for being lucrative after graduation. Despite there being a lot of students with disabilities at my university, there were few in the College of Business and even fewer in MIS. I think it got the guy's attention that I applied and got into "the program no one gets into." At the time it would make me happy hearing that – especially since I came from a high school where my IEP Team did not have high expectations for me.

Thinking back, I do appreciate how efficiently my case was handled by my university. However, I wish they had asked me "Do you know about this conference that could help you get a job after you leave us?" Had they realized how pushy I would need to be about getting the future that I wanted, and suggested, it could have changed my life! I would have attended such conferences when I was about to graduate. I would not have been daunted by travel or the fear of missing two days of school. I would have felt that that was my next step.

Of course, I would have flown coach, gotten the cheapest room, and contacted the conference's organizer to waive or reduce the fee due to my being a student. You need to be smart about spending your loan money. Only use loans for what you need, not for retail therapy or just a fling.

I did not find out about the US Business Leadership Network and its annual conference until years after graduation. By then all my SSI was going just to pay bills. I had no savings; I made too little to save. I was well past college, so I no longer had the option of going to student aid and explaining why I needed an extra thousand in student loans to go to a conference. I was on my own in the real world.

I was also very aware that some were a lot more on their own; I still had family to call if I needed something. When I found out about the conference, I had only a little time to get everything together to go. It would have been better if I could save up, plan and go next year. However, that was the last year that they had the career fair. If I had known about it as a student, I would have had a better shot at getting a job through going. Later, having been unemployed for a couple of years, I would have had to regenerate the momentum to get back in the game.

The event that you attend does not have to be disability related. It can be the big yearly event for your profession. The point is, after you graduate, unless you've managed to save some of your student loan money, you won't have that resource anymore. It gets harder and harder to pull yourself out of unemployment. Plan wisely!

Plan for Life After College
Just as you did when you prepared to go off to college, graduation means you will again need to consider how your disability will affect your work life, and *everything else*, which I'll call your home life.

Let's deal with home life first. After graduation, where are you going to live? Are you currently in campus housing which will kick you out within hours of receiving that all-important diploma? Or, do you live off-campus? The latter gives you more flexibility as to when you have to get out. You might even have the option to stay put if you can pay the rent. If you do not have a job and have to go somewhere; can you go back home? This can be temporary or more permanent, depending on your situation.

If you do go back home, don't feel bad! A study found that *85%* of all US college grads move back home for some period of time. Having a disability complicates your situation and may make moving back home even more natural. Even if you have a job, it may be best to move back home so you can focus on mastering working life, THEN re-tackle moving out. Living on your own is different from living at college.

Work Life Begins in Earnest

As for work, I have covered and will cover more topics that are directly related to job hunting. In this section I want to talk about re-assessing your situation one more time as college ends. What did college life let you "get away with" in terms of your disability that might be problematic in a job? What can you do to transition away from that while I am still in school?"

I will answer this for myself to illustrate what I mean. There were three areas in which being a college student made my disability a lot less of a problem, where it would have been a problem on the job: communication and not looking the part. These issues weren't a problem to the point of stopping me from being a decent and often even good student. But again, the real world out there is different. Let's see what I could have done in school to assuage the challenges of my three when I went to the next stage of life.

Communication

I have always had speech that is difficult to understand. Throughout my life it has affected me in various ways. In school, during my pre-college years, it freaked many teachers out. This caused them to lobby for a solution that I feel was not in the best interest of the greatest number of people.

The law prevented them from doing the equivalent of not hiring me. When I reached college, my professors were less up front about their discomfort. However, I am sure each one I encountered had their own thoughts about me, whatever those might have been. Professors have thoughts about all students – I am no different. My speech did make my campus life more difficult. I have no way of knowing how my social life would have been different if my speech were not impaired.

True-story...

One of my professors recommended to me a weekend, off-campus event that I could attend for extra credit. What happened illustrates the challenges that can happen when people are not successfully communicating.

I only half-understood the bus system, so I got off at the wrong spot – at night. I wasn't that far away from my dorm, so I decided to wheel my way home. The sidewalk on my side of the road came to a crumbling halt next to a multi-lane road. I wasn't going to jaywalk across to get to where the sidewalk picked up again. I just kept going on the shoulder of the road, thinking *This isn't cool.*

I could see that the sidewalk continued maybe 100 feet ahead. I could see the school's stadium; as soon as I was there, I would be on campus and feel safe, even though my dorm was on the opposite side of campus. I told myself, *"You're almost at the stadium, just keep going!"*

But it was not to be.

Two women who were driving by, pulled over, got out of their car, grabbed my chair and pulled me into the nearest parking lot.

"You're not safe," they told me. "We're calling the cops!"

I showed them my university ID and tried to explain. I was hoping that when they saw my ID, they'd realize that I was in college and able to reason as well as any other U of A student. That would lead them to let me go on...

But no, again. They called 911, and then actually lied to the dispatcher, telling her that they had found me wandering *in the middle of the road*, "nonverbal and agitated."

That was it! I became irate and just started to curse them out. When the cops got there I immediately calmed down. Cursing at the police would only make matters worse. My goal was still to get home in a reasonable amount of time that night, not be sent to some psych ward for an evaluation.

I told the cops what happened, as best I could. My motor functions and speech aren't too great, I said, but I am in college; my reasoning abilities are fine. They seemed to get it. One of them said, "My wife used to live in your dorm."

The way they were responding, I thought they were going to either let me go on my way or take me home. But again, no...

"You were probably fine, but since we were called, if we did let you go and something were to happen to you, we'd lose our jobs. We are calling the crisis van to take you home. We'll stay here, till the van arrives, and it will be fine."

I replied, "Great, thank you, Officer."

I was wondering why they couldn't just give me a ride home. But I thought they had their policies and procedures and at this point it would be best to go with the flow.

I had never felt such relief as I did when the van, carrying me, turned onto my block. Until that point, I was afraid they were lying to me, saying that they were taking me home only to keep me calm for as long as possible. Fearing that I was headed for the county psychiatric facility!

I cannot tell you how relived I felt when I realized that wasn't the case. I was really going to get to return to my dorm that night.

I wanted to tell my professor what great lengths I ended up going to earn extra credit in his course. I figured I had nothing to lose by trying, and it might help my grade. Unfortunately, once again there was a communication breakdown. He just couldn't understand me well enough. After just a few minutes of trying, it was clear that it was a lost cause.

Happy ending: throughout the semester I was able to communicate well enough to earn an 'A' in his class!

Back in the Real World?

In the world of employment, the laws are not nearly as powerfully on your side as they are in high school and college. True, an employer cannot legally decide not to hire me due to my speech if I can still do the job. But there's no law that guarantees me a job. They can give the job to someone else and either not say why or give another reason. They can hire me and then not promote me. If I am making employers sound evil, I don't mean to. Everyone puts their interests first; that is the way of the world!

How could I address this in college to make it less of a barrier to getting chosen by employers? I could have started using an augmentative and alternative communication device. These systems take a while to become used to using. College would have given me an opportunity to learn my system so when I went to get a job, I would have been a master. This illustrates that while you might have gotten to college without the help of something, as the game changes from education to employment, you may opt for it.

My case also illustrates that, just because you identify a problem and a possible solution, doesn't mean that you have to use that particular solution. I have thought about my communication issue. I feel that there would never be a situation where I am struggling that an augmentative communication device would make things easier! I have a laptop; I can just type it. There's text-to-speech software that I can load onto a laptop. I do not see why I need another device. I have spoken with others who agree with me that also have speech impairments. My family disagrees with me; they think an augmentative communication device would have made me more 'employer friendly.' I do not know who is right. I do know that the way I chose to handle this issue feels right for me.

Should I have felt that I needed an augmentative communication device, Vocational Rehab would have paid for it. That is another lesson, when it comes to equipment or evaluations that are needed to make you more employable, go to VR. When it comes to expenses anyone would incur, such as a wardrobe or travel to get employed, my experience has been student loans will allow a wider scope of what they will cover. If you want to submit everything to VR first, go ahead. Expect a no and be happy if you get a yes. I don't think VR would have covered my trip to specialized job fair, but I could have used student loan money for it.

Looking the Part

Compared to the other women in my office, I think hair and makeup are an area of weakness for me. On campus, again, things are more relaxed in this area of life. Professors must let you in their class even if they don't think you look good. Again, employers are prohibited from not hiring an applicant for not looking "good" (unless it's reasonable to consider appearance as relevant to performing the job, of course), but are not legally required to hire or promote anyone.

It matters how one looks on a job; it just does. I am not writing this to debate right or wrong. I am writing this from the standpoint of what I have encountered and what has been proven. How could I have worked on this during college? Simple, designate a time to practice. I am a night person. This meant I had some night classes. For me to incorporate a new set of behaviors into my routine – which is the goal when working on ADLs – I would have started blow-drying my hair and putting on makeup before every class even if it was at night. The goal of this would have been to get better at it *before* I really needed it and without having to learn a lot of *other* new behavior at the same time.

Your Turn

I've explained my barriers to employment and how I could have better addressed them in college. What are *your* barriers? What can you do in college to remove or lower yours so you can have the employment future that you deserve?

Planning for Graduate School

Grad school might be right for you for several reasons. First, you want to enter a profession that requires a graduate degree to be hired, such as doctor, lawyer or physical therapist. Second, you feel that the chances of your finding a job with only a bachelor's degree in your field are not great. This can be because of the economy, how you did as an undergraduate, or both. Three, you want or need more time with campus services to "get your life together" so you can have the best shot having a "typical" adulthood. By getting your life together I mean making use of anything I mentioned in chapters nine through twelve. By "typical adulthood" I mean being able to work, live and do whatever you want. There is no shame in going to grad school because you're not ready to work.

In my case, I was struggling the first two years with being at college. This meant I was not actively working on building a résumé. Another example of this is that my first and second year, I would have never talked to my professors about anything personal. I considered my goals and fears about employment personal. Toward the end of college, I finally felt secure enough to do so! The sooner you accept these issues without judging yourself for having them and start talking to anyone that you think might "get it" and be able to help you, the better off you will be.

Towards the end of college, I started to do more of what I needed to be doing to be a stronger applicant. One thing was talking to some of my professors. My struggles in high school, which led to struggles in my early college years, would have made a strong case to stay in school and get my master's. While doing so, I could have used that time in a way that would have given me the best chance at the adulthood I wanted. Remember, adulthood is really long. It is going to be the longest part of your life. Investing an extra two or three years in building a stronger foundation for the next four or five decades will be worth it.

I am not advocating either of your two options, enter the work force or go to grad school. You may be sick to death of writing papers and taking tests. You may also feel as prepared as you can be to move on to a career. It is entirely possible that there is nothing more you can do to address your disability and another two or three years in a slightly more flexible environment will not make any difference. You are wherever you are in terms of how your disability impacts you. If this sounds like you, going to work is your next logical step.

If your goal from the start was a graduate degree, then it will be a better plan to get a higher GPA in your undergrad program. Then worry more about résumé-building during your master's studies. If a bachelor's is as high as you need or want to go academically, then put more effort into the résumé as I described in Chapter 7. If you're going to go to law school, your best shot is to have a high GPA all the way through undergrad *and* law school. If you want to work for a top corporate law firm, they want graduates at the top of their class. On the other hand, if you are getting a master's in a liberal arts field to have more time on campus, your time while in grad school would be better used by becoming a more well-rounded job candidate. If you get a master's in literature, you could then apply for a wide range of jobs. This means making more contacts and being able to boast of more extracurricular achievements will serve you better.

If you go to grad school for either medicine or law, consider how you will be accommodated during work differently than during your undergraduate years. Prepare for it by knowing what to expect. If you get your undergrad degree in business administration and return to the same school for a master's in public administration, Disability Services will more than likely work the same way.

Most graduate programs require entrance exam scores. The kinds of accommodations you can be granted during these exams are the same as for the SAT/ACT. However, it might be a harder to get approved for such. Do your research and start early.

MCAT

http://testing.astate.edu/PDFs/mcatada.pdf

You must register to take the MCAT before requesting accommodations.

AAMC
MCAT Office of Accommodated Testing
Attn: Saresa Davis, Mailroom Supervisor
2450 N Street, NW
Washington, DC 20037

Inquiries and Decision Letter Requests:

Email: accommodations@aamc.org

GMAT

GMAT test takers requesting test accommodations are strongly encouraged to submit all of the required forms and information well in advance of the desired testing date. The forms and supporting documentation must be reviewed to determine whether the request is adequately supported and to identify appropriate accommodations, consistent with the Americans With Disabilities Act (ADA) or applicable law.

A decision regarding your accommodation request may take up to three (3) to four (4) weeks.

Express Mail / Courier Service
Pearson VUE
Attention: GMAT Disability Services
5601 Green Valley Drive, Ste. 220
Bloomington, MN 55437

GRE

ETS Disability Services
PO Box 6054
Princeton, NJ 08541–6054

Phone: 1-609-771-7780 or 1-866-387-8602
(toll-free for test takers in the United States, American Samoa, Guam, Puerto Rico, U.S. Virgin Islands and Canada)
TTY:1-609-771-7714
Fax: 1-609-771-7165
Email: stassd@ets.org

LSAT

LSAC Accommodated Testing
662 Penn Street
Newtown PA 18940-0995

Phone: (215) 968-1001
Fax: (215) 504-1420
Email: accom@LSAC.org

More about the LSAT

You must register and pay to take the test first, then request an accommodations packet.

Thanks to a YouTube video by The National Association of Law Students with Disabilities[17], I can tell you the following:

The application process for accommodations is particularly lengthy. If you are approved for any accommodations for your LSAT, you need to save the documentation. This is because if you apply for accommodations to take the bar exam, you'll be able to document the fact that you received accommodations throughout your education. You will be in for extra scrutiny when applying for accommodations for the LSAT and the bar exam. If you only have one doctor's note when applying for the bar exam and are not able to show a history of needing academic support, you will probably be denied.

I imagine that the extra difficulty has had to be imposed because admission to the bar is such a valuable career asset that it draws more cheaters than other tests.

Unlike undergraduate admissions tests, such as the SAT, at the time this book was written, LSAT score will be "flagged." This means the schools that you apply to will see that you received accommodations.

The National Association of Law Students with Disabilities offers more information on disability accommodations for both the LSAT and bar exam on their website.

---

[17]From: https://www.youtube.com/watch?v=Nzkl4m438jM

Points to Remember from Chapter 9

✓ As you near college graduation, you should pivot to more actively seeking what you want next: either your "dream *first* job" or graduate school.

✓ Don't let the momentum that you have worked so hard to achieve die by graduating without a plan.

✓ You might think "I just want to take some time off." You very well deserve it. However, it is usually better to make your plan and defer that time off, rather than defer making your plan.

✓ I have seen too many college grads with a variety of disabilities stagnate once they graduate. I wrote this entire book to try to stop you from running into that. The way to prevent that is to graduate with a plan. It does not have to be the perfect plan (thank goodness).

✓ College usually affords more latitude in terms of both flexibility and resources than the workforce. That could be enough reason for you to attend grad school. You very well could feel that you have mastered every aspect of life with a disability that you can. A few more years will not do anything for you. If that is the case, the work world is calling!

✓ Know that it is an option for any borrower to get their loans discharged due to disability. Meaning if a doctor fills out the appropriate paperwork saying that a borrower is unable to work due to a disability, they then do not have to repay the loan. Also know the system will only let you do this once. If you discharge your undergrad loan, then you get another loan for graduate school, you must pay it back. Whereas, if you attain a master's or PhD through continuous college attendance, you'll have (technically) only one loan to either (preferably) repay or get discharged. Finally, student loans are (usually) not dischargeable by declaring bankruptcy, so plan accordingly.

✓ As you face leaving your college campus, ask yourself *"What can I get done while I am still here?"* You don't want to regret any missed opportunities. If you move home after college, chances are you will not have the same access to the plethora of resources you had on campus.

Success Story: What Can I Offer Others?

By "Jane" (name withheld by request)

My name is "Jane," and I'm an appellate attorney who represents indigent criminal defendants. I was born in 1968. At the age of three months old, I contracted spinal meningitis through an ear infection. This led to fluid retention on the back part of my brain causing me to have cerebral palsy.

I could walk but only with assistance and I still had difficulty speaking and eating. Nonetheless, out of all the siblings, I was the only one tapped into the National Honor Society and initiated into the girls' social club, Anchor Club. Two days after high school graduation, I went to Florida Southern College in Lakeland, Florida where my peers gave me a sense of belonging as if my disability did not exist. They encouraged me to serve as a camp counselor during the summer at a Methodist youth camp in Leesburg, Florida, a rustic environment, alongside them. When I had doubts due to my disability, they encouraged me. That was the most physically challenging job but the best job I ever had! I did that job each summer until I graduated from college. my senior year, I was asked to be a Lil Sis of Lambda Chi Alpha fraternity and ended the year by being elected "Miss [Florida] Southern. "At Stetson College of Law in St. Petersburg, Florida, I worked a part-time job in the library to pay for groceries, and also worked fifteen hours a week as a Public Service Fellow which paid some of my tuition. I took a full load and went year-round. In law school, students were given three- and four-hour essay exams at the end of the semester which was the sole basis for the grade. I was accommodated by having twice the time and allowed to type my essays. I never knew that six to eight hours could pass so quickly.

I had one surgery in my third year, but only took a week to recover. It was the first time I experienced pain and fatigue. After I graduated and took the bar exam in 1994. The Florida Bar denied my request for accommodation initially, but then allowed me time and a half. The exam consisted of two parts which were six hours long each. Examinees without disabilities took the first part for six hours one day, and then returned the next day to take the second part. The Florida Bar allowed me nine hours on each part, but I had to complete each part in one day meaning nine hours of testing per day. I failed the second part. I took it over twice and missed the passing score by two points each time. I pleaded with the examiners to let me take only the second part of the test for six hours one day and return the next day for three hours to complete the exam. They granted my request, and I passed the Bar in 1996.

I was diagnosed with fibromyalgia in 1999. During the two years between graduation and passing the bar exam, I lived at home for eight months where I volunteered at a friend's law firm. Then, in 1995, I enrolled in the MBA program at Florida Southern College, and I lived with a couple who were longtime friends. After four months, I got an apartment in college housing for graduate students. My financial aid covered rent, and I lived on SSI for ten months until I passed the bar and got hired. Those ten months were difficult since the apartment was upstairs without an elevator. No washer or dryer. Every Saturday, I packed my dirty clothes in a suitcase to kick down the stairs, took a bus over to my friend's house and did laundry. I was volunteering two or three days a week at the Public Defender's Office in Bartow, a 25-mile drive by taxi, studying for the bar, and attending three-hour MBA classes four nights a week. Then, after I was hired, I worked from 7:30 am to 5:30 pm, went to class from 6:30 pm to 9:30 pm, ate a TV dinner and went to bed four nights a week. I kept that schedule for six months and then dropped out of the MBA program.

I was determined not to give in to fibromyalgia, maintaining my work schedule and social life until 2001. Then, I began to be a regular visitor at the ER with chest pain, bladder retention, and other symptoms of fatigue. So, I gave into working from home twice a week and resigned from the boards, but still clung to too many social obligations. My fibromyalgia became more prevalent, and the 25-mile commute to work and back was too hard; I had to walk about two blocks and take a regular Lakeland city bus to the bus station, and then wait a half-hour for the Bartow bus, which took me to the Bartow courthouse where my office was. It was an hour and a half one way. While working in Bartow, I argued four cases in the Second District Court of Appeal and one case in the Florida Supreme Court. From 1998 through 2001, I was also the mental health liaison for the office working with trial lawyers and mental health providers.

In 2003, I transferred to the Public Defender's Office in Tallahassee because I could work and live in the same town! I did very well here for three- or four-years health wise, but then, the fibromyalgia became worse. I hired help with housekeeping and errands and changed doctors. I tried pool therapy, different sleep schedules, different diets, but nothing seemed to help. In March of 2007, I reluctantly decided I needed to move into assisted living to have assistance with daily living activities so I could conserve energy for work. I sold my furniture, dishes, cookware, and every nonessential item to fit my bed, desk, filing cabinet in a small room. In 2012, I was strong enough to move back into an apartment and live independently with home health coming in every other day. I'm more active than I have been in twelve years. I still have fibromyalgia, and work from my home full-time. I volunteer once a week for four hours at hospice, and carefully select other activities so I avoid becoming too fatigued.

My advice to a young person with a disability consists of three principles; (1) take initiatives to make people without disabilities comfortable with you, (2) pick a career which meets your abilities with the least amount of accommodations, and (3) when an accommodation is necessary, think of the easiest method and be the one who proposes it. Remember, while it is not your fault you have a disability, it is also no one else's fault. By taking the initiative to put others at ease with you, you remove the invisible barrier of fear, pity, and guilt that non-disabled person may feel. Pick a career that meets your abilities, and not just your dreams. Very few people have dreams of jobs which meets their abilities. I never wanted to be a lawyer. I dreamed of being a teacher or a minister, but my speech ruled such careers out. I knew I could analyze research and write a paper; that is what I do when I write a brief as an appellate attorney. Remember also that the Americans With Disabilities Act is an equal opportunity law, not affirmative action. That means an employer can hire a person without disabilities if he or she has the same qualifications as you without violating the ADA, so long as the employer gave you "an equal opportunity" to apply for the job. Thus, it is wise to have an attitude of "what can I offer others," as opposed to "what do I need from others to succeed."

Part III: Getting a Job

Chapter 10: Finding a Job

I will not lie: the process of finding a job is usually not fun! It is one of the most trying experiences of a person's lifetime. It is a lot of work – and unpaid work at that. As with everything else in life, your disabilities might make it more challenging. But everyone gets through it eventually, if they keep looking. Eventually the process will end, and you will find a job. It might take longer for you, and it might not be your dream job, but you will get there.

The same principle applies to job seeking as anything else in life with a disability. Start the process as anybody else would. If you not making progress, there are resources that are specially designed to help people with disabilities find jobs and succeed in them.

You might be in a situation similar to that of lots of people in their twenties without disabilities. You graduate from college, then you take some time off. Then reality sets in; it feels like you were in a cap and gown just yesterday when it was several months ago. You feel the need for some cash flow to be coming in and that requires you to find a job. Eek, how do you start?

You might be a person who up until now has been minimally affected by your disability. Or you may be like me, ever since you were old enough to understand what was going on, your disability has impacted you. It doesn't matter. Each new life stage you enter, you might still wonder, "How will my disability impact my next venture into the unknown?"

Network

This is not the first time I have talked about networking. Why do I keep harping on it? Because it's vital! Research shows that networking is the most successful way to find a job. Hopefully you started networking in college or even before college. If you did, now is the time to start working those connections in earnest. Trust your gut about whom to contact. But there is no such thing as going too far back. If you feel your first-grade teacher will remember you and be happy to get a graduation announcement from you, send her one. She might very well respond with "What are you doing now?" That's a perfect opportunity to tell her you're looking for a job (and describe the kind of job). You never know who will know someone!

52% of adults with disabilities find their jobs through personal contacts

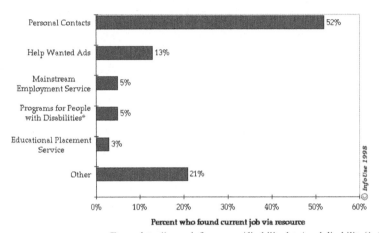

From: http://www.infouse.com/disabilitydata/workdisability/4_6.php.

More than half of employed adults with disabilities report that they found their jobs through personal contact. The percentage was highest among those who worked part-time – 62%, compared with those who worked full-time – 45%. One in five or 21% report finding jobs through means other than personal contact, help wanted ads, mainstream employment services, special programs for people with disabilities or college or training program placement programs.

You Are Only a New Grad for So Long!

I graduated in December. I should have started applying a couple weeks or a month later for internships for that following summer! What I failed to realize is many internship programs extend eligibility to applicants who are up to a year out of college. Meaning that they were still hiring someone as an intern if they graduated less than a year ago! If you are reading my book for the first time as a college graduate, don't assume you missed the opportunity to intern – not so.

The Workforce Recruitment program that I first spoke of in Chapter 2 also comes into play here. This program lets you interview through them up to a year after graduation! If I'd known about this in January or February after I graduated, I could still have benefited. I could have campaigned in the spring to bring the program to the University of Arizona, and then interviewed in the fall.

It makes sense to me why someone would not care about this program until after they graduated. I would have seen it as a useful tool when I was at my dad's after college, thinking, "Alright, this is what I'm facing. How am I going to deal with it?" It would have been great for me to have sprung into action to form a backup plan.

Just like you have only a year to take part in the Workforce Recruitment program and about the same amount of time to apply for most internship, this was vary depending on the internship. Your college or university almost certainly has a career services department or something with a similar name. This is an office department that you need to contact. Most schools have policies that provide students with career services for a while after graduation. So even if you didn't get very involved with them when you were a student, it might not be too late.

However, don't wait too long. This option will eventually be closed off to you. At the school I graduated from, the entire student population could participate in on-campus interviewing for a year after graduation. Yet, if you contact them in five years, they will not do anything for you.

USBLN Conference and Job Fair
The last thing I wish I had known about during the year after I graduated college is the USBLN's conference and job fair! I could have very easily put together a plan to go. Either of my parents would have been happy to let me live rent-free to save up for the trip and look for a job in the meantime!

Volunteer or Temp

The worst thing any unemployed person can do is nothing. By nothing, I mean sit at home using job-hunt strategies that are not working. How do you know if they are working? Simple: if you have been doing the same thing for longer than six months and you still do not have a job, or more than two interviews, it is not working. What do you do instead of sitting home? Anything you can! More specifically, volunteer or temp. Temping is where you work with an agency and they send you out to work at sites that request that they send them staff. These jobs could only last a day, or they could last several months.

When you get a position that lasts for months; this is a good thing. Companies often "try people out" through them temping but ultimately will hire a temp that they are happy with. Remember, companies prefer to hire from within. This means if you get an internship, temp position or are a volunteer somewhere, you are way more likely to get that job openings when it becomes available than someone on the outside. Even if you do not get offered a permanent position through your first temping job, you are still building skills, making contacts and extra income. It might take you awhile or several temp jobs to become a regular hire. So what? If you use this to keep working until you get a job offer, this will be your method to success in an increasingly tough job market.

Volunteering has all the same benefits as temping, except you do not get paid. However, when you volunteer you will probably be at the same work site (in contrast to temping, naturally). This can make volunteering easier if you do not drive. If you do not know where you will be working from one day to the next, it will be harder to arrange transportation. Volunteering can absolutely lead to a job! Yes, no one likes to work for free. However, in the long run it can be well worth the sacrifice.

Balancing

You might be thinking "Looking for a job is a full-time job." You are right! You might be thinking that you do not have time to volunteer or temp on top of that. To that I say, you are half-right. It is okay to your make job hunt the sole focus of your life for a definite period of time. However, at the end of that time, if you do not have a job, I say you need to be either volunteering, temping, going back to school, or a combination. One year from your college graduation you need to be doing *something*. Not just saying "I am looking." Volunteer or temp, even if it is just two days a week. That way you still have plenty of time to look for a paid position since you are not working full-time.

AmeriCorps

AmeriCorps engages more than 75,000 Americans in intensive service each year at nonprofits, schools, public agencies, and community and faith-based groups across the country.

Since the program's founding in 1994, more than 900,000 AmeriCorps members have contributed more than 1.2 billion hours in service across America while tackling pressing problems and mobilizing millions of volunteers for the organizations they serve.

While one can participate in national service at any time in their lives, many chose to do so right at of school, due to job experience and further education benefits.

AmeriCorps is a national *service* organization. When you work for them, you are considered a volunteer doing national service work, not an employee. However, all AmeriCorps positions do offer both a small living allowance and opportunities to get money for education. That is, if you work for them for an agreed-upon period, they will pay part of your tuition. This applies to both undergrad and graduate degrees.

One of AmeriCorps' many objectives are to increase the number of people with disabilities taking part in national service. This is the reason the HEART Act was passed. This act allows those who collect SSI to continue getting their full amount despite the fact they are earning a small living allowance and educational benefits.

The HEART Act only protects those who collect SSI. It does not apply to people who earn SSDI. AmeriCorps has several programs of national service. VISTA allows those on SSDI to keep their full amount and receive a living allowance. With the other programs, you need to be on SSI to have assurance that your benefits will not be affected.

AmeriCorps' different programs are each run differently, catering to different interests. Visit their website to see which program(s) are best for you.

VISTA

Today, more than 46 million Americans live in poverty. AmeriCorps VISTA taps the skills, talents and passion of more than 7,000 Americans annually to support community efforts to overcome poverty....

Members make a year-long, full-time commitment to serve on a specific project at a nonprofit organization or public agency. They focus their efforts to build the organizational, administrative, and financial capacity of organizations that fight illiteracy, improve health services, foster economic development, and otherwise assist low-income communities....

AmeriCorps VISTA is open to all U.S. citizens, nationals, or lawful permanent resident aliens age 18 and older. Members and Summer Associates receive a modest living allowance. Members who serve for a year also receive limited health benefit options, childcare, if needed, and other benefits. After successful completion of a term of service, members can choose to receive a Segal AmeriCorps Education Award or post-service stipend.

I think this is a fabulous way for new graduates (be it high school or college) to start getting work experience. It will also help you build a résumé and could lead to a job. If not, it's a good way to pay for more education. It's also a good way to start working without jeopardizing your SSI. Should things not work out, you do not have to go through the effort and stress of getting *back* on SSI!

Additionally, if you are having trouble finding a job, AmeriCorps is a great way to keep up your momentum and morale.

To start your AmeriCorps journey, contact:

Disability & Inclusion Advisor
Email: disability@cns.gov
For more information: https://www.nationalservice.gov/node/36515

Recap: What Should You Be Doing as a New Grad?

- ✓ **Look for Internships:** Many internship programs allow recently graduated students to participate. Do not feel this opportunity is gone when you wear a cap and gown. Also, be aware that you will probably only be able to be an intern for so long after you are a student
- ✓ **Check out the Workforce Recruitment Program:** Consider if that could help you land a job. Again, you have only one year to take part in this. Meaning you need to start efforts to bring it to the college that you graduated from, right after graduation.
- ✓ **Look into Your School's Alumni Career Program:** Every college or university has services to help their graduates find employment. However, again, some schools only offer the most extensive services to people who have graduated within two years. Find out what your school offers, are there time limits and use whatever's offered!
- ✓ **Attend Conferences:** The best time to go to a conference either for your industry or with the goal of increasing disability employment is when you are fresh out of school and ready to work.
- ✓ **Consider AmeriCorps:** Excellent way to get work experience, make contacts and earn founding for further education
- ✓ **Volunteer.**
- ✓ **Network.** This needs to be a lifelong practice. It is also what is most likely to find you a job and is a must for **ALL** new grads!

Keep Up Your Momentum!!!

The ADA and Employment

Title I of the ADA deals with employment. It reads as follows:

> The ADA states that a covered entity shall not discriminate against a qualified individual with a disability. This applies to application procedures, hiring, advancement and discharge of employees, workers' compensation, job training, and other terms, conditions, and privileges of employment. Covered entity can refer to an employment agency, labor organization, or joint labor-management committee, and is generally an employer engaged in interstate commerce and having 15 or more workers. Discrimination may include, among other things, limiting or classifying a job applicant or employee in an adverse way, denying employment opportunities to people who truly qualify, or not making reasonable accommodations to the known physical or mental limitations of disabled employees, not advancing employees with disabilities in the business, and/or not providing needed accommodations in training. Employers can use medical entrance examinations for applicants, after making the job offer, only if all applicants (regardless of disability) must take it and it is treated as a confidential medical record. Qualified individuals do not include any employee or applicant who is currently engaging in the illegal use of drugs when that usage is the basis for the employer's actions.[18]

That is the good news! There are laws that protect those with disabilities against employment discrimination. There is a common misconception that the ADA requires employers to hire those with disabilities. This is flat-out not true! You are not guaranteed to get the job that you are interviewing for just because you have a disability. Employers are NOT required to lower their job requirements because of an applicant's disability. If the job requires that you be able to lift so many pounds or type so many words per minute, the employer is not legally required to lower that or waive it due to an applicant's disability. However, the employer **cannot** tack on requirements that are not essential to the job. For example; an employer cannot require you have a driver's license or be able to lift fifty pounds for a simple office job. Conversely if a company is hiring a truck driver, they have the right to require that the applicant have a driver's license and can lift a minimum weight.

In the scenario that there are two candidates who are equally qualified, the ADA does not legally require that the applicant with a disability be given any extra "points" when making hiring decisions. The intent behind the ADA is to remove one's disability status as being a factor in the interviewing, hiring and employment. What the law provides for and what really happens are not always the same.

---

[18] Adapted From: http://en.wikipedia.org/wiki/Americans_with_Disabilities_Act_of_1990.

Limits of ADA

The ADA was designed to end discrimination based on disability. Has it? No. Has it helped? Probably. While I may sound pessimistic, I prefer to look at it as being real. I say no matter who you are, you are going to encounter discrimination sometime in your life. This is more possible when a person is job hunting. While there are plenty of laws that are in place to protect people from hiring discrimination, the truth is people who are hiring can hire whomever they want. When one is hiring, they are most likely to hire someone who they feel would either fit themselves or their company the best. Another way of looking at this is people like hiring people who are like them. This could include anything from age to appearance to religion to where one went to school to whether one is a parent. Now, it may not be fair, it is how it is. This is one reason why looking for a job is usually not fun.

One example: it's illegal to not hire someone based on their religion. However, it is legal to invite someone from your synagogue to interview, and you end up hiring that person for nonreligious reasons.

Another example: If two people respond to my ad and I hire one of them, legally it is almost impossible for the other to sue me for discrimination even though it is illegal to discriminate based on age or sex. As long as I didn't ask any illegal questions or say, "I am not hiring you because you are old," or "because you're a guy," or "I feel 20-year-olds are flaky." What I did was hire the person who made the best impression on me during the interview. That is legal. I contacted the other candidate and said thanks for your time, but I am going with another person. That's it; I did not give a reason why I did not hire them.

The fact that you are very rarely given a reason why you are not being hired is one reason why disability-based discrimination in hiring is hard to prove. Often, they did not hire you because of any one of thousands of factors. For you it *could* be your disability, but how do you prove it? Most often you have to say, "I just didn't get the job." It happens. It must not have been the right job for you. Every interview is an opportunity for you to improve.

Trust me, I know how difficult this is! Also trust me when I say that people without disabilities go through the same thing.

Even though discrimination is hard to prove, there are instances where it is clear-cut. For those times you can file a complaint with the Equal Employment Opportunity Commission (EEOC). See the section below.

Just consider before you file a complaint or a lawsuit, it will take up a lot of time and cost money should you chose to sue a company. Also know that courts do not have a good record in ruling in favor of the plaintiff in cases such as these. In fact, in more than 9 out of 10 cases, employers win when their employees file disability discrimination lawsuits against them. That does not mean you have no chance of winning, it just means overall the courts tend to rule on the employer's side. I am not telling you not to file a complaint. But I encourage you to consider carefully the strength of your case and whether it's worth the hassle.

You may encounter a situation where you suspect you were discriminated against by an employer, but you're not sure. In those instances, you can contact a client specialist at JAN:

> Phone: (800) 526-7234
> Website: http://askjan.org/links/contact.htm

JAN's office hours are 9 am to 6 pm Eastern, Monday through Friday. After working hours, calls are received by an answering machine and will be responded to by the next business day. If you are accessing JAN services after regular business hours, please leave your name, the purpose of your call, and an e-mail address or phone number (including area code). Please see the website on what information JAN needs to help you in a timely manner.

JAN can help you figure out if you were denied your rights based on the ADA. If yes, they can inform you on how to file a complaint. They can also help you figure out how to overcome the issue to go forward with the hiring process for that job or overcome a disability-related challenge so that you can get the next job that you apply for.

One instance, where I felt I was being denied proper accommodation during the interviewing process. I did not want to file a complaint with the EEOC, I wanted to fix the issue, so I could go forward with their hiring process. In other words, I still felt qualified and wanted the job! I did contact everyone at the company whom I had contact with to explain and ask for an in-person interview rather than just a phone interview. Due to my speech being impaired them substituting a face-to-face for a phone interview would have been a reasonable accommodation based on my disability. In my attempts to try to get the company to reconsider their decision not to pursue me as a candidate, which consisted of sending a couple well thought out emails. I also wished I had contacted JAN to see if they had any suggestions Even if contacting JAN did not lead to me getting the job, I would have known that I did whatever could to get what I needed. There is a certain satisfaction in knowing you did everything that you could dot regardless of how it turns out.

What Should I Do If I Think my ADA Rights Have Been Violated?

You should contact the nearest office of the Equal Employment Opportunity Commission (EEOC). Someone will help you determine whether you should file a charge of discrimination:

> http://www.eeoc.gov/
>
> Federal Sector Programs
> 1801 L Street, NW 8th Floor
> Washington, DC 205017
>
> Phone: (800) 669-4000
> TTY: (800) 669-6820
>
> There are strict time frames for filing charges of employment discrimination. In most states, you have 300 days from the time the alleged discrimination occurred to file a charge, but in some states, you may have only 180 days. The EEOC field office nearest you can tell you which time period applies to you. However, you should file a charge as soon as possible after you believe the discrimination occurred. [19]

You do not need an attorney to file a complaint. At is recommended that you file in person, when possible. You can also by telephone, or by mail. Before you file you should prepare the following:

1. *Yourself* (your name, address, and telephone number)

2. *How you qualify for the job* (your education, work experience, training, references, job performance reviews, and other documents that show that you can do the basic parts of the job. It is also a good idea to show your ability to work with other people, make good decisions, and be a good worker).

3. *Your disability* (what your disability is, how it limits major life activities, what records you have of being disabled, and how the employer thought of you as being disabled).

4. *The employer* (name of employer, address, telephone number, type of business, and, if you know, the number of employees).

5. The discrimination you experienced:

   a. The type of discrimination you experienced, including discrimination because of your disability, as well as other factors you think may be related to the discrimination such as your race, national origin, sex, religion, or age.

   b. The date, place, and people involved in the discrimination.

   c. The names and contact information of people who saw or knew about the discrimination.

---

[19] From: http://www.humancentereddesign.org/neada/pubdocs/pub_127.pdf.

6.   It is a good idea to have *written documents from other people* for things that are difficult to explain or prove, like a disability that is hidden, and how it limits your major life activities." [20]

"At the EEOC, after you file a complaint, the office will review it and give it a priority. There are three categories that your complaint can be put in:

- **Category A.** This is the highest priority and means that the office thinks that there is a strong case or even that there may be severe harm to the person filing. Most Category A complaints will be thoroughly investigated by the office.

- **Category B.** This is the next-highest priority and means that your complaint might not be as thoroughly investigated.

- **Category C.** This is the lowest category and means that your complaint will most likely be quickly dismissed or closed.

For the cases that will have some investigation done, a letter will be sent to you and the employer. The letter tells the employer that a complaint of employment discrimination has been filed. It will not include all the information in your written complaint. It will give the employer a deadline for responding to the complaint. It will also warn the employer not to retaliate against you because you filed the complaint.

After the office has reviewed the information from your complaint, any response from your employer and the results of the investigation, a decision will be made on your complaint. The decision will either be: (1) there is reason to think that the complaint is true (called "reasonable cause") or (2) it is found to be probably not true (called "no reasonable cause"). You will get a letter with this decision. If your complaint results in a decision of reasonable cause, then the EEOC will try to work with you and the employer to find a good result."[21]

Important to Remember: As of September 30, 2000, **ONLY** about 16 out of every 100 people received some kind of benefit from the employer as a result of filing a complaint." And then if you do file a lawsuit, your odds of winning are not good either.

---

[20] From: http://www.adaenforcementproject.unc.edu/adaguide.html.

[21] From: http://www.adaenforcementproject.unc.edu/adaguide.html.

What Are the Conditions of People Who Aare Helped by Vocational Rehabilitation?

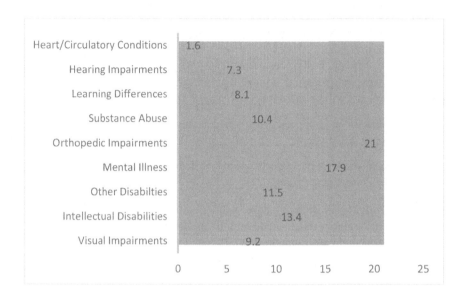

Heart/Circulatory Conditions: 1.6
Hearing Impairments: 7.3
Learning Differences: 8.1
Substance Abuse: 10.4
Orthopedic Impairments: 21
Mental Illness: 17.9
Other Disabilties: 11.5
Intellectual Disabilities: 13.4
Visual Impairments: 9.2

Based on: Rehabilitation Services Administration, program statistics (911 data based on FY 1995 cumulative case load report.)

Conclusion: Vocational Rehab (VR) mostly serves people with physical disabilities.

About 60% of successful rehabilitation clients worked a full work week

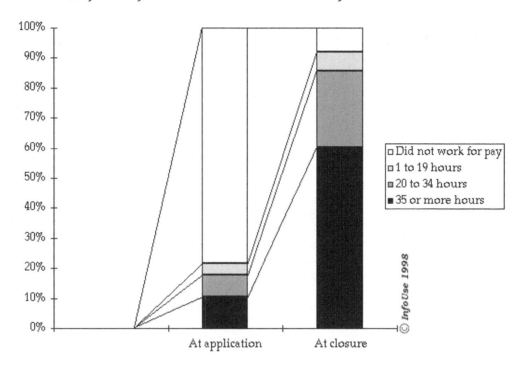

Source: Rehabilitation Services Administration, program statistics
(data based on FY 1995 cumulative case load)

My Thoughts on Vocational Rehab

There are some positives in Vocational Rehabilitation One, their services are free. Two, you can apply for services anytime. There is no stipulation about having to be in school or newly graduated. Three, they are used to working with those who are disabled. Some other reasons opt to go to VR are; you are finding that you disability is consistently causing the same obstacles to working, you want to return to work after either a decrease in function or acquiring a disability and are now not sure how you will perform the work you did prior or you want someone to help you navigate how working will affect benefits such as Medicaid and social security.

There are also some negatives to going through Vocational Rehab. I know in many states there is a waiting list of six months to a year before you can get services. This is because funding is always being cut. You need to prove your eligibility at the time you are placed on the waiting list, not at the time you receive benefits.

I had multiple experiences with a couple of different counselors. Thinking back on each encounter that I have had, I would rate each one poorly. But they paid for my books the last three years of college. This was a huge help!

When I tried to go to VR to find a job, this was two years after I graduated, it did not work for me. It was always the same; one pointless appointment after another after another. Despite my going to these appointments, nothing ever got done. That time ending in my case being closed, without my knowledge.

For me, VR did not work. I have concluded it's another case of "you get what you pay for." Vocational Rehab is free; to me it makes sense that they are not all that good at serving their clients. I needed them to help me get interviews. Whenever I said what I needed, their answer was "that's not how we do things." It was extremely frustrating! I feel that I gave them plenty of time to work with me and they did not do what I needed.

And they did not inform me, when I was in college, or after, about Schedule A, a government hiring initiative that I was qualified for and would have helped me get a job. Getting a job was the sole reason I opened a case with them after college.

I have also noticed that they don't model good job skills to their clients. They failed to keep appointments, and often did not maintain a professional demeanor. To me this was absurd, considering that they are supposed to be teaching people how to get and keep a job.

But just because vocational rehab did not work for me doesn't mean they won't help you. They are a resource at your disposal, and I want to inform you of all of your options.

Getting help finding a job is the same as getting anything you need from Vocational Rehab! You need time, everything will take forever. You need persistence, patience and understanding! This is because your counselor is only allowed to do what they are allowed to do! It is not their fault if they cannot provide you with good service because they themselves have a million procedures to follow. You need to go into the system knowing this and be able to keep working to get what you need.

Other Options for Career Counseling

As in all areas of life, just because you have a disability does not mean that you are relegated to using services only for the disabled. Most go from unemployed, to jobseeker, to employee without doing formal counseling pertaining to this part of their lives. An important note here, finding a job without professional help is *not* the same as finding a job without help! I believe everyone needs help when finding a job. Be it consulting books or internet resources to make a game plan, or having someone help them with their résumé, relying on their support network for advice on interview fashion, or just listening, or getting a position from networking: job-hunting is rarely a solo venture.

Some find themselves in a position where they have read books, talked to their friends and/or family and they are still at a loss to where to start. Others fall into a situation where they've been actively seeking work for over a year and don't feel they're getting anywhere. If either sound like you, you might want to get professional help.

There is a myriad of options out there for job seekers. Some examples are career counselors, job coaches, and placement firms (or "headhunters"). You'll need to decide what you need help with specifically, then do research on what is available both in your area and in your price range. Should you pay for services, really look into their success record as to whether they really do what they claim. There are going to be scams out there. If they promise to find you a job for $49.95, that is a red flag. You know the saying is if it is too good to be true...

When opting for a counselor without experience with those with disabilities, it is common sense you will need to let them know any relevant information about your disability as it pertains to either your job hunt or life on the job. You will also need to gain your own knowledge on both the ADA and if applicable how employment will affect your benefits. That said, private services could be better at serving your needs. Take me for example; my experience has led me to believe that I need private counseling for my career-related issues. I certainly feel I have a total awareness of how my disability impacts me, how the ADA works, as well as benefits issues.

Or Get Both...
Private counseling and vocational rehab are not mutuality exclusive. Your best bet might to go private to either find a job, determine your plan for a career change or to decide if you should go back to school for more job options. Then go to VR to find out if they will fund anything, or to make sure you know how to work without losing your personal attendant care. My uncle's a private college coach; I could probably think of ten things he'd do, such as help his clients find the best school for them. Most of what he does, a VR counselor probably would not do. My uncle probably feels a lot more vested in "his" kids' outcomes than a VR worker who is mandated to show up to an IEP.

That being said, if my uncle had a client with a physical disability going to Yale, he very well might refer them to VR to see what help in funding the client was eligible for. VR would probably know more about how to apply for state-funded attendant care than my uncle would. Plus, no matter how much my uncle loves his students, he's probably not going to buy their books throughout college. Neither will a VR counselor – but the VR counselor might be able to appropriate government funds for that.

Contact Your Elected Officials

This idea comes from the book, *Job Hunting for the So-Called Handicapped*, by Richard Nelson Bolles and Dale Susan Brown. It makes total sense if you are looking for a job to contact your elected officials. There are a lot of people in government! You could send the same letter and résumé out to almost a thousand people – including the president of the United States, all 50 governors and each Member of Congress. This could get results; however, it is not likely. The president gets thousands of letters and phone calls a day. Only a fraction of those reach the leader of the free world … who will respond to a very small percentage of that fraction. Same is true for governors and senators – the volume is only a little lower.

Your best bet would be to contact your congressional representatives in your congressional district. The more "local" the official, the more he or she will be able to respond to constituents. You will have the best chance if they are able to confirm that you are in their district right away. To ensure this, include your ZIP+4 area code at the top of your letter. You can look it up at: www.usps.com.

> Unless you have a personal, first-name relationship with a member of Congress or one of their staff members, the way you guarantee that your communication will be effective is to make sure the receiving office instantly can identify you as a constituent. If they can't, there is an excellent chance your communication will be discarded without being read. Start each communication with your name and address at the very top:

> Ms. Sally Jones
> 123 Main Street
> McAlester, OK 74501

> When writing a member of Congress, it's important to use the proper salutation. For senators it's "Dear Senator" (and the senator's last name: Dear Senator Lansing:). For members of the House of Representatives (according to House rules), the way to address female members of the House is "Congresswoman" and male members is "Congressman" (Dear Congresswoman Munster:). However, using "Dear Representative" (Dear Representative Hammond:) is acceptable.

> If you are sending an e-mail to a representative, you won't receive a response via e-mail but will receive one through the mail (rules of the House – however, you can communicate with House staff members via e-mail). Senators respond to e-mail with e-mail. If you follow these guidelines and establish a working relationship with the elected official or one of their staff, you might be sending and receiving e-mails on a regular basis.[22]

As in any cover letter, you need to be concise and positive. Your letter should be no longer than a page. The main point is that you have this type of disability and you are looking for a specific type of work. Use the rest of the letter to make them like you. An example is talking

---

[22] Reprinted with permission from the Oklahoma Association of REALTORS®.

about why you are committed to staying in their district by stating why it is a great place to live or you want to be a contributing member of that community.

If you have experienced discrimination during your job hunt, say so. But make sure the tone is positive. Do this by ensuring that for each sentence you use to describe the discrimination, write three sentences about why you are amply qualified for the exact type of position that you are seeking. Clarify that your intent in writing the letter is to ask them for advice in finding a position, not asking them to go after whomever you feel discriminated against you!

If you overcame sizable obstacles despite your disability to get your degree, that also could be how you fill up the page and get them to like you. Again, keep the tone positive.

Follow up with a phone call to their office to ask if they received your letter. Ask to speak to who is responsible for running daily operations at the office. If you can talk to someone on the person's staff, this can help get some attention to your letter.

Focus on no more than three government officials at a time. Tailor each letter just to the recipient and then follow up with their offices. Start local. If you still get no reply after follow-up, target two or three other officials, going from as local as you can, all the way up to the president. If you are trying to relocate, start with officials where you want to live. Say why you would like to live there that you want to become an asset to their community.

Finding Your Local Government Officials
http://www.contactingthecongress.org/

The link above does not list mayors. Do not forget to write either the mayor of your town or the town you want to work in! State in your letter that you are aware of vocational rehab, but you are trying to expand your job hunt beyond a reliance on any one agency. Remember, these people are elected to serve you; if approached correctly, that is what they will want to do.

Companies That Embrace Diversity

Another idea is to apply to companies that most value diversity. This list comes out often and is easy to find on the internet. You could also search for list of the best companies for (fill in the blank), to get still more lists of companies to apply to.

Granted, who knows how these companies really get on the "best" lists? When I look at these lists, I sometimes think, "That company gets sued every other week for sexual discrimination," or, "How nice, this other company got on the list despite my experience with them as a job applicant did not leave me with the impression that they value diversity. I consider myself a skeptic. Despite this, all companies are compelled to at least look like they're seeking diverse candidates. Some truly do want to honor that. Such lists could help you find companies that will have these values.

Apply in Person Sometimes

When one talks about job-hunting, the phrase "pounding the pavement" often gets used. There is something to be said for applying in person. If you show enough commitment to go there, it shows that you really want the position. This could work particularly well for smaller companies, in that there won't be 10 levels in the org chart separating you as the job applicant from anyone who can make any decisions. As a new grad don't overlook smaller companies! They could provide you with that opportunity out of school just as any larger company can. There also might be less competition and easier access to the hiring process.

As a person with a disability, applying in person may be more intimidating. If you deem that going there in person will be most effective in getting the job, then you just have to do it! Suit up, print out some résumés, grab your portfolio, and go get what is yours! Now, if this does not work out, of course you will feel some disappointment. This is part of life and certainly part of job hunting. But remember *it only takes one yes!* By *yes,* I mean a job offer. When you get that yes, it will not matter how many no's you heard before.

Placement Agencies and Other Resources for Jobseekers Disabilities

ABILITYJobs

http://www.abilityjobs.com

ABILITYJobs is an "employment resource for individuals with disabilities, corporations seeking a diversified work force, and rehabilitation service providers. Free services for job seekers include résumé posting and searchable job listings. Fee-based services for employers include job postings and résumé searching. Job seekers and students seeking internships can freely post their résumés and cover letters on the site with the knowledge that companies are actively seeking them for employment.

PO Box 10878
Costa Mesa, CA 92627
Phone: 949-854-8700
Fax: 949-548-5966
Email: hire@abilityjobs.com

ABILITYJobsPlus

http://www.abilityjobsplus.com

Ability Jobs Plus recognizes a serious lack of employment opportunities within the disabled community. Currently in the United States there is over 54 million unemployed (non-military) individuals, and over 3 million disabled unemployed Military Veterans. This is the reason why AbilityJobsPlus exists. Our main focus is to educate the community and the public in general. We want to help disabled individuals reintegrate into the work force and or enter the working world for the first time.

P.O. Box 6276
Kingman, AZ 86402-6276

Bender Consulting

http://benderconsult.com/

Bender Consulting Services, Inc.'s mission is to recruit and hire people with disabilities for competitive career opportunities in the public and private sectors.

3 Penn Center West, Suite 223
Pittsburgh, PA 15276

Phone: 412-787-8567
TTY/TDD Relay Service: 800-654-5988
Email: resume@benderconsult.com

Career Opportunities for Students with Disabilities (COSD)

http://www.cosdonline.org/home

The COSD website will provide background information on COSD and the work of COSD in assisting college students and recent graduates with disabilities in career development and attaining a career of their choice.

100 Dunford Hall
Knoxville, TN 37996-4010

Phone: 865-974-7148
Fax: 865-974-6497
Email: amuir@cosdonline.org

Damon Brooks Associates

http://www.damonbrooks.com

Damon Brooks is a talent agency that specifically represents performers and speakers who have disabilities. The Web site includes a list of the performers they represent as well as their clientele. Contact them directly for information about joining their roster.

Damon Brooks Associates
1601 Holly Avenue
Channel Islands Beach, CA 93036

Phone: 805-604-9017
Email: marc@damonbrooks.com

Disability Matters Radio Show

http://benderconsult.com/about-us/disability-matters-guests

Disability Matters with Joyce Bender focuses on the employment and empowerment of people with disabilities. It is one of the first international talk radio shows with real-time captioning. Hear prominent disability leaders such as Congressman Tony Coelho, Governor Dick Thornburgh, Andy Imparato and senior executives from the private sector.

Glance through the archives of this show; there are several guests who are in corporate America. Listen to those who you feel would be beneficial to send your résumé to – then do it! Hunt down their contact information on the internet, send them a cover letter mentioning where you heard them and that you are a person with disabilities with a degree in (whatever) … Then follow up!

JobAccess

https://www.jobaccess.gov.au/

JobAccess is dedicated to increasing the employment of people with disabilities. People with disabilities can post their résumés and search for employment opportunities. The site also offers a "Résumé Builder" tool that helps job seekers to build and post a professional looking résumé. Employers can browse for qualified job candidates and enter detailed search criteria to find job seekers with specific skill sets. Companies can post job descriptions and contact

information, and search the online résumé bank. In addition, the site offers extensive information on the ADA.

1001 W. 17th St.
Costa Mesa, CA 92627
Email: generalinquiries@jobaccess.org

Lime Connect

http://www.limeconnect.com

The Lime Network - our broader virtual program that prepares and connects students, and alumni, with disabilities for success regardless of their geographic location.

590 Madison Avenue, 21st Floor
New York, NY 10022
Phone: (212) 521-4469
Fax: (212) 521-4099

National Business and Disability Council

https://www.viscardicenter.org/nbdc/

The NBDC is the leading resource for employers seeking to integrate people with disabilities into the workplace and companies seeking to reach them in the consumer marketplace. The NBDC site contains a national résumé database for disabled individuals, job postings, accessibility surveys, an information hotline, audio/visual library addressing various issues pertaining to disabled employees, a monthly informational mailing, customized training services, information on conferences and seminars, and applicable links.

201 I.U. Willets Road
Albertson, NY 11507
Phone: (516) 465-1515
Fax: (516) 465-3730

Email: mcgowan@business-disability.com

The Sea Glass Group

http://theseaglassgroup.com/

We have developed a selective identification and recruitment process designed to ensure a custom fit with our client's needs and the candidate's qualifications. Our searches, by design, span multiple industries and disciplines; placements range from upper and mid-level management positions for established professionals, to career building leadership positions for recent college graduates.

Submit your résumé and cover letter to: resumes@theseaglassgroup.com

U.S. Business Leadership Network

https://www.ncil.org/usbln/

The U.S. Business Leadership Network (USBLN) is the national organization that supports development and expansion of its BLN affiliates across the country, serving as their collective voice. It is the only national disability organization led by business for business. The USBLN recognizes and promotes best practices in hiring, retaining, and marketing to people with disabilities. There are 53 Business Leadership Network affiliates in 31 states, including the District of Columbia, representing more than 5,000 employers across the U.S. The BLN uses a "business to business" approach to educate, promoting the business imperative of including people with disabilities in the workforce.

1310 Braddock Place, Suite 101
Alexandria, VA 22314
Phone: (800) 706-2710
Fax: (800) 706-1335
Email: info@usbln.org

Points to Remember from Chapter 10

- ✓ Network, Network, Network. It is the number one-way people find jobs!

- ✓ Consider volunteering; consider AmeriCorps.

- ✓ Think about everything you do online. Don't blow an opportunity because your prospective employer finds dirt on you.

- ✓ Contact your elected representatives could lead to a job.

- ✓ Vocational Rehab is at your disposal; decide if they are right for you.

- ✓ Know your rights under the ADA and your options should you feel they have been violated.

- ✓ Know and try out all the agencies that help jobseekers with disabilities.

- ✓ Most Effective Job-Hunting Strategy: Persist!!!

Remember, you only need one <u>YES</u>!!!

Chapter 11: Interviewing and Disclosure

The goal of any job interview is to get a job offer. How do you accomplish this? Simple: by using the interview to convince the decision-maker that you are the best person for the job! It is really that simple for any jobseeker, regardless of their situation. As in anything in life, the core of being successful is the same for you as it is for those who do not identify as having a disability. Your disability just might add a few factors to consider.

What Your Interviewer Really Wants to Know

A crucial part of preparing for an interview is to *put yourself in the interviewer's shoes*. I will be spending a lot of time in this chapter helping you do just that. Analyzing the situation from the other person's perspective will help you do the things that will help the interviewer see you as the "best fit" for the job.

No matter who you are or what job you want, your interviewer will be trying to answer for himself the questions below.

- Can you do the job as well as, or better than, anyone else I'm likely to find with the time I have?

- Will you add value to the company?

- Will I look good for having decided to hire you?

- Do you have the potential to help me get promoted?

- Can I depend on you?

That is all it comes down to. Your interview mission is to get the interviewer to answer these questions in the affirmative!

The most important difference between you and the nondisabled job applicant is that you might require some accommodations. We all know by now that discrimination based on disability is illegal. But obviously not everyone follows every law all the time.

It's in your best interest to minimize, first, the *emotional impact* of the idea that you will need accommodations. In a non-technical sense, we all "accommodate" people that we like most of the time. It's not all about the technicalities of the law and how much it will cost the employer to meet your particular needs. It's about removing any concern that your disability is going to be a constant inconvenience for your employer – something that the employer would regret having had to accommodate.

Now, just because I've expended more words on the question of accommodations than I have on any of the other considerations in the interviewer's mind, don't assume that means that every interviewer is going to be focused on this question more than on the others. Some human resources professionals are trained to be very well aware of disability issues, but others will put them out of their mind within just a few moments of sitting down with you (unless you explicitly bring it up).

Again, most interviewers are hoping you will be the first who can meet the needs of the position, so they can stop interviewing and "get back to work." They are not looking to shoot you down for the pleasure of it. Most interviewers will not even be thinking about disabilities unless they see a wheelchair or a cane.

People vary; how they do their job also will vary based on their personality. This is the way the world is. But the more you are "all business" – yet also appropriately warm – the more likely the interviewer will be, too.

When Disabilities Affect the Interview

When you have a disability, it's quite possible that you will have to adjust how you do things in order to be your best during an interview. This might go against the interview advice you've heard. I don't completely reject that advice, but I moderate it. My rule is: Comply with what the literature says about interviewing as best you can. But it's better to slightly change your interview plan, to best fit your disability. Remember, the goal is to make the best impression possible – not to do the *impossible*!

Examples from My Life

Conventional interview advice says do not bring water, much less coffee, into an interview. For my particular disability set, talking is harder when I do not have water. Having more trouble speaking would have greater and a more negative impact on an interviewer than my being prepared with a water bottle. After all, many people keep a water bottle at their desks and drink from it all day. So, it is very unlikely to even be seen as a negative if you have one with you during the interview.

Typically, your handshake is one of many things' interviewers will use to evaluate you – perhaps less consciously than how they evaluate other things about you. Well, of course if you are paralyzed or an amputee, you may have a handshake that is affected by your disability. You might not be able to shake hands at all. This will not count against you with any but the most boorish persons. Most interviewers will have sense enough to "get it" right away and move on. Make a good first impression in other ways, such as by giving a genuine but appropriately brief smile, with direct eye contact, also appropriately brief.

Present the Best *You*!

Clean, Working Equipment
As I explained in Chapter Eight, if you use a chair or other mobility aids, make sure you clean it thoroughly the night before! Remember, in the eyes of other people at least, *your chair is an extension of yourself.* Always make sure that your equipment is clean and is in good repair before you go for an interview. You would not go in wearing dirty shoes, so do not go in with a dirty wheelchair or cushion. And again, make no unnecessary last-minute changes. You're likely to be nervous about the interview itself; don't throw obstacles in your own path!

No Fumbling
If your briefcase is on the back of your chair, leave it there. In deciding whether you want to use your lap, under your chair or the back of the chair to put the things you need during your interview, do whatever's physically going to be easiest for you to access during the interview. You do not want to be struggling to pull out your résumé.

In fact, you want to keep any physical struggling to a minimum. Your disability may be apparent, and that is fine. But you do not want to be seen as having any more trouble functioning than you actually do just because you are nervous or failed to plan well. Let the interview see you at your physical best. It will be easier for your new employers to overlook physical awkwardness after you've already gotten the job and wowed them with your job performance.

Play the Game You Can Win
In an interview, it is all about selling yourself. While I can walk some, l always use my chair for interviews. This is simply because walking is a way bigger physical struggle for me than rolling. I feel best in my chair. How can I feel confident when I stumble into the interview with my "CP gait?" When I cannot stand long enough to shake hands firmly? I cannot. Walking into an interview will not get me any points. "Oh, she can walk, good for her." No. It will only make me lose points. They will know I am disabled, but I am going to make every choice I can to present my best self.

It's Just Business
None of this is about hating yourself for being disabled, or assuming that an interviewer will hate you for it. It's just about being honest and realistic. You've had some time to get used to your disability; the interviewer hasn't. Don't let your disability hog the stage, pushing your hard-earned job skills into the background! Keep them front and center.

It's no different than picking shoes or a handbag that you think looks best on you, is most appropriate for the occasion, or both.

Before the Interview: Arranging for Accommodations

The Americans with Disabilities Act (ADA) requires employers to provide reasonable accommodations during the interview process. An employer cannot refuse to consider you because you require a reasonable accommodation to compete for or perform a job.

If you need an accommodation during the interview, you have to ask for it before the interview. Your interviewer will need time to make arrangements. A request can either be made orally or in writing. The important thing is to notify the company or place you are interviewing as soon as possible. Be sure to reply promptly to any of their questions regarding your request.

The prospective employer can ask certain questions about your request. These fall into two categories:

1. Why is the requested accommodation needed?
2. Will our plan to honor the request work for you?

Just be friendly and work with the employer through this process. Don't assume there is negative intent behind such questions. Most people – especially human resources professionals – are pretty good at detecting defensiveness. Don't give them a reason not to hire you!

Examples of "reasonable accommodations" during the hiring process include (but are not limited to):

- Providing written materials in accessible formats, such as large print, braille, or audiotape

- Providing readers or sign language interpreters

- Ensuring that recruitment, interviews, tests, and other components of the application process are held in accessible locations

- Providing or modifying equipment or devices

- Adjusting or modifying application policies and procedures.

- Extra time for pre-qualifying tests for those with documented learning disabilities

- A face-to-face interview in lieu of a phone interview or use of Speech-To-Speech relay for those with speech-impairments [23]

---

[23]Adapted from: The Website of the U.S. Equal Employment Opportunity Commission

Informal Accommodation Request

Here is an example of an email message that I typically would send to tell an employer that I need an accommodation in the interviewing process.

> Hello Mr./Ms. Jones,
>
> I would like to take this opportunity to both thank you for the initial contact and to respond to your request for a phone interview.
>
> I have a physical disability that affects my articulation, making it harder for people to understand me on the phone. I prefer to use email to make it easier for those I am communicating with. I do not require any on-the-job accommodations for my disability. Generally, I keep my laptop available to use as a communication aid if needed.
>
> Obviously, this may pose a challenge to conducting a phone interview. I am willing to try, as some people have no trouble understanding me via phone. However, if you would rather use either email or instant messaging, these are options that I have used in the past. I look forward to "speaking" with you further about the position!
>
> Best regards,
>
> Julia Nelson

Formal Accommodation Request

This Sample Accommodation Request Letter (really just an outline of a letter) was downloaded from the Ask JAN website:

> The following is an example of what can be included in an accommodation request letter and is not intended to be legal advice.
>
> ---
>
> Date of Letter
>
> Your name
>
> Your address
>
> Employer's name
>
> Employer's address
>
> Dear (e.g., Supervisor, Manager, Human Resources, Personnel Department):
>
> Content to consider in body of letter:
>
> Identify yourself as a person with a disability
>
> State that you are requesting accommodations under the ADA (or the Rehabilitation Act of 1973 if you are a federal employee)
>
> Identify your specific problematic job tasks
>
> Identify your accommodation ideas
>
> Request your employer's accommodation ideas
>
> Refer to attached medical documentation if appropriate*
>
> Ask that your employer respond to your request in a reasonable amount of time
>
> Sincerely,
>
> Your signature
>
> Your printed name
>
> Cc: to appropriate individuals
>
> ---
>
> You may want to attach medical information to your letter to help establish that you are a person with a disability and to document the need for accommodation.
>
> Linda Carter Batiste, J.D.[24]

The second is more formal. Adapt whichever style that you feel would best serve you.

---

[24] From: http://askjan.org/media/accommrequestltr.html

I like this letter outline and would use it. However, I would not "state that you are requesting accommodations under the ADA (or the Rehabilitation Act of 1973 if you are a federal employee)." To my mind, such formal language would make me look litigious. One of employers' fears of dealing with or hiring those with disabilities is that they will be at greater risk for lawsuits. Remember, as a job seeker, your goal is to get the job! Simple. By telling employers I know the exact law, I may feed into their fears. Only after they refuse a reasonable accommodation request would I cite the law(s) that require them to comply with my request.

The 'Dreaded' Phone Interview

My disability affects my speech. I hate talking on the phone. It has been the source of many a melodramatic meltdown. Adding the stress of an interview to that is just over the top!

Phone interviews are also commonly used by companies as a tool to weed out applicants in less time than required by in-person interviews. The system is designed to eliminate less articulate candidates. I understand companies need to do this.

Yet you might, like me, be a member of a sub-group of the population whose lack of ability to speak over the phone in no way indicates how much skill and quality I would bring to my job. The thing about being in small groups is that we are often overlooked. From an employer's point of view, they are thinking in generalities when designing their hiring process. They are mostly not thinking about things from the applicants' point of view. In most cases they are more afraid of hiring a bad employee, than they are hoping to hire a good one. So how do you overcome this disadvantage?

Using Speech-to-Speech Relay on Phone Interviews

My answer is use speech-to speech relay for phone interviews.

Speech-to-Speech (STS) is one form of Telecommunications Relay Service (TRS). TRS is a service that allows persons with hearing and speech disabilities to access the telephone system to place and receive telephone calls. STS enables persons with a speech disability to make telephone calls using their own voice (or an assistive voice device). Like all forms of TRS, STS uses specially trained operators – called Communications Assistants (CAs) – to relay the conversation back and forth between the person with the speech disability and the other party to the call. STS CAs are specially trained in understanding a variety of speech disorders, which enables them to repeat what the caller says in a manner that makes the caller's words clear and understandable to the called party.

A person can make an STS call from any telephone. You simply call the relay center by dialing 711, and indicate you wish to make an STS call. You are then connected to an STS CA who will repeat your spoken words, making the spoken words clear to the other party. Persons with speech disabilities may also receive STS calls. The calling party calls the relay center by dialing 711 and asks the CA to call the person with a speech disability. STS users have the option of muting their voices during an STS call, so that the party to whom they are speaking hears only the voice of the STS CA, and not the voice of the STS user. If you wish to use this option, please inform the STS CA to mute your voice for the other party to the call. If you choose this option, the STS CA will still be able to hear what you are saying and will re-voice what you say to the other party.[25]

---

[25] From: http://www.fcc.gov/guides/speech-speech-relay-service

They Can't Ask You That

Simply put, employers cannot ask you "Are you disabled?" or "What is your disability?" This is the case even if you use a wheelchair or a white cane. I think this is silly. I mean, I am obviously disabled. To me it is no big deal if anyone asks, "Why do you use a wheelchair?" But regardless of my opinion on this point, the law is still the law. What employers can ask are questions to ascertain whether I can do the job with reasonable accommodations.

While the employer has a right to ask certain questions about the accommodations, that does not mean it's open season on every aspect of your disability or how it affects your life. The questions must be directly relevant to either the interview process or whether you can perform the "essential functions" of the job with "reasonable accommodations." These terms are defined in the ADA and of course in numerous court decisions interpreting the law.

I have "issues" with the way the law was written, but I understand why it was written the way it was. The majority of people who self-identify as having disabilities have "invisible disabilities." I can see why this law would offer them better protection.

Should You Mention Your Disability?

When someone with a visible disability interviews for a position they must also deal with the wild card of whether the prospective employer will be uncomfortable, either consciously or unconsciously, with the fact that I am disabled? Interviewing differs from daily life. In my daily life, if someone I meet gives me the sense that they cannot see beyond my disability. Oh well, that is life; we just don't "click" with everyone.

However, on an interview, they have something that I want and need: a job. Therefore, I have more motivation to try to make them comfortable with my disability. To me the only mentality that makes sense on an interview is to casually try to put the other person at ease with my disability with the goal of them seeing past it. Anyone who interviews for any position or job, goal number one is to show them what you can do for them. For me in order to achieve goal number one, I need to first make them see past my disability. How do I make them see past it? Get them comfortable with it. Again, for me, disclosure is not an issue since my disability is obvious to all who meet me. It then becomes not *do I tell?* but rather *how do I get people comfortable with it, without focusing on it?*

My Take

You may or may not agree with my thinking, that of needing to make those comfortable with you during an interview. You may feel there is nothing for them "to get comfortable with."

I hope my suggestions make sense and feel both practical and natural to you. If they do – great. Otherwise, don't do them. In an interview, it's important to come off self-assured (with the understanding that almost everyone is at least a little nervous during a job interview). If something feels awkward for you to say or do on an interview and you say or do it anyway, you might be perceived as awkward. That hurts your chances of landing the job. This book is all about figuring out what works for you to get the job!

As I have already written, you DO NOT have to bring up your disability in an interview! Employers can only ask whether you can do the essential functions of the job – that's it. They cannot ask what your disability is, again no matter how obvious it is. If you do not have to mention your disability, why would you? Every reader will answer this differently. Some will say "I do not have to talk about it, so it's best not to." That is completely fine!

The second half of this chapter deals with disclosure, with the goal of informing you of your options and helping you choose the best one for you. If you choose not to disclose until after you get hired, or never to do so, then you don't have to think about tit going into the interview.

But consider: People fear the unknown. This is also true of people who do not identify themselves having a disability when it comes to interacting with people who do. This is a fact of life. This is also easily worked around if you just look at it through their point of view.

Do what feels right to you. And if you either choose to disclose or are forced to have everyone know, your goal needs to be to make everyone comfortable!

Strategy One: Mention It in Advance

Generally, when one goes for an interview, they have some with the employer beforehand to confirm place, time and so on. A lot of you reading this may find it smart to mention the fact that you or in a chair, blind or an amputee right after you have scheduled the interview. While you are still on the phone say, "I just want to make sure your building is accessible because I am in a wheelchair." Great, most buildings are, and my being in a chair probably will not come up again. I just did not want to shock you when we meet."

I operate with the assumption that most public buildings are accessible. Despite being significantly disabled, I don't give much thought to accessibility. So, when I ask about it, it's really just an easy way to tell people, so that they're not surprised when I show up in a chair.

Strategy Two: Use Common Interview Questions
Interviewing is not a total unknown. In most interviews you'll be asked the same types of questions. Successful job hunters/interviewees familiarize themselves with the most common interview questions way in advance to form a plan of how they are going to answer to maximize their chances of getting job offer. A list of "common interview questions" can easily be found online. What I think works well is when I am going over these, because I have to anyway in order to best prep for the interview. I think which ones would lend themselves to mention my disability in a positive way.

A question that would did jump out at me is "Would you be able to travel." For me, this would be natural to say, yes. In fact, I love to travel. Some may assume, due to me being disabled it would be considerably harder. Not so, I have it down and love that I am able to board flights first. Even though I am in a wheelchair I am able to walk short distances. This in combination with the type of chair that I use negates my need for total accessibility. There are two steps to get into my home   to me is a natural way of talking about it and telling them a lot more than just am I open to travel.

The question of "What's your greatest weakness, strength," is one I would pass on. In other words, I would not mention my being disabled when answering this question. That would be putting too much emphasis on my disability itself. Even, if I spun it as a strength by either saying it has made me—or I have perfectly learned to do everything with it that I would have done as a non-disabled person. That just is not my style. Again, if it is not your style, it will not go over well!

Another one that I might use is "Why do you want to work here." If they have a good reputation for hiring those with disabilities, or honoring diversity, I would cite that as ONE reason. Not my ONLY reason, regardless of who you are you, should be able to articulate at least three reasons why you want to work anywhere you are interviewing. I also could use, "Tell me why you chose to go to (the colleges I attended)?" I would say "I love big schools; its program is contently nationally ranked for my major and I wanted a school that was accessible." "By going to a school with great disability services it enabled me to focus on my studies, grow as both a person and a perspective employee, as well as given me the confidence to independently coordinate accommodations in all areas in my life. I have no doubt these skills will translate to my work environment." I would end the question with "and the fact that Tucson averages over 300 days a year of sunshine also helped in the decision."

How I would handle these two questions demonstrates how I feel comfortable with making my disability only *one* of my reasons why I want to work for or went to my college. Not the main reason, not the only reason, not the first or the last reason. By doing it this way, I am setting the tone that I need to set about my disability. It's *there*, it's okay to mention or talk about it, but it's not a defining factor. I am there as a prospective employee. The primary focus always needs to remain on the fact that am I the best person for the job.

The last question I like is "What was your favorite course in college?" I could say a course that granted me the opportunity to improve on both my public speaking skills and confidence to use them despite my speech disability. These answers emphasis my abilities while giving some information about my disabilities. In other words, I would rather "spin" it my way as opposed to have people make assumptions that will lead them not to hire me!

Should you decide to use this strategy on the interview, preselect your own questions and answers based on your own situation.

Strategy Three: Use the Part Where *You* Ask Questions

Typical interviews towards the end they ask, "Do you have any questions for us?" Another rule is you always should ask two or three well thought out questions. Saying "Nope, I don't." is an interviewing no-no. From their end you seem uninterested. From your end, you waste an opportunity to prove you are intelligent, ambitious and knowledgeable about the position. There are other books/websites that tell you how to ask excellent questions on an interview to increase your chances of getting hired. I highly suggest that you use them to come up with a plan. Again, there is a science to good interviewing and a lot of it is simple preparation. This book is only dealing with one aspect, the disability aspect, of interviewing. You need to cover all aspects.

It is perfectly acceptable (even preferred) to ask two or three questions. By now maybe you guessed my pattern of having one question, reason, or whatever, be about disability and the others having nothing to do with it. Use one question to tackle this issue. Then for the other two pre-planned questions that have, you guessed it, nothing to do with disability.

Take the bull by horns and ask, "Do you foresee any area of the job that I may have trouble doing directly because of my disability, or are you curious about what accommodations that I would need if I were hired?" *Boom*, you are taking the lead and bringing it up. This tells them it is okay for them to admit their concerns and give you a chance to address them.

> ***Important:*** This is a good technique for two reasons. First, there are laws binding them from asking. But there is no law against you raising the issue – especially if you stick to how your disability will or won't impact your ability to do the job. That is exactly how the law is written. You now know the law. They might not. Therefore, it is up to you to lead them through it. I love this strategy!

One, usually you will be asked do you have any questions towards the end of the interview. This will give your interviewer(s) a chance to get to know you throughout the interview before you address the issue of your disability. Two, it is following the law. You are limiting the conversation to the legal area of whether you can perform the job with reasonable accommodations. But asking, "Do you have any questions about my spina bifida?" or whatever your disability is, would be inviting them to break the law. If they realize that, they could be quite uncomfortable with your question.

For me, the only accommodation I need for an office job is to use the phone as little as possible in performing my duties. I explain to them that I use email as much as possible. I laugh slightly after I say I prefer to email as opposed to calling my family. I then say for those times when I must use the phone, I can use a free, confidential service called "Speech-To-Speech relay." It works by my calling 711, giving them the number that I need to call and then a trained operator repeats what I say." I then give them a printout with basic information about this service. I offer to call them at a future time that they select so they can see how it works.

This is an example of being really specific about how you will complete the functions of the job! This is what they need to feel comfortable hiring you.

What If....

You might be asked how you will work around your disability to do something you had not thought of in terms of doing the job. Do not say "Oh, I don't know." Do not give them an answer you have not thought through. Instead, say "I apologize, I was not aware that that was part of the job description. Would it be possible to give me two business days to contact you with a plan?" Then explain what you intend to do – which is contact JAN. Tell them JAN is a national organization and one of their services is to advise people with disabilities as to the reasonable accommodations that might enable them to do a certain job function." You could then offer them a printout about the basics of JAN.

Immediately after your interview call:

> Phone: (800) 526-7234
> TTY: (877) 781-9403

Or go to their website for live chat and do what you told the interviewer you would. Hello, I have this disability, I want a job as a, how do I perform the task of? If you leave a message a JAN representative will get back to you the next business day. Ask JAN for a contact number in case your perceptive employer has questions.

After you talk to someone at JAN, follow up with your potential employer as soon as possible. Tell them exactly what Jan said, why this will work for you and offer them JAN's contact information. Tell the perspective employer JAN is also for any employer who has questions or wants information about hiring those with disabilities.

Strategy Four: Easing Employer Concerns

Do not read this list of concerns and assume that every interviewer will be thinking all these "bad" things about you. Of this list, only one or two may cross the minds of your potential employers. Bias still exists. I believe it is in your best interest to acknowledge this. There are two opportunities to use this strategy, during the interview itself and/or by handing them a "Disabilities MythBusters Sheet" (DMS) after the interview (more about this below). Each of the fears I cover will be better counteracted by one of these two methods.

Concern Number One: My Insurance Premiums Will Rise

This concern is more likely to be in the minds of smaller employers. To me this fear makes sense. Business by nature is concerned with the bottom line. That is just the way it is! Business owners covering fewer employees are more directly affected by who they cover than a Fortune 500 company with thousands of employees.

This issue probably won't come up explicitly doing your interview. Strict laws prohibit employers from asking about your health status or your history regarding workers comp claims. I have not been able to think of a natural way to raise and resolve this concern during the interview itself. Interviewers are well-trained to steer clear of it.

Still, you have a chance of laying this concern to rest by handing the interviewer the "DMS" *at the end of the interview*. This is a simple way to give your potential employers accurate information that will make them more comfortable with hiring you. Keep it simple, by sticking to facts and statistics.

Leave it at that. Don't get into your own medical history. Even if you have never been hospitalized, been on ongoing medication, or had anything beyond the occasional cold/flu that we all get. It's awkward and possibly illegal to talk about any of that while interviewing, so don't go there. A sample of this document can be found on page 356.

Concern Number Two: "This Person Will Not Get Along with My Other Employees or Fit in With Our Team"

When I first thought of this concern, I got a little angry. This comes from misconceptions I have dealt with my whole life. Especially in school, if you have a disability then you must be in Special Ed. We all know that is not true. The misconception goes on: if you are in Special Ed, then your behavior must also be adversely affected. We all also know this is not true. Everyone has a past, and everyone is affected by that in different ways. But it's not always easy to change the perspective on the way you see something. Sometimes it is almost impossible. This is one time when as soon as I changed how I thought about it, it didn't bother me anymore.

No matter who you are, when you are interviewing, your job is to be likable! People want to hire those like themselves.

Think about it, who would want to hire someone who is not pleasant and makes work less fun? Nobody! One of the main goals in an interview is likability. This should be the same for everyone, whether they self-identify as having a disability or not.

Unlike the last concern, this one is best nipped in the bud during the interview. Since there are no studies are statistics that state people with disabilities have as much chance as getting along with others as anyone else, there is no need to devote space to this on your "disability sheet." You will have ample opportunity to prove you get along with others! Half the questions will be designed to see how well you get along with others. Your job is to be Polly-positive and prove that you work well with others. Do not just say you are a people person, or I love people. Show it by how you talk about your experiences!

A good way to do this is elaborate on something from your résumé. Using myself as an example, I do this when I am asked about being president of my college dorm. I take the opportunity to say how great my fellow officers where, I could never have accomplished (insert a specific example) without them and how much fun we had while doing so.

Concern Number Three: Will They Really Be Able to Do the Job?

No matter how you feel about this, it a potential concern, especially if you are visibly disabled as I am. I simply tackle this one head-on when interviewing. I do this by asking them if they have any questions about how my disability impacts my performance in the work force. Again, I wait until they ask if I have any questions, and then I answer them in the way described above.

Concern Number Four: Changes in Either Job Description or Physical Abilities

Opportunities to address this will come up in interviews. You almost always asked to talk about your strengths. One should be that you adapt easily to new situations. Rehearse in advance a specific example to prove this! If you studied abroad, perfect. If not, talk about any time when things changed rapidly, and you were able to adapt to get the job done. This example should not mention your disability. Remember, your goal is not to make the interview about your disability. It is simply to get the job! Getting people comfortable with your disability is just a sub-goal of the one and only goal of getting the job!

If you bring your disability into everything, that could be a turn-off. Usually, in life, either extreme is bad. For me, being in a chair and having impaired speech, ignoring it would be just as awkward as if I were to bring the topic back to my disability no matter what they ask.

Focus on your experience in previous jobs or group projects in college. I have found that if you are lacking in work experience – and most new grads are – group project stories are great material for interview questions. Look for ways to work in the idea that you also responded well under stress. That will also gain points. Some might think that your disability may make it harder for you to cope with stress. Again, show rather than tell, with *specific stories* – again, carefully chosen and rehearsed in advance! – that prove you are the best for that job!

You can't say, "I haven't had any decrease in physical function nor am I at risk for any." Again, that gets into the zone of not being legal and could make someone who knows the law uncomfortable. You have to talk about your résumé in a way, so they conclude that medical issues do not hold you back. Also, by giving them Ask JAN info on your DMS, they will be able to see that if something does change with your physical abilities, there is someone you can go to.

Concern Number Five: Expense of Accommodations
You have already addressed this by asking "Do you foresee any area of the job that I may have trouble doing directly because of my disability or are you curious about what accommodations that I would need if I were hired?" Do not try to address it again during the interview by talking about the economic angle. This is one for your "disability sheet" since there are facts and figures to bolster what you are trying to accomplish.

If I were putting together a DMS in preparation for an interview for myself, I would state that I consider myself in the 20 percent of workers whose tools for circumventing disability to do my job are already provided to me. Example: A computer that I use in two additional ways because of my disability; one I use email instead of the phone whenever possible; two, I have text-to-speech software loaded onto my laptop for times when people do not understand me. (This software is available to download off the Internet, free and legal, so it can be loaded onto the employer's computer as well.) In event that my job requires me to use the phone, I can use Speech-To-Speech relay, which is also free.

I don't require any adaptations to my workstation (desk), any special computer or phone equipment. Nor do I require any architectural changes to use the restroom or any other facilities for employees.

I would word my statement that way because I feel people assume, I need more than I do. When it comes to perceptive employers, they assume my needs will cost them money; this is not true.

You could include the following chart on your DMS:

Sixty-nine percent (69%) of people with disabilities do not need special equipment or technology to do their jobs effectively.

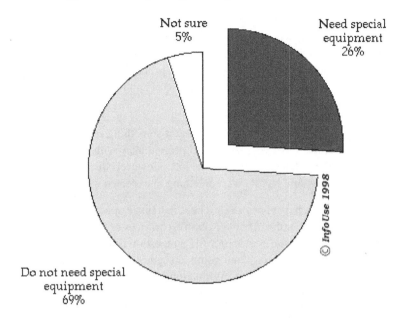

Source: N.O.D./Harris Survey of Americans with Disabilities (1994).
Surveys: Louis Harris and Associates, Inc.

Concern Number Six: Can I Get in Legal Trouble for Firing Them for Cause?

I understand this fear. Would you want to hire someone who would be difficult or impossible to fire without costing you a lot of time, money, and trouble? I know I wouldn't. Some people can fake their way through an interview. So, this might be in the mind of some potential employers.

This item goes on your "disability sheet" and does not get talked about during an interview. It is an interview, not an infomercial! Saying "you can fire me if I don't work out," does not convey that you are confidence in yourself or that you are committed to becoming an asset to that company. Both are crucial when interviewing.

An exception to this rule is if you are interviewing for a law firm. I would leave this off my "disability sheet." Lawyers should well know the law; you risk offending them by implying they don't.

Concern Number Seven: What If There's an Emergency and the Building Needs to Be Evacuated?

This is not likely to come up in an interview. Hence, it goes on your DMS as an attached checklist that details what you'll need if the building needs to be evacuated. Should you be hired, this can be reproduced, either by you or the company, for the appropriate parties.

I really wish I had provided such a checklist for my supervisor at one of my jobs! He told me one day, "I need a plan for you." I just said, "I can walk downstairs if I have to." Had I given him a real plan, it would have been more respectful and made him feel better. It would have impressed him that I was "on the ball" and a team player.

If you have a condition that is "invisible" such as epilepsy, asthma, or extreme food allergies, wait until after you have the job to decide whether you need to alert your co-workers. Do this if you feel, in the event of a medical emergency, those around you need to know what to do for your safety. If you have the condition basically under control, you probably don't need to tell people (other than always wearing the appropriate medical bracelet if applicable).

Concern Number Eight: I Am Alone in This!

No one likes to feel alone in anything. I feel better knowing that if something comes up, I have someone to call! An employer may love you, may be 85 percent okay with your disability. They may think you are completely perfect for the job. However, there may be a question in their mind as to how they would handle it if something unexpected were to happen.

Remember, all through school, your teachers always had school therapists or administrators to go to. In college your professors had either the office for disabled services or student affairs to go to. Where does an employer go, if an issue comes up? My suggestion is to give them something as a safety net. By now you guessed it, I am going to suggest you give them a brief description of the Ask JAN website, and their contact information.

You may be as I was when I started job hunting thinking, "Why can't I say if you have any questions about my disability, at any time, please feel free to ask." I have since learned that, in addition to saying that, it's helpful to provide employers with an objective information source. This is because the employer might feel more comfortable talking to a third party. There are a variety of reasons for this. One being people may be afraid of offending you even after you say, "Oh, it's fine."

They still might worry "What if I use the wrong language or ask the wrong thing, or is it even legal to ask this?" Also, I'm not objective! Think about it: if you are worried you could possibly get sued, would you ask the person who you are worried might sue you? Probably not!

Third, although I know my disability and how it affects me, I don't know the exact legal requirements for every disability-related question. Do I know how exactly wide a bathroom stall needs to be to meet ADA requirements? No. Do I know what exactly qualifies a company for a tax credit due to their having an employee with a disability, what that credit is called in the tax code and how to file for it? No.

What to Call the "Disabilities MythBusters Sheet"

First do not call it a "Disability MythBusters Sheet." I called it that to get the point across to you. Call it something natural and to the point, such as "Myths and Facts about Employees with Disabilities." Stay away from any negative words such as "stereotypes" or "fears." Would you ever want to have the assumption made about you that you hold stereotypical views of any group? No. That never feels good. Would you like it to be assumed that you are afraid? Probably not. Again, this is all about putting yourself in the would-be employer's shoes.

If this seems like the stuff of marketing or politicking, that's only because it is. When you are interviewing, YOU are the product you are trying to sell.

Assembling Your Disabilities MythBusters Sheet

Putting your Disabilities MythBusters Sheet together should take no more than an hour, probably less. It is basically a copy-and-paste task, not a writing task. It should only be a few pages long. Your evacuation plan should start on a separate page, at the back.

 Get the information to put together this sheet at:

> https://www.dol.gov/odep/pubs/fact/ada.htm

If this link does not work, search the web for "Myths and Facts About Workers with Disabilities."

You can use the same document after all your interviews. It should be on paper that matches your résumé and reference sheet in quality, if not in color.

You do not have to go into "What is your disability called?" "How does it impact you?" Nor should you define any medical terms. As you will see on the sample, I do not even mention the term "cerebral palsy."

When and How to Use Your DMS

I believe there are better and worse times to give the DMS to an employer. The most common time is towards the end of an interview. Usually when an interview is wrapping up, an applicant would offer a reference sheet. You can say, "Here are my references and *here* is some information, should you have any questions about my disability." This will work particularly well if you are visibly disabled and you did not bring it up in the interview

A second, less common, time to give this out is either at career fairs or information nights which precede a company conducting on-campus interviews. If you attend a fair and just drop résumés at each booth, not really talking to any of the recruiting reps, I would not bother. But if you go with a specific mission to make a strong connection with a handful of companies, then add a DMS to your packet. Part of the mission will be really trying to stand out to these companies' recruiters. This involves talking to them and using whatever time they give you to sell yourself.

Again, if you are in a wheelchair or otherwise visibly disabled, at the end of the conversation say "Here is some information in case you have any questions about my disability." Leave it with that. Same goes with company information nights on campus. Passive job hunters just go to these, listen and leave. Aggressive job hunters stay after to try and network with the people who spoke. In addition to the normal networking period towards the end, offer them the information sheet.

For people who require accommodations during the interview process, you need to let the employer know ahead of time to arrange them (but only after they've let you know that they want to interview you). Email them your accommodation request and write just a few words to draw their attention to it.

Whenever possible, my goal is to try and let someone to know me first, even if it is only for a few minutes, before offering them this kind of information. It just seems odd otherwise. I feel that you should never attach the Disability MythBusters Sheet to a follow-up to a networking event such as a career fair or a company information night, or as an attachment to a thank-you note for an interview. Such communications should be used as opportunities only to fortify the connection you have made. Therefore, I would not mention my disability in an interview thank-you letter. I dealt with the issue at the interview. If they want to ask any further questions about it afterwards, they know where to find me. It is all about presenting as, "a qualified candidate who happens to have a disability," not "a disabled candidate."

A Total Positive
Using this technique does not guarantee that you will get the job. You might do everything right, get lucky and get the first job you apply for. Most jobseekers go on several interviews before they get an offer.! Not getting a job that you interview for might not have anything to do with your disability. Most cases you might have a feeling but will not know definitively. To me this doesn't matter, because it's usually beyond both my knowledge and my control. The only thing that matters is that I know I'm everything I can to get what I want.

In my opinion, using the DMS will give you another opportunity that candidates without visible disabilities don't have, to prove that they have the qualities that employers wants. Employers want to hire people who are honest, in touch with the company's needs, proactive, and mature. Presenting them with the facts in a well-thought-out manner shows that you possess those qualities.

Myths and Facts about Employees with Disabilities (Sample)

Myth: It is too expensive to accommodate workers with disabilities.

FACT: Most workers with disabilities do not require any special accommodations. When accommodations are necessary, about 20 percent cost nothing, and 50 percent cost less than $500. There are a variety of national and community-based organizations that help employers identify low-cost or no-cost accommodation alternatives. Employers have always adjusted in the workplace to accommodate employees' needs. That same flexibility should be extended to people with disabilities.

Myth: If I hire someone with a disability, my workers' compensation insurance rates will skyrocket.

FACT: Employers' insurance rates are not based on whether workers have disabilities. They are based solely on the workplace's relative hazards and the company's accident experience. Supervisors report that workers with disabilities have higher safety rankings then their non-disabled peers, so there is no reason to expect rates to increase.

MYTH: Won't my medical insurance rates increase?

FACT: Employers are often surprised to learn that most disabilities do not require frequent ongoing doctor visits. The Americans with Disabilities Act requires that an employer treat a worker with disabilities the same as everyone else, and offer the same access to existing medical coverage as offered to other employees.

MYTH: Workers with disabilities will be absent more than others, and it will negatively affect my bottom line.

FACT: A DuPont Corporation study found that 85 percent of its employees with disabilities rated average or above on attendance. International Telephone and Telegraph surveyed a 2,000-employee plant and found that the workers with disabilities had fewer absences than their coworkers. Workers with disabilities are not absent any more than workers without disabilities.

Myth: Under the ADA, an employer cannot fire an employee who has a disability.

Fact: Employers can fire workers with disabilities under three conditions:

- The termination is unrelated to the disability or;
- The employee does not meet legitimate requirements for the job, such as performance or production standards, with or without a reasonable accommodation or;
- Because of the employee's disability, he or she poses a direct threat to health or safety in the workplace.[26]

right**(Continued on other side)**

---

[26] From: http://www.dol.gov/odep/pubs/fact/ada.htm

Myths and Facts about Employees with Disabilities (Sample Continued)

Should you hire me, these are the low-cost accommodations that I need to perform my job:

- To accomplish ___, the accommodation I would need is ___
- To accomplish ___, the accommodation I would need is ___
- To accomplish ___, the accommodation I would need is ___

Should you or any of your colleagues have any disability-related questions pertaining to your employees or workplace, contact JAN.

> http://askjan.org/JANonDemand.htm
>
> The Job Accommodation Network (JAN) is the leading source of free, expert, and confidential guidance on workplace accommodations and disability employment issues. Working toward practical solutions that benefit both employer and employee, JAN helps people with disabilities enhance their employability, and shows employers how to capitalize on the value and talent that people with disabilities add to the workplace.
>
> - By Phone: From 9 a.m. to 6 p.m. ET, customers can call JAN toll-free to speak with a workplace accommodation expert. (800) 526-7234 or (877) 781-9403 (TTY)
>
> - Via the Web: http://askjan.org/
>
> - JAN's online service provides customers with individualized e-mail responses to questions about accommodations and the ADA.

In addition, please feel free to ask me any questions about how my disability might impact me on the job.

Attached is a checklist I've created for you. It details my needs in case the building needs to be evacuated. Should I be hired, this can be reproduced, either by myself or the company, for the appropriate parties.

Emergency Checklist for Employees with Disabilities

FOR HEARING IMPAIRMENTS

In an emergency, I should be alerted by (check all possible options):

☐ Visual alarms, if building is equipped.

☐ Physical contact.

☐ Turning the lights on and off (flashing lights).

☐ A written note explaining the emergency.

☐ Gestures that indicate what is happening and what to do.

☐ Other: _____

_____

To get to safety, I would need (check all possible options):

☐ A volunteer to escort and guides me to the nearest evacuation route.

☐ A volunteer to relay verbal instructions being given through gesture or written note.

☐ A volunteer to relay environmental warnings and dangers.

☐ Other: _____

_____

Comments: _____

_____

FOR MOBILITY IMPAIRMENTS

From a first-floor location in an emergency, I should be assisted by (check all possible options):

☐ A volunteer to push my manual wheelchair.

☐ A volunteer to clear any obstacles obstructing my path to the nearest evacuation route.

☐ A volunteer to provide assistance while walking or running.

☐ A volunteer to assist opening doors.

☐ A volunteer to push me in a chair on roller-wheels.

☐ Two volunteers to carry me in locked-arm position.

☐ A team if two or three volunteers to carry me in a sturdy chair, preferably one with arms.

☐ Other: _____

_____

Comments: _____

_____

(Continued on other side)

359

From an upper floor, in an emergency, I should be assisted by (check all possible options):

- Ambulatory:

☐ Volunteers to assist me using the stairs, # of volunteers needed: _____

☐ Other: _____

_____

- Non-Ambulatory:

☐ Two volunteers to carry me in locked-arm position.

☐ If more than three flights, two relay teams of two or three volunteers to carry me in a sturdy chair, preferably one with arms.

☐ If more than three flights, two relay teams of two or three volunteers to carry me in my manual wheelchair.

☐ Other: _____

_____

- On a flight of stairs, I should be carried facing:

☐ Forward   ☐ Backward

☐ If a seatbelt is available, I should be secured with the seat belt before transporting.

☐ To transfer me from my wheelchair, volunteers should (list instructions):

_____

☐ Other: _____

_____

- After-Care Instructions (following the evacuation): _____

_____

FOR VISION IMPAIRMENTS

In an emergency, I should be assisted by (check all possible options):

☐ An auditory alarm, if building is equipped.

☐ A description of the emergency (the nature of the emergency).

☐ Precise verbal instructions.

☐ A volunteer to guide me by my taking his or her elbow.

Volunteers: give verbal warning of upcoming steps or other obstacles in the pathway.

☐ A volunteer to lead the way to the nearest evacuation route.

☐ Two volunteers to carry me in a locked-arm position or in a chair, if needed.

☐ If more than three flights of stairs, a relay team may be needed.

☐ Other: _____

_____

After-Evacuation Instructions:

☐ Reorient me to the new location.

☐ Offer guidance and assistance as needed.

☐ Other: _____

_____

Questions and Answers about Disclosure

Just to be clear, I am back to giving you information. This is not a document for you to give employers. Many who apply and get jobs have questions or are apprehensive about telling their employer about their disability. That is what disclosure is. It is the act of telling your employer, either verbally or in writing, that you either self-identify as having any type of disability or have a documented disability of any kind. For most it is both. I self-identify as a person living with a disability and it is also documented.

Q. Am I ever required, legally or otherwise, to disclose?

A. No. You never have to disclose. You only need to disclose your disability if you want to ask for an accommodation to complete the application process or to do job-related tasks." If you do not, it is your right to keep your disability status private.

Q. Why would I choose to disclose?

A. The main reason is you need an accommodation to do your job. Other reasons would be if you have a chronic condition, such as asthma or epilepsy that causes you to have safety concerns. Should you have a medical emergency, you need those around you to know what to do. Other reasons maybe it is obvious; for example, you are an amputee or a little person. And it just feels weird not to ever talk about, even if you do not need any accommodations. Or you might feel for whatever reason that "hiding" your disability would be too stressful.

Q. Are there laws in place to protect me against discrimination should I disclose?

A. Yes. Title I of the American with Disabilities Act states that a covered entity shall not discriminate against a qualified individual with a disability. Discrimination may include, among other things, limiting or classifying a job applicant or employee in an adverse way, denying employment opportunities to people who truly qualify, or not making reasonable accommodations to the known physical or mental limitations of disabled employees, not advancing employees with disabilities in the business, and/or not providing needed accommodations in training.[27]

Q. When should I disclose?

A. You can disclose at any point throughout the application process, after a job offer but before starting a job, or at any time after you start the job. Keep reading this chapter for pros and cons of disclosure in each stage of your hiring/employment process.

Q. Who should I disclose to?

A. It depends. For those who work for smaller employers, you will probably talk to your supervisor or their supervisor who you also consider to be your boss as well. Those who work for larger employers have the option of going to HR. Some employers will have procedures you will need to follow for requesting accommodations.

Q. Will my employer require proof of my disability?

---

[27]From: http://www.ada.gov/ada_title_I.htm

A. This also depends. It will vary based on the nature of your disability, if they have policies in place and what accommodations you are requesting. If you have a disability that is not obvious, or the accommodations for an "obvious disability" are not clearly connected to that disability or common, the employer may request documentation from you demonstrating that you have a disability and explaining why you need a reasonable accommodation. Under these conditions' employers are legally allowed to require proof disability once an accommodation request is made. If this sounds subjective, that is because it is.

Example where proof is **not** supposed to be required:

- You are in a wheelchair and need your desk raised.
- You have a visual impairment and need material in an alternative format or Jaws on your computer.

Example where proof is **can** be required:

- You are in a wheelchair or visually impaired and need to go against the dress code, i.e., wear jeans or sneakers to work.
- You have PTSD and need to bring a service animal to work.
- You have a learning disability, your job requires you to pass a certification test every so often, and you need extra time for these tests.

Q. What should I say if I disclose?

A. Start by saying, "because of my disability I need to talk with you about accommodations that I will need. This is what I need, and therefore." Pick a time when they available to talk and there is privacy. Be direct, open and go in with the goal of coming up with a solution that works for all involved. If talking to HR same thing followed up with are there any procedures that I need to follow?

The basic rule here, as with most business situations, is to simply be direct and keep it simple. There's no need to be embarrassed. But neither should you share more information than necessary. And this is the kind of conversation for which you would probably want some privacy. If you come into the office of a manager who has an open-door policy, ask permission to close the door behind you.

Q. Do my employers have to keep my disability status confidential?

A. Yes. Title I of the ADA also mandates that medical records are confidential. The basic rule is that with limited exceptions, employers must keep confidential any medical information they learn about an applicant or employee. Information can be confidential even if it contains no medical diagnosis or treatment course and even if it is not generated by a health care professional. For example, an employee's request for a reasonable accommodation would be considered medical information subject to the ADA's confidentiality requirements.

Q. Do you need to tell your employer everything when I disclose

A. No. Take me for example. I consider my cerebral palsy my primary disability. I also have dystonia as a secondary diagnosis. When I talk about my disability to employers, I only talk about cp.

The dystonia is not relevant. Any accommodations that I need can be justified by the fact that I have cp. If I get "sicker" in the future, I am eligible for the same medical leave as any other employee.

Now, my situation is more complex than the paragraph above! I self-identify as having a physical disability resulting from neurological impairment. I do not know if I agree that I have the exact conditions that I have been diagnosed with cerebral palsy and dystonia. I have several theories as to what I have or do not have. Does that mean I consider it a lie when people ask, and I answer, "I have cerebral palsy"? No. That is my official diagnosis. I do not want to spend twenty minutes explaining my thinking around whether my official diagnosis is correct. Nor do I feel most people want that. They want a simple answer. It is the same as when you ask an acquaintance how they are: do you really want to spend 15 minutes listening to every little detail? Some do, most don't. Now, why don't I just say, "I am physically disabled due to neurological impairment"? To me, that sounds evasive. People like labels. They like to be able to put people in organized boxes. Sometimes, in life you just must check a box. That is how life is – for everyone. Right now, my official "label" or diagnosis is cerebral palsy, so that is what I tell people. Should my official diagnosis ever change, then I would tell people I have whatever it is changed to.

Employers want the short story. There are a lot of things that are caused by my disability that does not affect my life at work. Therefore, I do not need to tell my supervisor or anyone that I work with about them. I am like every other adult on the planet: there are parts of my life, both past and present, that I consider private. Just because my disability is intertwined with those doesn't mean I need to tell everyone.

Pros and Cons of Disability Disclosure at Different Stages of Employment

Stage 1: On a resume

Pros

- If whoever looks at your résumé is a total bigot, it saves you from wasting time trying to go through that employer's hiring process.
- It can give you a jumping-off point to frame your disability positively at an interview; i.e., tell about… whatever you listed doing pertaining to the disabled community.

Cons

- It is really easy to not hear back when you send out your résumé; you'll never be able to prove that this disclosure was the reason.

My Thoughts...
Unless you have an obvious disability, do not even think about it. The main reason to do it is to not waste time on people who'd never hire you. This is risky, remember – you are both breaking protocol and disclosing when you are just a piece of paper to them.

Stage 2: Cover Letter

Pros

- Possible advantage for two types of positions: where the job is with a state or federal agency that must comply with affirmative action policies, or the job you are applying for directly relates to your experience as a person with a disability such as a rehabilitation counselor.
- Again, if it is that much of a problem for an employer, do you want to hear back from them if they are not open?

Cons

- Same as before, you can never prove this was why you got no response.

My Thoughts...
If you are applying for either a Schedule A government job, another government job, or a job working with those who are disabled – take the advantage! For all other jobs, if you have a visible disability, do whatever you feel would sell yourself the best. The goal of any cover letter is to get an interview. Give them no reason to turn you down.

Stage 3: When an employer calls for an interview

Pros

- You need to disclose if you need to arrange for an accommodation.
- You want peace of mind; to take away the surprise when you meet them: one less worry going in.
- They contacted you, so they like your cover letter/résumé and it will be harder for them to back out.

Cons

- It gives them room to make false assumptions or doubt your qualifications before you have a chance to dispel their concerns.

My Thoughts...

If you need an accommodation during the interview you need to disclose now.

If not, it just depends on you. Do you have the temperament to just show up in a chair and go from there in getting them to like you? Or does the thought of "surprising" people add to your anxiety?

Stage 4: During the interview

Pros

- You will seem confident, well-adjusted and comfortable with yourself!
- This is your chance to prepare and get employers comfortable with your disability on your terms!

Cons

- You need to be sensitive to their time frame, if they only schedule 15 minutes for an interview do not take up 30 by going on about your disability.
- You also need to be sensitive to the law! Even if you are comfortable with talking about your diagnosis-they may not be. Stick to topics that can be legally discussed that of can you do the job!

My Thoughts....

I covered this earlier in the chapter. If you have a visible disability; I feel it is a "no-brainer" to bring it up during the interview.

Prepare to do this, by reading this chapter. Stay positive and stick to discussing how you would do your job!

If I had an invisible disability I would wait 'til after I got the job to disclose. I am just being honest!

Stage 5: After you've accepted the job but before you start

Pros

- You can get accommodations set up right away so you can do your job to the best of your ability and make the best first impression you can!

Cons

- Your employer may be skeptical; some may think "Why didn't she say something sooner?", while others may think you want special treatment.

My Thoughts...

I feel most people will assume why you did not disclose during the hiring process; and if you frame it this is what I need to best serve you/the company it lessens the "special-treatment factor."

Stage 6: After you have started a job

Pros
- You get a chance to prove yourself before you ask for anything.
- You can get a sense of the atmosphere, who is who and who best to go to. This could be an asset for trying to nonchalantly get what you need.
- "If your disability doesn't impact job performance, but your employment situation somehow changes after disclosure, you may have legal recourse."[28]

Cons
- The longer you wait to disclose it may become harder; you could encounter "Why didn't he disclose earlier?" from bosses and/or co-workers.

My Thoughts...

If you choose to disclose only after you have been at a job for a period, come up with a reason why you waited.

---

[28] From: http://career.umn.edu/disability.html

Stage 7: After you have a disability-related issue on the job

Pros

- You may prove that you tried to do without "special treatment" and it did not work. This may make some think higher of you.
- It could be your only way to maybe save yourself from getting in trouble or fired.

Cons

- Your employer or your team of co-workers may be annoyed in instances where if you had disclosed and gotten an accommodation earlier a problem could have been avoided. People tend to value those who are proactive over those who are reactive.

My Thoughts...

This could go either way depending on the situation. Trying to manage on your own first, may make you look stronger and honest to some. However, if it causes a problem for anyone due to not telling sooner. You might face either skepticism or hostility.

Stage 8: Never

Pros

- If it does not affect your life at work, you have a right to your privacy.
- You do not have to deal with explaining, answering questions or people's reactions.

Cons

- You may or may not feel as if you are hiding something and that may be stressful.
- You can get fired if you cannot perform a job and do not use an accommodation so that you can perform that job.
- You could nullify some of your protections under the ADA. When an employer does not know, they cannot be then charged with discrimination.

My Thoughts...

Most workers have some issue that impacts their health or functioning in some small way. Examples are wearing glasses/contacts, vertigo, a bad back, arthritis in a joint, asthma, dysgraphia or nighttime anxiety. These things might not be labeled disabilities. It does not matter if it does not affect their job, so they have no need to formally discuss it at work.

In Conclusion

After you read the above, only you can decide what is going to be right for you! There are probably a million different permutations. Every person is different. Every disability is different. I always say that if you met one person who has whatever diagnosis, you have met one person with that diagnosis. Every profession is different. Every place of employment is different. Every supervisor is different. Every team of co-workers is different. You get my drift.

In making this decision it comes down to two main factors, accommodations and visible/invisible disabilities. First, whether you need accommodations and what type you need, will influence your choice how you handle this process.

Second, visible/invisible disabilities. My highly visible disability makes me feel as if the issue of disclosure is moot in my own life. Whenever someone sees or hears me, they know. This is just a fact of my life. I have often wished it were otherwise. This has led me to experience many emotions. One is "It's not fair! People with invisible disabilities have it so much easier." When I am in the midst of these emotions, it is all I am feeling. But when I think about it logically, we all have challenges. In the end, it is pretty much equal.

People with disabilities that are considered "hidden" often have a different set of logistical issues to figure out and may have different feelings about all that. It is a waste of energy to try to decide "who has it worse." In life, we get whatever we get, and it is then our job to make the best of it!

With this choice comes opportunity: the opportunity to formulate the best game plan you can! You are unique, as are the combination of factors that influence you. Use these to come up with a game plan that you feel will give you the "win." Whether or not you play sports, healthy attitudes toward life can be learned from successful sports figures. In sports, winners go in with a plan. Just as in sports, there is more than one game in life. Whether you win your first game or not, the game plan is always being adjusted, be it slightly or radically, to win the next. You will not do everything the same in regard to interviewing or dealing with your disability on the job. This is okay. Not only is it okay, it is good! Life is always changing. If something doesn't go over well, the next time you have a chance to do it differently.

Formulating a plan that is tailored to you and your goals will put you ahead of the game! Then adjust based on what works and what could be improved or needs to be different. Keep doing this and it will work!

Points to Remember from Chapter 11

- ✓ Know whether you need interview accommodations before you apply for jobs. As soon as a prospective employer contacts you for an interview, politely notify them of any accommodations you need.

- ✓ Decide if you want to mention your disability on an interview and how you want to do so.

- ✓ Consider providing your interviewers a "disability myth buster sheet" in case they want some information or support for hiring a qualified, talented person who happens to have a disability.

- ✓ You always have a choice about disclosing your disability to an employer Weigh the pros and cons of any choice you make and when you do so.

- ✓ Prepare for ALL aspects of interviewing, not just about your disability. Consult other sources to brush up on fashion advice and rehearse powerful responses to common interview questions.

Chapter 12: Working for the Government

The unemployment rate among people with disabilities is much higher than among those without disabilities. This problem is well known in the disability community. There have been multiple efforts by people with disabilities and industry leaders to solve this. Because this problem so profoundly affects one of our country's largest minority groups, governments at the state and federal levels continue to try and address it as well.

> Currently 11.89 percent of the total federal civilian workforce, over 219,000 people with disabilities, are employed by the federal government. Jobs for the disabled exist in most organizations and in hundreds of occupations. Total disabled employment has increased dramatically from 7% in 2010 to just under 12% of the total federal workforce in 2013. In 2013 16% of all new hires were disabled. The President signed Executive Order 13548 requiring agencies to increase federal employment of individuals with disabilities in 2010, the 20th anniversary of the signing of the American Disabilities Act (ADA). These orders and the ADA have increased awareness among managers within the federal sector of their disabled hiring options. The federal government is working aggressively to expand total disabled employment opportunities within government. All agencies are required to establish Selective Placement Program Coordinators and to develop outreach efforts to identify qualified candidates to meet agency workforce diversity goals.[29]

This means if you want a job working for the government your disability could be an asset in applying for a position that you are qualified for! Now, being disabled does not automatically give you a government job. But it can boost your chances of getting interviewed and hired. In the private sector there is no universal program to hire employees with disabilities.

---

[29] From: http://www.federaljobs.net/disabled.htm#Hiring_Options

What Are the First Things That You Need to Know?

First, you may be thinking you cannot apply for jobs with the federal government because you cannot or do not want to relocate to the Washington DC area. In reality, 84 percent of federal jobs are located outside the DC area!

> Federal government jobs can be found in every state and large metropolitan area, including overseas jobs in 140 countries. The average annual federal workers compensation, including pay plus benefits, is $123,049 compared to just $61,051 for the private sector according to the United States Bureau of Economic Analysis[30].

There are programs geared toward hiring new college graduates from every major.

---

[30] From: http://www.federaljobs.net/disabled.htm#Hiring_Options

Schedule A and B Hiring

There are three different programs that the federal government uses to hire those with severe physical or intellectual disabilities or psychiatric illnesses.

- **Schedule A, 5 CFR 213.3102(t)** for the hiring of people with [intellectual disabilities] who meet the eligibility requirements. Upon completion of 2 years of satisfactory performance the employee may qualify for conversion to the competitive service.

- **Schedule A, 5 CFR 213.3102(u)** for the hiring of People with Severe Physical Disabilities. Agencies can appoint persons with severe physical disabilities who: (1) under a temporary appointment can demonstrate their ability to complete duties satisfactorily; or (2) have been certified by a State vocational rehabilitation agency (SVRA) counselor or the Department of Veterans Affairs Vocational Rehabilitation Office as likely to succeed in the performance of specified duties. After successfully completing two years of satisfactory service under this schedule, the employee may qualify to be converted to the competitive service.

- **Schedule B, 5 CFR 213.3202(k)** for the Hiring of People Who Have Recovered from Mental Illness. This schedule permits appointments at up to the Grade GS-15 level when filled by individuals who: (1) are placed at a severe disadvantage in obtaining employment because of a psychiatric disability evidenced by outpatient treatment or hospitalization and have had a significant period of substantially disrupted employment because of the disability. [31]

Schedules A and B are intended to enable federal agencies to hire persons with severe disabilities without making them compete for the job. Using this allows such agencies to fill vacancies without making qualified applicants go through the traditional, and sometimes lengthy, competitive hiring process. I am assuming most of my readers will be applying for Schedule A, 5 CFR 213.3102(u), so that's mainly what I'll talk about when describing the process to obtain employment using these avenues.

Do I Have to Get Hired Under Schedule A?

No, you do not. The government has several different paths to employment. If you do not get hired under Schedule A or B, you still may seek Competitive employment. Competitive employment is when you apply for any opening you find and go through the application progress normally. Competitive employment is also how most government jobs are filled. Should you opt for this, you are always entitled to the same accommodations during this process, as you would be for any other position in the private sector. The Federal Job Opportunities Bulletin Board has 24-hour hotlines for finding open positions:

Phone: (912) 757-3000
TDD: (912) 744-2299

---

[31] From: http://www.federaljobs.net/disabled.htm#Hiring_Options

Or, you may use websites listed later in this chapter.

Non-competitive hiring is usually used for disabled veterans. They make up the majority of non-competitive hires. Persons hired under Schedule A or B are also considered to be non-competitive hires.

Those who are offered non-competitive jobs are still required to interview, pass a background check/obtain the needed level of security clearance, and in some cases pass a written test. After you successfully complete this process you are deemed eligible for the position that you are applied for. This means you are automatically offered the job if it is available. If the position is not available, you are placed on a waiting list until there is a vacancy for that specific position. This differs from "competitive employment" in that you are guaranteed a job if you fulfill all the qualifications.

How to Apply for Schedule A Jobs

There are two ways to apply for Schedule A jobs. First, you can apply to a position online and indicate that you are applying under Schedule A. If you do this, you'll need to be able to produce the documents that are discussed below when you are going through the interview process. When applying to government jobs, you should put that you are eligible for Schedule A hiring on the resume that you submit for that government position. Again, only note this if you are applying to a government job. If you are applying to a non-government job, or a job in the private sector, do not indicate that you are schedule A eligible on your resume.

Second, you can assemble a packet and send it directly to each agency. Many federal agencies have someone who serves as Selective Placement Program Coordinator (SPPC) or Disability Program Manager (DPM) . These are two titles for basically the same position. They are the ones who oversee Schedule A hiring for their agency. Follow the steps below to apply directly to certain agencies.

Step One: Obtaining Documents You Need

This is the group of documents that you need to either send out to the SPPC or DPM of each agency that you apply to; or you will need to produce if you apply for a position online under Schedule A.

- ✓ **Cover letter.** When you are sending out packets to different agencies each cover letter should be addressed to both that agency and its SPPC/DPM. The cover letter should indicate that you are applying under Schedule A as well as why you feel you are a good fit for that agency. You should end the letter asking to be contacted with further information on that agency's Schedule A hiring process.

- ✓ **Résumé.** You may be required to submit a regular résumé, or they may want a "Federal Résumé." Federal résumés are more detailed and can be two or three pages long, which can include:

  - Information about the opening

  - Your personal information

  - Education and coursework levels

- Work experience (including dates of employment, number of hours worked per week, location of position and a supervisor's contact information)

Other qualifications[32]

- Proof of disability. This is required and needs to be provided before you are hired. This is also not the norm when you apply for a job. Proof of disability will typically come in the form of a letter. You can get this letter from:

  o Your doctor,

  o A licensed medical professional,

  o A licensed rehabilitation professional, or

  o Any federal, state, District of Columbia, or US territory agency that issues or provides disability benefits.

The letter does NOT need to detail your medical history or your need for an accommodation. The simpler the letter, the better.

- ✓ **Certificate of Job Readiness.** Does not have to be a fancy-looking certificate. It can be obtained in three ways:

  - The agency which you are applying to can review your résumé and references and thereby certify your readiness for the position, or

  - Any of the people who approved to grant you a "proof of disability letter" can also write you a letter that you are able to work with your disability, or

  - When you don't have a certificate of job readiness, the SPPC or DPM can decide to start you as a temporary hire. Once you have proven that you can perform the job, you would be made a regular employee.

If you are applying under Schedule B, you are required to submit a two-year history of your mental illness and the treatments you received during that period. You also must have a psychologist or psychiatrist issue both your proof of disability and certificate of job readiness.

I suggest that you request a letter from your doctor saying that you have a severe disability, and another letter saying you can perform the essential functions of a job with reasonable accommodations. Again, the second letter does not have to be detailed.

Common sense might tell you that all a government employee would have to do to deem you ready to work would be to look at your résumé. Common sense might also make you think it is easier to get just one letter that says everything. However, when government is involved you often need to submit documentation in an exact way.

Because of this, despite not normally choosing the word "Severe" to describe my disability, if I were getting "Proof of Disability" from my doctor, I would instruct them to use "Severe." I know that my disability *is* severe, so I would not be asking my doctor to lie. All these terms

---

[32] From: http://www.makingthedifference.org/federaljobs/.

have some level of subjectivity to them. The legal, or government term, may be *severe*. So fine, I'll use that to get something that I qualify for. I would also advise you to do the same. It is called playing the game. We all do it at some point. However, in non-legal, everyday life, to me, "significant" means it impacts most aspects of my life. I like that word better and that's what I usually use to describe my level of disability.

It is less aggravation and work for you when are applying for this to get everything you need right the first time. You don't want to be sent back to get another document from your doctor, wait for an appointment, etc. Don't feel bad about being so specific in telling your doctor what you need. Just say "You know how the government is." They will know what you mean.

- Reference sheet. This is the same as any other reference sheet you would use for any job application or interview process.

- Your official transcripts.

Step Two: Decide Which Agencies You Want to Apply to First

At the time this book was written there were approximately 1,300 agencies that make up the federal government. That's a lot! I don't suggest that you try to apply to all of them. Imagine trying to send out 1,300 packets with the same information – much less trying to customize each of those applications to each job!

A better strategy is to pick five to ten agencies at a time and go through the process to apply to each one. This includes confirming the contact information of the office that handles Schedule A applications for that agency, then drafting a specialized cover letter for that agency. Most of your cover letters to each agency can be copies of the same letter with the exception of their address in the header, the salutation, and so on. In the first or second paragraph you want to demonstrate both that you know what that agency does and why you would be an asset.

After you have sent out your packets and allowed some time for the SPPC/DPM to review it, follow up.

After you go through that for five to ten agencies, pick the next batch of five or ten to do.

Keep doing this until you either have a position or are on a waiting list for a position in every federal agency where you would be willing to take a job.

Once you've been waitlisted, check in with each agency's SPPC/DPM every three months to let them know you are still interested. Also keep checking internet job sites for jobs in those agencies. If you find a position that you are qualified for, apply and then immediately contact the SPPC/DPM to whom you sent your information.

You might be wondering, "How do I pick five or ten out of 1,300?" I suggest applying three simple criteria. First, apply to the largest agencies first. Further limit the options by matching your academic major to the available jobs. You can further narrow things down and prioritize according to the geographic match, either based on where you live now or where you would like to relocate.

If you have a graphic design degree and your whole family lives in Long Island, does it make any sense to apply to some agency that employs five scientists to monitor some type of fish in Alaska? Yes, if you want the makings of a TV dramedy or you have tried everything else and are desperate for a job. Otherwise – probably not.

Step Three: Assemble, Confirm, Send

Once you have all your documents, make multiple copies of each! Put them in a folder. Never send your master or last copy of any document. Sometime in the process, someone will need you to send them something again! Way easier if you have it on hand.

After, you have plenty of copies of everything on your checklist, you then need manila envelopes and stamps. Assemble your documents in the order they are listed above, put them in the envelope and mail envelope to each federal agency c/o the name of that agency's SPPC/DPM.

Now, you want to find out a specific name and address for every packet that you send out. You can use the link below to do this:

https://www.opm.gov/policy-data-oversight/disability-employment/selective-placement-program-coordinator-directory/

If I were you, I would use this as a jumping-off point. Sure, you could send a packet to the person listed on the website. But you don't know how often the site is updated. To make sure that you are sending to the current person in that agency, I would either email or call what is listed on the site to confirm their contact information.

Say "Hi, I am trying to establish the correct person and address to send a Schedule A disability application packet to. Is it...?" (whoever's listed on the website). As long as you have the coordinator on the phone, you should ask if they mind answering two brief questions. One would be, would they rather a "traditional" résumé or a federal résumé be submitted? If they say they want a federal résumé, go online to figure out how to do one.

Next say, "I have a copy of my proof of disability and a certificate of job readiness; is there anything else I need to include?"

Afterwards, thank them so very much for their time. Tell them both they will be receiving a packet from, your name, soon and you will follow up within a month of the date you mail the application. Thanks, them again and tell them to have a great day!

For those of us with speech disabilities, we will use email to first attempt to both confirm the contact information we got from the website, as well as get our two questions answered. Many instances, this will work, and then we will promptly follow up with a "Thank you, I'll be sending out my packet to you within ..." Emails are often missed or ignored. This is another fact of life.

When one has a speech disability, this valuable tool is less useful. You have two options: speech-to-speech relay or have someone make the call for you. The choice is yours. If someone makes the call for you, I have some recommendations about how to do it.

Notice how I worded what you should say to the SPPC/DPM. Don't start off by introducing yourself; just start with "Hi, I am trying..." You can word it so that it is not obvious as to who is calling or why. When I was researching Schedule A, the literature said it makes a better impression to make the call yourself rather than having a parent or a VR counselor call. This makes good sense. However, it seems to me that Schedule A was not written with those with speech disabilities in mind. The authors apparently think that if someone does not take the initiative to call, themselves, then they can't do the job. It goes back to the issue about phone interviews I talked about. It seems to me that "the system" is not set up for those with my type of disability as much as it is for other types. But maybe people of every type of disability could make a case for that.

Whatever the reason for the law being the way it is, I still need to get done what I need to get done. This is the same for you! Sometimes for me, or possibly for you, this means finding a way to make the system work for me, or yourself, even if it is not the common way of doing something.

So, having your support person make the call for you might be what works best for you. By "support person" I mean whoever you lean on to get through life. Everyone has family/friends that help them through life at the same time as I help them through life.

Lots of people get help with their job hunt! You don't have to be any different and you don't have to feel bad because of the help you get. Should you decide you need someone to call for you, I would ask that he or she use the same tactic above, of keeping it ambiguous as to who is calling, or even pretending to be you (as long as the call does not turn into an interview).

Remember, with the first phone call you make your first impression. I have had people call and pretend they are me. Some instances this is the easier way to accomplish what I need. This book is about being honest and living in the "real world!" Should you decide to have someone call and have them be you, stick strictly to three goals:

- ✓ Obtaining accurate information.

- ✓ Confirming the type of résumé desired.

- ✓ Getting a complete list of the documents that need to be sent for your application to be evaluated.

That is, it! Your "representative" should not be selling you beyond sounding incredibly positive and polite. That is, they should not be, in any way, be interviewing as you.

Not all federal agencies have a SPPC/DPM. In that case, you need to contact HR and ask whom in that agency you should contact pertaining to Schedule A hiring for the disabled. You, or your "pretend you," need to use the word "disabled" when contacting HR. This is because there are numerous entities that are referred to as Schedule A within the government. You need to make sure whoever you are in contact with knows exactly what you mean!

After you have made sure you know where to send your packet, send it. Keep track of both which agencies you sent packets to and the replies you receive.

What *NOT* to Send to a Selective Placement Program Coordinator

There is something I would not include in your packet. In Chapter 11 I cover how to put together and use a "disability sheet" during the interviewing process. This should *not be* used when applying to a Schedule A job. The reason is simple: those who are going to decide if you are Schedule A-eligible, process your information, and make arrangements after you are hired, are used to working with employees who are disabled. They do not need the information I recommended that you provide in the last chapter. They already know it or should be expected to know it.

To be very clear: *Do not* bring either a Proof of Disability or Certificate of Job Readiness to an interview for any job in the private sector! The instructions in this chapter apply *only* to applying for Schedule A jobs. Know your audience and do not get confused. These are two separate things: applying for Schedule A and applying for all other jobs. Each category requires you to do things differently. This does not mean you can't do both at the same time. You can go on interviews for other jobs and do the techniques I talk about in the last chapter. During the same week you can be sending out Schedule A packets and following up with each agency's SPPC/DPM. Keep doing both until you find a job!

Do I Have to Go Through VR to Be Eligible for Schedule A?

No. The rules state you can get your Proof of Disability from several different sources. The way the guidelines read, anyone who is approved to give you a Proof of Disability can also give you a Certificate of Job Readiness. Therefore, there is nothing in writing saying you must be a VR client.

One person who is authorized to provide these documents is a physician. You may find it way easier to go through your doctor to get your documents. I say this based on my personal experience with Vocational Rehab Your doctor will at the most require you to come in once so that they can draft the documents that you need. If you know the doctor, they have seen you recently and are accommodating; they may be able to get you what you need by way of a phone call/email and a couple of days.

Vocational Rehab on the other hand, will require you to open a case and come into their office multiple times. To open a case, you will need to provide them with, you guessed it, "Proof of Disability." This same document will suffice for applying directly to Schedule A. So why would you need VR to apply for Schedule A?

Do not be passive and let anyone push you into a system that will only delay your goal of getting hired! We can understand their motives. VR is always trying not to get its funding cut. The more clients they have with either open cases or on the waiting list, the better their chances of keeping that funding. If they keep their funds, their staff gets to keep their jobs. Therefore, it is in government workers' interest to push people into the system. By knowing exactly how Schedule A works, you can get around being pushed into VR and better defend your own interests.

Every agency will have a different person that you will need to go through to be approved for Schedule A. Each person will interpret the rules a little differently. Some agencies will *require* you to go through VR, but most will not.

Why You Might Want to Go Through VR

There are a couple of reasons why you might want or need to go through VR to get your Certificate of Job Readiness. One is that you really want to work for a certain government agency, and their SPPC/DPM is strict about making Schedule A applicants go through VR. Second, you might need help to figure out what accommodations you need to be successful on the job after you get a position through Schedule A. Three, you want help with other employment-related issues from VR, so you chose to open a case anyhow; why not ask them to draft your documents? If you don't have health insurance or a doctor that you are on friendly terms with, you might note that going to VR is free, while a doctor's visit is not!

Or you could be reading this in college. In college I already was a client of VR to get my books paid for. It would have made sense for me to ask for my Proof of Disability and Certificate of Job Readiness from my counselor, so I could apply after I graduated to be eligible for Schedule A.

Should you opt to go to VR, you and your counselor will draw up an Individualized Plan of Employment (IPE). When you are drawing up your IPE with VR, let them know that that you want to apply to Schedule A and you need them to give you *both* a Proof of Disability and a Certificate of Job Readiness. They should be able to give you both without a problem.

As far as other help in getting your applications out, by all means ask for what you need. Take me for example. I need help in both making phone calls and addressing envelopes. So, I should tell my counselor that is what I need. Then ask can you help. When it comes to making phone calls to confirm the SPPC/DPM contact information, they will not pretend to be you! Don't even ask! They cannot do that; they could lose their job. I'm no fan of the system, but even I understand why someone is not going to risk their job for me. What you can do is say, "I need the phone calls made in a way such that it is ambiguous as to who's calling…" (as I described in the last section) … "Can you do it that way?"

If they say no, say, "Okay, I understand," and make the calls yourself. Do not get into more detail than you need. They might say "I can address envelopes for you if you provide the address list, the envelopes and stamps," which would have been great in my case. If not, my grandmother would have been a good person to get to help me with this task. Like all jobseekers, you need to figure out what you need help with and who will be best to help you.

You are entitled to ask VR for what you need! You are not entitled to expect them to deviate from their guidelines for you. It is that simple –with any system. It's not that people at VR are bad. Just remember they represent the state's interest, not yours. They have procedures they have to follow as to how they do everything, and I mean *everything*.

You Will Be Required to Complete a Probation Period
After you get hired under Schedule A or Schedule B you will have to complete a probationary period. Usually it is two years. During this period, you will be judged on job performance and will be expected to meet the same standards as any other employee in that position.

Expect More Regulations for Receiving Accommodations
As soon as your SPPC/DPM contacts you to offer you a position, and you accept, you need to tell them if you need any accommodations to perform your job. They expect this. They also expect you to notify them before you start so they have time to put in place what you need. This is slightly different than most jobs. The chart in Chapter 11 that discusses when you should disclose and request accommodations assumes that you are working for an employer with either no policies, or with looser policies, to support employees who are disabled. Schedule A is firmer in these policies; therefore, you will be expected to act accordingly. One example of this is to tell them as soon as you are hired what you need on the job.

You Can Wait to Apply
You can apply to be eligible under Schedule A at any point in your lifetime. It is not tied to within a certain time period of being a student or graduation. Nor do you need to have a college degree to be eligible.

If you are reading this near graduation and are daunted by with all the things you could be doing to find a job, I understand. If you are a person who just wants to find the best job you can with your degree – meaning you don't long for a job with the federal government –focus first on campus interviewing and other opportunities through career services, internships and companies programs for new graduates. I say this because you are only human. You can only focus on so many different things at once. It makes sense to pursue the opportunities that will expire a year or two after graduation first.

Resources for Finding a Government Job or Government Employees with Disabilities

Computer/Electronic Accommodations Program, U.S. Department of Defense

https://www.cap.mil/

There is a wonderful federal program housed within the Department of Defense. The Computer/Electronic Accommodations Program (CAP) provides assistive technology and services to people with disabilities throughout the federal government FREE OF CHARGE! That means you can tap this resource for help in accommodating an employee with a disability. CAP will do the needs assessment, buy the needed technology, train the employee on how to use it, and follow up.

5111 Leesburg Pike, Suite 810
Falls Church, VA 22041-3206
Phone: 703-681-8813
TTY: 703-681-0881
Fax: 703-681-9075
Email: cap@tma.osd.mil

Department of Energy Accommodations Program

https://www.energy.gov/cio/office-chief-information-officer/services/assistive-technology

Provides reasonable computer and related telecommunications accommodations to assist DOE headquarters employees with disabilities.

Bradley Shaff
Corporate Reasonable Accommodation Manager
Office of Economic Impact and Diversity (ED-30)
Phone: (918) 595-6696
Email: bradley.shaff@hq.doe.gov

Federal Jobs Net

http://www.federaljobs.net/index.htm

Federal Jobs Net also includes comprehensive Postal employment information, information about overseas jobs, law enforcement opportunities, and detailed information on Veteran's benefits, handicapped employment options, and special emphasis hiring programs.

FederalJobs.net Center
302 Scenic Court
Moon Township PA 15108

Phone: (412) 494-6926
Email: customerservice@federaljobs.net

FedWorld Federal Jobs Search

https://www.usajobs.gov/

The FedWorld.gov web site is a gateway to government information. This site is managed by the National Technical Information Service (NTIS) as part of its information management mandate.

FedWorld@NTIS
National Technical Information Service
5301 Shawnee Road
Alexandria VA 22312

Email: helpdesk@fedworld.gov

Govtjobs

http://www.govtjobs.com/

For the government agency, govtjobs.com is an opportunity to reach a pool of individuals who are actively seeking employment in the public sector. Agencies listing positions with govtjobs.com include cities, counties, states, executive search firms, advertising agencies and other governmental jurisdictions. Non-profits are also invited to advertise.

1820 Bennett Drive #44
West Des Moines, IA 50265

Phone: (860) 437-5700

Limited Examination and Appointment Program (LEAP)

https://www.edd.ca.gov/about_edd/leap_program.htm

The Limited Examination and Appointment Program (LEAP) is an alternate selection process designed to facilitate the recruitment and hiring of persons with disabilities, and to provide them with an alternative way to demonstrate their qualifications for employment than the traditional state civil service examining process. The information below provides more details about the program.

Phone: (916) 324-0970
Email: LEAP@calhr.ca.gov

Office of Personnel Management (OPM) Disability Employment Website

https://www.opm.gov/policy-data-oversight/disability-employment/

The Federal Government's centralized website for information about issues related to the recruitment, employment, and retention of Federal employees with disabilities, including guidance on reasonable accommodations.

200 Constitution Ave., NW
Room C-5515
Washington DC 20210

Phone: (202) 693-7765
TTY: (202) 693-7755
Fax: (202) 693-7761

Section508.gov

https://Section508.gov

A website to find guidance, tools, and resources for Section 508 with the goal of ensuring equal participation for people with disabilities by improving Information and Communication Technology (ICT) accessibility.

Teddy Dyer
DOE Section 508 Coordinator
Office of the Chief Information Officer, Office of IT Policy and Management (IM-22)
Phone: (202) 586-9698
Email: teddy.dyer@hq.doe.gov

The ABCs of SCHEDULE A

https://www.eeoc.gov/eeoc/publications/abc_applicants_with_disabilities.cfm

Tips for Applicants with Disabilities on Getting Federal Jobs

The Target Center

https://www.targetcenter.dm.usda.gov/

The U.S. Department of Agriculture (USDA) established the Technology & Accessible Resources Give Employment Today (TARGET) Center in 1992 to utilize the power of technology and provide impactful services related to improving accessibility and contributing to the complete employment experience of individuals with disabilities.

Room 1006-South Building, 1400 Independence Avenue
SW, Washington, DC 20250
Phone: 202-720-2600 or 844-433-2774 (toll-free nationwide)
Email: target-center@usda.gov

USAjobs

http://www.usajobs.gov/

This is one of the US government's official sites for jobs and employment information. It is current; and at my writing, contains almost 17,000 jobs. But it doesn't by any means show *all* the jobs available with the federal government. Many agencies use their own hiring resources, and you won't always find such jobs listed here.

Most Effective Job-Hunting Strategy: Persist!

In the last couple of chapters, I've offered several suggestions about how to find a job. You might be asking yourself, "Which one should I use?" My answer is simple: Whatever works for you! By *works* I mean whatever leads you to either the job that you want, or a job that will give you both income and experience so that you can eventually get the job you want. It doesn't matter how you achieve either goal. It does not matter whether you land a government job or a position in the private sector!

If this book gives you an idea that leads you to a job – great! If you use a strategy that is not talked about in this book to get a job – great! If it plays out that life leads to a job without using what is available to jobseekers with disabilities, that is no more or less great!

All that matters are you find what is right for you and use it to succeed! You might try several job-seeking strategies before one lead to a job. This is absolutely normal for jobseekers in every category imaginable. You are no different! The most important job strategy of all: don't give up!

When it comes to job hunting, instant gratification is rarely part of the process. Everyone faces rejection during this process! You are no exception. You may not get the first of couple jobs that you want. This might or might not be because of your disability.

You might run into some people's negative attitudes; you might for the first-time encounter prejudice due to your disability. That's not going to feel good. Let this be another people's loss, not yours. Should this happen to you, I encourage you to talk about it with whoever you are closest to. If you need a little counseling to deal with the feelings that keep coming up during this process, get it. Rejection is part of job hunting.

The most important thing is that you use all that is at your disposal to get through this process and get employed. As with anything, there's going to be a learning curve. If something doesn't work, use that to re-adjust your strategies. This is what any successful jobseeker does!

Keep emphasizing your abilities. You need to be confident that if you keep looking you will find a position that enables you to shine!

Remember, you only need one <u>YES</u>!!!

Points to Remember from Chapter 12

✓ Government at all levels seek qualified, talented applicants with disabilities. Your disability could be an actual asset for getting a government position.

✓ You can apply for government jobs like anyone else; you are not required to use Schedule A.

✓ Familiarize yourself with Schedule A; it is just another option to get the job you deserve.

✓ You do not have to go through Vocation Rehab to obtain the documents you need to apply through Schedule A. If there's a long waiting period to get an appointment with VR, don't let that slow you down. Conversely, if you are already established with VR, or feel the need to do so for other reasons, it would probably make the most sense to get your documents from their counselors.

✓ When applying through Schedule A, focus on five or ten government agencies at a time, as opposed to sending hundreds of packets out to every agency in existence. Make sure to confirm you have the right contact information, that the agency received it, and then follow up.

✓ Never bring your Schedule A documents to an interview for a position in the private sector. Do not include a Disability MythBusters Sheet when either applying or interviewing for a Schedule A position. Each has a specific time and reason for use; know the difference.

✓ When employed through the government, expect more rigid procedures for both disability disclosure and accommodation requests.

✓ If you are hired through Schedule A, you will be required to satisfactorily complete a probationary period, generally two years.

✓ Schedule A hiring is not tied to college graduation in any way; you can apply anytime during your lifetime.

✓ Don't quit! You **CAN** do this!

Success Story: Born to Code

Tim Marciniak

My Name is Tim Marciniak and I'm currently employed full time as the MnDOT Metro District Principal Application Programmer/Architect for the State of Minnesota. I'm honored to be featured on this book as a "Success Story."

I have Spastic Cerebral Palsy, and generally use a wheelchair, but can walk with a walker for limited distances around the house. I consider myself fairly outgoing but because of a stutter/stammer I prefer email and texting until I'm well acquainted with a person. I was raised by the Marciniak family among four older brothers and an adopted sister in foster care from the age of 3 months. I was given up to Catholic Charities at birth by my 17-year-old biological mother.

My first job was as a research aide at the U of M library counting and categorizing book search requests in 1981. I remember my co-worker Carla's never-ending obsession with the wedding of Prince Charles and Diana. I remember they hired an able-bodied person to occasionally check our work. I found that extremely demeaning and complained with no avail. The next summer I worked at a local public library shelving and later checking out books. I liked that job, but it was exhausting. During the next summer I moved out on my own to the Courage Center to learn if I could live independently. To me I was on my own before graduating high school!

I graduated high school in 1984 holding a 3.6 GPA and on the National Honor Society list taking AP English and math. This was especially challenging since I had real obligations to make in order to move out of the Courage Center and be truly on my own. In August of 1984 I move in to my first apartment and that fall I enrolled at Normandale Community College. I had won a few small scholarships, but I could go to any Minnesota State college free since I was a ward of the state until age 21. Seemed an obvious choice to me.

I enjoyed most of my classes at Normandale but was really just taking classes until I figured out a direction. Then I took a fascinating Pascal programming class. The teacher held good programming and programmers with such high esteem I was drawn to the in-depth problem solving and the pursuit of the most elegant solution possible. The level of control and flexibility I saw in the lines of code freed my mind somehow. I wanted to be the guy that could get the proverbial black box to bend to his will. After that one class God showed me my passion but didn't yet show me a way to pursue it.

At the end of 1985 my vocational advisor from high school contacted me about a vocational training program looking for potential students. This program was created, sponsored, and overseen by 26 of the largest Minnesota companies to train screened, effective programming interns with the skills needed in their companies. This was perfect for me! In December 1985 I passed the aptitude exam and interviewed with the Business Advisory Committee, then was accepted to the MRC Computer Training Program in January 1986. The best part was that the state picked up the cost since it was accredited by a local state college.

The training flew by; I knew I was learning what I would use; I was in my zone. I remember constantly putting family and friends off to study. I aced nearly every test (except my final exam). I completely enjoyed a 90-day internship at National Car Rental. In a surprise move for everyone, NCR's IT department was sold off and all interns were immediately let go late that December.

To make matters worse, on the last week of the internship I developed a staph infection in my right leg, just before my final exam! I was allowed to make it up after I was out of the hospital, and I needed to find a Job. I remember calling all my placement counselors and favorite members of the Business Advisory Council from my hospital bed. That next week, I didn't do as well as I expected on the final, but ended up graduating with a 4.0 GPA in January 1987. I landed at IDS Financial Services, not my first choice.

I started at IDS Financial Services in January 1987 working as the programmer on the Consolidated Tax Statements team. This used a COBOL generator called PACBASE. This was "paint by numbers" programming: I would just fill out a CICS (mainframe terminal) online form to generate the COBOL code. I hated it and it showed. After two years I found another job at IDS writing PC-based BASIC applications to help financial planners in the field sell and configure financial products. This was definitely better, but the pace and the ever-present stuffy people and impossible expectations stressed me to the limit.

I left IDS at the end of 1990. I knew my personality clashed with their environment and to them my performance was sub-par. I could do the work, but my management didn't understand giving me "other duties as assigned" would extend the timelines out for my main ongoing projects. I did get severance pay for time served and five sessions with a career counselor. I also had a five-year relationship end at that time. I needed a big change and I got it. I moved back into Section 8 housing because I could no longer afford my market rate apartment. I was scared but also happy to have a chance to start over.

I talked to that career counselor many times throughout 1990. I also bought a copy of Turbo C, a PC programming tool, to keep my mind sharp and learn another language. Within a few months I wrote a computer game version of the Mastermind board game. I had dreams of offering it as a shareware download but I was never satisfied enough with it to do that. During that year, I was constantly looking for work on my own and monitoring the progress of the placement specialist MRC had reassigned to me. I called her at least twice a week to remind her I was still looking, and she should be too. We were always happy to talk to each, but we often held each other accountable to get stuff done. After a while I learned I needed her contacts more than I needed her help but was happy to have both. She showed me that finding a job is real work over a long haul.

I was getting interviews and my qualifications were solid. However, when I was asked about why I left previous job, my demeanor would change drastically. I even used the word "fired" a few times. I knew I needed to come to grips with what happened at IDS. It took much of that year to stop agonizing about being let go and truly focus on any interview. IDS set it up officially as a layoff so I could collect unemployment. My career counselor assured me this sort of "gray layoff" happens enough to keep him feverishly employed. He also reminded me every employer has a different personality and mismatches happen all the time. Matching an employer with an employee can be a complex issue. We learned that I needed autonomy to feel successful and IDS micromanaged too much. We spent much time working out these issues so I understood that I really could call it a layoff without feeling that I was misleading my interviewer. Even though I understood what happened, it still took a long time to feel okay enough about it to ace an interview. Looking back on it, I see that I just needed to decide to stop looking back and keep moving forward.

In November of 1991 found a job as a part-time computer lab technician at a local high school. My job was to keep the room organized, plan lessons and teach disabled students PC skills and assess student progress. Also, in I found my biological mom and met her later the next year. I saw this job as a gift to notice what high school looks like 6 years after graduation.

By January 1992 I was all set to receive SSDI, but I borrowed money from my family to make it until I received my first check. Then I interviewed for the MnDOT job on my birthday. I knew I'd aced it! After a thank-you letter and waiting two weeks, I was on edge with anticipation. I called and learned that they really liked me but needed to interview more candidates because the two others canceled. In April 1992 I was finally hired at MnDOT's Metro District as a part-time (39 hours/week) entry-level EDP Programmer. Within two years I was promoted to a Full-Time Programmer/Analyst or ITS 3.

At MnDOT I got along great with almost everyone. A few co-workers in IT bullied me in 1994, and another from the business in 1999. Both made fun of my impressive startle reflexes. I never reported either to management, but I did say lines like "I expect better from adults in a workplace" and "I know how to report these issues and make your life hell if you want me to!" in the lunchroom while four friends witnessed it. I guess it scared them because it stopped immediately afterward.

I was almost "bumped" out of my job (forced to take a lower position) in 1995 by a lady with more seniority who came back from a temporary position to find that her old job was no longer there. My managers at the time fought to keep me. A very tense time turned out very reassuring afterward.

In early 1996 I received the coveted "You are no longer disabled" letter from the SSA. This letter indicated that from a financial standpoint I was no longer considered disabled by the Social Security Administration. I laughed as I said "Wow, I'm cured!"

MnDOT's facilities were generally accessible. However, up until 2002, for more than 10 years, I needed to use a handicapped stall with a door that didn't close behind me. I and many others complained. The lame facilities manager for most of that time was fired for other reasons, but his replacement in 2001 was much more diligent about these matters.

Just this May I became an ITS 4 (5 is the max), after having my job duties evaluated by HR and proving to them, I had performed the higher-level duties for quite some time because the position required it. Not the classic promotion with all the afterglow, but still a significant bump in pay and the politics that come with it. I still like my autonomy, but our policies and procedures are now mine to push on others! I oversee our local suite of applications, ensuring that changes to our infrastructure don't bring things to a screeching halt. So far, so good.

Life's Side Effects
1. Met Debbie in 1998 on Match.com
   a. Proposed September 1999
   b. Married in June 2001 in Rapid City, SD
   c. Honeymooned in Disney World
   d. Built an accessible house in 2002
2. Bought a new van in 2012
3. Cruised Eastern/Western Caribbean in 2011/2013
4. Installed a lift system to help extend my working years as long as possible.

What I've Leaned

Showing my success to encourage others or otherwise has had its drawbacks. This is truly difficult for me to understand. It really looks like disabled people struggle to push each other forward into gainful employment. It's not right to hold we back just because not everyone will come along. Here are some examples of the negative feedback I received when I've tried to help:

1. When I told people in passing about moving out of Section 8 housing in 1993 (I was paying market rate anyway) I was called shallow, lucky, and materialistic by others in the complex. Many others projected back that I'm either egomaniacal, trying to be or act "able bodied" or are "selling out". I have yet to learn who I sold out to.

2. In 2010 I created a "Working with CP" group on Facebook to share the experiences of those who have worked, are working, or want to work. In just a few days I received a mean-spirited message from a former roommate from 1984 on his wife's account. He claimed I was lying about having had a job for so long. His wife took over the conversation, also accusing me of boasting or belittling others that don't or can't work. She said that my remarks worked to divide the disabled community based on my "pure luck." It became a five-day Facebook nightmare that just dropped. So how do we support ourselves to find and hold jobs? I wasn't hurt, but I was shocked to learn that "our" successes are so widely seen that way. I closed the group shortly afterwards.

Instead of detailing everything that has frustrated me as a disabled person, I'm outlining some of my guiding principles that I try to live by when searching or on the job. These have evolved over the years and while I have not always followed these principles, they are my guides every day at work. Yes, in a perfect world, no one should need to do any of these, but the reality is that if you want to blaze a trail, you need to be okay with being uncomfortable and working harder than those who don't.

When searching for a job:
1. Be patient but assertive with yourself, your family, employers, coworkers, doctors, teachers, government workers, vocational advisors; we all learn as we go.

2. Ask everyone you know for help. Take what you need and forget the rest; it's just not tailored for you.

3. Practice interviews with others, and even apply for jobs you're overqualified for to get the interview practice.

When interviewing for a job:
1. Answer the questions your interviewers can't or are afraid to ask. HR folks know what they can and can't ask during an interview, but that won't help answer the questions that give them the confidence to hire you.

2. Walk them through a typical day on your job. Include the quirky things you need to do to be you. Outline why and how… but leave out the messy stuff. Everyone new to you will wonder how you stuff gets done.

3. Don't outline any behind-the-scenes complications of your disability to the interviewers. They likely won't understand the implications.

4. Don't ask about affirmative action or other programs. You're qualified or you wouldn't be here. Most companies will state their participation on the application.

5. Tell them enough to see the disability as a non-issue.

6. Don't ask them the favor of hiring you. Tell them they won't regret taking a chance on you.

7. Outline what accommodations you'll likely need as early as possible. End the mystery but don't get cocky. Keep it to the biggest needs and their most commonsense solutions.

8. Be excited about and desperately "want" every job you interview for, but never indicate that you "need" any job, even if you do.

On the job be prepared to be:
1. Underpaid and micro-managed. Work harder because others aren't really sure you can do the work. Make it obvious every day. No, it's not fair, but you are blazing the path for others.

2. Overqualified and undignified. Study or practice earlier in your career to gain the respect others already have. It'll pay off later.

3. Bullied, tested and targeted; understand people often treat what they don't understand with childish reactions. It's really a serious form of confusion about a social situation. Don't be afraid to set people straight right away. The longer you allow it to continue, the more others will deem it acceptable and even join in.

4. Blamed, left out, coddled, and scapegoated; get assertive here but don't project back. Just explain what you can honestly… and then solve the issue.

5. Confided in, trusted, hailed and loved; once people know you and how you work, you'll notice the turn quickly. Accept all positive feedback positively… or it will stop.

6. Protected, favored, and humanized; over time a disabled person in the workplace reminds every one of their humanity. It's good to witness, but if not appreciated others feel mistreated and it won't last.

7. Relied upon, needed, and counted on; this is the ultimate compliment for the disabled person on the job. It is the true contradiction to what we are often told or expect.

8. Funny and light… but real; Show how complex you are. It put you at the same level.

9. Paying back any SSI or SSDI checks you receive after about a year of full-time employment. I owed about $7000.

10. Mentally and physically exhausted every day; I see it as a good thing, as I sleep very well just because I am completely spent when I get home.

Once hired always try to:
1. Stay in generally forward direction. Just take the path of least resistance even if it's twice as long.

2. Handle situations directly instead of going to your supervisor/HR. No one likes getting others involved.

3. Understand that other people's anger at you or your performance is never about you, it's about how your actions remind them about themselves.

4. Be confident and realistic about your abilities, limitations, expectations, and deadlines so your word can be trusted.

5. Be assertive without being emotional, angry, or deflecting; it's difficult to treat you unfairly if you're always fair.

6. Be upfront but brief about your condition, health and availability; you need to prove you're realistic and reliable.

7. Work at a pace you can sustain; it avoids burnout, stress, and blown expectations.

8. Be available to hear other people's health issues; it helps everyone realize no one is perfectly healthy.

9. Be concise, precise and proactive about any reasonable accommodation. People want to help you be your best. Using their time and money wisely will pay dividends.

10. Be pro-active about your health and wellness. Aging is at best complicated by a disability. Get whatever you need to improve your heath when you can afford it. Use these tools to extend your career.

Never did I envision my adult life being as functionally "American" as it is now. All my life I paid attention and kept reaching forward for the opportunities I saw in front of me. I'm happy and know that I'm blessed, to be able to completely support myself and actively contribute to the household and the economy. I specifically want to encourage those who can and want to work to dream bigger than you imagine right now. You will grow and mature over time and you'll want to reach further and further. So, aim high, my friends!

Appendix A: Disability-Related Scholarships

As with all 'resource sections' in this book, please keep in mind that websites get taken down and web addresses get changed. Information was current within a few months before publication of this book. The program names you find here can be used to do internet searches of your own for up-to-date links.

Amputees

Bridge to Ability Scholarship

http://www.amputee-coalition.org/scholarship/bridge_to_ability/index.htmlhttp://www.amputee-coalition.org/events-programs/scholarships/

It is the goal of the Amputee Coalition through the Bridge to Ability Fund to reduce or eliminate the financial barriers to attending our national conference for new amputees.

Headquarters:
9303 Center Street, Suite 100
Manassas, VA 20110

Branch Office:
900 East Hill Avenue, Suite 290
Knoxville, TN 37915

Christina Skoski, M.D., Scholarship

http://www.amputee-coalition.org/events-programs/scholarships/skoski/index.html

This fund will provide a $1,000 scholarship to a full-time undergraduate student who has a congenital limb difference or an amputation *and* who is, or whose parent or legal guardian is, a *registered friend* of the Amputee Coalition.

Phone: 888/267-5669

Headquarters:
9303 Center Street, Suite 100
Manassas, VA 20110

Branch Office:
900 East Hill Avenue, Suite 290
Knoxville, TN 37915

Claude S. Weiler Scholarship for Amputee College Students

http://nationalamputation.org/scholar1.html

The National Amputation Foundation is proud to offer six (6) $500.00 scholarships to college students with a major limb amputation, who will be attending an accredited university as a full-time student. A major limb amputation is described as loss of limb beginning at or above the wrist or ankle.

National Amputation Foundation
Attn: Claude S. Weiler Scholarship Coordinator
40 Church Street
Malverne NY 11565

Phone: (516) 887-3600
Fax: (516) 887-3667
Email: amps76@aol.com

National Amputee Golf Association Educational Scholarship Grant
http://wagagolf.org/test-paypal-donation/

One of the goals of our Association is to provide educational assistance to an amputee member or his or her dependent(s). The primary purpose of this grant is to assist an amputee member or their dependent in the payment of tuition and fees while pursuing an undergraduate or two year vocational/technical degree at an accredited college, vocational/technical school or institution. The amount of the grant for a four-year Bachelors' degree will be $2,000.00/year (maximum). If an individual is selected, the grant will be issued each year for a maximum of four (4) years or until graduation, whichever occurs first. For a two-year non-bachelor's degree or technical/associates degree, the award will be for a maximum of $1,000/year or $500/semester.

Scholarship Grant Program
701 Orkney Ct
Smyrna TN 37167-6395

Peg-Leg Pirate Scholarship for Amputee Students
https://www.peglegpirate.org/

The goal of the scholarship program of "Ye Notorious Krew of the Peg-Leg Pirate" is to assist amputees in furthering their education. That education may be provided by an accredited college or university, community college, or vocational-trade-technical school that is state licensed. The scholarships have a value between $1000 and $2000.

Peg-Leg Pirate Scholarship Program
P.O. Box 1854
Ruskin, FL 33575

Autism and Autism Spectrum Disorder

AHEADD Scholarship for Students with Autism or Autism Spectrum Disorder

https://www.top10onlinecolleges.org/scholarships-for/autism-spectrum/

AHEADD (Achieving in Higher Education with Autism/Developmental Disabilities) is a private, community organization. It provides $500 scholarships to current high school and college students in the United States with Autism and Asperger's.

Phone: 1-877-AHEADD-1
Email: admin@aheadd.org

Schwallie Family Scholarship Program

http://www.researchautism.org/news/otherevents/scholarship.asp

OAR's scholarship program provides non-renewable $3,000 scholarships to students across the autism spectrum. OAR is pleased to invite applications from persons with an autism diagnosis (DSM-IV or later criteria) pursuing full-time, post-secondary, undergraduate education or vocational-technical training in any of the following:
- ✓ Four-year undergraduate college or university
- ✓ Two-year undergraduate college
- ✓ Trade, technical or vocational school
- ✓ Cooperative life skills programs

2000 North 14th Street, Suite 240
Arlington VA 22201
Phone: (703) 243-9710

Career-Specific

American Architectural Foundation

http://www.aia.org/education/AIAB081881

The American Architectural Foundation offers the Minority/Disadvantaged Scholarships in order to encourage diversity and equity in the architectural profession. These scholarships are open to high school seniors and college freshmen who plan to study architecture at a NAAB-accredited program. The scholarship program was established in 1970 by a grant from the Ford Foundation to aid students who would not otherwise have an opportunity to enter a professional degree program. Twenty awards are made per year and may be renewed for two additional years, ideally maintaining 60 students in the program in any given year. Scholarship amounts range between $500 and $2,500 and are determined by evaluation of financial need information provided by the student and the school.

Email: scholarships@aia.org

American Association of Health and Disability (AAHD) Scholarship

http://www.aahd.us/initiatives/scholarship-program/

In 2009, AAHD created the AAHD Scholarship Program, which will support students with disabilities who are pursuing higher education. Preference will be given to students who plan to pursue undergraduate/graduate studies in the field of public health, health promotion, disability studies, to include disability policy and disability research. Royalties from the DHJ will fund the first year of the AAHD Scholarship Fund. As 2009 is the first year of the scholarship program, funds are limited, and we anticipate that scholarships will be competitive. Scholarships will be limited to under $1,000.

Scholarship Committee
American Association On Health and Disability
110 N. Washington Street, Suite 328-J
Rockville MD 20850

American Library Association (ALA) Century Scholarship

http://www.ala.org/awardsgrants/ala-century-scholarship

The American Library Association's annual $2,500 ASCLA Century Scholarship will fund services or accommodation for a library school student or students with disabilities admitted to an ALA-accredited library school. The scholarship will fund services or accommodations that are either not provided by law or otherwise by the university that will enable the student or students to successfully complete the course of study for a master's or Doctorate in Library Science and become a library or information studies professional.

ALA Scholarship Clearinghouse
50 E. Huron St
Chicago, IL, 60611

Phone: (800) 545-2433 ext. 4279
Email: scholarships@ala.org

Caroline Simpson Maheady Scholarship Award

http://www.exceptionalnurse.com/scholarship.php

A $250.00 scholarship will be awarded to a nursing student with a disability. Preference will be given to an undergraduate student, of Scottish descent, who has demonstrated a commitment to working with people with disabilities.

Scholarship Committee
ExceptionalNurse.com
Palm Beach Gardens, FL 33410

College Scholarship Fund / Working Artists Fund

http://www.specialacademy.org/scholarships/

To assist the special needs community to achieve their artistic dreams, the Academy of Special Dreams will offer a limited number of cash scholarships to those participants who submit their artistic expressions in the competitions sponsored by the Special Academy.

Academy of Special Dreams
115 W. California Blvd. Suite 326 Pasadena, CA 91105

Donald W. Banner Diversity (Banner & Witcoff) Scholarship

http://www.bannerwitcoff.com/index.php?option=com_bwabout&task=view&id=12

Banner & Witcoff is proud to offer the Donald W. Banner Diversity Scholarship for law students. This scholarship is part of Banner & Witcoff's commitment to fostering the development of intellectual property lawyers from diverse backgrounds.

Donald W. Banner Diversity Scholarship
c/o Christopher Hummel
Banner & Witcoff, Ltd.
1100 13th Street NW, Suite 1200
Washington, DC 20005

Farella Braun + Martel Diversity Scholarship

http://www.fbm.com/Farella_Braun__Martel_Awards_2014_Diversity_Scholarships_04-23-2014/

As part of our commitment to diversity, Farella Braun + Martel also recognizes the value of increasing diversity within the legal profession as a whole, and we award Diversity Scholarships to support outstanding diverse Bay Area law students. As we have for the past nine years, Farella Braun + Martel will award a total of $25,000 in scholarship grants, to be divided equally between three to five law student recipients.

Scholarship applicants must be current first-year, full- or part-time (attending first-year classes) law students who are students of color, members of the lesbian, gay, bisexual, transgender and queer (LGBTQ) community, disabled, or whose background or experience would otherwise contribute to the diversity of the legal profession. Recipients must currently attend one of the following local law schools: University of California, Berkeley School of Law; University of California, Davis School of Law (King Hall); University of California, Hastings College of the Law;

Golden Gate University, School of Law; Stanford Law School; Santa Clara University, School of Law; or the University of San Francisco, School of Law.

Cheryl Loof
Farella Braun + Martel LLP
235 Montgomery Street
San Francisco CA 94104
Phone: (415) 954-4433
Email: cloof@fbm.com

FFA B.R.I.D.G.E. Endowment Scholarship

https://www.studentscholarshipsearch.com/scholarships/bridge-endowment-fund-ffa-scholarship

The B.R.I.D.G.E. Endowment Fund offers a $5,000 scholarship to physically disabled or handicapped students pursuing a two- or four-year degree in any area of agriculture. In addition to the individual scholarships, the B.R.I.D.G.E. Endowment Fund will make available a $200 cash award and plaque to the FFA chapter doing an excellent job of serving rural handicapped people in their community.

National FFA Organization
P.O. Box 68960, 6060 FFA Drive
Indianapolis IN 46268-0960
Phone: (317) 802-6060

Fish & Richardson 1L Diversity Fellowship

http://www.fr.com/diversity-about/

One key component of our ongoing initiative to recruit a diverse group of attorneys is the 1L Diversity Fellowship Program. Launched in 2005, the program provides fellowships to diverse first-year law students throughout the country annually. Each selected student receives a $5,000 academic scholarship, mentoring by members of the firm, and a paid Summer Associate position in the Fish office of the student's choice.

Email: careers@fr.com

Fredrikson Byron Foundation Minority Scholarships

http://www.fredlaw.com/firm/scholarship.htm

The Fredrikson & Byron Foundation Minority Scholarship Program sponsors educational opportunities for currently enrolled, first-year law students of diverse backgrounds. The Foundation offers one award of $10,000.

Grant Program for Students with Disabilities in Graduate Science Degree Programs (Foundation for Science and Disability)

http://www.stemd.org/ and http://ars.usda.gov/rmankin

A goal of the Foundation for Science and Disability is to increase opportunities in science for disabled students. To promote this goal, the foundation has established a Science Student Grant Fund, available to fourth year undergraduate (who have been accepted to graduate or professional school) and graduate students who have a disability. The students must be United States citizens. Awards of $1000 each will be made to college or university students for some special purpose in connection with a science project or thesis in any field of Mathematics, Science, Medicine, Engineering, or Computer Science. An award could be given for an assistive device or instrument, or as financial support to work with a professor on an individual research project or for some other special research need.

Past President and Chair, FSD Grants Committee:

Richard Mankin
USDA-ARS-CMAVE
1700 SW 23rd Dr
Gainesville, FL 32608

Phone: (352) 374-5774
Fax: (352) 374-5804
Email: rmankin1@ufl.edu

Injury Lawyer News Disability Scholarship Award
http://injurylawyer-news.com/scholarship/

Injury Lawyer News (ILN) believes strongly in helping students achieve their goals of higher education, especially when they are faced with challenges such as physical and learning disabilities. As advocates of higher education, ILN is proud to give back to the community through the Injury Lawyer News Disability Scholarship Award. Please review the eligibility information below and familiarize yourself with the application process.

The scholarship award is available to all pre-law and law school students. Students must be accepted to or already attending an accredited US college or university or accepted to or attending a fully accredited US law school. In addition, the scholarship is only available to students with a medically documented disability, which can be either a physical disability or a learning disability.

The scholarship will be awarded to three students; each student will receive $1000 to be used toward tuition, books or housing at an accredited US undergraduate college program or law school.

Email: scholarship@injurylawyer-news.com

Peter Gili Scholarship Award
http://www.exceptionalnurse.com/scholarship.php

A $500.00 scholarship will be awarded to a nursing student with a disability. This scholarship has been donated by family members and friends in memory of Peter Gili.

Scholarship Committee
ExceptionalNurse.com
13019 Coastal Circle
Palm Beach Gardens, FL 33410

Scholarship for Minority Accounting Students (AICPA)
http://www.aicpa.org/Career/DiversityInitiatives/Pages/smas.aspx

This program provides awards to outstanding minority students to encourage their selection of accounting as a major and their ultimate entry into the profession. Funding is provided by the AICPA Foundation, with contributions from the New Jersey Society of CPAs and Robert Half International. The AICPA awarded 94 accounting students with scholarships ranging in amounts from $1,500–$3,000 each for the 2009–2010 academic year.

Email: scholarships@aicpa.org

Worldstudio AIGA Scholarships
http://scholarships.worldstudioinc.com/

Each year, Worldstudio AIGA Scholarships receives hundreds of applications from young people in this very predicament – desperate to influence the world with their amazing talents but without the financial means to do so. Fortunately, with the support of generous individuals, organizations and corporations, Worldstudio AIGA Scholarships allow young people from minority and economically disadvantaged backgrounds not only to realize their artistic dreams, but also to give back to their communities.

Worldstudio AIGA Scholarships, AIGA
164 Fifth Avenue
New York, NY 10010

Contact Mark Randall, Worldstudio Foundation

Phone: (212) 366-1317 ext.11
Email: mrandall@worldstudioinc.com

400

Deafness/Hearing Loss

AG Bell Financial Aid and Scholarship Program
https://www.agbell.org/Connect/AG-Bell-College-Scholarship-Program

Thanks to generous donations from individuals over the years, AG Bell is able to offer several scholarships for full-time students who have a pre-lingual bilateral hearing loss in the moderately-severe to profound range, use listening and spoken language, and who are pursuing a bachelors, masters or doctorate (not law or public policy) [see below] degree at an accredited mainstream college or university. This is a merit-based scholarship program and award selection is extremely competitive; over the past six years approximately 12% of applicants were selected to receive an award.

George H. Nofer Scholarship for Law and Public Policy
https://www.agbell.org/Connect/NoferScholarship

The George H. Nofer Scholarship for Law and Public Policy is for full-time graduate students with a pre-lingual bilateral hearing loss in the moderately-severe to profound range, use listening and spoken language as their primary method of communication, and who are attending an accredited mainstream law school or a masters or doctoral program in public policy or public administration.

3417 Volta Place, NW
Washington, DC 20007
Phone: (202) 337-5220
TTY: (202) 337-5221

Gallaudet University Alumni Association Graduate Fellowship Fund
https://www.gallaudet.edu/alumni/alumni-association/the-centennial-funds/graduate-fellowship-fund

The Graduate Fellowship Fund (GFF) is one of three separate funds made possible by the half-million-dollar Centennial Fund that was presented by the Gallaudet University Alumni Association (GUAA) to Gallaudet in commemoration of its centennial anniversary (1964). This fund makes up half of the Centennial Fund. Its principal has been established by the University as a permanent endowment. Its investment is the responsibility of the GUAA Board of Directors.

Chair, GFF Committee
Peikoff Alumni House
Gallaudet University
800 Florida Avenue, NE
Washington, DC 20002-3695
Phone: 202-651-5060 (Voice/TTY)

Graeme Clark Scholarship
http://www.cochlearamericas.com/Support/2291.asphttp://www.cochlear.com/wps/wcm/connect/us/recipients/nucleus-6/nucleus-6-support-and-community/scholarships/scholarship-details

The Graeme Clark Scholarship is an award open to Nucleus® cochlear implant recipients around the world. Awarded by Cochlear, this Scholarship has been set up to help individuals further themselves by undertaking university studies. The Scholarship consists of financial assistance toward a minimum three-year undergraduate degree at an accredited university and is paid in annual installments on the completion of each year of study. It is available to those currently completing their final year of high school, to mature aged students who have been accepted into a university course and to current university students.

Cochlear Americas
The Graeme Clark Scholarship
13059 East Peakview Avenue
Centennial, CO 80111

Louise Tumarkin Zazove Foundation Scholarships for the Deaf and Hard of Hearing
https://www.ltzfoundation.org/

Any citizen or permanent resident of the United States with a significant bilateral hearing loss is eligible for consideration by the Foundation, regardless of age, sex, race, geographic location or ethnicity. We generally require at least a 50-dB unaided hearing loss in both ears and do consider applicants who have a cochlear implant. If there are extenuating circumstances documented in the application, we may consider applicants with less hearing loss. Criteria used for selection of scholarship recipients ensure that the mission of the Foundation is supported. Financial need will increase the possibility of being awarded funds but is only one of many criteria that are considered.

Barbara Reed
c/o LTZ Foundation
2903 Craig Rd
Ann Arbor MI 48103

Minnie Pearl (Hearing Bridges) Scholarship Program
https://www.scholarships123.com/award/minnie-pearl-scholarship-program

The Minnie Pearl Scholarship is a scholarship of up to $2,500 per year, for four years. This scholarship is only for undergraduate study and is to be used at any accredited junior college, college, university, or technical school in the United States.

Minnie Pearl Scholarship
935 Edgehill Ave
Nashville TN 37203

Phone: 800-545-7373 (HEAR)
Voice/TDD: 615-627-2724

Travelers Protective Association of America (TPA) Annual Scholarship Trust for the Hearing Impaired
http://www.tpahq.org/scholarshiptrust.html

In 1975 the Travelers Protective Association of America (TPA) established a scholarship trust for the deaf and near deaf. The intent and purposes of the trust are the giving of financial aid or assistance to US Residents who are deaf and hearing impaired who may benefit from medical, mechanical or specialized treatment or special education. Candidates must also demonstrate financial need. The patient pays for hearing aid(s) and applies for grant; awarded once a year (April); eligibility based on amount of hearing loss and need and dollars available for the trust for the year;

usually is a partial grant; also covers for education, interpreters, cochlear implants, assistive devices.

The Travelers Protective Association of America
2041 Exchange Drive
Saint Charles MO 63303

William C. Stokoe (National Association of the Deaf) Scholarship

http://www.nad.org

Graduate student will be awarded $1000. Applicants must be deaf or hard of hearing.

NAC: Stokoe Scholarship Secretary
814 Thayer Ave
Silver Spring MD 20910
Phone: (301) 587-1789 (TTY)

General

Access Technology Scholarship

http://www.caped.io/scholarships/2016-caped-scholarship-descriptions/

In memory of Penny Petersen, Assistive Technology Specialist from CSU Long Beach, who promoted and advocated for the technology needs of students with disabilities. The Access Technology Equipment Scholarship will award assistive technology software or hardware (up to $1000) to a student who uses this technology to access their college courses.

10073 Valley View St. #242
Cypress CA, 90630
Phone: (562) 397 2810
FAX: (866) 577 3387

Betty Bacon Memorial Scholarship

http://www.caped.io/scholarships/2016-caped-scholarship-descriptions/

To honor the memory of Betty Bacon, a Director of Disabled Student Services for over 25 years at San Diego State University and a consummate advocate for people with disabilities. Awarded to a college or university student with a disability.

10073 Valley View St. #242
Cypress CA, 90630
Phone: (562) 397 2810
FAX: (866) 577 3387

CAPED General Excellence Scholarship

http://www.caped.io/scholarships/2016-caped-scholarship-descriptions/

In celebration of student excellence. Awarded to a college student with a disability who demonstrates high academic achievement and is involved in his/her community as well as campus life.

10073 Valley View St. #242
Cypress CA, 90630

Phone: (562) 397 2810
FAX: (866) 577 3387

Central Intelligence Agency Undergraduate Scholarship Program

https://www.cia.gov/careers/student-opportunities/undergraduate-scholarship-program.html

The Undergraduate Scholar Program was developed, in part, to assist minority and disabled students, but application is open to all students who meet the requirements. The program offers unmatched experience. You'll complete work sessions during each summer break, increasing your knowledge and job responsibilities while assisting intelligence professionals and applying your academic skills. Once selected, recipients will be given an annual salary; a benefits package that includes health insurance, life insurance, and retirement; and up to $18,000 per calendar year for tuition, mandatory fees, books and supplies. They will be required to work at an Agency facility during summer breaks and to maintain full-time college status during the school year with a minimum cumulative 3.0/4.0 GPA. We will pay the cost of transportation between school and the Washington, DC area each summer and provide a housing allowance.

Central Intelligence Agency
Office of Public Affairs
Washington, D.C. 20505

Phone: (703) 482-0623
Fax: (571) 204-3800

Cindy Kolb Memorial Scholarship

http://www.caped.io/scholarships/2016-caped-scholarship-descriptions/

In memory of Cindy Kolb, a Director of Disabled Student Services at San Francisco State University. Awarded to a student with a disability attending a four-year college or university.

10073 Valley View St. #242
Cypress CA, 90630

Phone: +1 562 397 2810
FAX: +1 866 577 3387

Incight Go Getter Scholarship

https://www.incight.org/scholarship

Incight is providing scholarships for disabled students. The only two requirements for application are that the applicant have a documented disability (of any type, be it physical, learning, cognitive, etc.) and that s/he be a full-time student at any college, university, trade school, etc.

Incight
310 SW Fourth Ave., Suite 630
Portland, OR 97204
Phone: (971) 244-0305
Email: questions@incight.org

Inclusion Scholars Program

http://www.nafeonation.org/att-and-nafeo-announce-inaugural-hbcupbi-inclusion-institutions/

AT&T and NAFEO have joined forces to launch the Inclusion Scholars Program (ISP), a scholarship initiative that will award three NAFEO "Inclusion Institutions" a $36,000 grant to offer one incoming freshman a $9,000 award toward his or her tuition and fees for each of four consecutive years.

Contact: Tamisha Marsh at 202-552-3300 or tmarsh@nafeo.org
National Association for Equal Opportunity in Higher Education (NAFEO)
209 Third Street, SE
Washington, DC 20003
Phone: 202.552.3300
Fax: 202.552.3330

Jackie Robinson Foundation's Scholarship Program

https://www.jackierobinson.org/apply/

Through its Education and Leadership Development Program, the Jackie Robinson Foundation provides scholarships of up to $7,500 annually to minority high school students showing leadership potential and demonstrating financial need to attend an accredited 4-year college or university of their choice.

Jackie Robinson Foundation
One Hudson Square
75 Varick Street, 2nd Floor
New York, NY 10013-1917

Phone: (212) 290-8600
Fax: (212) 290-8081

Joe Cleres Memorial Scholarship

http://www.newoutlookpioneers.org

Application may be made either by a physically or mentally challenged student or by someone on their behalf. Each financial award is to be used solely for tuition support. Payment of the scholarship award will be made directly to the school that will provide the education for the physically or mentally challenged student. Only completed applications will be considered.

New Outlook Scholarship Administrator
Joe Cleres Memorial Scholarship
c/o Ms. Sara Huffman
930 15th St, 12th Floor
DENVER CO 80202

John Weir Scholarship

https://www.annarborcil.org/2018/02/23/2018-john-weir-scholarship-applications-now-available/

The Ann Arbor Center for Independent Living is now accepting applications from graduating high school seniors living or going to school in Washtenaw, Livingston and Monroe Counties for its John Weir Scholarship. The scholarship is open to seniors with all types of disabilities, including learning, cognitive, developmental,

405

physical, visual, and hearing disabilities, as well as autism/Asperger's, mental health and chronic health conditions, such as cancer. The scholarship is for those going to a two- or four-year college or a trade school after high school. The winner gets a $500 scholarship (with the possibility of an addition $500 for the following three years of college) and becomes the CIL's youth spokesperson. Runners-up receive smaller one-time scholarships.

Ann Arbor Center for Independent Living
3941 Research Park Drive Ann Arbor, MI 48108

Lynn M. Smith Memorial Scholarship
 https://caped.net/scholarships/

In memory of Lynn M. Smith, Career/Vocational counselor at De Anza Community College and Director of Disabled Student Services at San Francisco State University. Awarded to a Community College student with a disability who is pursuing a vocational career goal.

10073 Valley View St. #242
Cypress CA 90630
Phone: (562) 397-2810
Fax: (866) 577-3387

Patricia Sonntag Memorial Scholarship

http://www.caped.io/scholarships/2016-caped-scholarship-descriptions/

In memory of Patricia Sonntag, a Director of the Office of Services to Students with Disabilities from Sacramento State University. Awarded to a student with a disability attending a four-year college or university, who is majoring in a field related to policy formulation or service delivery to students with disabilities or is actively engaged in advocacy or leadership in campus, community or governmental organization that benefits individuals with disabilities regardless of major.

10073 Valley View St. #242
Cypress CA, 90630
Phone: (562) 397 2810
Fax: (866) 577 3387

Paul G. Hearne AAPD Leadership Award

http://www.aapd.com/what-we-do/education/higher-education/Scholarships/scholarships.html

Each year, we select up to two individuals whose work, life, and passion mirrors the life and legacy of Mr. Hearne to receive the annual Paul G. Hearne AAPD Leadership Awards. Hearne Award recipients are featured at the AAPD Leadership Gala in short documentary films chronicling their disability advocacy work. In addition, Hearne Award recipients each receive $10,000 to help them continue their progress as leaders and have an opportunity to meet and network with national disability leaders with AAPD. U.S. residents with any type of disability are eligible to apply.

American Association of People with Disabilities
2013 H St. NW, 5th Floor
Washington DC 20006

Special People in Need Scholarship

http://www.scholarships4students.com/special_people_in_need_scholarship.htm

The Special People in Need Scholarship is available to students with disabilities. You must demonstrate financial need to be considered for this award. Additionally, you must have your educational institution serve as your sponsor, with the institution serving as the award applicant. Two letters of recommendation are also required to be considered for this renewable award.

Fields of Interest: Elementary school, secondary schools, other institutions of education, health care organizations, higher education, hospitals, human services.

Special Populations: People with Disabilities and illness and people who are economically disadvantaged

Kinds of Support: General/Operating support, grants to individuals, program development, fellowships, scholarships funds, and scholarships to individuals.

Special People In Need
Attn: Irene S. Peterson

500 W. Madison St., Ste. 3700
Chicago, IL 60661-4591
Phone: (312) 715-5235

Steve Fasteau Past Presidents' Scholarship

http://www.caped.io/scholarships/2016-caped-scholarship-descriptions/

In honor of all the dedicated professionals who have served as President of CAPED. Awarded to a college student with a disability who has high academic achievement and has shown leadership and dedication to the advancement of students with disabilities in postsecondary (college or university) education.

10073 Valley View St. #242
Cypress CA, 90630
Phone: (562) 397 2810
Fax: (866) 577 3387

Through the Looking Glass for Students of Parents with Disabilities

http://www.lookingglass.org/scholarships/

Through the Looking Glass will award students of parents with disabilities two separate scholarship awards: one for graduating high school seniors who will be attending college, and one for currently enrolled college students. The application packet will be somewhat different than in previous years, and applicants will need to apply online.

3075 Adeline St., Ste. 120
Berkeley, CA 94703
Phone: (800) 644-2666
TTY: (510) 848-1005
Local: (510) 848-1112
Fax: (510) 848-4445

William May Memorial Scholarship

https://caped.net/scholarships/

In memory of William May, a CAPED Founder and a former Coordinator of Disabled Student Programs and Services at Riverside City College. Awarded to a college student with a disability.

10073 Valley View St. #242
Cypress CA, 90630
Phone: (562) 397 2810
Fax: (866) 577 3387

Health Impairments

Andre Sobel Award

http://andreriveroflife.org

The Andre Sobel Award is available to cancer survivors who are residents of the United States. To be eligible, you must write an essay of 1,500-words or less on the topic: "The letter I would like to have received from my best friend during my illness." The essay should be written in letter form from whomever you consider to be your best friend.

P.O. Box 361460
Los Angeles CA 90036
Phone: (310) 276-7111
Email: info@andreriveroflife.org

Beth Carew Memorial (Colburn-Keenan Foundation) Scholarship

http://www.colkeen.org/?page_id=123

The Beth Carew Memorial Scholarship is open to full-time undergraduates and entering freshmen who have hemophilia, von Willebrand disease, or another related, inherited bleeding disorder.

The Colburn-Keenan Foundation, Inc.
PO Box 811
Enfield CT 06083

Toll-Free Phone: 800-966-2431
Fax: 888-345-0259
Email: admin@colkeen.org

Biogen Idec Hemophilia Scholarship Program

https://www.scholarships.com/financial-aid/college-scholarships/scholarship-directory/employer/biogen-idec

Individual awards ranging from $2,500-$7,000. In 2013, a total of $50,000 was awarded to 11 recipients with hemophilia and with diverse educational goals. Biogen Idec is honored to continue its support of the community's dreams in 2014 by planning to once again donate a total of $50,000 to multiple winners. Individuals with hemophilia A or B who are pursuing a vocational or technical certificate, a 2- or 4-year degree program, or graduate degree are encouraged to apply.

Attention: Biogen Idec Grants Office
Phone: (617) 914-1299
Email: grantsoffice@biogenidec.com

BioRx/Hemophilia of North Carolina Educational Scholarship Program

https://www.diplomatpharmacy.com/resources/nc-scholarship

Intended for individuals who are diagnosed with hemophilia, VWD or other bleeding-associated factor deficiency, or their siblings, parents or caregivers living within the same household. At least one scholarship is awarded to an applicant pursuing education in a health-related field from an accredited college or university or certified training program.

Hemophilia of North Carolina
Attention: Chris Barnes
Phone: (866) 442-4679
Email: cbarnes@biorx.net

Cancer for College
http://cancerforcollege.org/

Cancer for College provides one-time and recurring scholarships to current and former cancer patients. Applicants must be a U.S. Citizen planning to enroll in an accredited four-year university, community college or graduate school. Awards vary from hundreds to thousands of dollars. The application period opens October 1st and closes January 31st. Awards are announced in July. Visit our website to submit the application. Cancer for College was founded in 1993 by Craig Pollard, a two-time cancer survivor and double amputee.

981 Park Center Drive
Vista, CA 92081
Phone: 760-599-5096
Email: info@cancerforcollege.org

Cancer Survivors' Fund Scholarship
http://www.cancersurvivorsfund.org/Applications/HowToApply.htm

The Fund awards four levels of scholarships to augment the expenses associated with the college educations of young cancer survivors. A selection committee chooses scholarship recipients based on the applicants' personal hardships, assessing their financial and emotional needs as well as their academic qualifications.

P.O. Box 792
Missouri City, TX 77459

Candice's Sickle Cell Scholarship
http://www.candicessicklecellfund.org/scholarships/

The goal of this scholarship is to help alleviate the financial pressures of college-bound students with sickle cell disease by providing three $1500 scholarships annually. These scholarships assist affected students with college or other post-high school education.

P.O. Box 672237
Bronx, NY 10467-0237
Phone: (646) 436-0477
Email: cscfinc@gmail.com

CHASA Scholarship for Childhood Stroke Survivors
http://www.chasa.org/scholarship.htm

The Children's Hemiplegia and Stroke Association offers college and vocational school scholarships to students with childhood hemiplegia or hemiparesis.

4101 W. Green Oaks, Suite 305, #149
Arlington, TX 76016

Children's Hemiplegia and Stroke Association Scholarship

http://www.chasa.org/scholarship.htm

The Children's Hemiplegia and Stroke Association Scholarship is available to students no older than 25 years of age who have experienced and continue to experience childhood hemiplegia, hemiparesis, or paralysis on one side. You must attend a post-secondary school or technical school leading to a degree or certification to be eligible for this award.

4101 W. Green Oaks, Suite 305, #149
Arlington, TX 76016

Christopher Mark Pitkin Memorial Scholarship

http://www.hemophilia.org/Community-Resources/Scholarships/Christopher-Mark-Pitkin-Memorial-Scholarship

All members of the hemophilia and bleeding disorders community, including spouses, siblings and children. Persons living with hemophilia and HIV, and their family members are encouraged to apply. Applicants must be pursuing a post-high school or college or technical/trade school education.

Hemophilia Foundation of Southern California (HFSC)
6720 Melrose Avenue
Hollywood CA 90038

Phone: (323) 525-0440
Email: ofcmgr@hemosocal.org

Cystic Fibrosis Scholarship Foundation

http://www.cfscholarship.org/applications.html

The mission of the Cystic Fibrosis Scholarship Foundation (CFSF) is to provide an opportunity for young adults with CF to further their education at a college or vocational school. This possibility is often out of reach for families with CF children because of the high cost of medical care from the time these students were babies. However, we at CFSF believe in the future of these young adults, their ability to achieve personal and educational goals, and their importance in making a long-term contribution to society on all levels. Scholarships are awarded based on educational achievement, leadership, and financial need as submitted by the student in the scholarship application form. In the first four years of the program scholarships were awarded to 250 young people from 40 states across the country. Most of the awards given were for a sum of $1,000.

Cystic Fibrosis Scholarship Foundation
1555 Sherman Avenue, #116
Evanston, IL 60201

Diabetes Scholars Foundation College Scholarship

http://www.diabetesscholars.org/

The Diabetes Scholars Foundation Scholarship Program is available to incoming freshmen seeking a higher education at an accredited four-year university, college,

411

technical or trade school. This scholarship recognizes students who are actively involved in the diabetes community, who have high academic performance, who participate in community and/or extracurricular activities and who have demonstrated that they are successfully managing the challenges of living with diabetes. Diabetes Scholars Foundation scholarships are not based on financial need.

Eligibility

- ✓ High School Seniors with type 1 diabetes seeking a higher education at an accredited four-year university, college, technical or trade school.
- ✓ U.S. citizen or permanent resident.
- ✓ Have contributed to diabetes research or advocacy through fundraising efforts, volunteering, public speaking, etc.
- ✓ Have demonstrated exemplary academic performance.
- ✓ Participates in community or extracurricular activities or sports.
- ✓ Endorsement from Physician or CDE that demonstrates that they are managing their diabetes. HbA1c is not a criterion.
- ✓ Letter of Recommendation from High School Counselor or Teacher.
- ✓ Complete a personal essay.

2118 Plum Grove Road, #356
Rolling Meadows, IL 60008
Phone: 312-215-9861
Fax: 847-991-8739
Email: m.podjasek@diabetesscholars.org

Doreen McMullan McCarthy Memorial Academic Scholarship for Women with Bleeding Disorders

https://www.fastweb.com/college-scholarships/scholarships/163353-doreen-mcmullan-mccarthy-memorial-academic-scholarship

Applicants must be female residents of the U.S. and have a diagnosed bleeding or clotting disorder. Note: this includes those with a diagnosis of von Willebrand disease, hemophilia, platelet disorder, or other factor deficiency, carrier status or clotting disorder.

National Hemophilia Foundation
116 West 32nd Street, 11th Floor
New York NY 10001
Attention: Sudha Sarode
Phone: (212) 328-3700
Email: ssarode@hemophilia.org

Education Advantage Scholarship Program

https://www.hemophiliafed.org/scholarships/education-advantage-scholarships-community/

Individuals with hemophilia A attending university, technical school or passing GED test. (Submissions for GED assistance may be on a rolling basis.)

See more at:

One Scholarship Way
Scholarship Management Services
Saint Peter, MN 56082
Phone: (877) 544-3018
Email: baxter@scholarshipamerica.org

Education is Power Scholarship

https://www.hemophiliafed.org/scholarships/education-power-scholarship/

Individuals living with hemophilia or von Willebrand disease and attending a community college, junior college, four-year college, university, or vocational school. Must also be a U.S. resident.

MedPro Rx, Inc.
Attention: Kathy Robinette-Stoneberg
140 Northway Court
Raleigh NC 27615-4916

Phone: 866.528.4963
Email: educationispower@medprorx.com

Elizabeth Nash Foundation (Cystic Fibrosis) Scholarship Program

http://www.elizabethnashfoundation.org/scholarships.html

The Elizabeth Nash Foundation (ENF) awards scholarships to assists persons with Cystic Fibrosis (CF) to pursue undergraduate and graduate degrees. Grants ranging from $500 to $2,000 are awarded annually. Since the program's inception in 2005, twenty-three individuals have received grants. The Elizabeth Nash Foundation Scholarship program is open to individuals with CF who are in-going or current undergraduate or graduate students at an accredited US-based college or university. Given limited resources, the program is currently only open to US citizens. Funds to support Associate Degrees are not currently available.

Elizabeth Nash Foundation
PO Box 1260
Los Gatos CA 95031-1260

Eric Delson Memorial Scholarship Program

https://gatewayhemophilia.org/our-programs/scholarship-program/

Three renewable $2,500 scholarships are awarded each year for new or current college or vocational-technical school students. Students clinically diagnosed with hemophilia or von Willebrand disease.

The Eric Delson Memorial Scholarship Program
One Scholarship Way
Saint Peter MN 56082
Phone: (866) 792-2731

Eric Delson Memorial Scholarship Program

https://gatewayhemophilia.org/our-programs/scholarship-program/

One renewable $1,500 scholarship is awarded to a student attending private school, grades 7-12. Students clinically diagnosed with hemophilia or von Willebrand disease.

The Eric Delson Memorial Scholarship Program
One Scholarship Way
Saint Peter MN 56082
Phone: (866) 792-2731

Eric Marder Scholarship / Immune Deficiency Foundation Program

https://primaryimmune.org/eric-marder-scholarship-fund-now-accepting-applications

The Immune Deficiency Foundation is honored to award scholarships to undergraduate students living with primary immunodeficiency diseases. The Eric Marder Scholarship Program is open to patients with a primary immunodeficiency as classified by the World Health Organization and is intended for undergraduate students attending or entering college or a technical training school.

IDF Eric Marder Scholarship Program
40 W. Chesapeake Avenue Suite 308
Towson, MD 21204

Friends of Scott Foundation Scott Delgadillo College Scholarship

http://www.friendsofscott.org/scholarship.aspx

The Friends of Scott Foundation (Friends to Children with Cancer) offers a scholarship each year to cancer patients currently on treatment or to survivors. Education was important to Scott. It was his dream to attend the University of Notre Dame. In his memory FSF offers a scholarship program for individuals who have been diagnosed with childhood cancer. We realize the importance of continuing education and know that pursuing this goal is difficult when given a life-threatening diagnosis.

6977 Navajo Rd #168
San Diego, CA 92119
Phone: 619.223.7268
Fax: 619.223.7002
Email: aztec.graphics@yahoo.com

Hemophilia Federation of America

http://hemophiliafed.org/ programs-and-services/educational-scholarships/

The Hemophilia Federation of America (HFA) is proud to offer ten educational scholarships of $1,500 each to members of the bleeding disorders community. Applications can be downloaded from our website. Previous scholarship recipients are encouraged to reapply. To qualify, an applicant must have Hemophilia or von Willebrand (VWD) and must be seeking a post-secondary education from a college, university, or trade school. The applicant must also be able to demonstrate a commitment to improving quality of life by pursuing his/her goals with determination.

Hemophilia Federation of America
210 7th Street SE, Suite 200 B
Washington, DC 20003
Phone: 800-230-9797

Hemophilia Health Services Memorial Scholarship Program

https://www.hemophilia.org/Community-Resources/Scholarships

The Hemophilia Health Services Memorial Scholarship is open to full-time undergraduate and graduate students with hemophilia, von Willebrand disease and other factor deficiencies. You must be a U.S. citizen and demonstrate financial need, academic achievement in relation to tested ability and involvement in extracurricular and community activities to be eligible for this award.

IASCNAPA Sickle Cell Scholarship

http://www.iascnapa.org/

The International Association of Sickle Cell Nurses and Physician Assistants, Inc. has established a college scholarship program to assist patients with Sickle Cell Disease who will be attending an institution of higher learning. The Association's Scholarship Committee has determined that selection of recipients will be based upon academic performance, financial need and additional criteria including character, school and community activities and proficiency in written expression. Applicants for IASCNAPA's $500 Scholarships must have a sickle hemoglobinopathy and be enrolled in or have been accepted by a recognized and accredited post-secondary school, including college, university, trade school, or other institution of higher learning.

Deborah Boger, RN, CPNP
IASCNAPA Scholarship Committee
Wake Forest Baptist Medical Center
Hematology/Oncology Dept.
Medical Center Blvd
Winston-Salem, NC 27157
Email: dboger@wakehealth.edu

Joshua Gomes Memorial Scholarship Fund

http://joshuagomes.org/scholarship/

The Joshua Gomes Memorial Scholarship Fund aims to lay a path for hope for young adults with HIV/AIDS by providing academic scholarships to universities of their choice. Each $1,000 scholarship we award will give the recipient a strong message.

The Joshua Gomes Memorial Scholarship Fund
45767 McKenzie Highway
Vida OR 97488

JustNebulizers.com Respiratory Care Scholarship

http://justnebulizers.com/respiratory-care-scholarship

Just Nebulizers – an online resource for nebulizer machines, accessories, and information – will be awarding the $1,000 JustNebulizers.com Respiratory Care Scholarship to a college or graduate student with a respiratory condition.

Keppra Family Epilepsy Scholarship Program
http://www.ucbepilepsyscholarship.com

The UCB Family Epilepsy Scholarship Program™ offers educational scholarships to people living with epilepsy, family members and caregivers who demonstrate academic and personal achievement. This year marks the 10th anniversary of the scholarship program. Since 2005, UCB has awarded $1,400,000 in scholarships to more than 275 deserving people who have applied their awards to undergraduate and graduate studies.

UCB Family Epilepsy Scholarship Program
c/o Summit Medical Communications
1421 E. Broad St., Suite 340
Furquay-Varina, NC 27526

Phone: (866) 825-1920
Email: ucbepilepsyscholarship@summitmedcomm.com

Kermit B. Nash (Sickle Cell Disease) Academic Scholarship
https://www.collegexpress.com/scholarships/kermit-b-nash-academic-scholarship/2016733/

The Kermit B. Nash Scholarship rewards academic achievement of individuals with sickle cell disease and promotes their pursuit of educational goals. The fund will award 4 people a total of $5,000 for 2 Academic Semesters. To qualify, you must be a graduating high school senior, United States citizens or permanent residents, and have sickle cell disease (individuals with sickle cell trait are not eligible).

Sickle Cell Disease Association of America, Inc.
3700 Koppers Street, Suite 570
Baltimore, Maryland 21227

Lawrence Madeiros Scholarship
https://www.hemophilia.org/node/8746

Student with an inherited bleeding disorder or other chronic disorder attending For students with an inherited bleeding disorder or other chronic disorder attending an accredited college or university.

The Lawrence Madeiros Scholarship
P.O. Box 11
Mayfield NY 12117
Phone: (518) 863-8998

Lupus Inspiration Foundation for Excellence (L.I.F.E.)
http://www.lifescholarship.org/about-the-scholarship/

The L.I.F.E. Scholarship will be awarded to one or more students in the month of August and/or January every year. Award recipients will receive a minimum award of $500.00 made payable to the educational institution at which they are enrolled for tuition, fees, and other educational-related expenses. Each applicant must be diagnosed with systemic lupus erythematosus (SLE) and be working towards a degree with a minimum of six credits per semester at an accredited United States college or university. The applicant must have a minimum GPA of 3.0 and be involved in at least one extracurricular activity (e.g., performance group, athletics, clubs/organizations, community service, employment, etc.).

Lupus Inspiration Foundation for Excellence
L.I.F.E. Scholarship Committee
P.O. Box 64088
Tucson, AZ 85728-4088

National Collegiate Cancer Foundation

http://collegiatecancer.org/scholarships/

The National Collegiate Cancer Foundation is proud to launch its first program to provide financial assistance to young adults pursuing their education who have lost a parent or guardian to cancer.

National Collegiate Cancer Foundation
4858 Battery Lane #216
Bethesda, MD 20814

Phone: (240) 515-6262
Email: info@collegiatecancer.orghttp://www.collegiatecancer.org/

National Multiple Sclerosis Society Scholarships

http://www.nationalmssociety.org/living-with-multiple-sclerosis/society-programs-and-services/scholarship/index.aspx

The MS Society is offering scholarships to provide between $1000 and $3000 to help with the expenses of: high school seniors with MS, high school seniors who have a parent or guardian with MS, and adults with MS who have never enrolled in a post-secondary institution. Decisions will be based on financial need, academic record and a personal essay discussing the impact of MS on the applicant's life. Last year, 332 scholarships were awarded for a total of $700,440.

National Multiple Sclerosis Society
733 Third Avenue
New York NY 10017
Phone: (800) 344-4867

Mike & Ron Scholarship

http://www.factorsupport.com/scholarships.htm

Factor Support Network is again pleased to offer the Mike Hylton & Ron Niederman Memorial Scholarship this year to MEN with bleeding disorders and their immediate family members. The award this year will be ten $1000 scholarships. This scholarship was established in 1999 to honor the memory of Mike Hylton (1945-1998) and Ron Niederman (1950-1999).

Attn: Scholarship Committee
Factor Support Network
900 Avenida Acaso, Suite A
Camarillo, CA 93012-8749

Fax: (805) 482-6324
Email: BeckyBouchet@FactorSupport.com

Millie Gonzalez Memorial Scholarship

https://www.collegexpress.com/scholarships/millie-gonzales-memorial-scholarships/5000672/

Women with hemophilia or von Willebrand disease. Applicant must be a US resident and either entering or attending a junior college, four-year college, university, or vocational school in Fall 2014.

Factor Support Network
900 Avenida Acaso, Suite A
Scholarship Committee
Camarillo CA 93012-8749

Attention: Linda Leigh Sulser

Phone: (877) 376-4968
Email: Scholarships@FactorSupport.com

PAF's Scholarships for Survivors

http://www.patientadvocate.org/index.php?p=69

The purpose of our scholarship program is to provide support to individuals, under the age of 25, who have been diagnosed with or treated for cancer and/or a chronic/life threatening disease within the past five years. The purpose of these scholarships is to provide support to patients seeking to initiate or complete a course of study that has been interrupted or delayed by a diagnosis of cancer or other critical or life-threatening disease.

- ✓ Must maintain an overall 3.0 GPA
- ✓ Must be a full-time student.
- ✓ Must sign an agreement to complete 20 hours of community service

Patient Advocate Foundation
Scholarship for Survivors
421 Butler Farm Road
Hampton, VA 23666

Phone: (800) 532-5274
Fax: (757) 873-8999

Patient Advocate Foundation Scholarship for Survivors

http://www.patientadvocate.org/events.php?p=69

The Patient Advocate Foundation Scholarship for Survivors is available to patients seeking to initiate or complete a course of study that has been interrupted or delayed by a diagnosis of cancer or other critical or life-threatening disease.

Patient Advocate Foundation
Scholarship for Survivors
421 Butler Farm Road
Hampton, VA 23666

Phone: (800) 532-5274
Fax: (757) 873-8999

Pfizer Epilepsy Scholarship Award

https://www.collegebasics.com/scholarships/pfizer-epilepsy-scholarship/

The Epilepsy Scholarship Award is a 1-year, $3000 scholarship honoring 25 outstanding students who have overcome the challenges of epilepsy, been successful in school, done well in activities outside the classroom or in the community, and shown a desire to make the most out of college or graduate school. You may apply for this award if you are under a doctor's care for epilepsy and in school as a high school senior who has applied to college, as a freshman, sophomore, or junior in college, or as a college senior who has applied to graduate school.

Pfizer Epilepsy Scholarship Award
c/o Adelphi Eden Health Communications
30 Irving Place, 10th Floor
New York, NY 10003
Phone: (800) 292-7373

Pfizer Soozie Courter Hemophilia Scholarship Programs 1 and 2

https://www.hemophiliavillage.com/hemophilia-scholarship-program

Scholarships will be awarded to applicants with hemophilia A or hemophilia B who present the best combination of a creative and persuasive essay, excellent recommendations, and superior academic standing. For the 2014-2015 academic year, Pfizer will award:

- ✓ Five $4,000 graduate scholarships
- ✓ Ten $2,500 college scholarships, including vocational schools

To be eligible, you must:

- ✓ Have been diagnosed with hemophilia A or hemophilia B, be a U.S. resident attending a school in the U.S. and meet one of the following educational criteria:
  - ○ Be a high school senior or graduate, or
  - ○ Have completed high school or an equivalent (e.g., general equivalency diploma [GED]), or
  - ○ Be currently accepted to or enrolled in a junior college, college (undergraduate or graduate), or vocational school

Hemophilia Scholarship Program
250 Greenwich Street, 36th Floor
New York, NY 10007
Attention: Porter Novelli
Email: pfizerscholarship@porternovelli.com

Professor Ulla Hedner Scholarship

https://nhfcentralohio.org/programs/academic-scholorships.html

For high school seniors and college or vocational students. This is a competitive scholarship. (Please Contact sponsor for additional information on eligibility–

Candidate may need to be affected by an inhibitor, acquired hemophilia or congenital factor VII deficiency).

Phone: (877) 668-6777

Sacks for Cystic Fibrosis Scholarship
http://www.sacksforcf.com/

For every sack recorded during NFL Monday Night Football games, Solvay Pharmaceuticals, Inc. will donate $1000 to the Boomer Esiason Foundation Scholarship Program. Through the BEF/SolvayCARES partnership, "Sacks for CF" funds will be awarded to 30 college students, based on their academic achievements and adherence to daily CF therapy.

Boomer Esiason Foundation Headquarters
483 10th Avenue, Suite 300
New York, NY 10018
Tel: 646.292.7930
Fax: 646.292.7945

SevenSECURE Adult Education Grant
https://www.collegescholarships.com/scholarships/detail/131956?/scholarships/detail/131956

Offers up to $2,500 in educational awards to take courses, continue training or learn skills for a new career. For adults with an inhibitor, acquired hemophilia or congenital factor VII deficiency, or a primary caregiver.

Scholarship Managers, Inc.
Phone: (877) 668-6777

Stony Wold-Herbert Fund Direct Service Grant
http://www.stonywoldherbertfund.com

The Stony Wold-Herbert Fund Direct Service Grant is available to students with respiratory ailments. You must have a pulmonary problem, live or go to school in the greater New York City area (within a 50-mile radius), and be at least 16 years old to be eligible for this award.

Cheri Friedman
Phone: (212) 753-6565
Email: director@stonywold-herbertfund.com

Ulman Cancer Fund for Young Adults
http://ulmanfund.org/scholarships

The Ulman Cancer Fund for Young Adults is committed to helping young adults continue their education after being affected by cancer through their own diagnosis or the diagnosis of a loved one. Many scholarships offered by UCF share similar applicant criteria. Applicants need only submit one application, which will be considered for any and all scholarships for which the student applies and is eligible.

Phone: (410) 964.0202
Fax: (888) 964.0402

Toll Free: (888) 393.FUND (3863)
Email: info@ulmanfund.org

Varun Bhaskaran (WAS) Scholarship Program of IDF

http://primaryimmune.org/services/idf-academic-scholarship-programs/

The Immune Deficiency Foundation is pleased to announce the new Varun Bhaskaran Scholarship of IDF for undergraduate or graduate students living with Wiskott-Aldrich Syndrome (WAS). Deepak and Ramya Bhaskaran created this scholarship in memory of their son Varun, who died of complications of Wiskott-Aldrich Syndrome. Varun touched the hearts and minds of many people during his very short lifetime.

The Varun Bhaskaran Scholarship Program
40 W. Chesapeake Avenue Suite 308
Towson, MD 21204

Learning Disabilities

Allegra Ford Thomas Scholarship

http://ncld.org/scholarships-and-awards

The Allegra Ford Thomas Scholarship is a $2,500 one-time scholarship awarded to a graduating high school senior with a documented learning disability who will be enrolled in a two-year community college, a vocational or technical training program, or a specialized program for students with LD in the fall of 2015.

National Center for Learning Disabilities
32 Laight Street, Second Floor
New York, NY 10013

Anne Ford Thomas Scholarships

http://www.ncld.org/about-us/scholarships-aamp-awards/the-anne-ford-and-allegra-ford-scholarship-awardhttp://www.ncld.org/scholarships-and-awards/

The Anne Ford Scholarship is a $10,000 scholarship ($2,500/year over four years) granted to a graduating high school senior with a documented learning disability who will be enrolled in a full-time bachelor's degree program in the fall of 2015.

National Center for Learning Disabilities
32 Laight Street, Second Floor
New York, NY 10013

Anne & Matt Harbison Scholarship

https://cps.academicworks.com/opportunities/2258

In keeping with the goals of P. Buckley Moss, who struggled with dyslexia during her school years, this grant represents the artist's dedication to the field of special education. Students with a learning disability.

P. Buckley Moss Foundation
Phone: (540)932-1728
Email: foundation@mossfoundation.org

Dick Griffiths Memorial Scholarship

http://www.caped.io/scholarships/2016-caped-scholarship-descriptions/

In memory of Richard (Dick) Griffiths, a Learning Disabilities Specialist and founder of CAPED from Cabrillo College. Awarded to a student with a learning disability who has been challenged in math. (In addition to completing the Student Scholarship Application, the student should complete the section in the student letter on strategies that s/he uses to overcome his/her math challenges, which will be published in the CAPED Communiqué to benefit other students with similar challenges).

10073 Valley View St. #242
Cypress CA, 90630
Phone: (562) 397 2810
Fax: (866) 577 3387
1

Judith Cary Leadership Memorial Scholarship

www.MossFoundation.org

The Judith Cary Leadership Memorial Scholarship (Cary Scholarship) is an up-to $750.00 award given annually to one student who is pursuing either a bachelor's or a master's degree in Special Education.

108 S. Wayne Ave
Waynesboro, VA 22980
Phone: (540) 932-1728
Fax: (540) 941-8865
Email: foundation@mossfoundation.org

LDA-IA Scholarships

http://ldaiowa.org/2019-scholarships/

The Learning Disabilities Association of Iowa will award three scholarships to high school seniors planning to obtain post-secondary education (college or vocational). Each award will be for $1,000.

LDA-IA
5665 Greendale Rd, Ste. D
Johnston IA 50131

Phone: (515) 280-8558

Novotni College Scholarship Fund

https://add.org/adhd-scholarships/

Attention Deficit Disorder Association (ADDA) established the Novotni College Scholarship Fund to assist college students with ADHD. The Scholarship was created in honor of Dr. Michele Novotni and her work in the field of ADHD.

Contact: Attention Deficit Disorder Association
Phone: (800) 939-1019
Email: adda@jmoadmin.com

Ralph D. Norman Scholarship Award

https://www.scholarships.com/financial-aid/college-scholarships/scholarship-directory/physical-disabilities/learning-disability/ralph-d-norman-scholarship

Available to Arkansas residents only. The Ralph G. Norman Scholarship fund was established to aid young adults with learning disabilities so they may obtain success in furthering their education. Two scholarships are awarded, each in the amount of $500.

Contact: Learning Disabilities Association of Arkansas
Phone: (501) 666-8777
Email: ldaarkansas@yahoo.com

Smart Kids with Learning Disabilities Youth Achievement Award

http://www.smartkidswithld.org/community/success-profiles/2014-fred-j-epstein-youth-achievement-awards/

This $1,000 award recognizing the strengths and accomplishments of young people with learning disabilities and ADHD is given to a student 19 or younger who has demonstrated initiative, talent, and determination resulting in a notable accomplishment in any field—including art, music, science, math, athletics or community service. Honorable Mentions will also be awarded.

Contact: Smart Kids with Learning Disabilities
Phone: (203) 226-6831
Email: Info@SmartKidswithLD.org

Susan Bunch Memorial Scholarship

http://www.caped.io/scholarships/2016-caped-scholarship-descriptions/

In memory of Susan Bunch, a Learning Disabilities Specialist from West Valley College. Awarded to a student with a learning disability who is pursuing a college degree.

10073 Valley View St. #242
Cypress CA, 90630
Phone: (562) 397-2810
Fax: (866) 577-3387

Theodore R. and Vivian M. Johnson Scholarship

http://www.johnsonscholarshipfoundation.com/

Available to students who enroll in a State University System of Florida institution. The Johnson Scholarship, funded by the Johnson Scholarship Foundation, is a competitively awarded program which is available to undergraduate students with disabilities with financial need who enroll in a State University System of Florida (SUS) institution. The dollar amount of the award is contingent upon the level of funding from the Johnson Scholarship Foundation and the Florida Legislature.

Johnson Scholarship Foundation
505 South Flagler Drive, Suite 810
West Palm Beach, Florida 33401

Phone: (561) 659-2005
Fax: (561) 659-1054
Email: wood@jsf.bz

Mental Illness

Alyssa McCroskey Memorial Scholarship

http://www.caped.io/scholarships/2016-caped-scholarship-descriptions/

Alyssa Rayne McCroskey "Aly McCroskey", granddaughter of Paula McCroskey, Coordinator of DSP&S in the Riverside Community College District for almost 26 years. Awarded to a student with a disability who is "making a positive difference" in the lives of other students who are struggling to maintain or regain their mental health. Aly died by suicide, in the summer of 2008, at the age of sixteen.

10073 Valley View St. #242
Cypress CA, 90630
Phone: (562) 397 2810
FAX: (866) 577 3387

Lilly Reintegration Scholarship

http://www.reintegration.com/

The Lilly Reintegration Scholarship is available to students with bipolar disorder, schizophrenia, schizophreniform disorder or schizoaffective disorder and be currently receiving medical treatment for the disease, including medications and psychiatric follow-up. You must also be a U.S. citizen and plan to attend a school in the U.S. and be actively involved in rehabilitative or reintegration efforts, such as clubhouse membership, part-time work, volunteer efforts or school enrollment to be eligible for this award.

Phone: 800-809-8202

Lilly Moving Lives Forward Reintegration Scholarships

http://www.reintegration.com/

The Lilly Moving Lives Forward Reintegration Scholarship is open to students who are diagnosed with schizophrenia, schizophreniform or schizoaffective disorder. You must be currently receiving medical treatment for the disease and be actively involved in rehabilitative or reintegrative efforts to be considered for this award.

The Center for Reintegration, Inc.
347 West 37th Street
New York, New York 10018

Phone: (212) 957-5090
Fax: (212) 974-0228

Physical/Mobility Impairment

1800Wheelchair.com Scholarship

http://www.1800wheelchair.com/scholarship/

1800Wheelchair.com is proud to announce our annual scholarship award. Established in 2006, the scholarship fund will award one $500 scholarship to an undergraduate student. The scholarship is open to students of any major or concentration. The winner's name, essay and photo will be posted on 1800wheelchair.com. Although not a requirement, preference will be given to students with mobility disabilities.

1800wheelchair.com
320 Roebling Street
Suite 515
Brooklyn, NY 11211

AmeriGlide Achiever Scholarship

http://www.ameriglide.com/Scholarship/

AmeriGlide is the leading supplier and distributor of home mobility products including wheelchair lifts and stair lifts. The AmeriGlide Achiever Scholarship is a program we offer to full time college students who use wheelchairs. Our goal is to help provide financial assistance for books or other school related supplies to deserving mobility challenged students. This $500 scholarship is available twice a year for the Fall and Spring Semesters.

AmeriGlide, Inc.
Raleigh NC 27610
2605 Atlantic Avenue
Raleigh NC 27604

Phone: (800) 790-1635
Fax: (800) 791-6524

Bryon Riesch Paralysis Foundation

http://brpf.org/scholarships/

A $1000 to $2000 scholarship shall be awarded to two to three individuals with neurological disabilities, or the child of that person, for post high school education.

Priority going to direct spinal cord injuries and diseases resulting in paralysis such as spinal tumors, strokes or aneurysms affecting the spinal cord, or spina bifida. Other diseases and disorders that would be considered include MS, traumatic brain injuries, Parkinson's and cerebral palsy.

- ✓ The applicant must have a high school or college GPA of 2.5 or higher.
- ✓ There are no income restrictions.
- ✓ The applicant must be college-bound; four-year degree or two-year associate degree.

Bryon Riesch Paralysis Foundation
P.O. Box 1388
Waukesha, WI 53187-1388
Phone: (262) 547-2083

CMMS Deshae Lott Ministries Inc Outreach Program

http://www.deshae.org/cmms/scholar.pdf

CMMS Deshae Lott Ministries Inc works to help American citizens with severe mobility limitations maintain hopeful, purposeful, engaged lives by providing some financial support for medically necessary home-health-care services not covered by insurance, private or governmental, and not covered by any other non-profit organization.

200 Glasgow Road
Edinboro, PA 16444
Phone: (814) 732-2462

Toll-Free: (888) 860-BORO
Fax: 814-732-2866

Jackson-Stricks Scholarship Fund

https://www.petersons.com/scholarship/jackson-stricks-scholarship-111_173020.aspx

The New York section of the National Council of Jewish Women awards the Jackson-Stricks Scholarships, which are available to students with physical challenges who are attending college in an undergraduate or graduate program in the New York Metropolitan Area. The scholarships, which range in value up to $3,000, are available to students with disabilities of all faiths.

National Council of Jewish Women
New York Section
241 W. 72nd Street
New York, NY 10023

Phone: (212) 687-5030
Email: info@ncjwny.org

Little People of America Scholarships

http://www.lpaonline.org/mc/page.do?sitePageId=84654&orgId=lpa

As part of our service to people with dwarfism and the community at large, LPA offers educational scholarships to prospective and current students attending college or vocational school in the United States. Awards can range from $250 to $1000 (sometimes more). A scholarship committee, headed by LPA's Vice President of Programs, will selectively review all scholarship application packets. Scholarships are given in order of preference to:

- ✓ Members of LPA who have a medically diagnosed form of dwarfism
- ✓ Immediate family members of dwarfs who are also paid members of LPA
- ✓ People with dwarfism who are not members of LPA
- ✓ Disabled students in general
- ✓ Non-disabled students who can demonstrate a need for financial educational assistance

Little People of America
250 El Camino Real Suite 211
Tustin, CA 92780

Take Stock in Children / Chair Scholars Foundation

http://takestocksarasota.org/apply/

Applicants Must: -

- ✓ Exhibit positive behavior in and out of school
- ✓ Attend school regularly
- ✓ Maintain satisfactory grades
- ✓ Be determined to succeed
- ✓ Demonstrate a financial need
- ✓ Must have a documented physical disability

Take Stock Sarasota
P.O. Box 48186
Sarasota, FL 34230
Phone: (941) 358-4407
Fax: (941) 358-4407

USA Funds Access to Education Scholarships

https://www.collegebasics.com/scholarships/usa-funds-access-to-education-scholarships/

USA Funds will award $1,500 scholarships to students with economic need through USA Funds Access to Education Scholarships. These scholarships are open to high school seniors, currently enrolled college students or incoming college students who plan to enroll or are enrolled in full- or half-time undergraduate or full-time graduate- or professional-degree coursework at an accredited two- or four-year college, university or vocational/technical school. GED recipients also are eligible. Fifty percent of the scholarship awards will be targeted to applicants who are members of an ethnic-minority group or have a documented physical disability. The scholarships are non-renewable. Previous scholarship recipients may apply each year for additional awards if the student maintains a 2.5 grade-point average on a four-point scale. Students will not be considered for additional awards if the total amount awarded to the student under this program reaches $6,000.

USA Funds
P.O. Box 6028
Indianapolis, IN 46206-6028

Visually Impaired

American Council of the Blind

The American Council of the Blind will present more than two dozen scholarships and awards to outstanding blind students. All legally blind, full-time students admitted to academic and vocational training programs at the post-secondary level are encouraged to apply for one of these scholarships. Part-time students who are working full-time are also invited to apply for the John Hebner Memorial Scholarship. A cumulative grade point average of 3.3 is generally required, but extenuating circumstances may be considered for certain scholarships. Applicants must be legally blind in both eyes. Applications may be completed online but supporting documentation must be submitted in hard copy print.

American Council of the Blind Scholarship Program
Attn: Dee Theien
6300 Shingle Creek Parkway, Suite 195
Brooklyn Center, MN 55430

Phone: 202-467-5081

Arthur E. and Helen Copeland (USABA) Scholarships

https://www.usaba.org/membership/scholarships/

The Arthur E. and Helen Copeland Scholarships are awarded annually to one male and one female member of the United States Association of Blind Athletes (USABA) who is legally blind and enrolling/enrolled at a two-year or four-year or technical institution or university as a full-time student. Applicants must have participated in USABA sports programs. Consideration will be given to students with good academic records, involvement in civic/extracurricular activities, academic goals/objectives and USABA involvement at various levels. Applicants must be United States citizens. Scholarship amount awarded is $500.

Send cover letter and transcripts to:
Matt Simpson
United States Association of Blind Athletes
1 Olympic Plaza
Colorado Springs, CO 80909

Phone: (719) 866-3019
Email: msimpson@usaba.org

Association of Blind Citizens Scholarship

http://www.blindcitizens.org

Applicants for the Association of Blind Citizens Scholarship must be legally blind to qualify. This is a $1,000 to $2,000 award. Applicants should provide a 300 to 500-word autobiographical sketch of yourself. Please include how the scholarship award would help you achieve your goal to attend college or a recognized vocational program.

The autobiographical sketch must be submitted by email to scholarship@blindcitizens.org.

A disk copy of the autobiographical sketch must be submitted along with the documents listed below:

- ✓ A high school or college transcript.
- ✓ A certificate of legal blindness or a letter from your ophthalmologist.
- ✓ Two letters of reference.
- ✓ A disk copy of your biographical sketch.
- ✓ Mail disk and documents listed above to:

Association of Blind Citizens
PO Box 246
Holbrook, MA 02343

Phone: (781) 961-1023
Fax: (781) 961-0004
Email: president@blindcitizens.org

California Council of the Blind

http://www.ccbnet.org/scholar.htm

The California Council of the Blind gives several awards to the most deserving blind student applicants residing in California who will enter or continue studies at an accredited college or university in either undergraduate or graduate status. These awards may be granted in two parts (1/2 each semester) upon receipt of proof of registration for each semester. You must be a legal California resident, who is legally blind, to apply. Awards will be granted on the basis of academic scholarship and other factors including financial need.

California Council of the Blind
1303 J Street, Suite 400
Sacramento, CA 95814-2900

Fax: (916) 441-2188
Email: ccotb@ccbnet.org

Carl Foley Graduate Scholarship Program

This program is for graduate students attending one of several colleges and universities which offer a degree in the field of low vision. Applicants need not be visually impaired. Application is made through the school directly.

Citizens with Low Vision International
c/o Annette Carter
2200 Wilson Boulevard, Suite 650
Arlington VA 22201-3354

Phone: (800) 733-2258
Email: president@cclvi.org

Christian Record Services (CRS) Scholarship

https://christianrecord.org/

Partial scholarships are offered to legally blind young people striving to obtain a college education. Scholarships are given on a limited basis to those who qualify. The amount Christian Record Services gives for scholarships varies from year to year. The actual amount given to each student is in proportion to the funds available.

CRSB / NCBC
PO Box 6097
Lincoln NE 68506-0097

Phone: (402) 488.0981

Christine H. Eide Memorial Scholarship for Blind Students

http://www.lighthouse.org

The Christine H. Eide Memorial Scholarship was established for legally blind students. The $500 scholarship is available to full-time undergraduate or graduate students entering or attending an accredited college or university, with a maximum of $1,000 per year for any individual.

111 E 59th St
New York NY 10022-1202

Phone: (800) 284-4422

Dale M. Schoettler Scholarship for Visually Impaired Students

https://www2.calstate.edu/impact-of-the-csu/support-the-csu/foundation/Pages/csu-scholarships.aspx

Sixty-five scholarships of $6,500 each are available for the 2014-2015 academic year for students who are visually disabled, as verified by a medical professional, and are enrolled in 6.1 units or more. Applications for this scholarship are accepted on a year-round basis. Please be sure to review the Fact Sheet and Checklist, and to complete the following two forms.

California State University, East Bay
25800 Carlos Bee Boulevard
Hayward, CA 94542
Phone: (510) 885-3000

Fred Scheigert (CCLVI) Scholarship Program

https://www.cclvi.org/scheigert-scholarship

The Council of Citizens with Low Vision International offers the Fred Scheigert Scholarship Program. This competitive scholarship is available to full-time college students with low vision, chosen from among those who meet the visual acuity and academic guidelines. For 2008, 3 awards of $3000 dollars were awarded.

Citizens with Low Vision International
c/o Annette Carter
2200 Wilson Boulevard, Suite 650
Arlington VA 22201-3354

Phone: (800) 733-2258
Email: president@cclvi.org

Georgia Council of the Blind Scholarship

http://www.georgiacounciloftheblind.org/scholarship.aspx

Each year, the Georgia Council of the Blind presents one or more scholarships of up to one thousand dollars to students who are legally blind, or to sighted students who are financially dependent on legally blind parent(s). Applicants must be accepted in one of the following levels of post-secondary education: (a) Vocational/technical school; (b) Junior or four-year College; (c) Master's or Doctoral program at an accredited University. Applicants must be legal residents of the state of Georgia.

Phone: (706) 410-1023
Toll-free: (877) 842-9733

There are chapters throughout the state. Below is for the Metro Atlanta chapter:

President, Brent Reynolds
Phone: (404) 814-0768
Email: jbr53@samobile.net

GuildScholar Award (Jewish Guild HealthCare)

http://www.petersons.com/scholarship/guildscholar-award-111_172628.aspx

Annual scholarship program for college-bound high school students who are legally blind. Applications will be accepted from students at the beginning of the senior year (September. 15th).

Eligibility Requirements:

- ✓ Must be an undergraduate student
- ✓ Must attend a university or a four-year college
- ✓ Must study full-time
- ✓ Must be a US Citizen
- ✓ Minimum 3.0 GPA
- ✓ Must currently be a high school student
- ✓ Restricted to applicants that have visual disabilities

How to Apply

Sign up for a Peterson's account and we'll tell you what you need and how to apply.

Lighthouse Scholarships

https://www.lighthouseguild.org/patients-families/scholarships/

The Scholarship & Career Awards (SCA) is a time-honored tradition that recognizes outstanding students who have overcome the challenges of vision loss by awarding them with scholarships for college and graduate studies. The program honors extraordinary corporate citizens committed to breaking down barriers in the workplace for people with vision loss.

Scholarship & Career Awards
111 E 59th St
New York NY 10022-1202

Phone: 212-821-9428
Toll-Free: (800) 284-4422

National Federation of the Blind (NFB) E.U. Parker Scholarship

https://nfb.org/programs-services/scholarships-and-awards/scholarship-program/scholarships

E. U. Parker Scholarship - Endowed by his wife, who joined him in a lifetime of Federations, this scholarship honors a long-time leader of the National Federation of the Blind whose participation stood for strong principles and strong support of the Federation's work.

National Federation of the Blind
200 East Wells Street
Baltimore, MD 21230

Phone: 410-659-9314
Fax: 410-685-5653

National Federation of the Blind (NFB) Jennica Ferguson Memorial Scholarship

https://nfb.org/programs-services/scholarships-and-awards/scholarship-program/scholarships

The Jennica Ferguson Memorial Scholarship was given to keep alive the memory of a young woman who dealt with her blindness and terminal illness with a grace and strength she frequently assured others she drew from the Federation and from her faith in God.

National Federation of the Blind
200 East Wells Street
Baltimore, MD 21230
Phone: 410-659-9314
Fax: 410-685-5653

National Federation of the Blind (NFB) Kenneth Jernigan Scholarship

https://nfb.org/programs-services/scholarships-and-awards/scholarship-program/scholarships

Kenneth Jernigan Scholarship - Given by the American Action Fund for Blind Children and Adults, a nonprofit organization which works to assist blind persons, in memory of the man who changed perceptions regarding the capabilities of the blind in this country and throughout the world.

National Federation of the Blind
200 East Wells Street
Baltimore, MD 21230
Phone: 410-659-9314
Fax: 410-685-5653

National Federation of the Blind (NFB) Kuchler-Killian Memorial Scholarship

https://nfb.org/programs-services/scholarships-and-awards/scholarship-program/scholarships

Kuchler-Killian Memorial Scholarship - Given in loving memory of her parents, Charles Albert Kuchler and Alice Helen Kuchler, by Junerose Killian, dedicated member of the NFB of Connecticut.

National Federation of the Blind
200 East Wells Street
Baltimore, MD 21230
Phone: 410-659-9314
Fax: 410-685-5653

National Federation of the Blind (NFB) Melva T. Owen Memorial Scholarships

https://nfb.org/programs-services/scholarships-and-awards/scholarship-program/scholarships

Given in memory of Melva T. Owen, who was widely known and loved among the blind. She and husband Charles Owen became acquainted with many blind people through their work in the "Voicepondence" Club. Charles Owen says: "There shall be no limitation as to field of study, except that it shall be directed towards attaining financial independence and shall exclude religion and those seeking only to further general or cultural education."

National Federation of the Blind
200 East Wells Street
Baltimore, MD 21230
Phone: 410-659-9314
Fax: 410-685-5653

Reggie Johnson Memorial Scholarship

http://www.blindcitizens.org

The Reggie Johnson Memorial Scholarship is available to blind or visually impaired students seeking a college degree. You must provide a certificate of legal blindness or a letter from your ophthalmologist, two letters of reference, a biographical sketch, and proof of acceptance to an accredited institution of higher learning. You must also be a legal US resident to be eligible for this award.

Association of Blind Citizens
PO Box 246
Holbrook, MA 02343

Phone: (781) 961-1023
Fax: (781) 961-0004
Email: president@blindcitizens.org

Walter Young Memorial Scholarship

http://www.caped.io/scholarships/2016-caped-scholarship-descriptions/

In memory of Walter Young, CAPED supporter and husband of Past President, Ellen Young. Awarded to a college student who is blind or visually impaired.

10073 Valley View St. #242
Cypress CA, 90630
Phone: (562) 397 2810
Fax: (866) 577 3387

William and Dorothy Ferrell (AER) Scholarship

https://aerbvi.org/resources/aer-scholarships/

AER proudly offers two scholarships, named in honor of William & Dorothy Ferrell. The scholarships are awarded in the even number years.

Cal State East Bay
Attn: Scholarship Coordinator/Financial Aid
25800 Carlos Bee Blvd
Hayward, CA 94542
Phone: 877-492-2708

Index

442

Made in the USA
Monee, IL
24 March 2022

93508172R00256